POVERTY IN THE UNITED STATES

Recent Titles in Documentary and Reference Guides

Culture Wars in America: A Documentary and Reference Guide
Glenn H. Utter

Civil Liberties and the State: A Documentary and Reference Guide
Christopher Peter Latimer

The Politics of Sexuality: A Documentary and Reference Guide
Raymond A. Smith

U.S. Election Campaigns: A Documentary and Reference Guide
Thomas J. Baldino and Kyle L. Kreider

U.S. Foreign Policy: A Documentary and Reference Guide
Akis Kalaitzidis and Gregory W. Streich

White-Collar and Corporate Crime: A Documentary and Reference Guide
Gilbert Geis

Homelessness: A Documentary and Reference Guide
Neil Larry Shumsky

Victims' Rights: A Documentary and Reference Guide
Douglas E. Beloof

Substance Abuse in America: A Documentary and Reference Guide
James A. Swartz

The Iraq War: A Documentary and Reference Guide
Thomas R. Mockaitis

Animal Rights and Welfare: A Documentary and Reference Guide
Lawrence W. Baker

Water Rights and the Environment in the United States: A Documentary and Reference Guide
John R. Burch Jr.

Endangered Species: A Documentary and Reference Guide
Edward P. Weber

9/11 and the War on Terror: A Documentary and Reference Guide
Paul J. Springer

Vaccination and Its Critics: A Documentary and Reference Guide
Lisa Rosner

Arab–Israeli Conflict: A Documentary and Reference Guide
Priscilla Roberts

Modern Slavery: A Documentary and Reference Guide
Laura J. Lederer

POVERTY IN THE UNITED STATES

A Documentary and Reference Guide

John R. Burch Jr.

Documentary and Reference Guides

An Imprint of ABC-CLIO, LLC
Santa Barbara, California • Denver, Colorado

Library of Congress Cataloging-in-Publication Data

Names: Burch, John R., 1968– compiler.
Title: Poverty in the United States : a documentary and reference guide / John R. Burch Jr.
Description: Santa Barbara, California : Greenwood, an Imprint of ABC-CLIO, LLC, [2018] | Series: Documentary and reference guides | Includes bibliographical references and index.
Identifiers: LCCN 2017046442 (print) | LCCN 2017053573 (ebook) | ISBN 9781440858505 (ebook) | ISBN 9781440858499 (hardcopy : alk. paper)
Subjects: LCSH: Poverty—Government policy—United States—History. | Public welfare—United States—History. | United States—Social policy. | United States—Economic policy. | Public welfare—Law and legislation—United States—History—Sources.
Classification: LCC HC110.P6 (ebook) | LCC HC110.P6 B865 2018 (print) | DDC 344.7303/25—dc23
LC record available at https://lccn.loc.gov/2017046442

ISBN: 978–1–4408–5849–9 (print)
978–1–4408–5850–5 (ebook)

22 21 20 19 18   1 2 3 4 5

This book is also available as an eBook.

Greenwood
An Imprint of ABC-CLIO, LLC

ABC-CLIO, LLC
130 Cremona Drive, P.O. Box 1911
Santa Barbara, California 93116-1911
www.abc-clio.com

This book is printed on acid-free paper ∞

Manufactured in the United States of America

CONTENTS

READER'S GUIDE TO RELATED DOCUMENTS AND SIDEBARS

Note: Some documents appear in more than one category.

Great Society and the War on Poverty

Housing

Medical Care

Mentally Ill

Military Veterans

New Deal

Presidents of the United States

State Politics

Temporary Assistance for Needy Families

U.S. Congress

U.S. Supreme Court

Urban Poverty

Wages

Women

PREFACE

In 2010, President Barack Obama's Patient Protection and Affordable Care Act (PPACA) was passed by Congress without one vote from a member of the Republican Party. Predictably, Republicans made the repeal of "Obamacare" their primary objective in subsequent elections. Donald Trump's ascension to the presidency in 2017 signaled that the PPACA was doomed. Among his first actions was signing the Executive Order Minimizing the Economic Burden of the Patient Protection and Affordable Care Act Pending Repeal. Trump had the benefit of having enough Republicans in both houses of Congress to repeal the law without any support from Democrats. When it came time to vote, a few members of the Republican Party who had campaigned for the repeal of the law had a change of heart and did not vote to repeal Obamacare. Their actions showed that there was a difference between using the PPACA as a tool to get elected and actually taking health insurance away from millions of U.S. citizens. Although Trump and many Republicans were incensed at the turn of events, history suggests that such an ending was inevitable. The U.S. government has never taken away an entitlement once it was established.

The compassion that was evident in keeping the PPACA as the law of the land confirmed the theme that guided the selection of documents for this reference tool over a year ago. Throughout the history of the United States, there has been a belief that society had an obligation to care for its most vulnerable members. Initially, charity began in the local community. The scope of the challenge quickly grew too much for individual towns, so responsibility was transferred first to the counties and eventually the states. The states, as shown by numerous documents contained herein, became laboratories where theories were tested. Successful initiatives were quickly imitated by other states.

The Civil War became a demarcation point as that is when the federal government began to wade into the treatment of the poor and infirm. It is somewhat startling to realize, but the Union really did not understand the human costs of war when the Civil War erupted. It was the needs of the maimed and the widowed that moved the government to begin its forays into medical care and pensions. The Pension Act of 1862 was the model that helped inform the construction of the Social Security Act of 1935 during President Franklin Delano Roosevelt's New Deal.

Inevitably, as the federal government's commitment to building an economic safety net grew, so did the political battles between Republicans and Democrats. As shown by the documents in the representative sections, the achievements of the Democrats ensconced in FDR's New Deal, JFK's New Frontier, and LBJ's Great Society were tempered by the rollbacks of the Reagan Revolution, which proved so transformational that Democrat Bill Clinton ran for president not as an heir of FDR or LBJ but as a "New Democrat" pledging to "end welfare as we know it." The political pendulum eventually reversed itself yet again, culminating in President Barack Obama's signature achievement, the Patient Protection and Affordable Care Act of 2010.

Each of the chronologically arranged documents included in this reference tool is accompanied by an analysis that contextualizes the document and illustrates its importance. In addition, there are suggestions for further reading. Interspersed throughout the volume are sidebars, which serve to highlight individuals or events related to the relevant time period. Other valuable features include the reader's guide to related documents and sidebars, a chronology, and a bibliography. Concluding the volume is the Index.

INTRODUCTION

Part 1: Native Americans

It has been said that the manner in which a community cares for the less fortunate is a reflection on society as a whole. That idea undergirds the construction of this reference tool. Part I examines the plight of American Indians, whose respective peoples endured the loss of land, cultures, and economic independence due to the machinations of the federal government. In the Indian Self-Determination and Education Assistance Act, it was stated that "the prolonged federal domination of Indian Service Programs has served to retard rather than enhance the progress of Indian people and their communities." The documents selected for inclusion in this section track the evolution of federal American Indian policy, beginning in 1830. The collective impact of the federal decisions contained herein helps explain how many of today's American Indian communities came to be mired in abject poverty.

The Indian Removal Act of 1830 led to one of the largest land grabs in U.S. history. It provided the president of the United States the authority to negotiate with American Indian peoples the exchange of their homelands for property in Indian Country. According to the legislation, American Indians had the right to refuse the overtures of the president. President Andrew Jackson determined that the act gave the United States the right to remove, forcibly if necessary, all Indians residing east of the Mississippi River to Indian Country. In the South, the removal of the Cherokees, Chickasaw, Choctaw, Creeks, and Seminoles made available some of the finest agricultural lands in the United States. It was that land that allowed for the massive expansion of the South's cotton economy. Removal was not limited to the South as the law also impacted Indian peoples of the Old Northwest, including the Sauk, Seneca, and Wyandots.

By the 1880s, the United States' manifest destiny had resulted in American citizens desiring the land that comprised Indian Country. The problem was that property belonged to the respective Indian tribes and could not be sold. The issue was solved with the General Allotment Act of 1887. Better known as the Dawes Act, it allowed individual Indians to own a piece of the reservation. Although the legislation did not allow Indians to sell their property for at least 25 years, that provision was not enforced. As a result, American Indian groups watched what little land they had left disappear with each sale.

Much of the land that the Indians had left was for all practical purposes useless due to the scarcity of water. The resulting food insecurity led to great suffering on the part of American Indians. Their plight became a concern for Secretary of the Interior Hubert Work. In 1926, he tasked Lewis Meriam and a team of researchers to conduct a study on the conditions endured by American Indians on the reservation. Two years later, they produced "The Problem of Indian Administration." The report proved to be very sympathetic to the native peoples. Among the conclusions reached was that the chronic shortages of water and the accompanying malnutrition resulted in higher mortality rates than in any other population in the country. The overarching theme of the document was that it was the fault of the federal government that many American Indians were destitute and in poor health. The report specifically blamed many of the problems on the Bureau of Indian Affairs. Many of the remedies recommended to reverse the situation became ensconced in the Indian Reorganization Act of 1934.

The Indian Reorganization Act, also known as the Wheeler-Howard Act, was a repudiation of the General Allotment Act of 1887, or Dawes Act. It took away the right of individual Indians to own a plot on the reservation, thereby once again making it impossible to sell tribal land. In addition, the act tasked the federal government with aiding federally recognized native groups in reacquiring the lands that had been lost, especially property with natural resources like water. A controversial provision allowed American Indians to write tribal constitutions. Many who opposed that provision believed that the concession was an acknowledgment that Indian groups had sovereign rights. To allow them even a modicum of sovereignty would provide the natives the justification to assert other rights in future years.

One of the reasons that there was a fear of native sovereignty was the activities of John Collier, who served as commissioner of the Bureau of Indian Affairs. He did not believe that the Indian Reorganization Act was adequate to address the many needs of American Indian peoples. He called for even more aid to compensate the respective peoples for the loss of land, cultures, and economic independence. His oratory proved catastrophic as key politicians came to view the act as an excuse to expand the Bureau of Indian Affairs' bureaucracy rather than helping deserving Indians. Congressional enmity toward him and the Bureau of Indian Affairs led to Collier's resignation in 1945.

Underpinning the Indian Reorganization Act was the idea that the United States owed American Indians aid and compensation for past injustices. Congress in 1953 signaled that the federal government owed native peoples nothing through House Concurrent Resolution 108. Congress determined to "terminate" all relationships between federal authorities and native groups, including all obligations that had been agreed to in treaties. Officials believed that cutting off all financial support would result in Indians leaving reservations and assimilating into the general population. Most of the native groups targeted for termination managed to avoid that fate. Among the groups that lost their reservations, treaty rights, and other assets were the Klamath Tribe of Oregon, Menominee Tribe of Wisconsin, Modoc, and Alabama-Coushatta.

Encouraged by the gains resulting from the African American civil rights movement, Native Americans began to demand recognition of their rights. President Lyndon Baines Johnson's administration aided the activists by supporting the Indian Civil Rights Act of 1968. The act extended to Native Americans rights, such as free speech, the right to assemble, and the right to a jury trial, that had long been enjoyed by other ethnic and racial groups in the United Nations. The new rights belonged to individuals, not American Indian Nations under threat of termination.

Termination was finally eliminated as a policy with the passage of the Indian Self-Determination and Education Assistance Act of 1975. With an acknowledgment that the federal government had failed miserably in its care of American Indian peoples, Congress made it a goal to allow native groups as much sovereignty as they could bear. For the first time in a century or more, American Indian leaders could make many of the day-to-day decisions that impacted their communities. The federal government pledged to serve as a partner by providing financial assistance and professional expertise as needed on issues such as the management of water resources. Also included in the legislation was a mechanism for tribes that had been terminated to have their federal recognition restored. Over time, the Indian Self-Determination and Education Assistance Act has succeeded in strengthening many American Indian nations as they have been allowed to plot their futures, but the harm of the past continues to haunt far too many communities.

Part 2: Early Local and State Perspectives

During the early 1800s, it was the local community that cared for the impoverished. That became a burden for local governments because the more aid that was provided to the poor, the more people asked for assistance. Politicians sought an explanation for the turn of events, as they had expected the number of people relying on public charity to decrease. The Massachusetts legislature in 1821 created a commission to study the issue. The commission's *Report of the Committee on the Pauper Laws of the Commonwealth* explained the conundrum by identifying two distinct groups among the impoverished. The "worthy" poor were truly incapable of caring for themselves. The other was comprised of able-bodied but lazy individuals who had come to view the charity provided to them as dependable income. The commission recommended that the citizenry reduce their charitable giving so that a permanent underclass of the undeserving was not created.

New York commissioned a similar study that was conducted by a committee led by New York secretary of state John Van Ness Yates. In the *Report of the Secretary of State in 1824 on the Relief and Settlement of the Poor*, the commission identified the same two groups of poor people that Massachusetts had described just three years earlier. In response to the commission's findings, the New York legislature passed the County Poorhouse Act of 1924. It called for the construction of poorhouses in each county so that the "worthy" poor could be housed and fed.

The identification of the undeserving poor in both the Massachusetts and New York studies fed into the idea that the poor were poor because of their personal failings, such as laziness or alcoholism. The consequence of the trope was that people did not give to charitable causes. In July 1833, Mathew Carey published his *Appeal to the Wealthy of the Land, Ladies as well as Gentlemen, on the Character, Conduct, Situation, and Prospects of Those Whose Sole Dependence for Subsistence Is on the Labour of Their Hands*, which made the case that poverty was the result of job shortages and the payment of low wages to those fortunate to find employment. He targeted the publication to the upper classes of society because he believed that it was their responsibility, through private charities, to help able-bodied individuals find jobs that paid a living wage.

In her 1843 *Memorial to the Legislature of Massachusetts*, Dorothea Dix recounted the poor treatment the mentally disabled received in communities around the state. Since towns had proven incapable of providing the necessary services, Dix called on the legislature to provide the facilities needed to ensure a decent quality of life for the mentally infirm. She proved extremely persuasive, as the Massachusetts legislature subsequently provided the funding required to construct the Worcester State Hospital. Her success in Massachusetts led her to launch similar campaigns in Kentucky, Maryland, New Jersey, New York, Ohio, Pennsylvania, and Tennessee.

Another group that was poorly treated was children. Many worked long hours for meager pay. Since their families required their incomes to subsist, they were not able to gain an education. Reformers in Pennsylvania who believed the children belonged in school convinced the Pennsylvania legislature in 1848 to enact the Minimum-Age Law. The law made it illegal for textile factories to employ children under the age of 12. The law was notable because it was the first minimum-age legislation enacted in the nation. It became the model for other states to emulate.

The Progressive Era, which began in the 1890s, found individuals concerned with the living conditions of the poor in urban areas. These areas had seen a large influx of immigrants who were essentially herded into tenement housing. One of the most famous publications about tenement house living during the period was Jacob Riis's *How the Other Half Lives*. Riis used text and haunting photographs to blame government officials and city elites for the squalor where too many people lived. The city, in his eyes, bore blame because it chose to ignore the plight of the immigrants. The upper class was directly responsible since that was the population that owned the respective slum housing.

A consequence of the massive immigration that occurred following the Civil War was that many children were being left to their own devices by their parents. Recognizing that these children needed guidance or other form of care, besides being incarcerated, Illinois created the first juvenile court in the nation. The Juvenile Court Law of 1899 endeavored to provide for children under 10 who had been abandoned or were homeless, beggars, or residing in establishments of ill repute so that they could be raised in a manner that would ensure they would become productive citizens. The law also addressed how delinquent children under 16 were to be treated. If they broke a law, they were to be punished. Should incarceration be necessary, they were separated from older offenders. This was due to the belief that since they were juveniles, they could be rehabilitated as they had not yet become hardened criminals. To house them with adults would result in their abuse as well as their falling under the influence of disreputable criminals.

Tenement houses once again came to the fore with the publication of the *Report of the New York State Tenement House Commission of 1900*. The report, which had been commissioned by Governor Theodore Roosevelt, reminded New York's citizenry that the conditions described a decade earlier by Jacob Riis in *How the Other Half Lives* continued to prevail in the city's poorest districts. Not coincidentally, the squalor and overcrowding in those very communities had fueled repeated outbreaks of tuberculosis and smallpox. The legislature responded to the commission's finding by passing the Tenement House Act of 1901, which among other requirements mandated that tenement houses have running water and courtyards to facilitate the circulation of air.

Although legislation like the Tenement House Act addressed the consequences of poverty, nothing had really been advanced to address the root causes of poverty. During the early years of the 1900s, statistician Lilian Brandt was studying the disease vectors that enabled the spread of tuberculosis in New York City. She noted that it was in the tenement houses that the disease persisted and thrived. In her report on her research, she made the connection that it was the lack of sanitation in the city's poorest neighborhoods that bred tuberculosis. City officials began addressing the sanitation issue and the outbreaks and their severity quickly declined. Buoyed by her success, she turned her attention to studying other facets of the city's poverty. In 1908, Brandt published her landmark article "The Causes of Poverty" in *Political Science Quarterly*, where she posited that poverty was the result of an imbalance in the prevailing economic system. To eradicate poverty, Brandt called for the end of child labor, the expansion of educational opportunities, the construction of medical facilities, improvement of housing, and the creation of decent paying jobs. Although controversial at the time, many of her proposals would find their way into federal legislation over the course of the twentieth century.

One of the most influential institutions of the Progressive Era was Hull House of Chicago, Illinois. Founded as a settlement house in 1889 by Jane Addams and Ellen Gates Starr, Hull House served as a place where immigrants, the working class, and the poor could receive necessary services such as childcare, English lessons, and citizenship classes. Hull House proved so successful that within two decades it encompassed more than 10 buildings. To commemorate Hull House's first two decades in operation, Jane Addams wrote *Twenty Years at Hull-House*. It served to spread the philosophies that subsequently undergirded the discipline of social work. Hull House also provided opportunities for many talented and influential women to hone their leadership skills. Its alumni included Edith and Grace Abbott, Florence Kelley, and Julia Lathrop, who worked together to convince the U.S. Congress to create the U.S. Children's Bureau in 1912.

As a harbinger of a national issue, Massachusetts in 1912 created a Minimum Wage Law for Women and Children. As such, it became the first state to mandate a minimum wage for these two groups. The momentum for the law was generated by a report commissioned by the legislature on the working conditions of women and children within the state. The findings described the many ways that employers exploited workers. Appalled, reformers set to write legislation that would improve working conditions and wages. Recognizing that the legislation was inevitable, probusiness forces ensured that the effect of the minimum wage law was muted.

The final version of the law called for a minimum wage that would be determined on a case-by-case basis by a Minimum Wage Commission, whose membership was selected by the governor. For all practical purposes, that meant the guaranteed wage really was not.

Part 3: The Civil War to the Roaring 1920s

In the early days of the Civil War, it was widely believed that the conflict would be of short duration. That belief was dashed by the carnage and panic of the first Battle of Bull Run. Understandably, the Union was soon facing problems getting men to enlist in the military. Congress offered an attractive inducement through the Pension Act of 1862, which offered a generous pension to any soldier who became disabled during his service. Should a soldier perish, his widow or surviving children up to the age of 16 received the pension. Over the course of the rest of the nineteenth century, the Civil War pensions became one of the federal government's most expensive obligations. Confederate veterans repeatedly had their legislators request to be added to the pension rolls to no avail.

Confederate veterans were also exempted from the Homestead Act of 1862. The act allowed for a head of household aged 21 or over of either sex to claim a plot of land 160 acres in size for $1.25 an acre plus the filing fee. In order to gain permanent title to the land, the homesteader had to live and farm the property for five years. They also had to improve the property by constructing a home. After the five years had passed, one needed two neighbors to confirm that the property had been improved plus pay another filing fee before the title was theirs. Initially, the Homestead Act looked like a great opportunity for poor people to achieve the American dream of homeownership. The problem was that many of the impoverished people who took that opportunity did not have the money to buy farm implements or construction materials. Even if they had enough revenue for initial expenses, a significant amount of the land did not contain a water source, thereby making agriculture impossible. By 1900, there had been 700,000 homestead claims made under the terms of the act. Less than 10 percent of the claimants ever received the title to their land.

The conclusion of the Civil War resulted in freedom for the former slaves held in Southern and border states such as Kentucky. To address their needs, Congress passed the Freedmen's Bureau Bill of 1865. It created the Freedmen's Bureau and put it under the leadership of General Oliver O. Howard. Among its activities was overseeing business relationships between the freedmen and their former masters, the provision of legal services, and the education of freedmen of all ages. Among the bureau's greatest achievements was the founding of some of the leading historically black colleges and universities, such as Fisk University in Nashville, Tennessee, and Howard University in Washington, D.C. The Freedmen's Bureau ceased operation in 1872.

The decades following the Civil War saw the population of the United States increase exponentially. A significant amount of that growth was the result of immigration. Congress wanted to ensure that the new immigrants were people who would be an asset to the country. Toward that end, it passed the Immigration Act of 1882. It levied a charge of 50 cents per foreign immigrant against the ship that transported the individuals to the United States. The revenue collected was used to staff immigration centers to block entry to criminals, people who could not care for themselves, and individuals deemed mentally deficient.

Thanks in part to the influence of Hull House, the welfare of children became a major focus of the federal government during the first decade of the twentieth century. In 1909, President Theodore Roosevelt convened the White House Conference on Dependent Children. The conference helped lead to the creation of the U.S. Children's Bureau in 1912. Julia Lathrop was selected to head the bureau, making her the first woman to ever serve at that level of the government. Like her, many of the people hired to work in the Children's Bureau were Hull House alumni.

After decades of work at the state level, the regulation of child labor became a national concern. In an effort to discourage the use of child labor, Congress passed the Keating-Owen Child Labor Act of 1916. The act forbade any products that utilized child labor in any form during the construction process to be sold over state lines. The law was declared unconstitutional in the 1918 majority decision in *Hammer v. Dagenhart*. Congress attempted a different strategy through the Child Labor Act of 1919. It levied a 10 percent tax on goods made by children. The act failed constitutional muster in the 1922 case *Bailey v. Drexel Furniture Company* because its purpose was not to raise revenue but instead punish companies hiring children.

An important landmark was the passage of the Promotion of the Welfare and Hygiene of Maternity and Infancy Act, better known as the Sheppard-Towner Maternity and Infancy Act of 1921. It created one of the first federal welfare programs. It authorized the U.S. Children's Bureau to distribute up to $1 million in matching funds to each state for the purpose of establishing programs to help keep women and their children healthy. The act proved a success. In the eight years that the program operated, there was an annual decline in the mortality rate of mothers and infants. The program ended because the American Medical Association convinced enough congressmen that the federal government did not have any business in medical fields.

In 1918, Congress returned to the subject of child labor. An act was passed that created a board tasked with setting the minimum wages for women and children in the District of Columbia. It was believed that people would keep from committing immoral acts if they were paid a decent wage. The act's constitutionality was weighed in the 1923 U.S. Supreme Court case *Adkins v. Children's Hospital*. The justices declared the act unconstitutional because it was designed to regulate the morality of women and children. If a law was passed to regulate how people behaved, it had to apply to the entire population, not just a segment.

With so many failed attempts to address the labor of children, Congress finally turned to the one method that was guaranteed to pass constitutional muster. It crafted the Child Labor Amendment of 1924. It has been ratified by 28 states, leaving it 10 short of becoming a part of the Constitution. It can technically still gain the needed votes because Congress failed to set a deadline for the ratification process to close. Its provisions became a moot point through the inclusion of child labor provisions in the Fair Labor Standards Act of 1938. That act had its constitutionality affirmed by the U.S. Supreme Court in the decision to the 1941 case *United States v. Darby Lumber Company*.

Part 4: The Great Depression and the New Deal

The Great Depression found President Herbert Hoover and his administration in denial over the gravity of the nation's economic straits. This was evidenced through his 1929 State of the Union address in which he attempted to assure the citizenry that the economy was not as troubled as it appeared. As the quality of life enjoyed by the citizenry declined precipitously, Hoover refused to use the resources of the federal government to allay their suffering. He believed that providing aid directly to the populace paved a direct road to socialism. His apparent indifference allowed political opponents to characterize him as uncaring about the plight of the common man. Hoover was unable to reverse that portrayal during his unsuccessful 1932 reelection bid.

Upon assuming the presidency in 1933, Franklin Delano Roosevelt in his first 100 days in office forced a number of measures through Congress in order to alleviate the suffering of many. The 1933 Agricultural Adjustment Act gave the secretary of agriculture the authority to set the prices of agricultural commodities in order to ensure farmers a dependable income. The Federal Emergency Relief Act created the Federal Emergency Relief Administration to distribute $500 million to the states so that they could provide direct payments to the unemployed.

While Roosevelt was in the initial stages of his New Deal with the citizenry, Upton Sinclair was campaigning to become governor of California. The centerpiece of his campaign was Immediate EPIC, which was intended to end poverty within the state. It was a working document that was constantly under revision as he met with voters at campaign events. Among the ideas in the final document was to seize lands that were not being used to distribute to the poor so that they could become farmers. Another proposal called for the repurposing of factories to produce foodstuffs for the general population. Political opponents used the more radical elements of Immediate EPIC to portray Sinclair as a Communist. That doomed Sinclair's prospects for the governorship. Despite his loss, parts of his bold plan later found their way into New Deal legislation.

Although the Federal Emergency Relief Act provided payments to the unemployed, it was strictly a short-term solution. What they truly required was employment. President Roosevelt began to address that need through his issuance of Executive Order 6101, which created the Civilian Conservation Corps (CCC). The CCC was designed for unmarried young men between the ages of 18 and 25 who hailed from families receiving some type of federal relief. Each man received $30 a week, with all but $5 going to their families. The CCC remained a component in the efforts to combat poverty until 1942, when it was defunded by Congress.

Another piece of legislation that had a labor component was the Tennessee Valley Authority Act of 1933, which created the Tennessee Valley Authority (TVA). The TVA's primary focus involved the control of flooding along the Tennessee River and providing cheap electrical power to fuel economic growth in the South. In order to meet the objectives, massive alterations to the local countryside were necessary. Dams were constructed along the entire expanse of the Tennessee River, which meant tens of thousands of jobs. A consequence was the burying of entire communities under water. As a direct result, many individuals were forced to migrate to urban centers such as Cincinnati, Ohio, and Chicago, Illinois. Although the TVA significantly improved the quality of life in such areas as Appalachia, its environmental and social costs ensured that no regional development project on such a grand scale would ever be undertaken in the country again.

The greatest achievement of the New Deal was the Social Security Act of 1935 (SSA). It created the Social Security Board, which was charged with the provision of old-age insurance, payments to the unemployed, assisting with the care of the blind and homeless, and aid to crippled and delinquent children. The initial success of the SSA proved mixed since it was created as a federal–state initiative. For example, in the case of the old-age insurance, the federal government would match the state contribution dollar for dollar up to $15. Some states contributed the maximum amount allowable, meaning that those over 65 in age received $30 per month. Other states opted not to participate in the program at all, which meant that their elderly population received nothing. The impact of the SSA benefit for the elderly proved transformational, as it established the right of employees to retire at the age of 65.

Other significant benefits for employees were established by the Fair Labor Standards Act of 1938 (FLSA). It initially set the minimum wage at 25 cents an hour and prescribed incremental increases over a seven-year period to 40 cents. It also established the 40-hour workweek. Through the FSLA, the federal government claimed the authority to regulate wages and working conditions. The constitutionality of the FLSA was challenged in the 1941 U.S. Supreme Court case *United States v. Darby Lumber Company*. At issue was whether the federal government had the authority to establish a minimum wage for all companies engaged in interstate commerce. The justices ruled in favor of the federal government.

By 1944, the New Deal had seen the populace largely recover from the horrors of the Great Depression. Despite that, there was a palpable fear that the standard of living that they had come to enjoy could once again be wiped out through another financial collapse. In his State of the Union address that year, President Franklin D. Roosevelt attempted to allay that anxiety through his "Economic Bill of Rights." It guaranteed that all Americans had the right to an education, job, housing, health care, and a comfortable retirement. His promise subsequently shaped the economic policies of the Democratic Party nationally into the twenty-first century.

The Servicemen's Readjustment Act of 1944 also continues to impact the nation today. It established the G.I. Bill, which provided World War II benefits to attend institutions of higher education, vocational training, and loan guarantees to purchase homes. It fueled one of the greatest economic expansions in the history of the United States. New G.I. bills would be enacted to benefit veterans of later wars, but they proved to be less generous than that forged during Roosevelt's presidency.

Part 5: The Post–World War II Era through the Carter Administration

During World War II, thousands of volunteers were denied admission into the military because they could not pass a physical. Since national defense was one of his primary responsibilities, President Harry S. Truman was determined to improve the health of the general populace. The National School Lunch Act of 1946 ensured that some of the nation's children received at least one nutritious meal a day.

Enacted the same year was the Hospital Survey and Construction Act, which was also known as the Hill–Burton Act. It endeavored to ensure a healthy pool of potential soldiers by specifically targeting services to men of age to serve and their families. Toward that end, the act financed the construction of hospitals in rural areas and funded the modernization of existing medical facilities. While the benefits of building or improving medical facilities were obvious, critics, including the American Medical Association, warned that the act was a step toward "socialized medicine." This charge would continue to emerge in later decades as the federal government expanded the nation's social safety net through legislation like the Patient Protection and Affordable Care Act of 2010, better known as "Obamacare."

Another outgrowth of World War II was the creation of the United Nations. It was envisioned as an intermediary to help solve problems between countries before open warfare erupted. One of the organization's first endeavors was the passage in 1948 of the Universal Declaration of Human Rights, which was heavily influenced by former First Lady of the United States Eleanor Roosevelt. Article 25 specifically addressed issues relating to poverty, including the right to food, housing, medical care, and security in old age.

Within the United States, the Housing Act of 1949 was enacted to construct more than 800,000 housing units within a six-year window. In order to create space for the new homes, dilapidated buildings were torn down. Many of those displaced were deeply impoverished, who did not have the means to obtain comparable housing. It had been envisioned by the planners of the legislation that any housing shortage would be short-lived due to the availability of the new housing units. The projections proved unrealistic since it took 20 years to complete construction of the homes.

The post–World War II era was a time of great prosperity within the nation, but by the 1960s it was evident that some did not share in that prosperity. One effort to uplift the economically disadvantaged was the Manpower Development and Training Act. It financed the retraining of laborers who had seen their jobs disappear through the automation of numerous industries. The first beneficiaries were predominantly white heads of households who were in the program for a year. During that period, they received a stipend to help support their families. Once that group had cycled through, the program was extended to African Americans and women. The change in demographics was accompanied by a different focus, which was aiding the impoverished in obtaining employment. The new charge provided ammunition to critics who alleged that what had been a successful employment initiative had devolved into a welfare program for minority groups.

It was during this period that Appalachian poverty came to the fore. It became a national issue because the impoverished were typically blamed for their state due to perceived deficiencies. To ascribe Appalachian poverty to the same deficiencies would be an affront to the Caucasian race. The explanation then became that Appalachians were "contemporary ancestors." They had missed out on prosperity due to the environment in which they resided. The solution was to connect them to the rest of the nation. Toward that end, a Joint Meeting of the Advisory Policy

Board to the Area Redevelopment Administration and the Conference of Appalachian Governors was convened by President John F. Kennedy on April 9, 1963. During that meeting, Kennedy proposed the creation of the President's Appalachian Research Commission. A year later, that body produced *Appalachia: A Report by the President's Appalachian Regional Commission 1964*. Its proposals included improving the region's infrastructure through initiatives like highway construction and the improvement of local educational systems. Those very ideas would shape the Appalachian Regional Development Act of 1965.

One of the initial challenges of poverty programs was determining who was "poor" in the country. In 1963, Mollie Orshansky, an economist for the Social Security Administration, published an article in the *Social Security Bulletin* that described an index she created to help determine the food needs of the poor. The index relied on a mathematical calculation that determined the minimum daily nutritional needs of a family for basic subsistence and then multiplied that number by three. Although Orshansky's index was not designed to measure poverty, since it solely focused on food, it would a year later become a major component of President Lyndon Baines Johnson's War on Poverty (WOP).

Upon assuming the presidency following the assassination of President John F. Kennedy in November 1963, Johnson determined that the eradication of poverty would be the centerpiece of his domestic agenda. In his first State of the Union address, he formally declared "unconditional war" on poverty. The president's rhetoric was supported by the *Economic Report of 1964*, prepared by his Council of Economic Advisers, which made the case that poverty could be eradicated by government-stimulated economic growth, which would inevitably result in the full employment of the nation's workforce. Congress responded by passing the Equal Opportunity Act of 1964, which created the Office of Economic Opportunity to administer many WOP programs, such as VISTA, the Job Corps, and the Community Action Program.

The WOP was a facet of what Johnson termed "The Great Society." It was a domestic program designed to build upon President Franklin Delano Roosevelt's New Deal. Whereas Roosevelt endeavored to provide the necessities required for the citizenry to subsist, Johnson wanted to improve the quality of life enjoyed by all. In 1964, Johnson demonstrated that the Great Society was for everyone through his successful efforts to get the Civil Rights Act of 1964 through Congress. Title VII of the act forbade discrimination against people searching for employment on the basis of race, color, religion, sex, or national origin. The drafters of the legislation included language that invoked the Commerce Clause of the Constitution, which made the law applicable to the public and private sectors.

A notable part of the WOP was the Housing and Urban Development Act of 1965 (HUDA). It created the Department of Housing and Urban Development to oversee housing programs aimed at moderate- and low-income families. This was a marked departure from older federal housing initiatives that primarily had benefited individuals from the middle and upper classes. The new department was charged with overseeing four agencies: Federal Housing Administration, the Federal National Mortgage Association, the Public Housing Administration, and the Urban Renewal Authority.

Arguably, the most popular and impactful program initiated during the WOP came out of the Social Security Amendments of 1965, namely Medicaid and Medicare. One of the reasons that these programs proved so successful was that they were well thought out and planned over time. While much of the WOP legislation was quickly drafted and passed through Congress in 1964 and 1965, the Social Security Amendments had been working their way through Congress in one form or another since they had been initially proposed by President Harry Truman's administration in the 1950s. By the time they were finally passed by Congress, they had been thoroughly vetted. Medicare was designed as an insurance policy for Americans already 65 years of age or older who were eligible for either Social Security benefits or Railroad Retirement benefits. In addition, the applicant would have had to work for a minimum of 10 years. An exception was made for people who were disabled, as they had to have worked for only two years and be eligible for Social Security Disability Insurance. Medicaid was intended to provide minimal health coverage for the impoverished. Since the states did not adopt Orshansky's index to determine who was poor, they had to means test all applicants using the standards of the state agency that was managing the federal Medicaid program at that level.

In 1966, the WOP harkened back to the National School Lunch Act. The 1946 legislation had shown over time that children who had a nutritious lunch functioned better than their peers who did not. The Child Nutrition Act of 1966 endeavored to ensure that all children received a nutritious meal by funding free lunches. The act also launched a pilot of the school breakfast program.

By 1968, the Great Society had fallen victim to the guns versus butter debate. The expenses and debates related to the escalating Vietnam War had left President Johnson's domestic agenda in tatters. To spur the federal government to reengage in the WOP, prominent economists, including John Kenneth Galbraith, proposed the establishment of a minimum income. It was to be set at a level that would elevate every citizen to at least the middle class. Although the plan was not adopted by the Johnson administration, elements of it would later emerge in President Richard Nixon's Family Assistance Plan (FAP).

Disenchantment with the results of the WOP had led to riots in more than 150 cities between 1965 and 1967. President Johnson in 1967 appointed the National Advisory Commission on Civil Disorders to produce a report explaining the causes of the violence. In February 1968, the commission issued the *Report of the National Advisory Commission on Civil Disorders*. Better known as the "Kerner Commission Report," so dubbed after Illinois governor Otto Kerner who headed the commission, it used culture-of-poverty theory to blame the rioting on the African American community.

The treatment of African Americans also became an issue in 1968 for the U.S. Supreme Court. In 1966, Alabama had withdrawn eligibility for Ms. Smith from the Aid to Families with Dependent Children (AFDC) program because the single mother had a lover at her home on weekends. Since he resided at the home during weekends, according to Alabama law, he was the man of the house. This meant he had assumed legal responsibility to care for Ms. Smith's children, despite the fact that he did not father any of them. The Supreme Court ruled in favor of Ms. Smith in the case *King v. Smith*. In their unanimous decision, the justices determined that children could not be denied benefits from AFDC due to the actions of a parent.

Another group being poorly treated in the United States at the time was borrowers. Many companies utilized predatory lending tactics such as bait and switch, which had lenders advertising a low interest rate to get people to their establishment but then assessing a much higher rate in the actual loan. Congress responded with the Truth in Lending Act of 1968. It required lenders to fully explain to their customers the total cost of the debt that was being offered to them. In order to limit the discretion of lenders, the legislation included language that prescribed how interest rates and fees were to be determined.

As the Republican Party candidate for the presidency in 1968, Richard Nixon pledged to dismantle President Lyndon Johnson's Great Society. His opening salvo in that effort was his Special Message to the Congress on the Nation's Antipoverty Programs. Issued on February 19, 1969, he detailed his intent to reform the Office of Economic Opportunity. In his June 10, 1970, statement announcing the extension of welfare reform proposals, Nixon provided specific details through his proposed FAP, which was a major revision of AFDC. The FAP called for a payment of $1,600 a month for a family of four plus $800 in food stamps. Democrats in Congress lauded Nixon for his version of the minimum income plan proposed by economists in 1968. Fellow Republicans were critical as they opposed direct payments to the poor. In order to appease the members of his party, he reduced the amount of money to be paid to poor families. In doing so, he alienated the Democrats who had pledged to support the FAP. Nixon ultimately failed to get the necessary support to get the FAP passed by Congress.

Due to Richard Nixon's resignation, President Gerald Ford was in office in 1975. Since the country was mired in a recession due to rampant inflation, he asked Congress to pass a stimulus package. His request resulted in the Tax Reduction Act of 1975. Ford was unhappy with the act because he had asked for measures that would only be in effect for the 1975 tax year. Instead, the act contained measures that were intended to become permanent, most notably the Earned Income Credit (EIC). The EIC was able to draw support from both Democrats and Republicans because it benefited the working poor. From their perspective, boosting the wages of those trying to improve their lot held the potential of encouraging the unemployed to find a job.

Two of the consequences of the inflation of the early 1970s were higher food prices and an increase in the number of people on food stamps. These factors combined to more than double the cost of the food stamp program to the federal government. To reduce costs, President Ford's administration increased the cost of food stamps. This hurt the poorest segment of the population since that was the group with the least amount of disposable income. Ford's decision became an issue when he launched his unsuccessful reelection campaign in 1975. Upon assuming office, President Jimmy Carter worked with Democrats in Congress to pass the Food Stamp Act of 1977. Its most notable provision was that it made foods stamps free. Republicans opposed free stamps because they believed that it would accelerate the growth in the number of beneficiaries. In a short matter of years, the Republicans were proven correct. But that was not necessarily a negative result since much of that growth was due to an increase in enrollment by the truly poor, as they were previously unable to benefit from the program due to their inability to pay the cost of the stamps.

Part 6: The Reagan Revolution through the Clinton Administration

Ronald Reagan's rise to political prominence began during the Great Society era. During that time, he established his conservative credentials by constantly criticizing President Lyndon Johnson's creation and expansion of entitlement programs. He charged that the welfare state robbed individuals of their freedom by making them wards of the federal government. His views at the time were to the right of prominent Republicans such as Richard Milhous Nixon. By 1980, Reagan's views on poverty were shared by the political mainstream of both major political parties, as evidenced by the support he received from Democrats in his first successful campaign for the presidency.

Reagan's influence on the electorate was confirmed when he ran for reelection in 1984 against the nominee of the Democratic Party, Walter Mondale. Mondale had joined the U.S. Senate in 1964, representing Minnesota. During President Lyndon Johnson's years as president, Mondale had been an ardent supporter of Great Society programs. Mondale's political bona fides as a champion of liberalism resulted in him becoming the vice president of the United States during President Jimmy Carter's term in office. That political background made it easy for Reagan to tie him to the welfare state that had come to be so despised by the electorate. In his remarks made in his speech accepting the presidential nomination at the Republican Convention in 1984, Reagan accused Mondale of contributing to the rampant inflation of the 1970s that had led to an economic recession, the growth of tax rates and budget deficits, teenage drug use, out-of-wedlock births, significant increases in crime, and spending billions of dollars on welfare programs that served to make the quality of life of recipients worse. Mondale was unable to convince many citizens that Reagan's allegations were not true, which led to one of the greatest electoral defeats in U.S. history.

Despite Reagan's reputation as an enemy of the poor, his accomplishments as president included the Emergency Medical Treatment and Active Labor Act of 1986 (EMTALA) and the Stewart B. McKinney Homeless Assistance Act of 1987. EMTALA addressed the problem of "patient dumping," which was a common practice of hospitals refusing emergency services to individuals without health insurance or other means to pay for treatment. The Stewart B. McKinney Homeless Assistance Act provided funding for nonprofit organizations and government agencies at the state or local levels to assist the homeless.

President Reagan was unsuccessful in his bid to significantly reform the AFDC through the Family Support Act of 1988 (FSA). The FSA was designed to encourage people to get the education and training that would allow them to find jobs that paid more than they were receiving from AFDC. To make AFDC even less appealing, the FSA required all beneficiaries to provide at least 16 hours of community service a week in exchange for their continued participation in AFDC. The fatal flaw in the act was that it was created as a joint federal and state program. Each state was to provide 60 percent of the funding for job training, but many did not have the funds to spare for that purpose. Without the states providing the monies to create the bureaucracy required to manage the initiative at the local level, there was nobody providing the necessary training or providing the confirmation that AFDC recipients were completing their community service responsibilities. The FSA proved so inefficient that the number of AFDC recipients actually grew over the years it was in effect.

Reagan's vice president of the United States, George H. W. Bush, succeeded him as president. Like his predecessor, Bush was concerned about the growth in spending by the federal government related to entitlement programs. At the same time, he wanted to be sure that the truly needy benefited from the nation's social safety net. His administration quickly discovered that the federal government did not have an accurate measure of hunger within the nation. Bush's administration worked with Congress to address the information void. The resulting National Nutrition Monitoring and Related Research Act of 1990 tasked the U.S. Departments of Agriculture and Health and Human Services to create a survey on food consumption, food insecurity, and the health of the nation. The resulting data was subsequently made available to both public and private interests to inform ongoing research initiatives and governmental programs at the local, state, and federal levels.

The success of the Reagan revolution was confirmed during the presidential campaign in 1992. Five-term governor of Arkansas William "Bill" Clinton ran for the Democratic Party nomination as a "New Democrat." He differentiated himself from his fellow Democrats by taking conservative stances on crime and welfare. Echoing President Ronald Reagan, Clinton promised to "end welfare as we know it." Clinton was challenged to keep his campaign promise through the Republican-sponsored Personal Responsibility and Work Opportunity Reconciliation Act of 1996 (PRWORA), which replaced the failed FSA. The PRWORA denied access to entitlement programs to noncitizens of the United States, fixed a maximum amount of welfare benefits that a family could receive over a five-year period, and required able-bodied adults to secure employment within two years of obtaining federal aid. The act also accomplished what Reagan had attempted—it replaced AFDC, the nation's largest welfare program, with Temporary Assistance for Needy Families (TANF). Democrats in Congress, led by Senator Daniel Moynihan of New York, urged Clinton not to sign the PRWORA because it promised to provide irreparable harm to families. Despite agreeing with his fellow Democrats that the act had serious flaws, Clinton signed the legislation into law. When running for reelection, he used the PRWORA as proof that he had followed through on his pledge to end welfare as we know it.

Part 7: The New Millennium

With the new century came a new type of Republican, the "Compassionate Conservative." Under that mantra, President George W. Bush made major structural changes to both the nation's schools and Medicare. Bush believed that the existing educational model utilized around the nation had failed because it created a significant achievement gap. In order to address that problem, Bush's administration worked with leaders in Congress to craft legislation that would ensure that all students received an education of comparable quality. Their work resulted in the No Child Left Behind Act of 2001 (NCLBA). The act required all schools receiving federal funding to adopt standards-based education. In order to assess whether schools were making progress toward that goal, educators were required to administer standardized tests to their students and make the results public. Although the early test results nationally suggested that the NCLBA had succeeded in improving student learning outcomes, Democrats and allied constituent groups like the National Education Association argued that the apparent improvement in student outcomes was due to teachers teaching only the content that would appear on the tests. Another criticism was that the tests were biased against minority groups and children from the lower economic and social classes.

Another controversial piece of legislation signed by Bush was the Medicare Prescription Drug, Improvement, and Modernization Act of 2003 (MPDIMA). The act created Medicare Part D, which was a voluntary prescription drug benefit for individuals enrolled in Medicare Parts A or B. The MPDIMA found critics from both sides of the political spectrum. Conservative Republicans were outraged by the creation of what they viewed as another unnecessary and expensive entitlement program. Democrats complained that Medicare Part D only covered a small segment of the population. They demanded that the benefit be extended to all Americans. The expansion of Medicare Part D became an issue of contention during the 2004 presidential campaign between Bush and Senator John Kerry, which saw the president elected to a second term.

Views on health care continued to mark a delineation between the Democratic and Republican Parties into the second decade of the twenty-first century. In 2010, President Barack Obama, a Democrat, successfully managed the passage of the Patient Protection and Affordable Care Act (PPACA), better known as "Obamacare." It enabled millions of Americans to obtain health insurance at a greatly reduced cost. The passage of the act was divisive, as no Republicans voted for the legislation. They opted to make the repeal of the PPACA a major campaign issue for years.

One cause that engendered great support among Democratic Party constituencies was Senator Bernie Sanders's 2015 push for a living wage. He had observed that too many people in urban areas could not afford to live where they worked. His remedy was detailed in Senate Bill 1832, which was not enacted due to Republican opposition. Rather than accept defeat, Sanders made the issue the centerpiece of his unsuccessful campaign for the presidency in 2016. Although Democrats in Congress continue to work on advancing federal living wage legislation, legislators in cities such as New York City, New York, and Portland, Oregon, opted not to wait for federal action and instead instituted their own live wage laws.

Although Sanders failed to receive the Democratic Party's nomination for the presidency, former secretary of state Hillary Clinton adopted a version of the living wage as part of her campaign platform against Republican Party nominee Donald Trump. Trump proved victorious in the general election. His victory was a setback for both supporters of the living wage and those dependent on the PPACA for their health insurance. One of Trump's first acts was to sign the Executive Order

Minimizing the Economic Burden of the Patient Protection and Affordable Care Act Pending Repeal. Although a symbolic step, it was a clear signal that Trump and the Republicans in Congress were going to revocate the PPACA. They certainly had the ability to do so, since the repeal could be passed by Congress with only Republican votes. Although most of the Republican members of Congress had run for office on a platform to repeal the PPACA, when they actually had the opportunity to do so, some changed their minds. In theory, getting rid of Obamacare was easy. From a pragmatic perspective, the vote meant taking health insurance from many of their constituents. That had the potential of hurting their reelection prospects. Although President Trump and Republican congressional leaders continue to seek a compromise that will attract the necessary number of votes for repeal, it appears that the PPACA may remain the law of the land. There is no precedent for the U.S. government's taking away a major federal entitlement once it has been established, and Obamacare had been established for seven years by the time the repeal efforts were launched by the Trump administration.

1

NATIVE AMERICANS

"To Provide for an Exchange of Lands with the Indians Residing in Any of the States or Territories"

- ***Document:*** Indian Removal Act of 1830
- ***Date:*** May 28, 1830
- ***Where:*** Washington, D.C.
- ***Significance:*** President Andrew Jackson utilized the Indian Removal Act of 1830 to force most of the Indians east of the Mississippi River to migrate to the Indian Territory, which was comprised of much of the present-day states of Kansas and Oklahoma.

DOCUMENT

CHAP. CXLVIII.—*An Act to provide for an exchange of lands with the Indians residing in any of the states or territories, and for their removal west of the river Mississippi.*

Be it enacted by the Senate and House of Representatives of the United States of America, in Congress assembled, That it shall and may be lawful for the President of the United States to cause so much of any territory belonging to the United States, west of the river Mississippi, not included in any state or organized territory, and to which the Indian title has been extinguished, as he may judge necessary, to be divided into a suitable number of districts, for the reception of such tribes or nations of Indians as may choose to exchange the lands where they now reside, and remove there; and to cause each of said districts to be so described by natural or artificial marks, as to be easily distinguished from every other.

SEC. 2. *And be it further enacted,* That it shall and may be lawful for the President to exchange any or all of such districts, so to be laid off and described, with any tribe or nation of Indians now residing within the limits of any of the states or territories, and with which the United States may have existing treaties, for the whole or any part or portion of the territory claimed and occupied by such tribe or nation, within the bounds of any one or more of the states or territories, where the land claimed and occupied by the Indians, is owned by the United States, or the United States are bound to the state within which it lies to extinguish the Indian claim thereto.

SEC. 3. *And be it further enacted,* That in the making of any such exchange or exchanges, it shall and may be lawful for the President solemnly to assure the tribe or nation with which the exchange is made, that the United States will forever secure and guaranty to them, and their heirs or successors, the country so exchanged with them; and if they prefer it, that the United States will cause a patent or grant to be made and executed to them for the same; *Provided always,* That such lands shall revert to the United States, if the Indians become extinct, or abandon the same.

SEC. 4. *And be it further enacted,* That if, upon any of the lands now occupied by the Indians, and to be exchanged for, there should be such improvements as add value to the land claimed by any individual or individuals of such tribes or nations, it shall and may be lawful for the President to cause such value to be ascertained by appraisement or otherwise, and to cause such ascertained value to be paid to the person or persons rightfully claiming such improvements. And upon the payment of such valuation, the improvements so valued and paid for, shall pass to the United States, and possession shall not afterwards be permitted to any of the same tribe.

SEC. 5. *And be it further enacted,* That upon the making of any such exchange as is contemplated by this act, it shall and may be lawful for the President to cause such aid and assistance to be furnished to the emigrants as may be necessary and proper to enable them to remove to, and settle in, the country for which they may have exchanged; and also, to give them such aid and assistance as may be necessary for their support and subsistence for the first year after their removal.

SEC.6. *And be it further enacted,* That it shall and may be lawful for the President to cause such tribe or nation to be protected, at their new residence, against all interruption or disturbance from any other tribe or nation of Indians, or from any other person or persons whatever.

SEC. 7. *And be it further enacted,* That it shall and may be lawful for the President to have the same superintendence and care over any tribe or nation in the country

DID YOU KNOW?

John Collier and Congress

John Collier, Office of Indian Affairs Commissioner, was not satisfied with the Indian Reorganization Act (IRA). He pushed Congress to do even more for native peoples. His fiery oratory blamed the United States for having robbed the Indians of their land, cultures, and economic independence. To many politicians, they had done more than enough to correct past sins and did not want to be reminded of them by Collier. The U.S. Senate's Indian Affairs Committee in 1939 began an investigation concerning the actions of the Bureau of Indian Affairs (BIA) since the passage of the IRA. It was determined that the law had allowed for the bureaucratic growth of the BIA, thereby expanding Collier's authority, but had otherwise yielded less than impressive results. Under political siege, Collier turned to the U.S. House of Representatives' Indian Affairs Committee and asked it to conduct an independent review. The committee acceded to his wishes. It its report, the committee acknowledged some of the successes accomplished through the IRA but also saw a political power grab by Collier. With no support forthcoming from Congress, Collier resigned in 1945.

FURTHER READING

Daily, David W. 2004. *Battle for the BIA: G. E. E. Lindquist and the Missionary Crusade against John Collier.* Tucson: University of Arizona Press.

to which they may remove, as contemplated by this act, that he is now authorized to have over them at their present places of residence: *Provided,* That nothing in this act contained shall be construed as authorizing or directing the violation of any existing treaty between the United States and any of the Indian tribes.

SEC. 8. *And be it further enacted,* That for the purpose of giving effect to the provisions of this act, the sum of five hundred thousand dollars is hereby appropriated, to be paid out of any money in the treasury, not otherwise appropriated.

APPROVED, May 28, 1830.

SOURCE: Indian Removal Act. *U.S. Statutes at Large* 4 (1830): 411.

ANALYSIS

The Indian Removal Act of 1830 had its beginnings with the Indian policy put into place by President Thomas Jefferson at the beginning of the nineteenth century. He pursued a two-pronged Indian policy of negotiation and acculturation. He dispatched agents to negotiate land transactions with Native American groups. Although this implied that the natives had a choice to sell or not to sell their lands, federal representatives such as William Henry Harrison encouraged successful negotiations through the use of military force. To entice native peoples to sell their real estate, Jefferson promised them a place in the nation if they became "civilized." Civilization meant abandoning their traditional cultures, embracing Christianity, and adopting the agricultural lifestyle pursued by the American yeoman farmers of the day. Jefferson believed that encouraging American Indians to acculturate would gradually make them disappear as distinctive peoples through assimilation. By the time Jefferson's presidency was concluded, his policy had resulted in the United States obtaining more than 200,000 square miles of land through treaties negotiated by his agents.

By the 1820s, many Americans were dissatisfied with the pace of land acquisition by government officials. In the Old Northwest and the South, there were demands for the federal government to begin forcibly removing native peoples from the land they occupied. In southern states, this meant a repudiation of Jefferson's Indian policy as many of the Creeks, Cherokees, Chickasaw, and Choctaw had become civilized by Jefferson's definition. The Cherokees even adopted a constitution modeled on that of the United States. The problem was that those groups also occupied some of the most fertile agricultural land, the very land that would soon thereafter become the basis for the South's cotton industry. The desire for native lands was championed by Andrew Jackson, who became president on March 24, 1829. Unlike Jefferson, Andrew Jackson did not see the Indians as future citizens of the United States, but rather as a foreign threat to the military security of the nation. As such, they needed to be removed west of the Mississippi River to Indian Territory, which consisted at the time of a significant portion of the present-day states of Kansas and Oklahoma.

President Jackson's administration and his supporters in Congress passed the Indian Removal Act of 1830 with the expressed purpose of moving all native peoples from the East to the West. Ostensibly, the federal government was required to negotiate an exchange of land with native peoples. For the title of the lands held in the East, the Indians were given land in the West. In practice, negotiations were unnecessary as Jackson empowered military officers to forcibly remove the natives from their homelands and force them west on the "Trail of Tears." When the respective native peoples arrived on their new lands, they found much of it arid and unsuitable for the agricultural lifestyle many had pursued in the East. In addition, the land was already claimed by the native peoples of the region who had lived there since time immemorial. They responded to their new neighbors with violence. By the end of the 1830s, U.S. Indian agents stemmed the animosity between the respective native groups by organizing intertribal councils where the natives negotiated treaties with each other and negotiated tribal boundaries.

The federal government was able to force all the natives to accommodate each other because most of the native peoples in Indian Territory had become dependent on the United States for the majority of the goods they required for subsistence, including food. Native dependency was not an accident, as the U.S. government in 1834 had created the Indian Office within the Department of War. The military could thus use the availability of needed supplies, like meat, as a tool to ensure that natives on the newly created reservations were controlled.

FURTHER READING

Bowes, John P. 2016. *Land Too Good for Indians: Northern Indian Removal.* Norman: University of Oklahoma Press.

Cave, Alfred A. 2003. "Abuse of Power: Andrew Jackson and the Indian Removal Act of 1830," *Historian* 65, no. 6: 1330–1353.

Garrison, Tim Alan. 2002. *The Legal Ideology of Removal: The Southern Judiciary and the Sovereignty of Native American Nations.* Athens: University of Georgia Press.

Haveman, Christopher D. 2016. *Rivers of Sand: Creek Indian Emigration, Relocation, and Ethnic Cleansing in the American South.* Lincoln: University of Nebraska Press.

Heidler, David S., and Jeanne T. Heidler. 1996. *Old Hickory's War: Andrew Jackson and the Quest for Empire.* Mechanicsburg, PA: Stackpole Books.

Littlefield, Daniel F., and James W. Parins, eds. 2011. *Encyclopedia of Indian Removal.* 2 vols. Santa Barbara, CA: Greenwood.

Miles, Tiya. 2010. *The House on Diamond Hill: A Cherokee Plantation Story.* Chapel Hill: University of North Carolina Press.

Perdue, Theda, and Michael D. Green. 2007. *The Cherokee Nation and the Trail of Tears.* New York: Viking.

Portnoy, Alisse. 2005. *Their Right to Speak: Women's Activism in the Indian and Slave Debates.* Cambridge: Harvard University Press.

Remini, Robert V. 2001. *Andrew Jackson and His Indian Wars.* New York: Viking.

Unrau, William E. 2007. *The Rise and Fall of Indian Country, 1825–1855.* Lawrence: University Press of Kansas.

"To Provide for the Allotment of Lands in Severalty to Indians on the Various Reservations"

- ***Document:*** General Allotment Act of 1887, also known as the Dawes Act
- ***Date:*** February 8, 1887
- ***Where:*** Washington, D.C.
- ***Significance:*** The General Allotment Act allowed individual Indians to own reservation land, thereby creating a mechanism for them to also sell it to non-Indians.

DOCUMENT

An Act to provide for the allotment of lands in severalty to Indians on the various reservations, and to extend the protection of the laws of the United States and the Territories over the Indians, and for other purposes.

Be it enacted by the Senate and House of Representatives of the United States of America in Congress assembled, That in all cases where any tribe or band of Indians has been, or shall hereafter be, located upon any reservation created for their use, either by treaty stipulation or by virtue of an act of Congress or executive order setting apart the same for their use, the President of the United States be, and he hereby is, authorized, whenever in his opinion any reservation or any part thereof of such Indians is advantageous for agricultural and grazing purposes, to cause said reservation, or any part thereof, to be surveyed, or resurveyed if necessary, and to allot the lands in said reservation in severalty to any Indian located thereon in quantities as follows:

To each head of a family, one-quarter of a section;
To each single person over eighteen years of age, one-eighth of a section;
To each orphan child under eighteen years of age, one-eighth of a section; and
To each other single person under eighteen years now living, or who may be born prior to the date of the order of the President directing an allotment of the lands embraced in any reservation, one-sixteenth of a section:

Provided, That in case there is not sufficient land in any of said reservations to allot lands to each individual of the classes above named in quantities as above provided, the lands embraced in such reservation or reservations shall be allotted to each individual of each of said classes pro rata in accordance with the provisions of this act: And provided further, That where the treaty or act of Congress setting apart such reservation provides the allotment of lands in severalty in quantities in excess of those herein provided, the President, in making allotments upon such reservation, shall allot the lands to each individual Indian belonging thereon in quantity as specified in such treaty or act: And provided further, That when the lands allotted are only valuable for grazing purposes, an additional allotment of such grazing lands, in quantities as above provided, shall be made to each individual.

Sec. 2. That all allotments set apart under the provisions of this act shall be selected by the Indians, heads of families selecting for their minor children, and the agents shall select for each orphan child, and in such manner as to embrace the improvements of the Indians making the selection. where the improvements of two or more Indians have been made on the same legal subdivision of land, unless they shall otherwise agree, a provisional line may be run dividing said lands between them, and the amount to which each is entitled shall be equalized in the assignment of the remainder of the land to which they are entitled under his act: Provided, That if any one entitled to an allotment shall fail to make a selection within four years after the President shall direct that allotments may be made on a particular reservation, the Secretary of the Interior may direct the agent of such tribe or band, if such there be, and if there be no agent, then a special agent appointed for that purpose, to make a selection for such Indian, which selection shall be allotted as in cases where selections are made by the Indians, and patents shall issue in like manner.

Sec. 3. That the allotments provided for in this act shall be made by special agents appointed by the President for such purpose, and the agents in charge of the respective reservations on which the allotments are directed to be made, under such rules and regulations as the Secretary of the Interior may from time to time prescribe, and shall be certified by such agents to the Commissioner of Indian Affairs, in duplicate, one copy to be retained in the Indian Office and the other to be transmitted to the Secretary of the Interior for his action, and to be deposited in the General Land Office.

Sec. 4. That where any Indian not residing upon a reservation, or for whose tribe no reservation has been provided by treaty, act of Congress, or executive order, shall make settlement upon any surveyed or unsurveyed lands of the United States not otherwise appropriated, he or she shall be entitled, upon application to the local land-office for the district in which the lands arc located, to have the same allotted to him or her, and to his or her children, in quantities and manner as provided in this act for Indians residing upon reservations; and when such settlement is made upon unsurveyed lands, the grant to such Indians shall be adjusted upon the survey of the lands so as to conform thereto; and patents shall be issued to them for such lands in the manner and with the restrictions as herein provided. And the fees to which the officers of such local land-office would have been entitled had such lands been entered under the general laws for the disposition of the public lands shall be paid to them, from any moneys in the Treasury of the United States not otherwise appropriated, upon a statement of an account in their behalf for such fees by the Commissioner of the General Land Office, and a certification of such account to the Secretary of the Treasury by the Secretary of the Interior.

Sec. 5. That upon the approval of the allotments provided for in this act by the Secretary of the Interior, he shall cause patents to issue therefor in the name of the allottees, which patents shall be of the legal effect, and declare that the United States does and will hold the land thus allotted, for the period of twenty-five years, in trust for the sole use and benefit of the Indian to whom such allotment shall have been made, or, in case of his decease, of his heirs according to the laws of the State or Territory where such land is located, and that at the expiration of said period the United States will convey the same by patent to said Indian, or his heirs as aforesaid, in fee, discharged of said trust and free of all charge or incumbrance whatsoever: Provided, That the President of the United States may in any case in his discretion extend the period. And if any conveyance shall be made of the lands set apart and allotted as herein provided, or any contract made touching the same, before the expiration of the time above mentioned, such conveyance or contract shall be absolutely null and void: Provided, That the law of descent and partition in force in the State or Territory where such lands are situate shall apply thereto after patents therefor have been executed and delivered, except as herein otherwise provided; and the laws of the State of Kansas regulating the descent and partition of real estate shall, so far as practicable, apply to all lands in the Indian Territory which may be allotted in severalty under the provisions of this act: And provided further, That at any time after lands have been allotted to all the Indians of any tribe as herein provided, or sooner if in the opinion of the President it shall be for the best interests of said tribe, it shall be lawful for the Secretary of the Interior to negotiate with such Indian tribe for the purchase and release by said tribe, in conformity with the treaty or statute under which such reservation is held, of such portions of its reservation not allotted as such tribe shall, from time to time, consent to sell, on such terms and conditions as shall be considered just and equitable between the United States and said tribe of Indians, which purchase shall not be complete until ratified by Congress, and the form and manner of executing such release prescribed by Congress: Provided however, That all lands adapted to agriculture, with or without irrigation so sold or released to the United States by any Indian tribe shall be held by the United States for the sale purpose of securing homes to actual settlers and shall be disposed of by the United States to actual and bona fide settlers only tracts not exceeding one hundred and sixty acres to any one person, on such terms as Congress shall prescribe, subject to grants which Congress may make in aid of education: And provided further, That no patents shall issue therefor except to the person so taking the same as and homestead, or his heirs, and after the expiration of five years occupancy thereof as such homestead; and any conveyance of said lands taken as a homestead, or any contract touching the same, or lieu thereon, created prior to the date of such patent, shall be null and void. And the sums agreed to be paid by the United States as purchase money for any portion of any such reservation shall be held in the Treasury of the United States for the sole use of the tribe or tribes Indians; to whom such reservations belonged; and the same, with interest thereon at three per cent per annum, shall be at all times subject to appropriation by Congress for the education and civilization of such tribe or tribes of Indians or the members thereof. The patents aforesaid shall be recorded in the General Land Office, and afterward delivered, free of charge, to the allottee entitled thereto. And if any religious society or other organization is now occupying any of the public lands to which this act is applicable, for religious or educational work among the Indians, the Secretary of the Interior is hereby authorized to confirm such occupation to such society or organization, in quantity not exceeding one hundred and sixty acres in any one tract, so long as the same shall be so occupied, on such terms as he shall deem just; but nothing herein contained shall change or alter any claim of such society for religious or educational purposes heretofore granted by law. And hereafter in the employment of Indian police, or any other employees in the public service among any of the Indian tribes or bands affected by this act, and where Indians can perform the duties required, those Indians who have availed themselves of the provisions of this act and become citizens of the United States shall be preferred.

Sec. 6. That upon the completion of said allotments and the patenting of the lands to said allottees, each and every member of the respective bands or tribes of Indians to whom allotments have been made shall have the benefit of and be subject to the laws, both civil and criminal, of the State or Territory in which they may reside; and no Territory shall pass or enforce any law denying any such Indian within its jurisdiction the equal protection of the law. And every Indian born within the territorial limits of the United States to whom allotments shall have been made under the provisions of this act, or under any law or treaty, and every Indian born within the territorial limits of the United States who has voluntarily taken up, within said limits, his residence separate and apart from any tribe of Indians therein, and has adopted the habits of civilized life, is hereby declared to be a citizen of the United States, and is entitled to all the rights, privileges, and immunities of such citizens, whether said Indian has been or not, by birth or otherwise, a member of any tribe of Indians within the territorial limits of the United States without in any manner affecting the right of any such Indian to tribal or other property.

Sec. 7. That in cases where the use of water for irrigation is necessary to render the lands within any Indian reservation available for agricultural purposes, the Secretary of the Interior be, and he is hereby, authorized to prescribe such rules and regulations as he may deem necessary to secure a just and equal distribution thereof among the Indians residing upon any such reservation; and no other appropriation or grant of water by any riparian proprietor shall permitted to the damage of any other riparian proprietor.

Sec. 8. That the provisions of this act shall not extend to the territory occupied by the Cherokees, Creeks, Choctaws, Chickasaws, Seminoles, and Osage, Miamies and Peorias, and Sacs and Foxes, in the Indian Territory, nor to any of the reservations of the Seneca Nation of New York Indians in the State of New York, nor to that strip of territory in the State of Nebraska adjoining the Sioux Nation on the south added by executive order.

Sec. 9. That for the purpose of making the surveys and resurveys mentioned in section two of this act, there be, and hereby is, appropriated, out of any moneys in the Treasury not otherwise appropriated, the sum of one hundred thousand dollars, to be repaid proportionately out of the proceeds of the sales of such land as may be acquired from the Indians under the provisions of this act.

Sec. 10. That nothing in this act contained shall be so construed to affect the right and power of Congress to grant the right of way through any lands granted to an Indian, or a tribe of Indians, for railroads or other highways, or telegraph lines, for the public use, or condemn such lands to public uses, upon making just compensation.

Sec. 11. That nothing in this act shall be so construed as to prevent the removal of the Southern Ute Indians from their present reservation in Southwestern Colorado to a new reservation by and with consent of a majority of the adult male members of said tribe.

SOURCE: Dawes Act of 1887. *U.S. Statutes at Large*, 24 (1887): 388–91.

ANALYSIS

Senators Richard Coke and Henry L. Dawes arguably created the most devious document ever enacted by the federal government in the General Allotment Act of 1887, better known as the Dawes Act. The act appeared to be a generous move by federal authorities to allow individual Indians to become landowners. This was a significant change in policy as reservation lands were previously tribally owned. In truth, it was designed to destroy the ability of tribes to maintain the few lands they still retained. If individual Indians could own land, they could also sell it. The government pretended to protect the lands for the Indians by making it illegal to sell the land for at least 25 years but that rule was not stringently enforced. Basically, the federal government had invented a way to legally obtain land for American citizens that had previously been unavailable to them. The federal government hoped that by breaking up reservations, Indians and American citizens would live alongside each other. Over time, this would result in Indians being assimilated into the general population, thereby eliminating the "Indian problem."

Since tribal reservation land had to be subdivided to create individual allotments, native groups were required to record the names of each member of the tribe on forms provided by federal Indian agents. Since fewer people meant more land, some native groups decided to redefine membership in their tribe. Many biracial Indians of African descent suddenly ceased to be Indians by the stroke of a pen and lost their share of the land.

The impact of the Dawes Act was catastrophic to American Indians. The act contained a clause that allowed the federal government to purchase unallotted excess land on the reservations. Since the federal government did the allotting, significant amounts of land became available as surplus. In 1871, Indians held more than 155,600,000 acres of land. By 1900, their landholdings had been reduced to approximately 77,865,000 acres. The legality of the land seizure was upheld by the decision in the 1903 U.S. Supreme Court case *Lone Wolf v. Hitchcock*, where the justices declared that Congress had the constitutional right to dispose of native lands as they saw fit without having to gain the approval of the affected tribe(s).

The abuses of the federal government in the allotment process came to the fore on February 21, 1928, with the publication of *The Problem of Indian Administration*, also known as the Meriam Report. It documented numerous instances of federal agents utilizing the Dawes Act to deprive Indians of their land, leaving many destitute. In 1934, Congress replaced the Dawes Act with the Indian Reorganization Act, or the Wheeler-Howard Act.

FURTHER READING

Banner, Stuart. 2005. *How the Indians Lost Their Land: Law and Power on the Frontier*. Cambridge, MA: Belknap Press of Harvard University Press.

Genetin-Pilawa, C. Joseph. 2012. *Crooked Paths to Allotment: The Fight over Federal Indian Policy after the Civil War*. Chapel Hill: University of North Carolina Press.

Greenwald, Emily. 2002. *Reconfiguring the Reservation: The Nez Percés, Jicarilla Apaches, and the Dawes Act*. Albuquerque: University of New Mexico Press.

Hoxie, Frederick E. 1984. *A Final Promise: The Campaign to Assimilate the Indians, 1880–1920*. Lincoln: University of Nebraska Press.

McDonnell, Janet A. 1991. *The Dispossession of the American Indian, 1887–1934*. Bloomington: Indiana University Press.

Meriam, Lewis, et al. 1928. *The Problem of Indian Administration: Report of a Survey Made at the Request of Honorable Hubert Work, Secretary of the Interior, and Submitted to Him, February 21, 1928*. Baltimore: The Johns Hopkins University Press. http://files.eric.ed.gov/fulltext/ED087573.pdf (accessed January 7, 2016).

Meyer, Melissa L. 1994. *The White Earth Tragedy: Ethnicity and Dispossession at a Minnesota Anishinaabe Reservation, 1889–1920*. Lincoln: University of Nebraska Press.

Prucha, Francis Paul. 1984. *The Great Father: The United States Government and the American Indians*. Lincoln: University of Nebraska Press.

"An Overwhelming Majority of the Indians Are Poor, Even Extremely Poor"

- ***Document:*** *The Problem of Indian Administration* (Excerpts)
- ***Date:*** February 21, 1928
- ***Where:*** Washington, D.C.
- ***Significance:*** *The Problem of Indian Administration*, also known as the Meriam Report, documented the poverty and its consequences suffered by American Indians during the 1920s. Its findings were used to reform the Bureau of Indian Affairs.

DOCUMENT

The Conditions Among the Indians. An overwhelming majority of the Indians are poor, even extremely poor, and they are not adjusted to the economic and social system of the dominant white civilization.

The poverty of the Indians and their lack of adjustment to the dominant economic and social systems produce the vicious circle ordinarily found among any people under such circumstances. Because of interrelationships, causes cannot be differentiated from effects. The only course is to state briefly the conditions found that are part of this vicious circle of poverty and maladjustment.

Health. The health of the Indians as compared with that of the general population is bad. Although accurate mortality and morbidity statistics are commonly lacking, the existing evidence warrants the statement that both the general death rate and the infant mortality rate are high. Tuberculosis is extremely prevalent. Trachoma, a communicable disease which produces blindness, is a major problem because of its great prevalence and the danger of its spreading among both the Indians and the whites.

Living Conditions. The prevailing living conditions among the great majority of the Indians are conducive to the development and spread of disease. With comparatively few exceptions the diet of the Indians is bad. It is generally insufficient in quantity, lacking in variety, and poorly prepared. The two great preventive elements in diet, milk, and fruits and green vegetables, are notably absent. Most tribes use fruits and vegetables in season, but even then the supply is ordinarily insufficient. The use of milk is rare, and it is generally not available even for infants. Babies, when weaned, are ordinarily put on substantially the same diet as older children and adults, a diet consisting mainly of meats and starches.

The housing conditions are likewise conducive to bad health. Both in the primitive dwellings and in the majority of more or less permanent homes which in some cases have replaced them, there is great overcrowding, so that all members of the family are exposed to any disease that develops, and it is virtually impossible in any way even partially to isolate a person suffering from a communicable disease. . . .

Sanitary facilities are generally lacking. Except among the relatively few well-to-do Indians the houses seldom have a private water supply or any toilet facilities whatever. Even privies are exceptional. Water is ordinarily carried considerable distances from natural springs or streams, or occasionally from wells. In many sections the supply is inadequate, although in some jurisdictions, notably in the desert country of the Southwest, the government has materially improved the situation, an activity that is appreciated by the Indians.

Economic Conditions. The income of the typical Indian family is low and the earned income extremely low. From the standpoint of the white man the typical Indian is not industrious, nor is he an effective worker when he does work. Much of his activity is expended in lines which produce a relatively small return either in goods or money. He generally ekes out an existence through unearned income from leases of his land, the sale of land, per capita payments from tribal funds, or in exceptional cases through rations given him by the government. . . .

The main occupations of the men are some outdoor work, mostly of an agricultural nature, but the number of real farmers is comparatively small. A considerable proportion engage more or less casually in unskilled labor. By many Indians several different kinds of activity are followed spasmodically, a little agriculture, a little fishing, hunting, trapping, wood cutting, or gathering of native products, occasional labor and hauling, and a great deal of just idling. Very seldom do the Indians work about their homes as the typical white man does. . . .

In justice to the Indians it should be said that many of them are living on lands from which a trained and experienced white man could scarcely wrest a reasonable living. In some instances the land originally set apart for the Indians was of little value for agricultural operations other than grazing. In other instances part of the land was excellent but the Indians did not appreciate its value. Often when individual allotments were made, they chose for themselves the poorer parts, because those parts were near a domestic water supply or a source of firewood, or because they furnished some native product important to the Indians in their primitive life. Frequently the better sections of the land originally set apart for the Indians have fallen into the hands of the whites, and the Indians have retreated to the poorer lands remote from markets. . . .

Suffering and Discontent. Some people assert that the Indians prefer to live as they do; that they are happier in their idleness and irresponsibility. The question may be raised whether these persons do not mistake for happiness and content an almost oriental fatalism and resignation. The survey staff found altogether too much evidence of real suffering and discontent to subscribe to the belief that the Indians are reasonably satisfied with their condition. The amount of serious illness and poverty is too great to permit of real contentment. The Indian is like the white man in his affection for his children and he feels keenly the sickness and the loss of his offspring.

The Causes of Poverty. The economic basis of the primitive culture of the Indians has been largely destroyed by the encroachment of white civilization. The Indians can no longer make a living as they did in the past by hunting, fishing, gathering wild products, and the extremely limited practice of primitive agriculture. The social system that evolved from their past economic life is ill suited to the conditions that now confront them, notably in the matter of the division of labor between the men and the women. They are by no means yet adjusted to the new economic and social conditions that confront them.

Several past policies adopted by the government in dealing with the Indians have been of a type which, if long continued, would tend to pauperize any race. Most notable was the practice of issuing rations to able-bodied Indians. Having moved the Indians from their ancestral lands to restricted reservations as a war measure, the government undertook to feed them and to perform certain services for them which a normal people do for themselves. The Indians at the outset had to accept this aid as a matter of necessity, but promptly they came to regard it as a matter of right, as indeed it was at the time and under the conditions of the inauguration of the ration system. They felt, and many of them still feel, that the government owes them a living, having taken their lands from them, and that they are under no obligation to support themselves. They have thus inevitably developed a pauper point of view.

When the government adopted the policy of individual ownership of the land on the reservations, the expectation was that the Indians would become farmers. Part of the plan was to instruct and aid them in agriculture, but this vital part was not pressed with vigor and intelligence. It almost seems as if the government assumed that some magic in individual ownership of property would in itself prove an educational civilizing factor, but unfortunately this policy has for the most part operated in the opposite direction. Individual ownership has in many instances permitted Indians to sell their allotments and to live for a time on the unearned income resulting from the sale. Individual ownership brought promptly all the details of inheritance, and frequently the sale of the property of the deceased Indians to whites so that the estate could be divided among the heirs. To the heirs the sale brought further unearned income, thereby lessening the necessity for self-support. Many Indians were not ready to make effective use of their individual allotments. Some of the allotments were of such a character that they could not be effectively used by anyone in small units. The solution was to permit the Indians through the government to lease their lands to the whites. In some instances government officers encouraged leasing, as the whites were anxious for the use of the land and it was far easier to administer property leased to whites than to educate and stimulate Indians to use their own property. The lease money, though generally small in amount, gave the Indians further unearned income to permit the continuance of a life of idleness.

Surplus land remaining after allotments were made was often sold and the proceeds placed in a tribal fund. Natural resources, such as timber and oil, were sold and the money paid either into tribal funds or to individual Indians if the land had been allotted. From time to time per capita payments were made to the individual Indians from tribal funds. These policies all added to the unearned income of the Indian and postponed the day when it would be necessary for him to go to work to support himself.

Since the Indians were ignorant of money and its use, had little or no sense of values, and fell an easy victim to any white man who wanted to take away their property, the government, through its Indian Service employees, often took the easiest course of managing all the Indians' property for them. The government kept the Indians' money for them at the agency. When the Indians wanted something they would go to the government agent, as a child would go to his parents, and ask for it. The government agent would make all the decisions, and in many instances would either buy the thing requested or give the Indians a store order for it. Although money was sometimes given the Indians, the general belief was that the Indians could not be trusted to spend the money for the purpose agreed upon with the agent, and therefore they must not be given opportunity to misapply it. At some agencies this practice still exists, although it gives the Indians no education in the use of money, is irritating to them, and tends to decrease responsibility and increase the pauper attitude.

The typical Indian, however, has not yet advanced to the point where he has the knowledge of money and values, and of business methods that will permit him to control his own property without aid, advice, and some restrictions ; nor is he ready to work consistently and regularly at more or less routine labor.

SOURCE: Meriam, Lewis, et al. 1928. *The Problem of Indian Administration: Report of a Survey Made at the Request of Honorable Hubert Work, Secretary of the Interior, and Submitted to Him, February 21, 1928*. Baltimore: The Johns Hopkins University Press.

ANALYSIS

In 1926, Secretary of the Interior Hubert Work charged Lewis Meriam and his nine-member team of researchers at the Institute for Government Research to study the day-to-day existence of American Indians on the reservation. Two years of work culminated in the publication of *The Problem of Indian Administration*. The more than 870-page document proved very embarrassing as it concluded that poverty was the gravest calamity impacting American Indians, and the cause of much of the suffering was the federal government itself.

Among the issues identified by Lewis and his team was that American Indians had far higher mortality rates than any other population in the United States. A factor identified as a cause was that the reservations tended to be on marginal lands far from water. Without water, raising animals and crops was virtually impossible. This led to malnutrition, which made individuals more susceptible to diseases like tuberculosis. Many died from survivable illnesses because physicians were rarely available.

Great criticism was levied by Meriam toward the boarding schools that many American Indian children were forced to attend. The purpose of those schools was to strip away the native identity and culture of the children so that they would assimilate into society. Since their purpose was to, as Captain Richard Henry Pratt famously exclaimed, "kill the Indian, and save the man," the children lived in squalid and overcrowded facilities, which bred misery and disease. Predictably, Indian children perished in droves. The problem was generally ignored by society at large since it was a by-product of "civilizing" the natives.

By bringing the plight of American Indians to the fore in *The Problem of Indian Administration*, Lewis Meriam made the misery of Indians the nation's problem. In making the federal government culpable, the document also made it the government's responsibility to address. The report went into so much depth that it identified specific flaws in the function of the Bureau of Indian Affairs along with suggestions for remedies. Many of the policy suggestions made by Meriam and his associates became law through the Indian Reorganization Act of 1934.

FURTHER READING

Critchlow, Donald T. 1981. "Lewis Meriam, Expertise, and Indian Reform." *The Historian* 43, no. 3: 325–344.

Fear-Segal, Jacqueline, and Susan D. Rose, eds. 2016. *Carlisle Indian Industrial School: Indigenous Histories, Memories, & Reclamations*. Lincoln: University of Nebraska Press.

Parman, Donald L., and Lewis Meriam. 1982. "Lewis Meriam's Letters during the Survey of Indian Affairs 1926–1927 (Part I)." *Arizona and the West* 24, no. 3: 253–280.

Parman, Donald L., and Lewis Meriam. 1982. "Lewis Meriam's Letters during the Survey of Indian Affairs 1926–1927 (Part II)." *Arizona and the West* 24, no. 4: 341–370.

"To Conserve and Develop Indian Lands and Resources"

- ***Document:*** Indian Reorganization Act of 1934 (Excerpts)
- ***Date:*** June 18, 1934
- ***Where:*** Washington, D.C.
- ***Significance:*** The Indian Reorganization Act of 1934 reversed the Indian policy enacted by the General Allotment Act of 1887. This meant that rather than reducing land ownership among the natives, the federal government acted to strengthen native sovereignty and assist in the process of reacquiring lands lost in previous decades.

DOCUMENT

AN ACT

To conserve and develop Indian lands and resources; to extend to Indians the right to form business and, other organizations; to establish a credit system for Indians; to grant certain rights of home rule to Indians; to provide for vocational education for Indians; and for other purposes.

Be it enacted by the Senate and House of Representatives of the United States of America in Congress assembled, That hereafter no land of any Indian reservation, created or set apart by treaty or agreement with the Indians, Act of Congress, Executive order, purchase, or otherwise, shall be allotted in severalty to any Indian.

SEC. 2. The existing periods of trust placed upon any Indian lands and any restriction on alienation thereof are hereby extended and continued until otherwise directed by Congress.

SEC. 3. The Secretary of the Interior, if he shall find it to be in the public interest, is hereby authorized to restore to tribal ownership the remaining surplus lands of any Indian reservation heretofore opened, or authorized to be opened, to sale, or any other form of disposal by Presidential proclamation, or by any of the public land laws of the United States: *Provided, however*, That valid rights or claims of any persons to any lands so withdrawn existing on the date of the withdrawal shall not be affected by this Act: *Provided further*, That this section shall not apply to lands within any reclamation project heretofore authorized in any Indian reservation: . . .

SEC. 4. Except as herein provided, no sale, devise, gift, exchange or other transfer of restricted Indian lands or of shares in the assets of any Indian tribe or corporation organized hereunder, shall be made or approved: *Provided, however*, That such lands or interests may, with the approval of the Secretary of the Interior, be sold, devised, or otherwise transferred to the Indian tribe in which the lands or shares are located or from which the shares were derived or to a successor corporation: . . .

SEC. 5. The Secretary of the Interior is hereby authorized, in his discretion, to acquire through purchase, relinquishment, gift, exchange, or assignment, and interest in lands, water rights or surface rights to lands, within or without existing reservations, including trust or otherwise restricted allotments whether the allottee be living or deceased, for the purpose of providing land for Indians. . . .

SEC. 7. The Secretary of the Interior is hereby authorized to proclaim new Indian reservations on lands acquired pursuant to any authority conferred by this Act, or to add such lands to existing reservations: *Provided*, That lands added to existing reservations shall be designated for the exclusive use of Indians entitled by enrollment or by tribal membership to residence at such reservations.

SEC. 19. The term "Indian" as used in this Act shall include all persons of Indian descent who are members of any recognized Indian tribe now under Federal jurisdiction, and all persons who are descendants of such members who were, on June 1, 1934, residing within the present boundaries of any Indian reservation, and shall further include all other persons of one-half or more Indian blood. For the purposes of this Act, Eskimos and other aboriginal peoples of Alaska shall be considered Indians. The term "tribe" wherever used in this Act shall be construed to refer to any Indian tribe, organized band, pueblo or the Indians residing on one reservation. The words "adult Indians" wherever used in this Act shall be construed to refer to Indians who have attained the age of twenty one years.

SOURCE: Kappler, Charles J., comp. 1941. *Indian Affairs: Laws and Treaties: Vol. 5 (Laws) Compiled from December 22, 1927, June 29, 1938.* Washington, D.C.: United States Government Printing Office.

ANALYSIS

In 1933, Secretary of the Interior Harold Ickes and Office of Indian Affairs Commissioner John Collier began work on what became the Indian Reorganization Act of 1934 (IRA), also known as the Wheeler-Howard Act. The new law ended the allotment process established by the General Allotment Act of 1886, or Dawes Act, which had become unwieldy due to the subdivision of the original allotments to numerous heirs. In direct response to that previous policy, provisions were included that protected native lands from purchase by non-Indians. Further, the Secretary of the Interior was granted the authority to purchase former Indian lands and hold them in trust for the natives. By not returning the land directly to its Indian owners, the federal government could shield them from state taxes and laws designed to impinge on both tribal authority and economic security.

The IRA also provided the opportunity for federally recognized tribes residing on reservations to write their own constitutions in an effort to help them reassert their sovereignty. Many politicians and their constituents disagreed with the concession to the Indians because they believed it implied that they had rights as sovereign governments. Although the new constitutions empowered tribal organizations within the boundaries of their respective reservations, the federal government still retained its right to control the land and resources contained on native reservations.

FURTHER READING

Daily, David W. 2004. *Battle for the BIA: G. E. E. Lindquist and the Missionary Crusade against John Collier*. Tucson: University of Arizona Press.

Deloria, Vine, Jr., ed. 2002. *The Indian Reorganization Act: Congresses and Bills*. Norman: University of Oklahoma Press.

Prucha, Francis Paul. 1984. *The Great Father: The United States Government and the American Indians*. 2 vols. Lincoln: University of Nebraska Press.

Rusco, Elmer R. 2000. *A Fateful Time: The Background and Legislative History of the Indian Reorganization Act*. Reno: University of Nevada Press.

Taylor, Graham D. 1980. *The Indian New Deal and American Indian Tribalism: The Administration of the Indian Reorganization Act, 1934–1945*. Lincoln: University of Nebraska Press.

Wilkins, David E. 2013. *Hollow Justice: A History of Indigenous Claims in the United States*. New Haven, CT: Yale University Press.

"The Following Named Indian Tribes and Individual Members Thereof, Should Be Freed from Federal Supervision and Control"

- ***Document:*** House Concurrent Resolution 108
- ***Date:*** August 1, 1953
- ***Where:*** Washington, D.C.
- ***Significance:*** House Concurrent Resolution 108 made it federal policy to "terminate" the relationship between the federal government and sovereign American Indian groups. By withdrawing all federal support and abandoning promises made through treaties, Congress hoped to force American Indians to leave the reservations and assimilate into the nation's general population.

DOCUMENT

Whereas it is the policy of Congress, as rapidly as possible, to make the Indians within the territorial limits of the United States subject to the same laws and entitled to the same privileges and responsibilities as are applicable to other citizens of the United States, to end their status as wards of the United States, and to grant them all of the rights and prerogatives pertaining to American citizenship; and

Whereas the Indians within the territorial limits of the United States should assume their full responsibilities as American citizens: Now, therefore, be it

Resolved by the House of Representatives (the Senate concurring),

That it is declared to be sense of Congress that, at the earliest possible time, all of the Indian tribes and the individual members thereof located within the States of California, Florida, New York, and Texas, and all of the following named Indian tribes and individual members thereof, should be freed from Federal supervision and control and from all disabilities and limitations specially applicable to Indians: The Flathead Tribe of Montana, the Klamath Tribe of Oregon, the Menominee Tribe of Wisconsin, the Potowatamie Tribe of Kansas and Nebraska, and those members of the Chippewa Tribe who are on the Turtle Mountain Reservation, North Dakota. It is further declared to be the sense of Congress that, upon the release of such tribes and individual members thereof from such disabilities and limitations, all offices of the Bureau of Indian Affairs in the States of California, Florida, New York, and Texas and all other offices whose primary purpose was to serve any Indian tribe or individual Indian freed from Federal supervision should be abolished. It is further declared to be the sense of Congress that the Secretary of the Interior should examine all existing legislation dealing with such Indians, and treaties between the Government of the United States and each such tribe, and report to Congress at the earliest practicable date, but not later than January 1, 1954, his recommendations for such legislation as, in his judgement, may be necessary to accomplish the purposes of this resolution.

SOURCE: Kappler, Charles. 1975. *Kappler's Indian Affairs: Laws and Treaties, United States, Vol.* 6. 2nd ed. Washington, D.C.: United States Department of the Interior.

ANALYSIS

The roots of the Termination policy espoused in House Concurrent Resolution 108 can be found in the 1946 creation of the Indian Claims Commission. The commission was ostensibly created to allow for the federal government to atone for its centuries of mistreatment of American Indians by encouraging tribes to bring claims in order to be compensated for lands that had been wrongly seized from them at some point in their relationship with the federal government. In order to advance their respective claims, the tribes had to demonstrate that they actually owned the land in question. If that test was met, the commission compensated the tribe using the value of that land at the time the land transaction had been made. If the treaty was negotiated in 1720, it was the 1720 valuation that was used, not the value of the land in 1946. This meant the tribes that successfully pursued their claims received a pittance. Unbeknownst to the natives, the federal government saw this compensation process as the end of its commitment to support American Indian groups. They had been compensated for past injustices and thus the federal government had no further reason to treat them any differently from any other citizen of the United States.

American Indians discovered that the federal government was ending its commitments to them through the issuance of House Concurrent Resolution 108. It not only made the Termination policy official, but also identified its first potential victims. Although the Flathead Tribe of Montana, the Potowatamie Tribe of Kansas and Nebraska, and the Chippewa Tribe on the Turtle Mountain Reservation, North Dakota, were targeted for termination, they were able to avoid that fate. The Klamath Tribe of Oregon and the Menominee Tribe of Wisconsin were not as fortunate. These groups lost their tribal government apparatus, all of their treaty rights, lands, and other assets.

Approximately a month later, Public Law 280 was passed, which transferred the jurisdiction of legal matters on the Indian reservations in California, Minnesota, Nebraska, Oregon, and Wisconsin from the federal government to state authorities. Provisions were soon made to make the same transfer of judicial authority in other states. With state officials seeing an opportunity to seize tribal lands and assets within their jurisdictions, they urged their representatives in the United States Congress to terminate other native groups. Among those targeted were the Cherokees and Seminoles, but peoples like them with large populations were able to protect themselves through their economic and political power. Smaller groups, such as the Modoc and the Alabama-Coushatta, were successfully terminated.

The Termination policy was not formally rebuked until the early 1970s, when Congress passed legislation that allowed terminated native groups through "restoration acts" to petition for federal recognition. Some terminated groups, such as the Menominee, were able to get their sovereignty as a nation re-recognized. Others were not successful. One unexpected consequence of the Termination policy was the rise of new native leaders as the 1960s dawned, determined to retain, and in some cases regain, their cultures and identity.

FURTHER READING

Beck, David R. M. 2005. *The Struggle for Self-Determination: History of the Menominee Indians since 1854*. Lincoln: University of Nebraska Press.

Fixico, Donald L. 1986. *Termination and Relocation: Federal Indian Policy, 1945–1960*. Albuquerque: University of New Mexico Press.

Metcalf, R. Warren. 2002. *Termination's Legacy: The Discarded Indians of Utah*. Lincoln: University of Nebraska Press.

Philip, Kenneth R. 1999. *Termination Revisited: American Indians on the Trail to Self-Determination, 1933–1953*. Lincoln: University of Nebraska Press.

Ulrich, Roberta. 2010. *American Indian Nations from Termination to Restoration, 1953–2006*. Lincoln: University of Nebraska Press.

Wilkinson, Charles. 2005. *Blood Struggle: The Rise of Modern Nations*. New York: W. W. Norton.

Wilkinson, Charles. 2010. *The People Are Dancing Again: The History of the Siletz Tribe of Western Oregon*. Seattle: University of Washington Press.

"The Prolonged Federal Domination of Indian Service Programs Has Served to Retard Rather Than Enhance the Progress of Indian People and Their Communities"

- ***Document:*** Title I of the Indian Self-Determination and Education Assistance Act (Excerpts)
- ***Date:*** January 4, 1975
- ***Where:*** Washington, D.C.
- ***Significance:*** The act marked a significant change in federal American Indian policy. Recognizing that federal decisions such as the Dawes Act and House Concurrent Resolution 108 had done extreme harm to native peoples, the act empowered the Secretary of the Interior to transfer decision-making powers that had formally resided in the Bureau of Indian Affairs to sovereign Indian nations.

DOCUMENT

AN ACT

To provide maximum Indian participation in the Government and education of the Indian people; to provide for the full participation of Indian tribes in programs and services conducted by the Federal Government for Indians and to encourage the development of human resources of the Indian people; to establish a program of assistance to upgrade Indian education; to support the right of Indian citizens to control their own educational activities; and for other purposes.

Be it enacted by the Senate and House of Representatives of the United States of America in Congress assembled, That this Act may Indian be cited as the "Indian Self-Determination and Education Assistance Act."

CONGRESSIONAL FINDINGS

SEC. 2. (a) The Congress, after careful review of the Federal Government's historical and special legal relationship with, and resulting responsibilities to, American Indian people, finds that—

(1) the prolonged Federal domination of Indian service programs has served to retard rather than enhance the progress of Indian people and their communities by depriving Indians of the full opportunity to develop leadership skills crucial to the realization of self-government, and has denied to the Indian people an effective voice in the planning and implementation of programs for the benefit of Indians which are responsive to the true needs of Indian communities; and

(2) the Indian people will never surrender their desire to control their relationships both among themselves and with non-Indian governments, organizations, and persons.

(b) The Congress further finds that—

(1) true self-determination in any society of people is dependent upon an educational process which will insure the development of qualified people to fulfill meaningful leadership roles;

(2) the Federal responsibility for and assistance to education of Indian children has not effected the desired level of educational achievement or created the diverse opportunities and personal satisfaction which education can and should provide; and

(3) parental and community control of the educational process is of crucial importance to the Indian people.

DECLARATION OF POLICY

SEC. 3. (a) The Congress hereby recognizes the obligation of the United States to respond to the strong expression of the Indian people for self-determination by assuring maximum Indian participation in the direction of educational as well as other Federal services to Indian communities so as to render such services more responsive to the needs and desires of those communities.

(b) The Congress declares its commitment to the maintenance of the Federal Government's unique and continuing relationship with and responsibility to the Indian people through the establishment of a meaningful Indian self-determination policy which will permit an orderly transition from Federal domination of programs for and services to Indians to effective and meaningful participation by the Indian people in the planning, conduct, and administration of those programs and services.

(c) The Congress declares that a major national goal of the United States is to provide the quantity and quality of educational services and opportunities which will permit Indian children to compete and excel in the life areas of their choice, and to achieve the measure of self-determination essential to their social and economic well-being.

. . .

TITLE I—INDIAN SELF-DETERMINATION ACT

SEC. 101. This title may be cited as the "Indian Self-Determination Act."

CONTRACTS BY THE SECRETARY OF THE INTERIOR

SEC. 102. (a) The Secretary of the Interior is directed, upon the request of any Indian tribe, to enter into a contract or contracts with any tribal organization of any such Indian tribe to plan, conduct, and administer programs, or portions thereof, provided for in the Act of April 16, 1934 (48 Stat. 596), as amended by this Act, any other program or portion thereof which the Secretary of the Interior is authorized to administer for the benefit of Indians under the Act of November 2, 1921 (42 Stat. 208), and any Act subsequent thereto: *Provided however,* That the Secretary may initially decline to enter into any contract requested by an Indian tribe if he finds that: (1) the service to be rendered to the Indian beneficiaries of the particular program or function to be contracted will not be satisfactory; (2) adequate protection of trust resources is not assured, or (3) the proposed project or function to be contracted for cannot be properly completed or maintained by the proposed contract: *Provided further,* That in arriving at his finding, the Secretary shall consider whether the tribe or tribal organization would be deficient in performance under the contract with respect to (A) equipment, (B) bookkeeping and accounting procedures, (C) substantive knowledge of the program to be contracted for, (D) community support for the contract, (E) adequately trained personnel, or (F) other necessary components of contract performance. (b) Whenever the Secretary declines to enter into a contract or contracts pursuant to subsection (a) of this section, he shall (1) state his objections in writing to the tribe within sixty days, (2) provide to the extent practicable assistance to the tribe or tribal organization to overcome his stated objections, and (3) provide the tribe with a hearing, under such rules and regulations as he may promulgate, and the opportunity for appeal on the objections raised. (c) The Secretary is authorized to require any tribe requesting that he enter into a contract pursuant to the provisions of this title to obtain adequate liability insurance: *Provided, however,* That each such policy of insurance shall contain a provision that the insurance carrier shall waive any right it may have to raise as a defense the tribe's sovereign immunity from suit, but that such waiver shall extend only to claims the amount and nature of which are within the coverage and limits of the policy and shall not authorize or empower such insurance carrier to waive or otherwise limit the tribe's sovereign immunity outside or beyond the coverage and limits of the policy of insurance.

CONTRACTS BY THE SECRETARY OF HEALTH, EDUCATION, AND WELFARE

SEC. 103 (a) The Secretary of Health, Education, and Welfare is directed, upon the request of any Indian tribe, to enter into a contract or contracts with any tribal organization of any such Indian tribe to carry out any or all of his functions, authorities, and responsibilities under the Act of August 5, 1954 (68 Stat. 674), as amended: *Provided however,* That the Secretary may initially decline to enter into any contract requested by an Indian tribe if he finds that: (1) the service to be rendered to the Indian beneficiaries of the particular program or function to be contracted for will not be satisfactory; (2) adequate protection of trust resources is not assured; or (3) the proposed project or function to be contracted for cannot be properly completed or maintained by the proposed contract: *Provided further,* That the Secretary of Health, Education, and Welfare, in arriving at his finding, shall consider whether the tribe or tribal organization would be deficient in performance under the contract with respect to (A) equipment, (B) bookkeeping and accounting procedures, (C) substantive knowledge of the program to be contracted for, (D) community support for the contract, (E) adequately trained personnel, or (F) other necessary components of contract performance.

(b) Whenever the Secretary of Health, Education, and Welfare declines to enter into a contract or contracts pursuant to subsection (a) of this section, he shall (1) state his objections in writing to the tribe within sixty days; (2) provide, to the extent practicable, assistance to the tribe or tribal organization to overcome his stated objections; and (3) provide the tribe with a hearing, under such rules and regulations as he shall promulgate, and the opportunity for appeal on the objections raised.

(c) The Secretary of Health, Education, and Welfare is authorized to require any tribe requesting that he enter into a contract pursuant to the provisions of this title to obtain adequate liability insurance: *Provided, however,* That each such policy of insurance shall contain a provision that the insurance carrier shall waive any right it may have to raise as a defense the tribe's sovereign immunity from suit, but that such waiver shall extend only to claims the amount and nature of which are within the coverage and limits of the policy and shall not authorize or empower such insurance carrier to waive or otherwise limit the tribe's sovereign immunity outside or beyond the coverage and limits of the policy of insurance.

GRANTS TO TRIBAL ORGANIZATIONS

SEC. 104. (a) The Secretary of the Interior is authorized, upon the request of any Indian tribe (from funds appropriated for the benefit of Indians pursuant to the Act of November 2, 1921 (42 Stat. 208), and any Act subsequent thereto) to contract with or make a grant or grants to any tribal organization for—

(1) the strengthening or improvement of tribal government (including, but not limited to, the development, improvement, and administration of planning, financial management, or merit personnel systems; the improvement of tribally funded programs or activities; or the development, construction, improvement, maintenance, preservation, or operation of tribal facilities or resources);

(2) the planning, training, evaluation of other activities designed to improve the capacity of a tribal organization to enter into a contract or contracts pursuant to section 102 of this Act and the additional costs associated with the initial years of operation under such a contract or contracts;

(3) the acquisition of land in connection with items (1) and (2) above: Provided, That in the case of land within reservation boundaries or which adjoins on at least two sides lands held in trust by the United States for the tribe or for individual Indians, the Secretary of Interior may (upon request of the tribe) acquire such land in trust for the tribe; or

(4) the planning, designing, monitoring, and evaluating of Federal programs serving the tribe.

(b) The Secretary of Health, Education, and Welfare may, in accordance with regulations adopted pursuant to section 107 of this Act, make grants to any Indian tribe or tribal organization for—

(1) the development, construction, operation, provision, or maintenance of adequate health facilities or services including the training of personnel for such work, from funds appropriated to the Indian Health Service for Indian health services or Indian health facilities; or

(2) planning, training, evaluation or other activities designed to improve the capacity of a tribal organization to enter into a contract or contracts pursuant to section 103 of this Act.

(c) The provisions of any other Act notwithstanding, any funds made available to a tribal organization under grants pursuant to this section may be used as matching shares for any other Federal grant programs which contribute to the purposes for which grants under this section are made.

SOURCE: U.S. Congress. 1975. Public Law 93-638, *88 Stat. 2203*.

ANALYSIS

Presidents Lyndon Baines Johnson and Richard Nixon believed that the federal relationship with American Indians needed to evolve from one where the government functioned in a paternalistic manner to a partnership. Toward that end, Nixon's administration helped enact the Indian Financing Act of 1974 to help native entrepreneurs build their businesses. American Indian groups at the time were also moving into gaming as a source of revenue. Nixon supported the expansion into casinos as that would help make American Indians less dependent on the federal government to fund their activities.

Nixon's enthusiastic support also paved the way for the passage of the Indian Self-Determination and Educational Assistance Act of 1975. The act allowed Indian nations to contract with the United States Secretary of the Interior to assume responsibility for some of the activities that up to that point had been managed by the Bureau of Indian Affairs. The contracts proved such a success that in 1988, Congress set up a test program that allowed native nations to petition the secretary of the interior to become self-governing. This meant allowing them to manage all of the programs that had formerly been administrated by the federal government. Up to 20 tribes a year were allowed to become self-governing. The initiative became permanent in 1994.

FURTHER READING

Ball, Dewi Ioan. 2016. *The Erosion of Tribal Power: The Supreme Court's Silent Revolution*. Norman: University of Oklahoma Press.

Castile, George Pierre. 1998. *To Show Heart: Native American Self-Determination and Federal Indian Policy, 1960–1975*. Tucson: University of Arizona Press.

Cobb, Daniel M. 2008. *Native Activism in Cold War America: The Struggle for Sovereignty*. Lawrence: University Press of Kansas.

Den Ouden, Amy E., and Jean M. O'Brien. 2013. *Recognition, Sovereignty Struggles, and Indigenous Rights in the United States: A Sourcebook*. Chapel Hill: University of North Carolina Press.

Harvard Project on American Indian Economic Development. 2007. *The State of the Native Nations: Conditions under U.S. Policies of Self-Determination*. New York: Oxford University Press.

Prucha, Francis Paul. 1984. *The Great Father: The United States Government and the American Indians*. Lincoln: University of Nebraska Press.

Strommer, Geoffrey D., and Stephen D. Osborne. 2014. "The History, Status, and Future of Tribal Self-Governance under the Indian Self-Determination and Education Assistance Act." *American Indian Law Review* 39, no. 1: 1–75.

2

EARLY LOCAL AND STATE PERSPECTIVES

"There Must Be, in the Nature of Things, Numerous and Minute Shades of Difference Between, the Pauper, Who, Through Impotency, Can Do Absolutely Nothing, and the Pauper, Who Is Able to Do Something, but That, Very Little."

- ***Document:*** *Report of the Committee on the Pauper Laws of This Commonwealth* (Excerpts)
- ***Date:*** 1821
- ***Where:*** Boston, Massachusetts
- ***Significance:*** The *Report of the Committee on the Pauper Laws of This Commonwealth*, also known as the Quincy Report, was an early study of poverty at the state level. It identified the presence of two types of paupers in Massachusetts. One group was incapable of caring for itself, while the other was comprised of able-bodied individuals who came to treat aid as a dependable form of salary.

DOCUMENT

The principle of pauper laws is that of a state, or public, or, as sometimes called, a compulsory provision for the poor. The poor are of two classes. 1. The impotent poor; in which denomination are included all, who are wholly incapable of work, through old age, infancy, sickness or corporeal debility. 2. The able poor; in which denomination are included all, who are capable of work, of some nature, or other;

but differing in the degree of their capacity, and in the kind of work, of which they are capable.

With the respect to the first class; that of poor, absolutely impotent, were there none other than this class, there would be little difficulty, either as to the principle, or as to the mode of extending relief.

But another class exists; that of the able poor; in relation to which, and from the difficulty of discriminating between this class and the former, and of apportioning the degree of public provision to the degree of actual impotency, arise all the objections to the principle of the existing pauper system. The evils, also, which are attributed to this system, of diminishing the industry, destroying the economical habits and eradicating the providence of the laboring class of society may all be referred to the same source;—the difficulty of discriminating between the able poor and the impotent poor and of apportioning the degree of public provision to the degree of actual impotency.

This difficulty, cannot, apparently, be removed by any legislative provision. There must be, in the nature of things, numerous and minute shades of difference between, the pauper, who, through impotency, can do absolutely nothing, and the pauper, who is able to do something, but that, very little. Nor does the difficulty of discrimination, proportionally, diminish as the ability, in any particular pauper, to do something, increases. There always must exist, so many circumstances of age, sex, previous habits, muscular, or mental, strength, to be taken into the account, that society is absolutely incapable to fix any standard, or to prescribe any rule, by which the claim of right to the benefit of the public provision shall absolutely be determined. The consequence is that the admission, or rejection, of the claim to such relief is necessarily left to the discretion of Overseers; or to those, who are entrusted by law, with the distribution of the public charity.

The necessity of entrusting this discretion, the class of society to which it must be entrusted to men in good, generally in easy, circumstances; that is, to the prosperous class of society. "The humanity natural to this class, will never see the poor, in any thing like want, when that want is palpably and visibly brought before it, without extending relief." Much less will this be the case, when they have means, placed in their hands by society itself, applicable to this very purpose. In executing the trust, they will, almost unavoidably, he (sic) guided by sentiments of pity and compassion, and be very little influenced by the consideration of the effect of the facility, or fullness, of provision, to encourage habits of idleness, dissipation and extravagance among the class, which labor. "They first give necessaries, then comforts; and often, in the end, pamper rather than relieve."

If the means, placed under their control, are confined to provision for the poor, in public poor, or alms houses, the effect of these dispositions and feelings appears, in the case, with which admission is obtained; the kindness with which the poor are treated, during their residence, and in the superiority of the food of the public table, to that, to which they have been accustomed. If those means consist in Funds, the same temper and feelings predominate, in their distribution. It is laborious to ascertain the exact merit of each applicant. Supply is sometimes excessive; at others misplaced. The poor begin to consider it as a right; next, they calculate upon it as an income. The stimulus to industry and economy is annihilated, or weakened;

temptations to extravagance and dissipation are increased, in proportion as public supply is likely, or certain, or desirable. The just pride of independence, so honorable to man, in every condition, is thus corrupted by the certainty of public provision; and is either weakened, or destroyed according to the facility of its attainment, or its amount.

View of this kind, connected with the experience of England, under the operation of her poor laws; have led some of her most distinguished statesmen and writers on public economy, to denounce all public, or compulsory provision for the poor, as increasing the evil they pretend to remedy, and augmenting the misery they undertake to prevent. Thus the Earl of Sheffield, in his observations on the English poor laws, published in 1818, declares that "the tendency of parochial relief is to encourage the worthless and audacious: to suppress the feelings of pity towards the poor; to lessen their honest exertions; to deprave their morals; to destroy the notions of a provident spirit; to multiply their number; offering a premium for indolence, prodigality, and vice; and stopping that course of things, by which want leads to labor, labor to comfort, the knowledge of comfort to industry, and its consequent virtues, and neglecting that respectable poverty, which shrinks from public view; it encourages all those abominable arts, which make beggary and parish relief a better trade than labor."

The celebrated Henry Brougham, also, in a letter to Sir Samuel Romilly, published in the same year, on the abuse of public charities, lays it down as "a principle, which will admit of no contradiction, that the existence of any permanent fund for the support of the poor, the appropriation of any revenue, however raised, which must be peremptorily expended, in maintaining such as have no other means of subsistence, has, upon the whole, a direct tendency to increase their numbers." . . .

Your Committee in placing, in this strong light the objections to the entire principle of our existing pauper laws, have had no intention to recommend, nor any idea that their investigations ultimately result in, an abolition of those laws altogether in Massachusetts. But they have been induced to this statement from a consideration that to any effectual attempt to ameliorate the present system of the Pauper laws a distinct apprehension of the nature of the objects to them should be attained; and the real nature of the evils as well as the manner, in with the causes, which induce them, operate, should be, known and made familiar to our fellow citizens. It is apparent, also, not only from the remarks of the Overseers of the Poor, of the Town of Richmond, in the document annexed, but also from expressions in returns from other towns, that a similar train of thoughts exists in some parts of the Commonwealth.

. . .

While, therefore, your Committee on the one hand are of opinion, that no subject more imperiously claims the attention and solicitude of the Legislature:—that it is the duty of society by general arrangements, to attempt to diminish the increase of pauperism, as well as to make provision for that which is inevitable;—that diminution of the evil, is best, and 'most surely to be effected by making Alms Houses, Houses of Industry, and not abodes of idleness, and denying for the most part all supply from public provision, except on condition of admission into the public institution;—and that of all modes of employing the industry of the poor, the best is in agriculture; yet on the other hand, they are also of opinion, that no ultimate system should be founded upon these principles, until they have been laid before their fellow citizens, for their contemplation. Certainly and general satisfaction, being, in cases of this nature, much more important that expedition.

Your Committee, therefore, only recommend that measures should be adopted to communicate to their fellow citizens in the several towns the results of this investigation; that measures should be taken to insure returns, from the several towns of the gross aggregate of their several expenses on account of paupers, for at least one year, and also, the whole number of paupers by each town supported during that year; and that a Committee should be appointed, instructed to report at the next session, a system of Town, or District Alms Houses, with such rules, regulations and provisions for their management and government, as shall be best adapted to promote the great objects contemplated in this report, and conformable to its general principles, in the form of a bill or bills; having a reference to placing the whole subject of the poor in the Commonwealth, under the regular and annual superintendence of the Legislature.

For the Committee,
JOYIAH [*sic*] QUINCY, *Chairman.*

SOURCE: Quincy, Josiah. 1821. *Report of the Committee to Whom Was Referred the Consideration of the Pauper Laws of the Commonwealth.* Boston: Shaw and Shoemaker.

ANALYSIS

The *Report of the Committee on the Pauper Laws of This Commonwealth* is widely known as the "Quincy Report," because Josiah Quincy, the mayor of Boston, Massachusetts, served as the chairperson of the commission that produced the study. The commission was charged by the Massachusetts legislature with studying the growth of poverty within the state's towns and cities. The obvious growth of the impoverished population since the beginning of the nineteenth century had vexed the politicians because the more aid that communities provided to the poor, the more individuals who asked for help. The legislators assumed that an increase in aid should have resulted in a decrease in the number of poor people.

Among the conclusions made in the Quincy Report was that the provision of aid to the poor was one factor leading to the growth of poverty. The generosity of the working class had created an underclass that came to view charity as a dependable source of income. In essence, being poor became their job. This finding proved problematic to Josiah Quincy personally, because he believed that the working class was extremely benevolent, but in order to alleviate the growth of the poor, they were going to have to harden their hearts to the plight of the impoverished. He demonstrated that English writers who studied poverty came to conclusions that mirrored those of the commission. Once it was determined in England that generosity grew the "evils" associated with poverty, the English eradicated all charitable activities toward the poor. Although Quincy suggested that a similar solution might help alleviate local poverty, he also stated that the people of Massachusetts did not have to be so cruel to their citizens.

Quincy's concerns about cruelty also extended to the treatment of the poor during the same period within the commonwealth. He was critical about how some communities in Massachusetts empowered "overseers of the poor," to care for the local underclass. Some overseers sold the labor of their charges in exchange for money. The overseers benefited financially, while the poor were compensated with the very aid that they were supposed to receive sans the work requirement.

The most recognized observation of the Quincy Report dealt with there being two types of poor. The "worthy" poor were truly incapable of caring for themselves, while the other group was comprised of able-bodied individuals who did not deserve to be compensated for their laziness in any form. While the commission was not interested in caring for the latter group, there was discussion of how to best provide for those needing care, including lodging. Almshouses, or poorhouses, were seen as a possible solution by the commission, among others, but a firm recommendation ultimately was not made. The commission instead suggested that the Commonwealth of Massachusetts convene other committees to further weigh issues related to the poor.

The Quincy Report proved influential to other states, most notably Pennsylvania and New York, as a model to conduct statewide studies of poverty. Unlike Massachusetts, New York, in the Yates Report, not only identified the challenges faced by the poor and the communities that served them, but also prescribed remedies.

FURTHER READING

Katz, Michael B. 1996. *In the Shadow of the Poorhouse: A Social History of Welfare in America.* Rev. ed. New York: Basic Books.

Trattner, Walter I. 1989. *From Poor Law to Welfare State: A History of Social Welfare in America.* New York: Free Press.

"Very Clear and Decided Evidence of, the Success of the Poor House System"

- ***Document:*** Report of the Secretary of State in 1824 on the Relief and Settlement of the Poor (Excerpts)
- ***Date:*** February 9, 1824
- ***Where:*** Albany, New York
- ***Significance:*** The Report of the Secretary of State in 1824 on the Relief and Settlement of the Poor, best known as the "Yates Report," concluded that many able-bodied individuals were unfairly benefiting from relief intended for the poor. In response, New York's legislators passed the County Poorhouse Act of 1924, which recommended that counties construct poorhouses for the "worthy" poor.

DOCUMENT

The poor of this state consist of two classes—the permanent poor, or those who are regularly supported, during the whole year, at the public expense; and the occasional, or temporary poor, or those who receive occasional relief, during a part of the year, chiefly in the autumn or winter.

Of the first class, according to the official reports and estimates received, there are, in this state, 6,896; and of the last, 15,215; making a grand total of 22,111 paupers. Among the permanent pauper, there are 446 idiots and lunatics; 287 persons who are blind; 928 who are extremely aged and infirm; 797 who are lame, or in such a confirmed state of ill health, as to be totally incapable of labor; 2604 children, under 14 years of age, and 1789 paupers of both sexes, all of whom, though not in the vigor of life, may yet be considered capable of earning their subsistence, if proper labor were assigned, and suitable means used to induce them to perform it, and whose labor might produce at least 150,000 dollars annually to the state. Of the whole number of permanent paupers, the returns and estimates will warrant the assertion, that at least 1585 male persons were reduced to that state by the excessive use of ardent spirits; and of consequence, that their families, (consisting of 989 wives, and 2167 children,) were reduced to the same penury and want; thus presenting strong evidence of the often asserted fact, that "Intemperance has produced more than two-thirds of all the permanent pauperism in the state:" and there is little hazard in adding, that to the same cause may be ascribed more than one half of the occasional pauperism. Of the whole number of both classes of paupers, 10,523 are males, and 11,588 females, (being an excess of 1065 female paupers:) 5883, including their children in that number, are either aliens or naturalized (sic) foreigners; and 16,228, including also their children, are native citizens.

There are 8753 children of both classes under 14 years of age, the greater number of whom is entirely destitute of education, and equally in want of that care and attention, which are so necessary to inculcate correct moral habits: It is feared that this mass of pauperism, will at no distant day form a fruitful nursery for crime, unless prevented by the watchful superintendance of the legislature.

In eighteen counties bordering on the ocean, and on the Hudson river, with a population of only 582,225 souls, being somewhat more than a third of our entire population, no less than 12,270 permanent and occasional paupers, are maintained or relieved, being far more than one half of all the paupers in the state. The city of New-York alone maintains 1698 permanent paupers, and relieves 7858 occasional paupers, being more than three sevenths of all the paupers of both classes, and nearly one fourth of all the permanent poor.

It will hardly be necessary to explain the cause of this great disparity. It will be found in the dense population of that city, and of the large villages and towns, which, from their convenient situation for navigation and commerce, allure to their haunts and recesses, the idle and dissolute of every description.

. . .

The next branch of this subject, is the amount of the whole pauper expense which has been borne by the state for several years past.

In the year 1815, according to the returns and estimates received, the whole pauper expense in this state, derived from taxation and the excise duties, amounted to 245,000 dollars.

In the year 1810, it had increased to 368,645 dollars, and in 1822, to 470,000. The excise duties, during the year 1822, are computed to exceed 66,600 dollars, and the costs and expenses of justices, overseers, and constables, in examining and removing paupers, and in other duties incident thereto, together with the expenses of appeals from orders of removal, exceeded 64,450 dollars. This amount of expense, (which, with ordinary management and care alone, would be sufficient to maintain at least 2148 paupers in an alms house for a whole year,) is certainly too large a deduction from our pauper funds, not to call for correction, especially when we consider the benevolent purposes for which our poor laws were professedly instituted. 1796 paupers, among whom were more than 600 children and 320 women were removed (and many of them while sick and diseased,) during the year 1822, to different parts of the state, under orders or warrants of justices, at an expense far exceeding 25,000 dollars; a sum if it had been applied for their support instead of their removal, would have maintained 833 of those paupers for a whole year, being nearly half the number removed. From these orders of removal, there were no less than 127 appeals to the courts of general sessions of the peace, the management and defence of which, cost the litigant parties upwards of 13,500 dollars, a sum equal to the support of 450 paupers for a year.

With respect to the amount necessary for the support of a pauper in an alms house, it appears to be variously estimated, as much depends on the skill, fidelity, and management of the keeper, the number of paupers supported and able to work, the expense of fuel, the contiguity of the institution to a market town, the economy of the house, and the conveniences for agricultural labour, connected with it. It is believed that with proper care and attention, and under favorable circumstances, the average annual expense in an alms house, having a convenient farm attached to it, will not exceed from 20 to 35 dollars for the support of each pauper, exclusive of the amount of labour he may perform; while out of an alms house, it will not be less than from 33 to 65 dollars, and in many instances where the pauper is old and infirm, or diseased, from 80 to 100 dollars, and even more.

There are few regular and well established poor houses in this state. In the year 1820, authority was given to erect a house of industry in the county of Rensselaer, and that institution which has been established, and is in full operation, has completely fulfilled, if not surpassed the expectation of its founders.

It would perhaps be proper to mention in this place, that the judicious and satisfactory report made of its management and economy, furnishes very clear and decided evidence of, the success of the poor house system.

SOURCE: Journal of the Senate of the State of New York. 1901. *Documents of the Senate of the State of New York. One Hundred and Twenty-Fourth Session. 1901. Vol. VI.-No. 26-Part 1.* Albany, NY: James B. Lyon, State Printer: 939–946.

ANALYSIS

In 1821, Massachusetts issued its *Report of the Committee on the Pauper Laws of This Commonwealth,* which explored the manifestations of poverty within its borders. Authored by Josiah Quincy, it determined that there were two types of poor. One group was incapable of caring for itself and the other was comprised of able-bodied people who were unfairly benefiting from aid. Influenced by Massachusetts, New York launched a similar study. Headed by Secretary of State John Van Ness Yates, it too found the same two classes of the impoverished. Whereas Massachusetts identified the problem, New York proposed a solution, which was to construct poorhouses, or "almshouses."

During the early 1800s, it was widely believed that poverty was caused by immoral activities such as the consumption of alcoholic beverages. With that assumption treated as fact, Yates separated the poor deserving of aid from those who could work but instead preferred to subsist at public expense. The worthy poor primarily consisted of children, women without a spouse, and the elderly. Everybody else was capable of working and the state expected them to do so. In order to address the needs of both types of poor people, Yates proposed changing the type of aid that was available to them. Prior to the passage of the County Poorhouse Act of 1924, cities and towns delivered "outdoor relief" to the impoverished. This relief consisted of commodities like money and food that could be taken to the home. Although they depended on the charity, which was a burden for a small community, it was alleged by the working class that the poor saw it as their right. Their lack of appreciation bred contempt among the general populace who saw that their effort encouraged laziness among the entitled poor.

The construction of poorhouses by individual counties solved a multitude of issues. First, it shifted the financial responsibility for helping the poor from individual communities to counties. With management centralized at the county level, state funding was easier to provide. It was also believed that at the county level, more services could be delivered to the poor for far less of an expense than was possible under the outdoor relief system. Since it was anticipated that each poorhouse would have a farm, the residents could work to grow the foodstuffs they required, thereby further reducing cost for both the county and the state.

Those physically capable of supporting themselves were pressured to find their own accommodations elsewhere rather than depending on the poorhouse. An unintended consequence was that exodus of able-bodied individuals rendered many of the farms useless since many of the worthy poor were not physically capable of performing the work that was required. The problem resulting from the shortage of food was compounded during the winter when many of the able-bodied poor moved into the poorhouse for the season, a period when their opportunities for work were minimal.

The poorhouses were not the panacea anticipated by New York. The state ultimately concluded that it cost more to provide care for the poor in almshouses than it would have if they had been left in their original residences. Once the poor residents were out of their homes, the state was not able to ignore them. New York, and other states that had emphasized the construction of similar institutions, thus had responsibility for a population that was largely unable to provide for itself. The states were unable to effectively divest themselves of their poorhouses until the passage of the Social Security Act of 1935, which created various welfare programs aimed at the needs of children, women, and the elderly.

FURTHER READING

Hannon, Joan Underhill. 1984. "Poverty in the Antebellum Northeast: The View from New York State's Poor Relief Rolls." *Journal of Economic History* 44, no. 4: 1007–1032.

Katz, Michael B. 1996. *In the Shadow of the Poorhouse: A Social History of Welfare in America.* Rev. ed. New York: Basic Books.

Trattner, Walter I. 1989. *From Poor Law to Welfare State: A History of Social Welfare in America.* New York: Free Press.

Wagner, David. 2005. *The Poorhouse: America's Forgotten Institution.* Lanham, MD: Rowman & Littlefield.

"Consider the Case of Those Whose Services Are So Inadequately Remunerated"

- ***Document:*** *Appeal to the Wealthy of the Land, Ladies as Well as Gentlemen, on the Character, Conduct, Situation, and Prospects of Those Whose Sole Dependence for Subsistence Is on the Labour of Their Hands* (Excerpt)
- ***Date:*** July 1833
- ***Where:*** Philadelphia, Pennsylvania
- ***Significance:*** During a time that most believed that poverty was caused by personal failings such as alcoholism, Mathew Carey argued that it was the result of factors like the shortage of jobs and the low wages being paid to those who were successful in attaining employment.

DOCUMENT

ESSAY I.

I propose in these essays to consider, and attempt to refute, certain pernicious errors which too generally prevail respecting the situation, the conduct, the characters, and the prospects of those whose sole dependence is on the labour of their hands—who comprise, throughout the world, two-thirds, perhaps three-fourths, of the human race—and on whose services the other third or fourth depend for their necessaries, their comforts, their enjoyments, and their luxuries.

According to these calculations, the number of persons in the United States depending on wages for their support must be eight or nine millions. This is a deeply interesting view of the subject, and fully proves its immense importance; and how solicitous we should be to guard against errors in discussing it—errors which may perniciously affect the interests and happiness of so large a portion of the human family. Whatever concerns their comfort or happiness—whatever tends to increase or decrease then comforts—to improve or deteriorate their morals, demands the most serious attention of the friends of humanity, of all whose views extend beyond their own narrow selfish concerns, and who, without the services of this class, would be forlorn and helpless.

The class in question is susceptible of two great subdivisions—those who are so well remunerated for their labours, as to be able, not merely to provide, when employed, for seasons of stagnation and sickness, but by industry, prudence, and economy, to save enough in the course of a few years, to commence business on a small scale on their own account. With this fortunate description, which is numerous and respectable, I have no concern at present. My object is to consider the case of those whose services are so inadequately remunerated, owing to the excess of labour beyond the demand for it, that they can barely support themselves while in good health and fully employed; and, of course, when sick or unemployed, must perish, unless relieved by charitable individuals, benevolent societies, or the guardians of the poor. I use the word "perish" with due deliberation, and a full conviction of its appropriate application to the case, however revolting it may seem to the reader; for as these people depend for daily support on their daily or weekly wages, they are, when those wages are stopped by whatever means, utterly destitute of wherewith to support their existence, and actually become paupers, and therefore, without the aid above stated, would, I repeat, "perish" of want.

The crisis of suffering through which this class about three years since passed here and elsewhere, and the occurrence of similar suffering in all hard winters (and, in other seasons, from sickness and destitution of employment), often without receiving that extra aid which such a state of things loudly demands, appears to require a sober and serious investigation, in order to probe to the bottom so deplorable a state of things, whereby the comfort and happiness of such a large portion of human beings are so cruelly shipwrecked, and to ascertain what are the causes of the evil, and whether it be susceptible of any remedy.

The erroneous opinions to which I have alluded are—

1. That every man, woman, and grown child, able and willing to work may find employment.
2. That the poor, by industry, prudence, and economy, may at all times support themselves comfortably, without depending on eleemosynary aid—and, as a corollary from these positions,
3. That their sufferings and distresses chiefly, if not wholly, arise from their idleness, their dissipation, and their extravagance.
4. That taxes for the support of the poor, and aid afforded them by charitable individuals, or benevolent societies, are pernicious, as, by encouraging the poor to depend on them, they foster their idleness and improvidence, and thus produce, or at least increase, the poverty and distress they are intended to relieve.

These opinions, so far as they have operated—and, through the mischievous zeal and industry of the school of political economists by which they have been promulgated, they have spread widely—have been pernicious to the rich and the poor. They tend to harden the hearts of the former against the sufferings and distresses of the latter,—and of course prolong those sufferings and distresses.

Many wealthy individuals, benevolent and liberal, apprehensive lest by charitable aid to persons in distress, they might produce evil to society, are, by these pernicious and cold-blooded doctrines, prevented from indulging the feelings of their hearts, and employing a portion of their superfluous wealth for the best purpose to which it can be appropriated—that purpose which, at the hour of death, will afford the most solid comfort on retrospection—that is, "to feed the hungry; to give drink to the thirsty; to clothe the naked; to comfort the comfortless." The economists in question, when they are implored by the starving poor for "bread," tender them "a stone." To the unfeeling and uncharitable of the rich (and such unhappily there are), these doctrines afford a plausible pretext, of which they are not slow to avail themselves, for withholding their aid from the poor. They have moreover tended to attach a sort of disrepute to those admirable associations of ladies and gentlemen, for the relief of the poor, on which Heaven looks down with complacence, and which form a delightful oasis in the midst of the arid deserts of sordid selfishness which on all sides present themselves to the afflicted view of the contemplative observer.

In entering on this discussion, it is necessary to consider the character and conduct of the classes whose case I have undertaken to review. Both are, I am persuaded, greatly and perniciously mistaken.

There is scarcely any propensity more universal among mankind, than the tendency to generalize from inadequate particulars. From the good or the bad qualities of half a dozen persons or things, most people are disposed to draw general conclusions affecting the whole species or genus to which the half dozen belong. It is not therefore wonderful, although greatly to be regretted, that on beholding a number of worthless, poor, so many superficial persons feel disposed to set down the mass as worthless. A little reflection "will prove the folly and injustice of this procedure. The estimable part of the poor, who struggle with their poverty, who resist the temptations to fraud and transgressions of every kind, are generally in the background—they escape notice. Hundreds of them may be within a few squares of us, and never attract our attention. Let us suppose a case. A man has, in the course of a year, dealings with five hundred of those persons who depend on their labour for support: among this large number, he discovers ten or a dozen tricky and worthless, who are on the watch to cheat and deceive him. Will he not, in his conversation about his affairs (and how many are there who have no other subject of conversation?) dwell more on the frauds and tricks of these, than on the correct conduct of the four hundred and eighty or four hundred and ninety? And will not superficial persons be disposed to generalize and stigmatize the whole from his statements?

Far from being surprised that among the poor there are to be found many worthless persons, it appears, that the surprise, all things considered, ought to be, that there are so few. In the first place, it is well known that we are the creatures of education and example; and how lamentably deficient the mass of the poor are in point of education and example, we all know. No small proportion have had no education;

others only a mere smattering: and the examples which they are to copy, are, alas too generally ill qualified to form them as useful or estimable members of society.

The higher orders of society have generally enjoyed the advantages of a good education and good examples: the censorial eye of the public is on them, and serves as a curb to restrain them from guilt: regard to character has a powerful operation. Nevertheless, do we not unfortunately see considerable numbers of them who lapse from the paths of rectitude? How powerfully do such lapses tend to extenuate those of the poor, who are under no such controlling or restraining circumstances, and have so much stronger incentives to aberration!

The population of Philadelphia is about 160,000 souls, of whom about 100,000 depend on the labour of their hands; 40,000 are probably labourers, hodmen, seamstresses, families of workmen on the canals and rail-roads. The utmost industry and economy they can employ will scarcely suffice to sustain them, if not unremittingly employed; and few of them are so fortunate as to be employed through the year. These last descriptions of persons are those whose case I have undertaken to consider.

Philadelphia, June 20 1833

SOURCE: Carey, Mathew. 1833. *Appeal to the Wealthy of the Land, Ladies as Well as Gentlemen, on the Character, Conduct, Situation, and Prospects of Those Whose Sole Dependence for Subsistence Is on the Labour of Their Hands*. 2nd ed. Philadelphia: L. Johnson: 5–7.

ANALYSIS

Born in Dublin, Ireland, on January 28, 1760, Mathew Carey was trained as a bookseller and publisher. In 1783, he began publication of the *Volunteer's Journal*. Its anti-English sentiments brought him to the attention of English authorities. After the publication of a cartoon in 1784 that mocked a British official, Carey was arrested and charged with sedition. Although the charge was eventually dropped, legal issues related to the incident led Carey to immigrate to Philadelphia, Pennsylvania. Thanks to his relationships with Benjamin Franklin and the Marquis de Lafayette, he was able to establish another newspaper focusing on political topics. In what would mark his career, his publishing proved both influential and controversial. Even after he left the publishing business, he continued shaping public opinion through writing pamphlets and newspaper articles.

Carey's interest in the poor had its origins with the Panic of 1819. A severe economic decline that could be traced to a lack of regulations on banks and the collapse of exports to Europe became a full-blown depression because the laissez-faire economic theory that guided authorities suggested that the economic issues should be allowed to correct themselves without any government intervention. Seeing the carnage that was being wrought to small business owners and their employees, Carey argued that government intervention was critical as many were suffering and could not afford to wait for relief. He published more than 50 essays and 30 newspaper articles calling for state and federal governments to begin regulating the activities of businesses in order to provide economic stability.

His writings led the city of Philadelphia, Pennsylvania, to offer him the position of "Guardian of the Poor" in 1827. His interactions in this post with the poor led him to conclude that poverty was not the result of poor morals, but was caused by the very economic problems that led to the Panic of 1819. Since companies were not required to pay their employees a living wage, they paid as little as possible. Economic forces kept wages suppressed because there were far more workers available than there were jobs. Recognizing that market forces were at the heart of the poverty issue, Carey began writing pamphlets and articles on the subject, with the *Appeal to the Wealthy of the Land, Ladies as Well as Gentlemen, on the Character, Conduct, Situation, and Prospects of Those Whose Sole Dependence for Subsistence Is on the Labour of Their Hands* being among the most widely read. Unlike his writings that grew directly out of the Panic of 1819, Carey did not call for government to expand its responsibilities to the poor beyond helping those who were incapable of working. He saw the responsibility to aid the able-bodied impoverished falling on private charities, hence the need to appeal to the wealthy.

Carey continued his political activity until his death on September 16, 1839. His prolific writing, philanthropy, and civic participation brought him admirers such as James Madison, but also brought him significant numbers of critics. Regardless of whether one agreed or disagreed with him, he brought issues to the fore in a manner that caused great debate and influenced both government policymakers and influential private citizens.

FURTHER READING

Carter, Edward C. 1962. "The Political Activities of Mathew Carey, Nationalist, 1760–1814." PhD diss., Bryn Mawr College.

Green, James N. 1985. *Mathew Carey, Publisher and Patriot.* Philadelphia: Library Company of Philadelphia.

Matson, Cathy. 2013. "Mathew Carey's Learning Experience: Commerce, Manufacturing, and the Panic of 1819." *Early American Studies* 11, no. 3: 455–485.

"I Refer to Idiots and Insane Persons, Dwelling in Circumstances Not Only Adverse to Their Own Physical and Moral Improvement, but Productive of Extreme Disadvantages to All Other Persons Brought into Association with Them"

- ***Document:*** *Memorial to the Legislature of Massachusetts* (Excerpts)
- ***Date:*** January 1843
- ***Where:*** Boston, Massachusetts
- ***Significance:*** In her report *Memorial to the Legislature of Massachusetts*, Dorothea Dix made the case that the state had the responsibility for the care of the mentally ill rather than local communities. Dix's document was circulated nationwide and proved influential in improving the treatment of individuals with mental issues.

DOCUMENT

MEMORIAL

To the Legislature of Massachusetts.

GENTLEMEN,

I RESPECTFULLY ask to present this Memorial, believing that the cause, which actuates to and sanctions so unusual a movement, presents no equivocal claim to public consideration and sympathy. Surrendering to calm and deep convictions of duty my habitual views of what is womanly and becoming, I proceed briefly to explain what has conducted me before you unsolicited and unsustained, trusting, while I do so, that the memorialist will be speedily forgotten in the memorial.

About two years since leisure afforded opportunity, and duty prompted me to visit several prisons and almshouses in the vicinity of this metropolis. I found, near Boston, in the Jails and Asylums for the poor, a numerous class brought into unsuitable connexion with criminals and the general mass of Paupers. I refer to Idiots and Insane persons, dwelling in circumstances not only adverse to their own physical and moral improvement, but productive of extreme disadvantages to all other persons brought into association with them. I applied myself diligently to trace the causes of these evils, and sought to supply remedies. As one obstacle was surmounted, fresh difficulties appeared. Every new investigation has given depth to the conviction that it is only by decided, prompt, and vigorous legislation the evils to which I refer, and which I shall proceed more fully to illustrate, can be remedied. I shall be obliged to speak with great plainness, and to reveal many things revolting to the taste, and from which my woman's nature shrinks with peculiar sensitiveness. But truth is the highest consideration. *I tell what I have seen*—painful and shocking as the details often are—that from them you may feel more deeply the imperative obligation which lies upon you to prevent the possibility of a repetition or continuance of such outrages upon humanity. If I inflict pain upon you, and move you to horror, it is to acquaint you victims of legalized barbarity.

I come to present the strong claims of suffering humanity. I come to place before the Legislature of Massachusetts the condition of the miserable, the desolate, the outcast. I come as the advocate of helpless, forgotten, insane and idiotic men and women; of beings, sunk to a condition from which the most unconcerned would start with real honor; of beings wretched in our Prisons, and more wretched in our Alms-Houses. And I cannot suppose it needful to employ earnest persuasion, or stubborn argument, in order to arrest and fix attention upon a subject, only the more strongly pressing in its claims, because it is revolting and disgusting in its details.

I must confine myself to few examples, but am ready to furnish other and more complete details, if required. If my pictures are displeasing, coarse, and severe, my subjects, it must be recollected, offer no tranquil, refined, or composing features. The condition of human beings, reduced to the extremest states of degradation and misery, cannot be exhibited in softened language, or adorn a polished page.

I proceed, Gentlemen, briefly to call your attention to the present state of Insane Persons confined within this Commonwealth, in *cages, closets, cellars, stalls, pens! Chained, naked, beaten with rods*, and *lashed* into obedience!

As I state cold, severe *facts*, I feel obliged to refer to persons, and definitely to indicate localities. But it is upon my subject, not upon localities or individuals, I desire to fix attention; and I would speak as kindly as possible of all Wardens, Keepers, and other responsible officers, believing that *most* of these have erred not through hardness of heart and wilful cruelty, so much as want of skill and knowledge, and want of consideration. Familiarity with suffering, it is said, blunts the sensibilities, and where neglect once finds a footing other injuries are multiplied. This is not all, for it may justly and strongly be added that, from the deficiency of adequate means to meet the wants of these cases, it has been an absolute impossibility to do justice in this matter. Prisons are not constructed in view of being converted into County Hospitals, and Alms-Houses are not founded as receptacles for the Insane. And yet, in the face of justice and common sense, Wardens are by law compelled to receive, and the Masters of Alms-Houses not to refuse, Insane and Idiotic subjects in all stages of mental disease and privation.

It is the Commonwealth, not its integral parts, that is accountable for most of the abuses which have lately, and do still exist. I repeat it, it is defective legislation which perpetuates and multiplies these abuses.

. . .

I have seen many who, part of the year, are chained or caged. The use of cages all but universal; hardly a town but can refer to some not distant period of using them: chains are less common: negligences frequent: wilful abuse less frequent than sufferings proceeding from ignorance, or want of consideration. I encountered during the last three months many poor creatures wandering reckless and unprotected through the country. Innumerable accounts have been sent me of persons who had roved away unwatched and unsearched after; and I have heard that responsible persons, controlling the almshouses, have not thought themselves culpable in sending away from their shelter, to cast upon the chances of remote relief, insane men and women. These, left on the highways, unfriended and incompetent to control or direct their own movements, sometimes have found refuge in the hospital, and others have not been traced. But I cannot particularize; in, traversing the state I have found hundreds of insane persons in every variety of circumstance and condition; many whose situation could not and need not be improved; a less number, but that very large, whose lives are the saddest pictures of human suffering and degradation.

. . .

Men of Massachusetts, I beg, I implore, I demand, pity and protection, for these of my suffering, outraged sex!—Fathers, Husbands, Brothers, I would supplicate you for this boon but what do I say? I dishonor you, divest you at once of Christianity and humanity—does this appeal imply distrust. If it conies burthened with a doubt of your righteousness in this Legislation, then blot it out; while I declare confidence in your honor, not less than your humanity. Here you will put away the cold, calculating spirit of selfishness and self-seeking; lay off the armor of local strife and political opposition; here and now, for once, forgetful of the earthly and perishable, come up to these halls and consecrate them with one heart and one mind to works of righteousness and just judgment. Become the benefactors of your race, the just guardians of the solemn rights you hold in trust. Raise up the fallen; succor the desolate; restore the outcast; defend the helpless; and for your eternal and great reward, receive the benediction. . .. "Well done, good and faithful servants, become rulers over many things!"

But, gentlemen, I do not come to quicken your sensibilities into short-lived action, to pour forth passionate exclamation, nor yet to move your indignation against those, whose misfortune, not fault, it surely is to hold in charge these poor demented creatures, and whose whole of domestic economy, or prison discipline, is absolutely overthrown by such proximity of conflicting circumstances, and opposite conditions of mind and character.

. . .

A communication from the warden of the Cambridge prison affords the following opinions, results of his experience:—"As to the expediency or propriety of holding for safe keeping, in the jails or houses of correction, insane persons or idiots, I must say that I consider it both inexpedient and decidedly wrong that the insane, or idiots, or any other persons, should be confined in prisons, except those who have been convicted for crimes, or who are so strongly suspected that it is necessary they should beholden for safe keeping until they can be tried for the offences for which they stand charged. Any person having the least experience in prison-keeping, must, I think, be fully sensible of the demoralizing and pernicious influences insane persons must have on the order and discipline of a prison, nor can it be doubted that the punishment of all sane persons is very much enhanced and aggravated by their exposure to the ravings of the insane. Neither can the keepers or other officers of prisons be selected with a view to their fitness to take care of the insane, consequently they are in want of those qualifications which make them suitable for the management of such persons, be they curable or incurable."

From the Sheriff of Dukes county I have testimony, corresponding to that elsewhere received, and from which I am obliged to make extracts, when the entire letters would be valuable:—"I beg leave to say that I am decidedly of opinion that such confinement, even if it were in some cases 'expedient,' is not in accordance with the principles of sound enlightened philanthropy. Humanity shudders at the thought that those whom God in his providence has bereft of the light of reason, should be confined within the narrow bounds of a prison, deprived of the enjoyment of the pure air of heaven; of necessary exercise; of the comforts to which they have been used, comforts which their peculiar circumstances render so necessary; and made companions of felons, and the worthless outcasts of society.

"With proper care and attention, lunatics may not only be made comfortable, but in many instances restored again to society with sound minds. But this care and attention cannot be expected from those who have charge of prisons, worthy men though many of them be; it requires a union of qualifications rarely found in one individual, to manage successfully those from whom that, which chiefly distinguishes man from the brute creation, is taken away.

"I conclude with expressing the hope that the wisdom of our Legislature may devise a remedy for the evils now attending the unfortunate pauper lunatic and idiot."

The warden of one of the best conducted prisons in this or any other country, I refer to that at South Boston, writes:—"I affirm, most decisively, that jails and houses of correction are not fit places for the safe keeping of lunatics and idiots, and, as far as my experience goes, the officers are not qualified to take charge of lunatics."

The master of the Plymouth almshouse writes, in a letter containing many clear views,—"I hope to hear people are awake on this subject, and trust they will not rest till they have compelled the public to provide suitable places for that unfortunate class of demented persons. They should never be received in almshouses."

It is not few but many, it is not a part but the whole, who bear unqualified testimony to this evil. A voice strong and deep comes up from every almshouse and prison in Massachusetts where the insane are or have been, protesting against such evils as have been illustrated in the preceding pages.

Gentlemen, I commit to you this sacred cause. Your action upon this subject will affect the present and future condition of hundreds and of thousands.

In this legislation, as in all things, may you exercise that "wisdom which is the breath of the power of God."

Respectfully submitted,
D. L. Dix.

85 MT. VERNON STREET, BOSTON.
January, 1843

SOURCE: Dix, Dorothea Lynde. 1843. *Memorial. To the Legislature of Massachusetts [In Behalf of the Pauper Insane and Idiots in Jails and Poorhouses throughout the Commonwealth. Jan. 1843]*. Boston: Munroe & Francis.

ANALYSIS

Dorothea Dix (April 4, 1802–July 17, 1887) was a prominent social reformer who began her career in Massachusetts as a school teacher while a teenager. She contracted tuberculosis in 1827 but refused to let the disease prevent her from working. Dix wrote a number of books for children before returning to the classroom in 1831. Her exhaustive schedule led to her succumbing to severe hemorrhaging in 1836, which caused her to lose one of her lungs. She went to Liverpool, England, to recover her strength. While there, she became acquainted with the work of both William Tuke and Philippe Pinel, Europeans who had been advocates for the mentally disabled.

Upon her return to Massachusetts, Dix endeavored to compare the treatment of the mentally impaired in the state to their counterparts in Europe. She first visited a jail in 1841 in Cambridge where she met with some female inmates. During their discussion, Dix discovered that the "insane" inmates were housed in dank and filthy cells. With the support of prominent citizens, such as Horace Mann and Charles Sumner, Dix went on a tour of additional facilities to investigate the conditions of other mentally infirm individuals. She discovered such inhumane treatment as chaining them to walls. Upon completion of her investigation, she presented her results to the Massachusetts's legislature through her *Memorial to the Legislature of Massachusetts*. Her efforts resulted in funding for the Worcester State Hospital to treat the mentally ill.

Her success in Massachusetts led Dix to lead similar campaigns in the states of Kentucky, Maryland, New Jersey, New York, Ohio, Pennsylvania, and Tennessee. By 1848, she had changed tactics, opting to challenge the U.S. Congress to pass legislation to benefit the mentally handicapped. Years of her lobbying resulted in the passage of "An Act Making a Grant of Public Lands to the Several States for the Benefit of Indigent Insane Persons" in 1854. President Franklin Pierce vetoed the bill because he believed that it would result in requiring the nation to care for not only those who were truly mentally ill but also the other poor.

FURTHER READING

Brown, Thomas J. 1998. *Dorothea Dix: New England Reformer*. Cambridge, MA: Harvard University Press.

Cutter, Barbara. 2003. *Domestic Devils, Battlefield Angels: The Radicalism of American Womanhood, 1830–1865*. DeKalb, IL: Northern Illinois University Press.

Gollaher, David. 1995. *Voice for the Mad: The Life of Dorothea Dix*. New York: Free Press.

Pierce, Franklin. n.d. "Veto Message, May 3, 1854." Online by Gerhard Peters and John T. Wooley. *The American Presidency Project*. http://www.presidency.ucsb.edu/ws/?pid=67850 (accessed February 27, 2017).

Vacek, Heather H. 2015. *Madness: American Protestant Reaction to Mental Illness across Three Centuries*. Waco: Baylor University Press.

"The Boundary Line of the Other Half Lies through the Tenements"

- ***Document:*** *How the Other Half Lives* (Excerpt)
- ***Date:*** 1890
- ***Where:*** New York City, New York
- ***Significance:*** Through text and photographs, Jacob Riis exposed the horrors of the living conditions endured by the poor living in New York City's Lower East Side tenement houses during the late 1800s.

DOCUMENT

INTRODUCTION

Long ago it was said that "one half of the world does not know how the other half lives." That was true then. It did not know because it did not care. The half that was on top cared little for the struggles, and less for the fate of those who were underneath, so long as it was able to hold them there and keep its own seat. There came a time when the discomfort and crowding below were so great, and the consequent upheavals so violent, that it was no longer an easy thing to do, and then the upper half fell to inquiring what was the matter. Information on the subject has been accumulating rapidly since, and the whole world has had its hands full answering for its old ignorance.

In New York, the youngest of the world's great cities, that time came later than elsewhere, because the crowding had not been so great. There were those who believed that it would never come; but their hopes were vain. Greed and reckless selfishness wrought like results here as in the cities of older lands. "When the great riot occurred in 1863," so reads the testimony of the Secretary of the Prison

Association of New York before a legislative committee appointed to investigate causes of the increase of crime in the State twenty-five years ago, "every hiding-place and nursery of crime discovered itself by immediate and active participation in the operations of the mob. Those very places and domiciles, and all that are like them, are to-day nurseries of crime, and of the vices and disorderly courses which lead to crime. By far the largest part—eighty per cent, at least—of crimes against property and against the person are perpetuated by individuals who have either lost connection with home, life, or never had any, or whose *homes had ceased to be sufficiently separate, decent, and desirable to afford what are regarded as ordinary wholesome influences of home and family*. . . . The younger criminals seem to come almost exclusively from the worst tenement house districts, that is, when traced back to the very places where they had their homes in the city here." Of one thing New York made sure at the early stage of the inquiry: the boundary line of the Other Half lies through the tenements.

It is ten years and over, now, since that line divided New York's population evenly. To-day three-fourths of its people live in the tenements, and the nineteenth century drift of the population to the cities is sending ever-increasing multitudes to crowd them. The fifteen thousand tenant houses that were the despair of the sanitarian in the past generation have swelled into thirty-seven thousand, and more than twelve hundred thousand persons call them home. The one way out he saw—rapid transit to the suburbs—has brought no relief. We know now that there is no way out; that the "system" that was the evil offspring of public neglect and private greed has come to stay, a storm-centre forever of our civilization. Nothing is left but to make the best of a bad bargain.

What the tenements are and how they grew to what they are, we shall see hereafter. The story is dark enough, drawn from the plain public records, to send a chill to any heart. If it shall appear that the sufferings and the sins of the "other half," and the evil they breed, are but as a just punishment upon the community that gave it no other choice, it will be because that is the truth. The boundary line lies there because, while the forces for good on one side vastly outweigh the bad—it were not well otherwise—in the tenements all the influences make for evil; because they are the hot-beds of the epidemics that carry death to rich and poor alike; the nurseries of pauperism and crime that fill our jails and police courts; that throw off a scum of forty thousand human wrecks to the island asylums and workhouses year by year; that turned out in the last eight years a round half million beggars to prey upon our charities; that maintain a standing army of ten thousand tramps with all that that implies; because, above all, they touch the family life with deadly moral contagion. This is their worst crime, inseparable from the system. That we have to own it the child of our wrong does not excuse it, even though it gives it claim upon our utmost patience and tenderest charity.

What are you going to do about it? is the question of to-day. It was asked once of our city in taunting defiance by a band of political cutthroats, the legitimate outgrowth of life on the tenement-house level. Law and order found the answer then and prevailed. With our enormously swelling population held in this galling bondage, will that answer be forgiven? It will depend on how fully the situation that prompted the challenge is grasped. Forty per cent of the distress among the poor, said a recent official report, is due to drunkenness. But the first legislative committee ever appointed to probe this sore went deeper down and discovered its roots. The "conclusion forced itself upon it that certain conditions and associations of human life and habitation are the prolific parents of corresponding habits and morals," and it recommended "the prevention of drunkenness by providing for every man a clean and comfortable home." Years after, a sanitary inquiry brought to light the fact that "more than one-half of the tenements with two-thirds of their population were held by owners who made the keeping of them a business,*generally a speculation*. The owner was seeking a certain percentage of his outlay, and that percentage very rarely fell below fifteen per cent, and frequently exceeded thirty. . . . The complaint was universal among the tenants that they were entirely uncared for, and that the only answer to their requests to have the place put in order by repairs and necessary improvements was that they must pay their rent or leave. The agent's instructions were simple but emphatic: 'Collect the rent in advance, or, failing, eject the occupants' " Upon such stock grew this upas-tree. Small wonder the fruit is bitter. The remedy that shall be an effective answer to the coming appeal for justice must proceed from the public conscious. Neither legislation nor charity can cover the ground. The greed of capital that wrought the evil must itself undo it, as far as it can now be undone. Homes must be built for the working masses by those who employ their labor; but tenements must cease to be "good property" in the old, heartless sense. "Philanthropy and fiver per cent" is the penance exacted.

If this is true from a purely economic point of view, what then of the outlook from the Christian standpoint? Not long ago a great meeting was held in this city, of all denominations of religious faith, to discuss the question how to lay hold of these teeming masses in the tenements with Christian influences, to which they are now too often strangers. Might not the conference have found in the warning of one Brooklyn builder, who has invested his capital on this plan and made it pay more than a money interest, a hint worth heeding: "How shall the love of God be understood by those who have been nurtured in sight only of the greed of man?"

SOURCE: Riis, Jacob A. 1890. *How the Other Half Lives: Studies among the Tenements of New York*. New York: Charles Scribner's Sons.

ANALYSIS

The words and photographs included in Jacob Riis's *How the Other Half Lives* focused on the living conditions within the tenement houses in New York City's Lower East Side. Although Riis chose to work within the buildings in that one area, what he described was emblematic of similar structures throughout the city. In his publication, he vividly captured the economic and class divides within New York City, as approximately 25 percent of the population enjoyed the extravagances of one of the world's great cities, while the impoverished, which made up the remaining residents, wasted away in filthy, disease-ridden tenements.

Riis, an immigrant from Denmark, was personally offended by the plight of the poor as a majority were newcomers who had come to the United States in hope of a new beginning. Instead they found themselves barely subsisting in tenement houses while being taken advantage of by greedy landlords. Riis photographed his subjects while they were engaged in their day-to-day activities. In addition to pictures within the tenement houses, his images included individuals involved in backbreaking work in sweatshops and at play in beer halls. Ostensibly his pictures were authentic in that they captured his subjects in the midst of their normal activities. In truth, he framed the pictures that he wanted and altered lighting conditions to make the photos much darker and grimier. The sensationalized photographs effectively served to convey suffering and violence.

The book and separate exhibitions of the photographs proved effectual in placing the blame on both government officials and the city's elites for allowing so many citizens to live in absolute squalor. City officials had abrogated their responsibility for ensuring that tenement houses were well maintained and sanitary. They had also not provided enough law enforcement to protect those residing in the buildings. This was a substantial amount of neglect considering there were as many as 300,000 people living in tenement houses within just a one-mile radius. The wealthy elite class also bore blame because many in their midst owned the tenements and thus were the very profiteers that Riis so despised. Riis hoped to shame this group into using their political and economic clout to ease the suffering of the impoverished majority through the construction of model tenement homes. Among his ideas were to allow far more light and fresh air into the buildings, which would help moderate temperatures. He also proposed that affordable rents be set that allowed families to acquire the amount of space they needed to live comfortably without facing financial ruin. Riis believed that if the government and elite class worked together to elevate the impoverished, the city as a whole would ultimately benefit from the creation of a better quality of citizenry.

FURTHER READING

Dolkart, Andrew S. 2012. *Biography of a Tenement House in New York City: An Architectural History of 97 Orchard Street*. 2nd ed. Charlottesville: University of Virginia Press.

Gandal, Keith. 1997. *The Virtues of the Vicious: Jacob Riis, Stephen Crane, and the Spectacle of the Slum*. New York: Oxford University Press.

Yochelson, Bonnie. "The Jacob A. Riis Collection: Photographs for Books and Lantern Lectures." In Ludwig Vogl-Bienek and Richard Crangle, eds. *Screen Culture and the Social Question 1880–1914, KINtop3*. Bloomington: Indiana University Press and John Libbey Press, 83–95.

"To Regulate the Treatment and Control of Dependent, Neglected and Delinquent Children"

- ***Document:*** Illinois's Juvenile Court Law of 1899
- ***Date:*** July 1, 1899
- ***Where:*** Springfield, Illinois
- ***Significance:*** The passage of the law created the first juvenile court in the nation.

DOCUMENT

A BILL

For an act to regulate the treatment and control of dependent, neglected and delinquent children.

Be it enacted by the People of the State of Illinois represented in the General Assembly.

Section 1. (Definitions.) This act shall apply only to children under the age of sixteen years not inmates of a State institution, or some institution incorporated under the laws of this state. For the purposes of this act the words dependent child and neglected child shall mean any child who for any reason is destitute or homeless or abandoned; or dependent upon the public for support; or who habitually begs or receives alms; or who is found living in any house of ill fame or with any vicious or disreputable person; or whose home, by reason of neglect, cruelty or depravity on the part of its parents, guardian or such person in whose care it may be, is an unfit place for such a child; and any child under the age of eight years, who is found

DID YOU KNOW?

Pennsylvania's 1848 Minimum-Age Law

During the nineteenth century, the textile industry in Pennsylvania depended on children to make up a significant part of its workforce. They were prized because they could be paid half the wages of an adult. Reformers in the state believed that children belonged in school so they lobbied the legislature to enact minimum-age legislation. In 1848, their campaign resulted in the passage of the Minimum-Age Law, which made it illegal for textile factories to employ children under the age of 12. The law's passage proved a pyrrhic victory since the legislation did not include enforcement provisions. Although the law did not accomplish its goals within Pennsylvania, as the first law of its kind within the United States, it became a model to be emulated in other locales.

FURTHER READING

Holleran, Philip M. 1996. "Explaining the Decline of Child Labor in Pennsylvania Silk Mills, 1899–1919." *Pennsylvania History: A Journal of Mid-Atlantic Studies* 63, no. 1: 78–95.

Speakman, Joseph M. 2002. "The Inspector and His Critics: Child Labor Reform in Pennsylvania." *Pennsylvania History: A Journal of Mid-Atlantic Studies* 69, no. 2: 266–286.

peddling or selling any article or singing or playing any musical instrument upon the street or giving any public entertainment.

The words delinquent child includes any child under the age of sixteen years who violates any law of this State or any city or village ordinance.

The word child or children may mean one or more children and the word parent or parents may be held to mean one or both parents when consistent with the intent of this act.

The word association shall include any corporation which includes in its purposes the care or disposition of children coming within the meaning of this act.

. . .

Sec. 2. (Jurisdiction.) The circuit and county courts of the several counties in this State, shall have original jurisdiction in all cases coming within the terms of this act. Proceedings under this act shall conform as nearly as may be to the practice in chancery: PROVIDED, that in cases where a criminal offense is charged, the accused shall have the right to trial by jury. When a case is being heard, all persons not officers of the court or witnesses, and those having direct interest in the case being heard, shall be excluded from the court room.

. . .

Sec. 3. (Juvenile Court.) In counties having over 500,000 population, the judges of the circuit court shall, at such times as they shall determine, designate on or more of their number, whose duty it shall be to hear all cases coming under this act. A special court room to be designated as the juvenile court room, shall be provided for the hearing of such cases, and the findings of the court shall be entered in a book or books, to be kept for that purpose, and known as the "Juvenile Record," and the court may for convenience be called the "Juvenile Court."

Sec. 4. (Petition to the Court.) Any reputable person being a resident in the county, having knowledge of a child in his county, who appears to be either neglected, dependent, or delinquent, may file with the clerk of a court having jurisdiction in the matter, a petition in writing, setting forth the facts, verified by affidavit. It shall be sufficient that the affidavit is upon information and belief.

Sec. 5. (Summons). Upon the filing of the petition a summons shall issue requiring the person having custody or control of the child or with whom the child may be, to appear with the child at a place and time stated in your summons, which time shall be not less than twenty-four hours after service. The parents of the child if living and their residence if known or its legal guardian, if one there be, or if there is neither parent or guardian or if his or her residence is not known, then some relative if there be one and his residence is known, shall be notified of the proceedings and in any case the judge may appoint some suitable person to act on behalf of the child. If the person summoned as herein provided shall fail without reasonable cause to appear and abide the order of the court or to bring the child he may be proceeded against as in the case of contempt of court. In case the summons can not be served or the party served fails to obey the same and in any case when it shall be made to appear to the court that suchhons will be ineffectual a warrant may issue on the order of the court, either against the parent or guardian or the person having custody of the child or with whom the child may be or against the child itself. One the return of the summons or other process or as soon thereafter as may be the court shall proceed to hear and dispose of the case in a summary manner.

. . .

Sec. 6. (Probation Officers.) The court shall have authority to appoint or designate one or more discreet persons of good character to serve as probation officers, during the pleasure of the court; said probation officers to receive no compensation from the public treasury. In case a probation officer shall be appointed by any court, it shall be the duty of the clerk of the court, if practicable, to notify the said probation officer in advance, when any child is to be brought before the said court; it shall be the duty of the said probation officer to make such investigation as may be required by the court; to be present in court in order to represent the interests of the child when the case is heard; to furnish to the court such information and assistance as the judge may require; and to take such charge of any child before and after trial as may be directed by the court.

Sec. 7. (Dependent and Neglected Children.) When any child under the age of fourteen (14) years shall be found to be dependent or neglected within the meaning of this act, the court may make an order committing the child to the care of some suitable State institution or to the care of some reputable citizen of good moral character, or to the care of some training school or an industrial school, as provided by law, or to the care of some association willing to receive it, embracing in its objects the purpose of caring or obtaining homes for dependent or neglected children, which association shall have been accredited as hereinafter provided.

. . .

Sec. 8. (Children Not to be Kept in Poor Houses.) It shall be unlawful to retain any child of sound mind and body, between the ages of two (2) and fourteen (14) years, in any poor house, and it shall be the duty of the superintendent of any poor house, or any member of the county board, who shall have knowledge of the presence of any such child in any poor house, to make petition to the circuity or county court, in the manner provided in Section 5 of this act. And the court shall have like power as in other cases of dependent children. When any child dependent upon a county for support is committed by the court to the care of an association, to be placed in a family home, the court may award a reasonable compensation for such services, to be paid by the county, including necessary expenses, provided that the compensation so allowed shall not exceed the sum of fifty (50) dollars in the case of any one child. If it shall prove impracticable to place or keep such child in a family home on account of incorrigibility, or any mental or physical defect, the child may be returned to the county authorities. In such case the court may require the association to refund to the county treasury such portion of the money paid by the county for the care of such child as may in the opinion of the court be equitable.

. . .

Sec. 10. (Disposition of Delinquent Children.) In the case of a delinquent child, the court may continue the hearing from time to time and may commit the child to the care and guardianship of a probation officer duly appointed by the court, and may all said child to remain in its own home, subject to the visitation of the probation officer; such child to report to the probation officer as often as may be required, and subject to be returned to the court for further proceedings, whenever such action may appear to be necessary; or the court may commit the child the care and guardianship of the probation officer to be placed in a suitable family home, subject to the friendly supervision of such probation officer; or it may authorize the said probation officer to board out the said child in some suitable family home, in case provision is mad by voluntary contribution or otherwise for the payment of the board of such child until a suitable provision may be made for the child in a home without such payment. . . . Or if the child is found guilty of any criminal offense and the judge is of the opinion that the best interest requires it, the court may commit the child to any institution within said county incorporated under the laws of this State for the car of delinquent children, or provided by a city for the care of such offenders, or may commit the child if a boy over the age of ten years to the State reformatory, or if a girl over the age of ten years to the State Home for Juvenile Female Offenders. . . .

Sec. 12. (Children Under Twelve Years Not to Be Committed to Jail.) Nor court or magistrate shall commit a child under twelve (12) years of age to a jail or police station, but if such child is unable to give bail, it may be committed to the care of the sheriff, police officer or probation officer, who shall keep such child in some place outside of the enclosure of any jail or police station; and the court may award such compensation for the care of such child as it deems suitable, not exceeding fifty (50) cents per day. When any child shall be sentenced to confinement in any institution to which adult convicts are sentenced, it shall be unlawful to confine such child in the same building with adult convicts, or to confine such child in the same yare or enclosure with such adult convicts, or to bring such child into any yard or building in which such convicts may be present.

SOURCE: Hurley, T. D., comp. 1907. *Origin of the Illinois Juvenile Court Law: Juvenile Courts and What They Have Accomplished.* 3rd ed. Chicago: The Visitation and Aid Society, 26–34.

ANALYSIS

The Illinois Juvenile Court Law had its origins with reformers in Hull House and the Chicago Woman's Club. These groups had a great interest in the welfare of children and among their causes was the treatment of child delinquents. Since they believed that delinquency was the by-product of poor or nonexistent parenting, they contended that a child placed in a compassionate and nurturing environment would conform to societal expectations. Such an atmosphere was not possible in a judicial system designed to punish hardened adult criminals. They proposed that a separate court be designed that would provide children the love, guidance, and discipline to grow into responsible citizens. It took approximately a decade of persistent activism for them to garner the political support necessary for the passage of the Juvenile Court Law.

The law did not create a separate judicial system for children because that would have been unconstitutional. Instead, existing county and circuit courts assigned judges to serve on a juvenile court. Some charges were litigated in adult courts, as there was no requirement to transfer children to the juvenile system. Despite its imperfections, the juvenile court marked a true achievement. The judicial system was forced to recognize that young children were still in the developmental stages and thus needed to be judged in a different manner than adults. When in detention areas, the children were kept separate from adults. One of the more notable achievements was the use of probation officers to provide guidance to the children they oversaw. The efficiency of the probation officers was due primarily to Hull House and the Chicago Woman's Club. The original legislation created the position of probation officer but did not provide the monies required for salaries. The members of the two groups stepped into the breach to raise the necessary funds to pay them. With the Chicago juvenile court firmly established, Illinois began opening courts in other counties. Legislators at other states subsequently enacted legislation using Illinois as a model. This resulted in 22 states operating juvenile courts inside of a decade.

FURTHER READING

Clapp, Elizabeth J. 1998. *Mothers of All Children: Women Reformers and the Rise of Juvenile Courts in Progressive Era America*. University Park, PA: Penn State University Press.

Getis, Victoria. 2000. *The Juvenile Court and the Progressives*. Urbana: University of Illinois Press.

Sutton, John R. 1988. *Stubborn Children: Controlling Delinquency in the United States, 1640–1981*. Berkeley: University of California Press.

"The Tenement House System Has Become Fraught with So Much Danger to the Welfare of the Community"

- ***Document:*** Report of the New York State Tenement House Commission of 1900 (Excerpt)
- ***Date:*** 1900, Reprinted in 1903
- ***Where:*** New York City, New York
- ***Significance:*** The report's vivid descriptions of the squalor found in the average New York City tenement house helped build the political momentum at the state level required for the passage of the landmark Tenement House Act of 1901.

DOCUMENT

THE TYPICAL NEW YORK TENEMENT

Some knowledge of the prevailing kind of New York tenement house must necessarily precede any consideration of its evils and their remedies. It is known as the "double-decker," "dumb-bell" tenement, a type which New York has the unenviable distinction of having invented. It is a type unknown to any other city in America or Europe.

Although the housing problem is one of the leading political questions of the day in England, the conditions which exist there are ideal compared to the conditions in New York. The tall tenement house, accommodating as many as 100 to 150 persons in one building, extending up six or seven stories into the air, with dark, unventilated rooms, is unknown in London or in any other city of Great Britain. It was first constructed in New York about the year 1879, and with slight modifications has been practically the sole type of building erected since, and is the type of the present day. It is a building usually five or six or even seven stories high, about 25 feet wide, and built upon a lot of land of the same width and about 100 feet deep. The building as a rule extends back 90 feet, leaving the small space of ten feet unoccupied at the rear, so that the back rooms may obtain some light and air. This space has continued to be left open only because the law has compelled it. Upon the entrance floor there are generally two stores, one on each side of the building, and these sometimes have two or three living rooms back of them. In the centre is the entrance hallway, a long corridor less than 3 feet wide and extending back 60 feet in length. This hallway is nearly always totally dark, receiving no light except that from the street door and a faint light that comes from the small windows opening upon the stairs, which are placed at one side of the hallway. Each floor above is generally divided into four sets of apartments, there being seven rooms on each side of the hall, extending back from the street to the rear of the building. The front apartments generally consist of four rooms each and the rear apartments consist of three rooms, making altogether fourteen upon each floor, or in a seven-story house eighty-four rooms exclusive of the stores and rooms back of them. Of these fourteen rooms on each floor, only four receive direct light and air from the street or from the small yard at the back of the building. Generally, along each side of the building is what is termed an "air shaft," being an indentation of the wall to a depth of about 28 inches, and extending in length for a space of from 50 to 60 feet. This shaft is entirely enclosed on four sides and is, of course, the full height of the building, often from 60 to 72 feet high. The ostensible purpose of the shaft is to provide light and air to the five rooms on each side of the house which get no direct light and air from the street or yard; but as the shafts are narrow and high, being enclosed on all four sides, and without any intake of air at the bottom, these rooms obtain, instead of fresh air and sunshine, foul air and semi-darkness. Indeed it is questionable whether the rooms would not be more habitable and more sanitary with no shaft at all, depending for their light and air solely upon the front and back rooms into which they open; for each family, besides having the foul air from its own rooms to breathe, is compelled to breathe the emanations from the rooms of some eleven other families; nor is this all, these shafts act as conveyors of noise, odors, and disease, and when fire breaks out serve as inflammable flues, often rendering it impossible to save the buildings from destruction.

A family living in such a building pays for four rooms of this kind a rent of from $12 to $18 a month. Of these four rooms only two are large enough to be deserving of the name of rooms. The front one is generally about 10 feet 6 inches wide by 11 feet 3 inches long; this the family use as a parlor, and often at night, when the small bedrooms opening upon the air shaft are so close and ill-ventilated that sleep is impossible, mattresses are dragged upon the floor of the parlor, and there the family sleep, all together in one room. In summer the small bedrooms are so hot and stifling that a large part of the tenement house population sleep on the roofs, the sidewalks, and the fire-escapes. The other room, the kitchen, is generally the same size as the parlor upon which it opens, and receives all its light and air from the "air shaft," or such a supply as may come to it from the front room. Behind these two rooms are the bedrooms, so called, which are hardly more than closets, being each about 7 feet wide and 8 feet 6 inches long, hardly large enough to contain a bed. These rooms get no light or air whatsoever, except that which comes from the "air shaft," and except on the highest stories are generally almost totally dark. Upon the opposite side of the public hall is an apartment containing four exactly similar rooms, and at the rear of the building there are, instead of four rooms on each side of the hallway but three, one of the bedrooms being dispensed with. For these three rooms in the rear the rent is generally throughout the city from $10 to $15 a month. In the public hallway, opposite the stairs, there are provided two water closets, each water-closet being used in common by two families and being lighted and ventilated by the "air shaft," which also lights and ventilates all the bedrooms. In the newer buildings there is frequently provided, in the hallway between the two closets, a dumb-waiter for the use of tenants.

It is not to be wondered at, therefore, that with such a kind of tenement house repeated all over the different parts of this city, and forming practically the only kind of habitation for the great mass of the people, the tenement house system has become fraught with so much danger to the welfare of the community. The effect upon the city population of the form of congregated living found in our tenement houses is to be seen, not only in its results upon the health of the people, but upon their moral and social condition as well. The public mind is just now especially aroused over the manifestation of one special form of vice in tenement districts. It is not to be wondered at that vice in various forms should manifest itself in the tenements; the wonder is that there is not more vice in such districts. The tenement districts of New York are places in which thousands of people are living in the smallest space in which it is possible for human beings to exist—crowded together in dark, ill-ventilated rooms, in many of which the sunlight never enters and in most of which fresh air is unknown. They are centres of disease, poverty, vice, and crime, where it is a marvel, not that some children grow up to be thieves, drunkards, and prostitutes, but that so many should ever grow up to be decent and self-respecting. All the conditions which surround childhood, youth, and womanhood in New York's crowded tenement quarters make for unrighteousness. They also make for disease. There is hardly a tenement house in which there has not been at least one case of pulmonary tuberculosis within the last five years, and in some houses there have been as great a number as twenty-two different cases of this terrible disease. From the tenements there come a stream of sick, helpless people to out hospitals and dispensaries, few of whom are able to afford the luxury of a private physician, and some houses are in such bad sanitary condition that few people can be seriously ill in them and get well; from them also comes a host of paupers and charity seekers. The most terrible of all the features of tenement house life in New York, however, is the indiscriminate herding of all kinds of people in close contact, the fact, that, mingled with the drunken, the dissolute, the improvident, the diseased, dwell the great mass of the respectable working-men of the city with their families.

SOURCE: DeForest, Robert W., and Lawrence Veiller, eds. 1903. *The Tenement House Problem: Including the Report of the New York State Tenement House Commission of 1900.* New York: Macmillan Company, 7–10.

ANALYSIS

One of the by-products of the Industrial Revolution was the need for laborers in factories. Many flocked to urban centers during the nineteenth century for the available jobs, only to discover that decent, affordable housing was nonexistent. Developers in New York City sought to address the need through the construction of tenement houses. These were buildings, five to eight stories in height, which were constructed on lots that measured 25 × 100 feet. Landlords viewed them as rich sources of income as each structure could be subdivided to accommodate 10–16 families, depending on the number of floors. Relative to the income generated, they were cheap to build, so they quickly permeated entire city blocks. Predictably, many of the tenements were inhabited by a far greater number of families than they were designed to accommodate. The overcrowding, combined with minimal ventilation and a shortage of lavatories, made for wretched living conditions. Under these circumstances, diseases ran rampant.

In 1865, the New York Council of Hygiene and Public Health issued a report decrying the diseases that were being spawned through the accumulation of human waste and garbage in tenements. The city responded with the passage of the 1867 Tenement House Act. Among its requirements was that each tenement have a fire escape, be properly ventilated, and contain at least one bathroom for every 20 people residing therein. The law proved ineffectual for several reasons. Despite horrid conditions, tenants had no affordable alternative to the tenements. Without having to fear the loss of residents, there was no incentive for the building owners to make improvements. With residents and owners satisfied with the status quo, city officials opted to turn a blind eye to violations of the law. Another Tenement House Act followed in 1879 with similar results.

The 1890s saw the public mood shift toward effective regulation. The publication of Jacob Riis's *How the Other Half Lives* in 1890 drew widespread attention through text and photographs to the substandard living conditions endured by the poor in the tenements. The consequences of the squalor became apparent soon thereafter with smallpox and tuberculosis outbreaks that were exacerbated by the sheer number of people living in such proximity.

The final stroke was an 1899 exhibition organized by Lawrence Veiller, secretary of the New York Charity Organization Society's Tenement House Committee, which focused on the tenements of New York City's Lower East Side. The Tenement House Exhibit was presented at a studio on 5th Avenue, a gathering place for the upper class during that era. Among the prominent politicians who were introduced to tenement living through the exhibit was Governor Theodore Roosevelt. Veiller's obvious expertise resulted in his appointment to lead the New York State Tenement House Commission. The commission's 1900 report, much of it written by Veiller, was utilized by New York State's legislature to craft the Tenement House Act of 1901. Among the law's features was a requirement that new tenements have a courtyard, for the purpose of providing enough air to ventilate the building. Also mandated was running water in each apartment. Enforcement of the law was ensured through the creation of the Tenement House Department.

Although Veiller assumed a leadership position within the new agency, he was not content with just making regulatory changes in New York. He published books that encouraged housing reformers in other states to use the Tenement House Act of 1901 as a model for similar legislation. His influence at the national level led him to become a founder of the National Housing Association.

FURTHER READING

Day, Jared N. 1999. *Urban Castles: Tenement Housing and Landlord Activism in New York City, 1890–1943*. New York: Columbia University Press.

Dolkart, Andrew S. 2012. *Biography of a Tenement House in New York City: An Architectural History of 97 Orchard Street*. 2nd ed. Charlottesville: University of Virginia Press.

Foglesong, Richard E. 1986. *Planning the Capitalist City: The Colonial Era to the 1920s*. Princeton: Princeton University Press.

Henderson, A. Scott. 2000. *Housing and the Democratic Ideal: The Life and Thought of Charles Abrams*. New York: Columbia University Press.

Kohn, Edward P. 2010. *Hot Time in the Old Town: The Great Heat Wave of 1896 and the Making of Theodore Roosevelt*. New York: Basic Books.

"The Wealth of the Rich Is Their Strong City; the Destruction of the Poor Is Their Poverty"

- ***Document:*** "The Causes of Poverty" (Excerpt)
- ***Date:*** December 1908
- ***Where:*** New York City, New York
- ***Significance:*** Lilian Brandt made the case in this influential article that poverty had structural causes which could be addressed, such as a shortage of jobs paying decent wages.

DOCUMENT

Knowledge of causes is indispensable to good work in either direction, whether in helping an individual or in improving social conditions. This has been said again and again, but when it comes to applying this maxim our ideas have been rather confused. "Distress cannot be permanently relieved except by removal of the causes of distress" is the principle we have clung to. If this is as true as it sounds, then a knowledge of causes is of use only in preventing the development of poverty. It will make us improve housing conditions, prohibit child labor, provide a rational system of education, clean the streets, purify the water supply, forbid all home work in the tenements, checker the map of the city with small parks, abolish quack medicines, build hospitals of all sorts and keep in them the people who ought to be there, ensure the purity of drugs and foods, revise our entire correctional system and, perhaps, even regulate wages. In our care of individual families it will keep us alert to recognize the existence of causes that have not yet begun to show effects; it will make us urge and aid families to move from dark basements to well-ventilated rooms, to keep their children in school until they can safely go to work, to go to the hospital or sanatorium when they need to do so and before it is too late, to learn how to buy and how to prepare nutritious food. But if it is true that "distress cannot be permanently relieved except by removal of the causes of distress," we must infer either that a knowledge of causes is of no help in our efforts to relieve existing poverty, or that the conditions which we are trying to change, the symptoms of poverty which we are trying to remove, are in reality causes. The second alternative is the true explanation. There has hardly been a discussion of causes of poverty that has not contained a reference to Oliver Wendell Holmes's oracular statement that it is necessary to begin two hundred years ago to cure some cases of disease. This is always quoted to show that the existing conditions are not the "underlying causes," and that, in order to decide in a given case what the cause is, you must look back two hundred years. No fault can be found with this statement when it is applied to increase our understanding of present conditions or to impress us with the necessity of looking ahead two hundred years from the present in making our plans; but if it is applied to the problems of relieving existing poverty it leads to despair. The underlying causes of two hundred years ago, or even of the preceding generation, may be crystal clear to us, but we cannot affect them; the existing conditions are what we have to deal with, and our practice has been to deal with them more hopefully than our theories would warrant. The results have justified the hopefulness; and a new theory is now emerging, namely, that there is in human nature recuperative power of such strength that the removal of the existing visible effects of the "underlying causes" will do almost as well, as far as the individual case is concerned, as the removal of the causes themselves; or, in other words, that poverty is itself one of the most potent causes of poverty and one of those most responsive to treatment. This is a truth that Mr. Bernard Shaw happened upon the other day in London, when he said that the whole trouble with the poor was their poverty, and that this could be made all right by dividing among them the money contributed for charity without any intermediate waste in salaries. The newspapers of the better sort sprang to the defense of the relief methods which require salaried services, and ridiculed Mr. Shaw's pronouncement as a begging of the question. It did not beg the question; and, however naive his practical application of it was, it contained a truth which had been stated long before: "The wealth of the rich is their strong city; the destruction of the poor is their poverty."

For practical purposes, the important thing for us to know, in relation to a dependent family or in relation to a community burdened with dependents, is: What adverse conditions are present which can be corrected? In the community these adverse conditions are "underlying causes." In the single families they are the results of the previous action of these or of earlier underlying causes, but they are also certain causes of future poverty. They must be corrected and their recurrence must be provided against.

The first step, therefore, in the treatment of a family or a city is to find out what adverse conditions are present and to what extent; and this is the first step also in the rational study of the causes of poverty. These adverse conditions are facts, and they are ascertainable facts. They either do or do not exist in the family or in the city. Their prevalence can be measured.

We have already a pretty definite idea what conditions are adverse, what conditions breed poverty, in a family or in a city; but of the extent and relative importance of these conditions we have little accurate knowledge.

Our ideas as to what constitutes an adverse condition in a family are the result of a study of the characteristics of families which have become dependent. Our ideas of what constitutes an adverse condition in a city are acquired in another way: we begin, for some reason or other, generally from our observation of individual cases, to view with suspicion some feature of the city's life, and we study that feature, trying to ascertain what bad effects it produces and why it produces these effects and what can be done about it.

The basis for a statement of the adverse elements present in the circumstances of dependent individuals and families is general observation, which is really an unconscious collection of statistics. Only conscious collections, of which we have few as yet on this subject, can give accurate knowledge of the relative importance of the various elements, but the unconscious collections may be trusted to the extent of basing on them a mere enumeration. The adverse conditions tending to involve dependence which have been observed are these: absence of natural care for children; lack of provision for old age; physical disability; mental defects; certain forms of criminality and moral obliquity; and inefficiency.

Dependence is the normal state of children and of the aged, but this normal dependence is on relatives. Childhood, however, may be deprived of natural care by the death of one or both parents if other relatives are lacking or are inaccessible, and also by neglect or maltreatment on the part of parents; and old age may lack the children or friends or savings that are its normal accompaniments. Both of these periods, during which dependence is the normal state, are lengthening at the expense of the working period. The tendency among well-to-do families to prolong their children's preparation for life has its counterpart in the legislation which is compulsorily prolonging that of the poorest. Simultaneously the upper limit of the working age is apparently being depressed. There is certainly a tendency to begin work at a later age; there is apparently a tendency to stop work at an earlier age. The latter tendency is one which counteracting influences may and should eventually overcome; but in many occupations it has been a conspicuous feature of modern industry. At the same time the average age at death is increasing. There are thus three factors tending to decrease, absolutely or relatively, the portion of life in which a man may work, and to increase, absolutely or relatively, the periods of dependence. Until wages have fully responded by an increase that will enable the average man not only to support his children for a longer time, but also to provide in a shorter working period for a longer old age, or until the effective working period has been materially lengthened, this adverse condition will persist. In it we find the reason why the problem of old-age pensions has become acute; from it comes much of the misery which gives point to radical socialistic proposals. Physical disability may either incapacitate the wage-earner or merely increase the family expenses. It may consist of permanent defects, permanent or temporary injury from accident, industrial or otherwise, or acute or chronic illness. Sickness and physical disability in its various forms give to the workers among the poor in their own homes their chief occupation, and to social workers for the improvement of general conditions their best opportunity.

Mental defects tending to involve dependence vary from insanity and feeble-mindedness down to peculiarities of temperament, such as obstinacy or a quick temper, which interfere with economic success. While this field of work is less encouraging, so far as improvement of the individual is concerned, there is here even greater need for a wise system of institutional care, and there is here an opportunity to introduce radically preventive measures. Crime and moral defects are adverse conditions in the family from an economic standpoint when they result in imprisonment of the wage-earner or inability to keep work or evasion of family obligations. Desertion, intemperance and vagrancy are from this point of view more significant than the more startling crimes.

Inefficiency (not amounting to defects) may be physical, mental or moral; and it may be due to such varied causes as malaria, intemperance, neglected teeth, defective education or unaccustomed surroundings. It may be environmental rather than personal, and it constitutes the first point of attack for all thorough-going reforms in the educational system.

Public disasters, such as fire, flood, earthquake, volcanic eruption or tornado, produce conditions not merely adverse but wholly abnormal. Of somewhat the same nature are the abnormal industrial conditions at times of financial crisis or widespread strike, when men in the prime of life, of reasonable education, health, industry and capacity, find it impossible to support a normal family of the average size. But even in normal times there are adverse conditions in every American city. There are insanitary houses, over-crowded apartments, ill-ventilated factories, germ-laden dust in the streets and germ-laden water in the mains. Little children are in glass-works or selling papers, when they should be at school or in bed. Men and women are working over-long hours in disease-breeding surroundings. The police are conniving with criminals; the courts are imposing sentences that confirm tendencies to crime. Men are exploiting, for their own profit, the weaknesses of their fellows, both as employees and as consumers. The study of causes, enlightening to the student, indispensable to the statesman, elementary to the social worker, beneficent to the poor, need not wait for hard times or times of great calamity, but may proceed at all times, under the most favorable conditions yet known in any community.

Study of the causes of poverty at this stage of our knowledge should consist of investigations into the prevalence of adverse conditions. What we need to know, for practical purposes, is not whether twenty per cent or thirty per cent or fifty per cent of the poverty in existence is due to illness, but how much illness there is, of what kinds it is, how much of it is unnecessary and by what means we may eliminate the unnecessary part. What we need to know about congestion is not what percentage of criminality and dependence is attributable to it, for that we can never find out, but where the congested districts are, how far the adverse features of life in them may be overcome, and what can be done to induce or to compel people to move elsewhere. In the language of current philosophical discussion, pragmatism affords our best working program. We are to look away from "first things, principles, categories, supposed necessities" and look towards "last things, fruits, consequences," facts.

We are to look for those particular ideas and facts which will "help us to get into satisfactory relation with other parts of our experience."

SOURCE: Brandt, Lilian. 1908. "The Causes of Poverty." *Political Science Quarterly* 28, no. 4: 637–651.

ANALYSIS

Lilian Brandt was an economist who began working with the New York Charity Organization Society in 1902 as a statistician on its Committee on the Prevention of Tuberculosis. Within three years, her work had resulted in two pioneering publications on the disease that identified the socioeconomic factors that allowed tuberculosis to not only persist but also thrive. Many of the disease vectors she analyzed were prevalent in New York City's poorer communities. Not coincidently, it was in these very locales that tuberculosis was most prevalent. As city officials began addressing the sanitation issues common to the respective impoverished communities, the number of people suffering from tuberculosis gradually declined.

The apparent success of the tuberculosis initiative led her to research other issues that plagued poorer communities. Her work was guided by the structural theory of poverty, which argued that poverty was the result of an imbalance in the prevailing economic system. The inherent inequality in the economy ensured that there would always be a class of impoverished people. This also meant that poverty, like tuberculosis, could be greatly reduced, or even eradicated, should officials choose to address the conditions that allowed it to persist. Among Brandt's prescriptions were the elimination of child labor, the provision of educational opportunities, the improvement in the quality of available housing, and the construction of hospitals to improve public health. She controversially also called for wages to be regulated in order to ensure that workers received the monies required to provide for themselves and their families. Although some of the ideas espoused by Brandt were gradually adopted in communities around the country, an underclass remained mired in incessant poverty.

FURTHER READING

Katz, Michael B. 2015. "What Kind of a Problem Is Poverty? The Archaeology of an Idea." In Ananya Roy and Emma Shaw Crane, eds. *Territories of Poverty: Rethinking North and South.* Athens: University of Georgia Press, 39–78.

"The Poor Creature Who Clung So Desperately to Her Chest of Drawers Was Really Clinging to the Last Remnant of Normal Living—a Symbol of All She Was Asked to Renounce."

- ***Document:*** Jane Addams's *Twenty Years at Hull-House* (Excerpts)
- ***Date:*** 1910
- ***Where:*** Chicago, Illinois
- ***Significance:*** Hull House was an extremely influential settlement house whose residents provided services to immigrants, the working class, and the impoverished of Chicago's Nineteenth Ward.

DOCUMENT

PROBLEMS OF POVERTY

That neglected and forlorn old age is daily brought to the attention of a Settlement which undertakes to bear its share of the neighborhood burden imposed by poverty, was pathetically clear to us during our first months of residence at Hull House. One day a boy of ten led a tottering old lady into the House, saying that she had slept for six weeks in their kitchen on a bed made up next to the stove; that she had come when her son died, although none of them had ever seen her before; but because her son had "once worked in the same shop with Pa she thought of him when she had nowhere to go." The little fellow concluded by saying that our house was so much bigger than theirs that he thought we would have more room for beds. The old woman herself said absolutely nothing, but looking on with that gripping fear of the poorhouse in her eyes, she was a living embodiment of that dread which is so heart-breaking that the occupants of the County Infirmary themselves seem scarcely less wretched than those who are making their last stand against it.

This look was almost more than I could bear for only a few days before some frightened women had bidden me come quickly to the house of an old German woman, whom two men from the county agent's office were attempting to remove to the County Infirmary. The poor old creature had thrown herself bodily upon a small and battered chest of drawers and clung there, clutching it so firmly that it would have been impossible to remove her without also taking the piece of furniture. She did not weep nor moan nor indeed make any human sound, but between her broken gasps for breath she squealed shrilly like a frightened animal caught in a trap. The little group of women and children gathered at her door stood aghast at this realization of the black dread which always clouds the lives of the very poor when work is slack, but which constantly grows more imminent and threatening as old age approaches. The neighborhood women and I hastened to make all sorts of promises as to the support of the old woman and the county officials, only too glad to be rid of their unhappy duty, left her to our ministrations. This dread of the poorhouse, the result of centuries of deterrent Poor Law administration, seemed to me not without some justification one summer when I found myself perpetually distressed by the unnecessary idleness and forlornness of the old women in the Cook County Infirmary, many of whom I had known in the years when activity was still a necessity, and when they yet felt bustlingly important. To take away from an old woman whose life has been spent in household cares all the foolish little belongings to which her affections cling and to which her very fingers have become accustomed, is to take away her last incentive to activity, almost to life itself. To give an old woman only a chair and a bed, to leave her no cupboard in which her treasures may be stowed, not only that she may take them out when she desires occupation, but that her mind may dwell upon them in moments of revery, is to reduce living almost beyond the limit of human endurance.

The poor creature who clung so desperately to her chest of drawers was really clinging to the last remnant of normal living—a symbol of all she was asked to renounce. . . .

The lack of municipal regulation already referred to was, in the early days of Hull-House, paralleled by the inadequacy of the charitable efforts of the city and an unfounded optimism that there was no real poverty among us. Twenty years ago there was no Charity Organization Society in Chicago and the Visiting Nurse Association had not yet begun its beneficent work, while the relief societies, although conscientiously administered, were inadequate in extent and antiquated in method.

As social reformers gave themselves over to discussion of general principles, so the poor invariably accused poverty itself of their destruction. I recall a certain Mrs. Moran, who was returning one rainy day from the office of the county agent with her arms full of paper bags containing beans and flour which alone lay between her children and starvation. Although she had no money she boarded a street car in order to save her booty from complete destruction by the rain, and as the burst bags dropped "flour on the ladies' dresses" and "beans all over the place," she was sharply reprimanded by the conductor, who was further exasperated when he discovered she had no fare. He put her off, as she had hoped he would, almost in front of Hull-House. She related to us her state of mind as she stepped off the car and saw the last of her wares disappearing; she admitted she forgot the proprieties and "cursed a little," but, curiously enough, she pronounced her malediction, not against the rain nor the conductor, nor yet against the worthless husband who had been sent up to the city prison, but, true to the Chicago spirit of the moment, went to the root of the matter and roundly "cursed poverty."

. . . Mr. Stead was much impressed with the mixed goodness in Chicago, the lack of rectitude in many high places, the simple kindness of the most wretched to each other. Before he published "If Christ Came to Chicago" he made his attempt to rally the diverse moral forces of the city in a huge mass meeting, which resulted in a temporary organization, later developing into the Civic Federation. I was a member of the committee of five appointed to carry out the suggestions made in this remarkable meeting, and our first concern was to appoint a committee to deal with the unemployed. But when has a committee ever dealt satisfactorily with the unemployed? Relief stations were opened in various parts of the city, temporary lodging houses were established, Hull-House undertaking to lodge the homeless women who could be received nowhere else; employment stations were opened giving sewing to the women, and street sweeping for the men was organized. It was in connection with the latter that the perplexing question of the danger of permanently lowering wages at such a crisis, in the praiseworthy effort to bring speedy relief, was brought home to me. I insisted that it was better to have the men work half a day for seventy-five cents than a whole day for a dollar, better that they should earn three dollars in two days than in three days. I resigned from the street cleaning committee in despair of making the rest of the committee understand that, as our real object was not street cleaning but the help of the unemployed, we must treat the situation in such wise that the men would not be worse off when they returned to their normal occupations. The discussion opened up situations new to me and carried me far afield in perhaps the most serious economic reading I have ever done.

A beginning also was then made toward a Bureau of Organized Charities, the main office being put in charge of a young man recently come from Boston, who lived at Hull-House. But to employ scientific methods for the first time at such a moment involved difficulties, and the most painful episode of the winter for me came from an attempt on my part to conform to carefully received instructions. A shipping clerk whom I had known for a long time had lost his place, as so many people had that year, and came to the relief station established at Hull House four or five times to secure help for his family. I told him one day of the opportunity for work on the drainage canal and intimated that if any employment were obtainable, he ought to exhaust that possibility before asking for help. The man replied that he had always worked indoors and that he could not endure outside work in winter. I am grateful to remember that I was too uncertain to be severe, although I held to my instructions. He did not come again for relief, but worked for two days digging on the canal, where he contracted pneumonia and died a week later. I have never lost trace of the two little children he left behind him, although I cannot see them without a bitter consciousness that it was at their expense I learned that life cannot be administered by definite rules and regulations; that wisdom to deal with a man's difficulties comes only through some knowledge of his life and habits as a whole; and that to treat an isolated episode is almost sure to invite blundering.

. . .

In the latter part of the summer of 1895, I served as a member on a commission appointed by the mayor of Chicago, to investigate conditions in the county poorhouse, public attention having become centered on it through one of those distressing stories, which exaggerates the wrong in a public institution while at the same time it reveals conditions which need to be rectified. However necessary publicity is for securing reformed administration, however useful such exposures may be for political purposes, the whole is attended by such a waste of the most precious human emotions, by such a tearing of living tissue, that it can scarcely be endured. Every time I entered Hull-House during the days of the investigation, I would find waiting for me from twenty to thirty people whose friends and relatives were in the suspected institution, all in such acute distress of mind that to see them was to look upon the victims of deliberate torture. In most cases my visitor would state that it seemed impossible to put their invalids in any other place, but if these stories were true, something must be done. Many of the patients were taken out only to be returned after a few days or weeks to meet the sullen hostility of their attendants and with their own attitude changed from confidence to timidity and alarm.

This piteous dependence of the poor upon the good will of public officials was made clear to us in an early experience with a peasant woman straight from the fields of Germany, whom we met during our first six months at Hull-House. Her four years in America had been spent in patiently carrying water up and down two flights of stairs, and in washing the heavy flannel suits of iron foundry workers. For this her pay had averaged thirty-five cents a day. Three of her daughters had fallen victims to the vice of the city. The mother was bewildered and distressed, but understood nothing. We were able to induce the betrayer of one daughter to marry her; the second, after a tedious lawsuit, supported his child; with the third we were able to do nothing. . . .

We early learned to know the children of hard driven mothers who went out to work all day, sometimes leaving the little things in the casual care of a neighbor, but often locking them into their tenement rooms. The first three crippled children we encountered in the neighborhood had all been injured while their mothers were at work: one had fallen out of a third-story window, another had been burned, and the third had a curved spine due to the fact that for three years he had been tied all day long to the leg of the kitchen table, only released at noon by his older brother who hastily ran in from a neighboring factory to share his lunch with him. . . .

With all of the efforts made by modern society to nurture and educate the young, how stupid it is to permit the mothers of young children to spend themselves in the coarser work of the world! It is curiously inconsistent that with the emphasis which this generation has placed upon the mother and upon the prolongation of infancy, we constantly allow the waste of this most precious material. I cannot recall without indignation a recent experience. I was detained late one evening in an office building by a prolonged committee meeting of the Board of Education. As I came out at eleven o'clock, I met in the corridor of the fourteenth floor a woman whom I knew, on her knees scrubbing the marble tiling. As she straightened up to greet me, she seemed so wet from her feet up to her chin, that I hastily inquired the cause. Her reply was that she left home at five o'clock every night and had no opportunity for six hours to nurse her baby. Her mother's milk mingled with the very water with which she scrubbed the floors until she should return at midnight, heated and exhausted, to feed her screaming child with what remained within her breasts. These are only a few of the problems connected with the lives of the poorest people with whom the residents in a Settlement are constantly brought in contact.

SOURCE: Addams, Jane. 1910. *Twenty Years at Hull-House with Autobiographical Notes.* New York: The Macmillan Company.

ANALYSIS

The inspiration for Hull House was Toynbee Hall in London, England, which was the first settlement school in the world upon its founding in 1884. The residents of Toynbee's establishment were educated young men who hoped to address the social ills resulting from industrialization and urbanization by providing assistance and educational opportunities to immigrants and the impoverished who had arrived in the city to find employment. Among the early visitors to Toynbee Hall were Jane Addams and Ellen Gates Starr, who were inspired to start their own settlement school but with female residents. On September 18, 1889, Hull House was established in Chicago, Illinois. It was among the first settlement schools in the United States and served as a model for the more than 400 settlement schools that were subsequently created.

Hull House was located in Chicago's Nineteenth Ward, which was largely populated with European immigrants who worked in local factories. Many resided with their families in overcrowded tenements. The residents of Hull House initially sought to entertain their neighbors by offering them instruction in art, music, and theater. It quickly became obvious that the ward's working class had greater needs than gaining an appreciation for the arts. They required assistance caring for and educating their children. This led to the creation of a daycare and kindergarten at Hull House. Since most of the immigrants barely spoke English, language lessons were created. The staff also began offering classes designed to enable the immigrants to obtain U.S. citizenship. Hull House's successes serving thousands of people a week not only brought attention to its staff but also attracted financial support. Within two decades of its founding, Hull House had grown to encompass 13 buildings. The 20-year mark also saw Jane Addams document her work at Hull House in her first memoir. Her efforts during that period would help in future years to shape the field of social work.

Although Hull House's primary purpose was to aid the people of Chicago's Nineteenth Ward, it also worked through the political process to advance causes at the state level, including the creation of the first juvenile court in the United States.

Through its social and political endeavors, Hull House provided opportunities for talented women, including Edith and Grace Abbott, Florence Kelley, and Julia Lathrop, to develop their leadership skills. Members of that group would use those very proficiencies to convince a skeptical Congress to create the U.S. Children's Bureau in 1912. In fact, Julia Lathrop became the highest-serving female in the history of the federal government when she became the bureau's director.

In 1931, Jane Addams became the first woman to win the Nobel Peace Prize, "for her social reform work" and "leading the Women's International League for Peace and Freedom." She had also cofounded the American Civil Liberties Union in 1920 along with nine other activists. The Jane Addams Hull House Association fell into bankruptcy and closed in 2012. All that remains on the site at the University of Illinois at Chicago is the Jane Addams Hull-House Museum: http://www.hullhousemuseum.org/.

FURTHER READING

Brown, Victoria Bissell. 2003. *The Education of Jane Addams*. Philadelphia: University of Pennsylvania Press.

Deegan, Mary Jo. 1988. *Jane Addams and the Men of the Chicago School, 1892–1918*. New Brunswick, NJ: Transaction Publishers.

Elshtain, Jean Bethke. 2001. *Jane Addams and the Dream of American Democracy: A Life*. New York: Basic Books.

Elshtain, Jean Bethke. 2002. *The Jane Addams Reader*. New York: Basic Books.

Hamington, Maurice. 2009. *The Social Philosophy of Jane Addams*. Champaign: University of Illinois Press.

Knight, Louise W. 2005. *Citizen: Jane Addams and the Struggle for Democracy*. Chicago: University of Chicago Press.

Knight, Louise W. 2010. *Jane Addams: Spirit in Action*. New York: W.W. Norton.

Ladd-Taylor, Molly. 1994. *Mother-Work: Women, Child Welfare, and the State, 1890–1930*. Urbana: University of Illinois Press.

Platt, Harold L. 2000. "Jane Addams and the Ward Boss Revisited: Class, Politics, and Public Health in Chicago, 1890–1930." *Environmental History* 5, no. 2: 194–222.

Sklar, Kathryn Kish. 1995. *Florence Kelley and the Nation's Work: The Rise of Women's Political Culture, 1830–1900*. New Haven, CT: Yale University Press.

"To Provide for the Determination of Minimum Wages for Women and Minors"

- ***Document:*** Massachusetts's 1912 Minimum Wage Law for Women and Children
- ***Date:*** June 4, 1912
- ***Where:*** Boston, Massachusetts
- ***Significance:*** Massachusetts became the first state in the nation to mandate a minimum wage for children and women.

DOCUMENT

CHAPTER 706.

AN ACT TO ESTABLISH THE MINIMUM WAGE COMMISSION AND TO PROVIDE FOR THE DETERMINATION OF MINIMUM WAGES FOR WOMEN AND MINORS.

SECTION 1. There is hereby established a commission to be known as the Minimum Wage Commission. It shall consist of three persons, one of whom may be a woman, to be appointed by the governor, with the advice and consent of the council. One of the commissioners shall be designated by the governor as chairman. The first appointments shall be made within ninety days after the passage of this act, one for a term ending October first, nineteen hundred and thirteen, one for a term ending October first, nineteen hundred and fourteen, and one for a term ending October first, nineteen hundred and fifteen; and beginning with the year nineteen hundred and thirteen, one member shall be appointed annually for the term of three years from the first day of October and until his successor is qualified. Any vacancy that may occur shall be filled in like manner for the unexpired part of the term.

SECTION 2. Each commissioner shall be paid ten dollars for each day's service, in addition to the traveling and other expenses incurred in the performance of his official duties. The commission may appoint a secretary, who shall be the executive officer of the board and to whose appointment the rules of the civil service commission shall not apply. It shall determine his salary, subject to the approval of the governor and council. The commission may incur other necessary expenses not exceeding the annual appropriation therefor, and shall be provided with an office in the state house or in some other suitable building in the city of Boston.

SECTION 3. It shall be the duty of the commission to inquire into the wages paid to the female employees in any occupation in the commonwealth, if the commission has reason to believe that the wages paid to a substantial number of such employees are inadequate to supply the necessary cost of living and to maintain the worker in health.

SECTION 4. If after such investigation the commission is of the opinion that in the occupation in question the wages paid to a substantial number of female employees are inadequate to supply the necessary cost of living and to maintain the worker in health, the commission shall establish a wage board consisting of not less than six representatives of employers in the occupation in question and of an equal number of persons to represent the female employees in said occupation, and of one or more disinterested persons appointed by the Commission to represent the public, but the representatives of the public shall not exceed one half of the number of representatives of either of the other parties. The commission shall designate the chairman from among the representatives of the public, and shall make rules and regulations governing the selection of members and the modes of procedure of the boards, and shall exercise exclusive jurisdiction over all questions arising with reference to the validity of the procedure and of the determinations of the boards. The members of wage boards shall be compensated at the same rate as jurors; they shall be allowed the necessary traveling and clerical expenses incurred in the performance of their duties, these payments to be made from the appropriation for the expenses of the commission.

SECTION 5. The commission may transmit to each wage board all pertinent information in its possession relative to the wages paid in the occupation in question. Each wage board shall take into consideration the needs of the employees, the financial condition of the occupation and the probable effect thereon of any increase in the minimum wages paid, and shall endeavor to determine the minimum wage, whether by time rate or piece rate, suitable for a female employee of ordinary ability in the occupation in question, or for any or all of the branches thereof, and also suitable minimum wages for learners and apprentices and for minors below the age of eighteen years. When two thirds of the members of a wage board shall agree upon minimum wage determinations, they shall report such determinations to the commission, together with the reasons therefor and the facts relating thereto, and also the names, so far as they can be ascertained by the board of employers who pay less than the minimum wage so determined.

SECTION 6. Upon receipt of a report from a wage board, the commission shall review the same, and may approve any or all of the determinations recommended, or may disapprove any or all of them, or may recommit the subject to the same or to a new wage board. If the commission approves any or all of the determinations of the wage board it shall, after not less than fourteen days' notice to employers pay a wage less than the minimum wage approved, give a public hearing to such employers, and if, after such public hearing, the commission finally approves the determination, it shall enter a decree of its findings and note thereon the names of employers, so far as they may be known to the commission, who fail or refuse to accept such minimum wage and to agree to abide by it. The commission shall, within fourteen days thereafter, publish the names of all such employers in at least four newspapers in each county in the Commonwealth, together with the material part of its findings, and a statement of the minimum wages paid by every such employer. Any employer upon filing a declaration under oath in the supreme judicial or superior court to the effect that compliance with such decree would endanger the prosperity of the business to which the same is made applicable, shall be entitled to a stay of execution of such decree, and a review thereof with reference to the question involved in such declaration. Such review shall be made by the court under the rules of equity procedure, and if it shall be found by the court that compliance with such decree is likely to endanger the prosperity of the business to which the same is applicable, then an order shall issue from said court, revoking the same. The type in which the employers' names shall be printed shall not be smaller than that in which the news matter of the paper is printed. The publication shall be attested by the signature of at least a majority of the commission.

SECTION 7. In case a wage board shall make a recommendation of a wage determination in which a majority but less than two thirds of the members concur, the commission, in its discretion, may report such recommendation and the pertinent facts relating thereto to the general court.

SECTION 8. Whenever a minimum wage rate has been established in any occupation, the commission may upon petition of either employers or employees, re convene the wage board or establish a new wage board, and any recommendation made by such board shall be dealt with in the same manner as the original recommendation of a wage board.

SECTION 9. For any occupation in which a minimum time rate only has been established, the commission may issue to any woman physically defective a special license authorizing the employment of the licensee for a wage less than the legal minimum wage: provided, that it is not less than the special minimum wage fixed for that person.

SECTION 10. The commission may at any time inquire into the wages paid to minors in any occupation in which the majority of employees are minors, and may, after giving public hearings, determine minimum wages suitable for such minors. When the commission has made such a determination, it may proceed in the same manner as if the determination had been recommended to the commission by a wage board.

SECTION 11. Every employer of women and minors shall keep a register of the names and addresses of all women and minors employed by him, and shall on request permit the commission or any of its members or agents to inspect the register. The commission shall also have power to subpoena witnesses, administer oaths and take testimony, and to examine such parts of the books and records of employers as re late to the wages paid to women and minors. Such witnesses shall be summoned in the same manner and be paid from the treasury of the commonwealth the same fees as witnesses before the superior court.

SECTION 12. Upon request of the commission, the director of the bureau of statistics shall cause such statistics and other data to be gathered as the commission may require, and the cost thereof shall be paid out of the appropriation made for the expenses of the commission.

SECTION 13. Any employer who discharges or in any other manner discriminates against any employee because such employee has testified, or is about to testify, or because the employer believes that the employee may testify, in any investigation or proceeding relative to the enforcement of this act, shall be deemed guilty of a misdemeanor, and upon conviction thereof shall be punished by a fine of twenty-five dollars for each offence.

SECTION 14. The commission shall from time to time determine whether employers in each occupation investigated are obeying its decrees, and shall publish in the manner provided in section six, the name of any employer whom it finds to be violating any such decree.

SECTION 15. Any newspaper refusing or neglecting to publish the findings, decrees and notices of the commission at its regular rates for the space taken shall, upon conviction thereof, be punished by a fine of not less than one hundred dollars for each offence.

SECTION 16. No member of the commission and no newspaper publisher, proprietor, editor or employee thereof, shall be liable to an action for damages for publishing the name of any employer in accordance with the provisions of this act, unless such publication contains some willful misrepresentation.

SECTION 17. The commission shall annually, on or before the first Wednesday in January, make a report to the general court of its investigations and proceedings during the preceding year.

SECTION 18. This act shall take effect on the first day of July in the year nineteen hundred and thirteen.

SOURCE: Commonwealth of Massachusetts, Bureau of Statistics. 1912. *Massachusetts Labor Bulletin: Volume XVII*. Boston: Wright & Potter Printing Co., State Printers.

ANALYSIS

In 1912, the Massachusetts legislature commissioned a study on the working conditions endured by women and children in the state. The resulting report showed that both groups were being exploited by employers in the state. They endured harsh working conditions that were extremely harmful to their health and welfare for wages that barely provided enough to minimally subsist. Upon receipt of the report, divisions within the legislature quickly appeared. One faction pushed for legislation mandating a minimum wage. Pro-business legislators opposed such an effort as an increase in wages would result in smaller profit margins for employers. The 1912 Minimum Wage Law for Women and Children proved a compromise measure. While it prescribed wage minimums for women and children, it left the determination of the requisite amount per occupation to a Minimum Wage Commission, whose membership was appointed by the governor.

"To Provide for the Partial Support of Mothers Whose Husbands Are Dead or Have Become Permanently Incapacitated for Work by Reason of Physical or Mental Infirmity"

- ***Document:*** Illinois's Mothers' Pension Law
- ***Date:*** 1913
- ***Where:*** Springfield, Illinois
- ***Significance:*** The act providing for the payment of mothers' pensions was one of the first pieces of legislation of its kind to be enacted in the United States.

DOCUMENT

AN ACT *to provide for the partial support of mothers whose husbands are dead or have become permanently incapacitated for work by reason of physical or mental infirmity, when such mothers have children under fourteen years of age, and are citizens of the United States of America and residents of the county in which application for relief is made. And, also, to provide for the probationary visitation, care and super vision of the family for whose benefit such support is provided.*

SECTION 1. JURISDICTION.] *Be it enacted by the People of the State of Illinois, represented in the General Assembly:* The juvenile court, or, where there is no juvenile court, the county court in the several counties in the State, shall have original jurisdiction in all cases coming within the terms of this Act.

§ 2. A woman whose husband is dead or whose husband has become permanently incapacitated for work by reason of physical or mental infirmity, may file an application for relief under this Act, provided such woman is a citizen of the United States of America and has a previous residence for three years in the county where such application is made and is the mother of a child or children.

§3. OFFICIAL INVESTIGATION AND REPORT.] Whenever an application for relief is filed the home of the applicant shall be visited by an officer of the court having jurisdiction of the matter, and the facts set forth in such application shall be investigated by such officer under the direction of the court, and a report and recommendation of the approval or disapproval of such application shall be made in writing by such officer to the court without any unnecessary delay.

§ 4. PETITION-FORM OF.] After the investigation of such application for relief by an officer of court and the filing of the report and recommendation thereon of such officer, such officer of court or any reputable and responsible person who has a residence in the county may file, with the clerk of the court having jurisdiction of the matter, a petition in writing duly verified by affidavit setting forth such facts as are necessary under this Act to give the court jurisdiction of the parties and of the subject matter, and setting forth such other facts, which, when found by the court to be true, shall be the basis upon which the order of relief is entered. It shall be sufficient that the affidavit is upon knowledge, information and belief. A separate petition shall be filed for each child. The mother of such child and the county board of the county in which the petition is filed shall be made parties respondent to such petition.

§ 5. SUMMONS.] Upon filing of such petition a summons returnable not less than three days nor more than ten days after the date thereof shall issue to the respondents named in such petition requiring the mother with such child and all the respondents to appear at a place and time stated in the summons, which time shall be on the return day of such summons.

§ 6. SERVICE.] Service of summons shall be made in the same manner as is provided for the service of a summons in an Act entitled "An Act to regulate practice in courts of chancery," approved March 15, 1872, in force July 1, 1872.

§ 7. NEW PROCESS.] Whenever process shall not be returned executed on or before the return day thereof, the court may direct the clerk to issue an *alias*, *pluries* or other process, returnable at a time ordered by the court.

§ 8. APPEARANCE—HEARING.] The filing of a written appearance by a respondent shall render the service of summons on such respondent unnecessary. The court shall proceed to hear the cause upon the return day of the summons or upon a day thereafter to be fixed by the court without the formality of the respondents filing answers: *Provided*, all the respondents have either been served with summons or have their written appearance in said cause.

§ 9. HEARING—ORDER or PAYMENT—DUTY OF COUNTY BOARD.] Upon the hearing in court of a petition under this Act, the court, being fully advised in the premises; finding the facts alleged in the petition to be true may make an order upon the county board of the county to pay to the mother of the child or children in whose behalf the petition or petitions are filed an amount of money necessary to enable such mother to properly care for such child or children. It thereupon shall be the duty of the county board, through its county agent or otherwise, to pay to such mother at such times as said order may designate the amount so specified for the care of such child or children until the further order of the court.

§ 10. AMOUNT OF ALLOWANCE.] The allowance made to such mother shall not exceed fifteen dollars per month when such mother has but one child under the age of fourteen years, and, if she has more than one child under such age, the relief granted shall not exceed ten dollars per month for each of the other children: *Provided*, that in no event shall the relief granted for any one mother and children exceed the sum of fifty dollars per month.

§ 11. CONDITIONS UPON WHICH RELIEF IS GRANTED.] Such relief shall be granted by the court only upon the following conditions:

(1) The child or children for whose benefit the relief is granted must be living with the mother of such child or children; (2) the court must find that it is for the welfare of such child or children to remain at home with the mother; (3) the relief shall be granted only when in the absence of such relief the mother would be required to work regularly away from her home and children and when by means of such relief she will be able to remain at home with her children, except that she may be absent for work a definite number of days each week to be specified in the court's order, when such work can be done by her without the sacrifice of health or the neglect of home and children; (4) such mother must, in the judgment of the court, be a proper person, physically, mentally and morally fit, to bring up her children; (5) the relief granted shall, in the judgment of the court, be necessary to save the child or children from neglect; (6) a mother shall not receive such relief who is the owner of real property or personal property other than the household goods; (7) a mother shall not receive such relief who is not a citizen of this country and who has not resided in the county where the application is made at least three years next before making such application; (8) a mother shall not receive such relief if her child or children have relatives of sufficient ability to support them.

§ 2. RELIEF FOR CHILD BETWEEN 14 AND 16 YEARS.] Whenever any child shall arrive at the age of fourteen years any relief granted to the mother for such child shall cease:*Provided*, if a child of fourteen years of age be ill or is incapacitated for work, the mother shall receive funds for his care during such illness or incapacity for work until such child is sixteen years of age. The court may, in its discretion, at any time before such child reaches the age of fourteen years, modify or vacate the order granting relief to any mother and for any child.

§ 13. PRESENCE OF HUSBAND.] Whenever relief is granted or is about to be granted to a mother whose husband is permanently incapacitated for work by reason of physical or mental infirmity and the presence of such husband in the family is a menace to the physical and moral welfare of the mother or children, then the court may require that such husband be removed from the home and provision for his care made elsewhere, or failing to remove such husband or upon his refusal to be separated from his family, the court may, in its discretion, vacate the order granting relief, or refuse the relief asked for.

§ 14. PROBATION OFFICERS—THEIR PAY.] The court having jurisdiction in proceedings coming within the provisions of this Act shall have the power to appoint one or more qualified persons of good character, who shall serve and be known as probation officers, during the pleasure of the court, and who shall be paid a suitable compensation by the county for their services, the amount thereof to be determined by the county board.

§ 15. DUTY OF PROBATION OFFICERS.] It shall be the duty of such officers to investigate all applications for relief and make a written report of such investigation with their recommendations. After granting of relief to any mother for the support of her children it shall be the further duty of such officers to visit and supervise, under the direction of the court, the families to which such relief has been granted and to advise with the court and to perform such other duties as the court may direct in order to maintain the integrity of the family and the welfare of the children.

§ 16. The county board in each county shall levy a tax of not to exceed three-tenths of one mill on the dollar annually on all taxable property in the county, such tax to be levied and collected in like manner with the general taxes of the county, and to be known as a mothers' pension fund: *Provided*, that said tax shall not be included in the aggregate of all the taxes required to be reduced under the provisions of an Act entitled, "An Act concerning the levy and extension of taxes," approved May 9, 1901, in force July 1, 1901, and Acts amendatory thereof.

§ 17. PARTIAL RELIEF.] Should the fund herein authorized be sufficient to permit an allowance to only a part of the mothers coming within the provisions of this Act, the court shall select, in its discretion, those in most urgent need of such allowance.

§18. PENALTY FOR FRAUD.] Any person or persons fraudulently attempting to obtain or fraudulently obtaining any allowance for relief under this Act shall be deemed guilty of a misdemeanor and on conviction thereof shall be punished by a fine of not less than five dollars nor more than two hundred dollars, or imprisoned in the county jail for a period of not to exceed six months, or both.

§ 19. All Acts or parts of Acts inconsistent herewith are hereby repealed.

SOURCE: Bowen, A. L., ed. 1913. "Illinois' New Mothers Pension Law." *Institution Quarterly* 4, no. 3: 35–37.

ANALYSIS

During the Progressive Era of the early twentieth century, "maternalists" began advocating for laws benefiting women and children. They argued that society at large benefited from children being nurtured by their mothers because they would grow to be better citizens than if they were left alone to range through seedy streets. The government should thus provide those mothers the financial wherewithal to conduct their domestic duties rather than joining the workforce. Toward that end, Illinois enacted in 1911 the Funds to Parents Act, which is often referred to as the first piece of legislation of its kind enacted in the United States. Although providing for mothers was ostensibly its primary purpose, language was also included that allowed for poor fathers to also obtain benefits under the act. Juvenile judges were granted a great amount of discretion under the law in how much aid to award and to whom, which resulted in significant malfeasance and costs that far exceeded the expectations of the state legislature. To address the rampant corruption, state legislators passed the Mothers' Pension Act of 1913. Unlike the earlier legislation, it not only narrowed eligibility to single women with children but also set the maximum amount that could be provided to a family. The provision of mothers' pensions had two unintended consequences. At a time when women were moving into professional jobs such as nursing and social work, it sent the message that a woman's place was in the home. The other issue was that while some states were providing the mothers a pension, the monies were barely enough for a family to subsist. The result was these mothers and their children were locked into poverty by the state.

FURTHER READING

Dahlquist, Amanda. 2013. "Legislating Motherhood: The History of Mothers' Aid in Montgomery County." *Journal of the Illinois State Historical Society* 106, no. 1: 129–154.

Goodwin, Joanne. 1997. *Gender and the Politics of Welfare Reform: Mothers' Pension in Chicago, 1911–1929*. Chicago: University of Illinois Press.

Ladd-Taylor, Molly. 1994. *Mother-Work: Women, Child Welfare, and the State, 1890–1930*. Champaign: University of Illinois Press.

Nackenoff, Carol. 2016. "Toward a More Inclusive Community: The Legacy of Female Reformers in the Progressive State." In Stephen Skowronek, Stephen M. Engel, and Brucke Ackerman, eds. *The Progressives' Century: Political Reform, Constitutional Government, and the Modern American State*. New Haven: Yale University Press, 219–242.

Skocpol, Theda. 1992. *Protecting Soldiers and Mothers: The Politics of Social Provision in the United States, 1870s–1920s*. Cambridge, MA: Harvard University Press.

Ward, Deborah E. 2005. *The White Welfare State: The Racialization of U.S. Welfare Policy*. Ann Arbor: University of Michigan Press.

3

THE CIVIL WAR TO THE ROARING 1920s

An Act to Grant Pensions

- ***Document:*** Pension Act of 1862 (Excerpts)
- ***Date:*** July 14, 1862
- ***Where:*** Washington, D.C.
- ***Significance:*** The Pension Act of 1862 provided benefits to soldiers that had been disabled while serving in the military. If they perished, the pension that they earned was provided to the widow or surviving children up to their 16th birthday.

DOCUMENT

Be it enacted by the Senate and House of Representatives of the United States of America in Congress assembled, That if any officer, non-commissioned officer, musician, or private of the army, including regulars, volunteers, and militia, or any officer, warrant, or petty officer, musician, seaman, ordinary seaman, flotilla-man, marine, clerk, landsman, pilot, or other person in the navy or marine corps, has been, since the fourth day of March, eighteen hundred and sixty-one, or shall hereafter be, disabled by reason of any wound received or disease contracted while in the service of the United States, and in the line of duty, he shall, upon making due proof of the fact according to such forms and regulations as are or may be provided by or in pursuance of law, be placed upon the list of invalid pensions of the United States, and be entitled to receive, for the highest rate of disability, such pension as is hereinafter provided in such cases, and for an inferior disability an amount proportionate to the highest disability, to commence as hereinafter provided, and continue during the existence of such disability. The pension for a total disability for officers, non-commissioned officers, musicians, and privates employed in the military service of the United States, whether regulars, volunteers, or militia, and in the marine corps, shall be as follows, viz: Lieutenant-colonel, and all officers of a higher rank, thirty dollars per month; major, twenty-five dollars per month; captain, twenty dollars per month; first lieutenant, seventeen dollars per month; second lieutenant, fifteen dollars per month; and noncommissioned officers, musicians, and privates, eight dollars per month. The pension for total disability for officers, warrant, or petty officers, and others employed in the naval service of the United States, shall be as follows, viz: Captain, commander, surgeon, paymaster, and chief engineer, respectively, ranking with commander by law, lieutenant commanding, and master commanding, thirty dollars per month; lieutenant, surgeon, paymaster, and chief engineer, respectively, ranking with lieutenant by law, and passed assistant surgeon, twenty-five dollars per month; professor of mathematics, master, assistant surgeon, assistant paymaster, and chaplain, twenty dollars per month; first assistant engineers and pilots, fifteen dollars per month; passed midshipman, midshipman, captains' and paymasters' clerk, second and third assistant engineer, masters' mate, and all warrant officers, ten dollars per month; all petty officers, and all other persons before named employed in the naval service, eight dollars per month; and all commissioned officers, of either service, shall receive such and only such pension as is herein provided for the rank in which they hold commissions.

SEC. 2. *And be it further enacted*, That if any officer or other person named in the first section of this act has died since the fourth day of March, eighteen hundred and sixty-one, or shall hereafter die, by reason of any wound received or disease contracted while in the service of the United States, and in the line of duty, his widow, or, if there be no widow, his child or children under sixteen years of age, shall be entitled to receive the same pension as the husband or father would have been entitled to had he been totally disabled, to commence from the death of the husband or father, and to continue to the widow during her widowhood, or to the child or children until they severally attain to the age of sixteen years, and no longer.

SEC. 3. *And be it further enacted*, That where any officer or other person named in the first section of this act shall have died subsequently to the fourth day of March, eighteen hundred and sixty-one, or shall hereafter died, by reason of any wound received or disease contracted while in the service of the United States, and in the line of duty, and has not left or shall not leave a widow nor legitimate child, but has left or shall leave a mother who was dependent upon him for support, in whole or in part, the mother shall be entitled to receive the same pension as such officer or other person would have been entitled to had he been totally disabled; which pension shall commence from the death of the officer or other person dying as aforesaid: *Provided, however*, That if such mother shall herself be in receipt of a pension as a widow, in virtue of the provisions of the second section of this act, in that case no pension or allowance shall be granted to her on account of her son, unless she gives up the other pension or allowance: *And provided, further*, That the pension given to a mother on account of her son shall terminate on her remarriage: And provided, further, That nothing herein shall be so construed as to entitle the mother of an officer or other person dying, as aforesaid, to more than one pension at the same time under the provisions of this act.

SEC. 4. *And be it further enacted*, That where any officer or other person named in the first section of this act shall have died subsequently to the fourth day of March, eighteen hundred and sixty-one, or shall hereafter die, by reason of any wound received or disease contracted while in the service of the United States, and in the line of duty, and has not left or shall not leave a widow, nor legitimate child, nor mother, but has left or may leave an orphan sister or sisters, under sixteen years of age, who were dependent upon him for support, in whole or in part, such sister or sisters shall be entitled to receive the same pension as such officer or other person would have been entitled to had he been totally disabled; which pension to said orphan shall commence from the death of the officer or other person dying as aforesaid, and shall continue to the said orphans until they severally arrive at the age of sixteen years, and no longer: *Provided, however*, That nothing herein shall be so construed as to entitle said orphans to more than one pension at the same time, under the provisions of this act: *And provided, further*, That no moneys shall be paid to the widow, or children, or any heirs of any deceased soldier on account of bounty, back pay, or pension, who have in any way been engaged in or who have aided or abetted the existing rebellion in the United States; but the rights of such disloyal widow or children, heir or heirs of such soldier, shall be vested in the loyal heir or heirs of the deceased, if any there be.

SEC. 5. *And be it further enacted*, That pensions which may be granted, in pursuance of the provisions of this act, to persons who may have been, or shall be, employed in the military or naval service of the United States, shall commence on the day of the discharge of such persons in all cases in which the application for such provision is filed within one year after the date of said discharge; and in cases in which the application is not filed during said year, pensions granted to persons employed as aforesaid shall commence on the day of filing of the application.

. . .

SEC. 10. *And be it further enacted*, That the pilots, engineers, sailors, and crews upon the gunboats and war vessels of the United States, who have not been regularly mustered into the service of the United States, shall be entitled to the same bounty allowed to persons of corresponding rank in the naval service, provided they continue in service to the close of the present war; and all persons serving as aforesaid, who have been or may be wounded or incapacitated for service, shall be entitled to receive for such disability the pension allowed by the provisions of this act, to those of like rank, and each and every such person shall receive pay according to corresponding rank in the naval service: Provided, That no person receiving pension or bounty under the provisions of this act shall receive either pension or bounty for any other service in the present war.

SEC. 11. *And be it further enacted*, That the widows and heirs of all persons described in the last preceding section who have been or may be employed as aforesaid, or who have been or may be killed in battle, or of those who have died or shall die of wounds received while so employed, shall be paid the bounty and pension allowed by the provisions of this act, according to rank, as provided in the last preceding section.

SEC. 12. *And be it further enacted*, That the Secretary of the Interior be, and he is hereby, authorized to appoint a special agent for the Pension Office, to assist in the detection of frauds against the pension laws, to cause persons committing such frauds to be prosecuted, and to discharge such other duties as said Secretary may require him to perform; which said agent shall receive for his services an annual salary of twelve hundred dollars, and his actual travelling expenses incurred in the discharge of his duties shall be paid by the government.

SEC. 13. *And be it further enacted,* That all acts and parts of act inconsistent with the provisions of this act be, and the same are hereby repealed.

SOURCE: Sanger, George P., ed. 1863. *The Statutes at Large, Treaties, and Proclamations of the United States of America from December 5, 1859 to March 3, 1863: Vol. XII.* Boston: Little, Brown and Company.

ANALYSIS

In 1862, the federal government was preparing for a prolonged conflict with the Confederate States of America and was having difficulty finding enough recruits to bolster its forces. As a recruiting inducement, Congress passed the Pension Act. It was an extremely generous pension that not only provided for the Union veterans should they become disabled due to their wartime service but also paid benefits to their widows or children up to the age of 16 should the individual succumb to his wounds. The pension benefits were not uniform, as the amount provided depended on the rank of the soldier at the time of disability or death. In practice, low-ranking soldiers received far less than officers. Over the course of the Civil War, with so many men and women maimed or killed in the fighting, the pension benefits helped many to economically recover. One group that did not receive enough to subsist was women with dependent children. It was not until 1873 that the federal government allowed for extra benefits to be paid to them. Former Confederates were envious of the Union pensions and had their legislators in Congress try to include them in the beneficiary class for the Pension Act but were ultimately denied.

FURTHER READING

Holmes, Amy E. 1990. "Such Is the Price We Pay: American Widows and the Civil War Pension System." In Maris A. Vinovskis, *Toward a Social History of the American Civil War: Exploratory Essays.* New York: Cambridge University Press, 171–196.

Johnson, Russell L. 2011. " 'Great Injustice': Social Status and the Distribution of Military Pensions after the Civil War." *Journal of the Gilded Age and Progressive Era* 10, no. 2: 137–160.

Marten, James. 2014. *America's Corporal: James Tanner in War and Peace.* Athens: University of Georgia Press.

McClintock, Megan J. 1996. "Civil War Pensions and the Reconstruction of Union Families." *Journal of American History* 83, no. 2: 456–480.

An Act to Secure Homesteads to Actual Settlers on the Public Domain

- ***Document:*** Homestead Act of 1862
- ***Date:*** May 20, 1862
- ***Where:*** Washington, D.C.
- ***Significance:*** The Homestead Act of 1862 allowed a head of household aged 21 or above of either sex to claim a plot of land 160 acres in size for $1.25 per acre plus a filing fee. Those desiring a smaller plot could buy 80 acres of land for $2.50 per acre plus the filing fee.

DOCUMENT

Be it enacted by the Senate and House of Representatives of the United States of America in Congress assembled, That any person who is the head of a family, or who has arrived at the age of twenty-one years, and is a citizen of the United States, or who shall have filed his declaration of intention to become such, as required by the naturalization laws of the United States, and who has never borne arms against the United States Government or given aid and comfort to its enemies, shall, from and after the first January, eighteen hundred and. sixty-three, be entitled to enter one quarter section or a less quantity of unappropriated public lands, upon which said person may have filed a preemption claim, or which may, at the time the application is made, be subject to preemption at one dollar and twenty-five cents, or less, per acre; or eighty acres or less of such unappropriated lands, at two dollars and fifty cents per acre, to be located in a body, in conformity to the legal subdivisions of the public lands, and after the same shall have been surveyed: Provided, That any person owning and residing on land may, under the provisions of this act, enter other land lying contiguous to his or her said land, which shall not, with the land so already owned and occupied, exceed in the aggregate one hundred and sixty acres.

SEC. 2. And be it further enacted, That the person applying for the benefit of this act shall, upon application to the register of the land office in which he or she is about to make such entry, make affidavit before the said register or receiver that he or she is the head of a family, or is twenty-one years or more of age, or shall have performed service in the army or navy of the United States, and that he has never borne arms against the Government of the United States or given aid and comfort to its enemies, and that such application is made for his or her exclusive use and benefit, and that said entry is made for the purpose of actual settlement and cultivation, and not either directly or indirectly for the use or benefit of any other person or persons whomsoever; and upon filing the said affidavit with the register or receiver, and on payment of ten dollars, he or she shall thereupon be permitted to enter the quantity of land specified: Provided, however, That no certificate shall be given or patent issued therefor until the expiration of five years from the date of such entry; and if, at the expiration of such time, or at any time within two years thereafter, the person making such entry; or, if he be dead, his widow; or in case of her death, his heirs or devisee; or in case of a widow making such entry, her heirs or devisee, in case of her death; shall prove by two credible witnesses that he, she, or they have resided upon or cultivated the same for the term of five years immediately succeeding the time of filing the affidavit aforesaid, and shall make affidavit that no part of said land has been alienated, and that he has borne rue allegiance to the Government of the United States; then, in such case, he, she, or they, if at that time a citizen of the United States, shall be entitled to a patent, as in other cases provided for by law: And provided, further, That in case of the death of both father and mother, leaving an Infant child, or children, under twenty-one years of age, the right and fee shall ensure to the benefit of said infant child or children; and the executor, administrator, or guardian may, at any time within two years after the death of the surviving parent, and in accordance with the laws of the State in which such children for the time being have their domicil, sell said land for the benefit of said infants, but for no other purpose; and the purchaser shall acquire the absolute title by the purchase, and be entitled to a patent from the United States, on payment of the office fees and sum of money herein specified.

SEC. 3. And be it further enacted, That the register of the land office shall note all such applications on the tract books and plats of, his office, and keep a register of all such entries, and make return thereof to the General Land Office, together with the proof upon which they have been founded.

SEC. 4. And be it further enacted, That no lands acquired under the provisions of this act shall in any event become liable to the satisfaction of any debt or debts contracted prior to the issuing of the patent therefor.

SEC. 5. And be it further enacted, That if, at any time after the filing of the affidavit, as required in the second section of this act, and before the expiration of the five years aforesaid, it shall be proven, after due notice to the settler, to the satisfaction of the register of the land office, that the person having filed such affidavit shall have actually changed his or her residence, or abandoned the said land for more than six months at any time, then and in that event the land so entered shall revert to the government.

SEC. 6. And be it further enacted, That no individual shall be permitted to acquire title to more than one quarter section under the provisions of this act; and that the Commissioner of the General Land Office is hereby required to prepare and issue such rules and regulations, consistent with this act, as shall be necessary and proper to carry its provisions into effect; and that the registers and receivers of the several land offices shall be entitled to receive the same compensation for any lands entered under the provisions of this act that they are now entitled to receive when the same quantity of land is entered with money, one half to be paid by the person making the application at the time of so doing, and the other half on the issue of the certificate by the person to whom it may be issued; but this shall not be construed to enlarge the maximum of compensation now prescribed by law for any register or receiver: Provided, That nothing contained in this act shall be so construed as to impair or interfere in any manner whatever with existing preemption rights: And provided, further, That all persons who may have filed their applications for a preemption right prior to the passage of this act, shall be entitled to all privileges of this act: Provided, further, That no person who has served, or may hereafter serve, for a period of not less than fourteen days in the army or navy of the United States, either regular or volunteer, under the laws thereof, during the existence of an actual war, domestic or foreign, shall be deprived of the benefits of this act on account of not having attained the age of twenty-one years.

SEC. 7. And be it further enacted, That the fifth section of the act entitled "An act in addition to an act more effectually to provide for the punishment of certain crimes against the United States, and for other purposes," approved the third of March, in the year eighteen hundred and fifty-seven, shall extend to all oaths, affirmations, and affidavits, required or authorized by this act.

SEC. 8. And be it further enacted, That nothing in this act shall be construed as to prevent any person who has availed him or herself of the benefits of the first section of this act, from paying the minimum price, or the price to which the same may have graduated, for the quantity of land so entered at any time before the expiration of the five years, and obtaining a patent therefor from the government, as in other cases provided by law, on making proof of settlement and cultivation as provided by existing laws granting preemption rights.

SOURCE: Act of May 20, 1862 (Homestead Act), Public Law 37-64, 05/20/1862; Record Group 11; General Records of the U.S. Government; National Archives.

ANALYSIS

As early as the 1840s, the U.S. Congress had seen the introduction of bills designed to encourage poor citizens and immigrants to migrate to the West by promising them an opportunity to receive some land. The proposals went for naught as congressmen from southern states would not support the initiatives due to the slavery issue. They believed any new states that were formed in the wake of the migration would enter the Union under the banner of free soil. It was not until after the outbreak of the Civil War, which saw southern legislators leave Congress, that the Homestead Act would find the political support necessary for its passage. The Civil War actually was referenced in the act, as people who had borne arms against the United States were ineligible to receive a homestead.

The Homestead Act of 1862 allowed a head of household aged 21 or above of either sex to claim a plot of land 160 acres in size for $1.25 per acre plus a filing fee. Those desiring a smaller plot could buy 80 acres of land for $2.50 per acre plus the filing fee. In order to gain permanent title to the property, the homesteader had to live on and farm the land for five years and improve the property through activities such as constructing a home. After five years, the head of household could obtain a title by having two neighbors verify that the land had been improved and then pay another filing fee.

The act had a mixed legacy. It provided an avenue for impoverished men or women to be able to obtain land and build a future for their households. For immigrants, it not only allowed for land ownership but granted a title after five years citizenship. Freedmen from the South were also granted access to a homestead, thereby providing them the ability to farm their own property. By 1900, approximately 700,000 claims for homesteads had been made under the terms of the 1862 act. Less than 10 percent of those claims resulted in the homesteader gaining title to the land. There were a multitude of reasons for the inability of people to succeed on their land. One of the most prevalent was the quality of the land that they received. Much of the land in the West was arid, which made farming almost impossible. Even if a homesteader received a decent claim, many did not have the money required after paying for land and filing fees to invest in seeds and farming implements. The inability to pay for the materials they required to improve their homestead led many to make financial arrangement for the items they required with unscrupulous individuals who were actually engaged in land speculation. When the homesteaders defaulted on their commitment, the speculator would obtain their property and promptly resell it. Although it was technically illegal for speculators to sell land that was originally obtained through the Homestead Act, few were ever prosecuted for their transgression.

By the early 1900s, the number of people seeking claims under the act had declined significantly. Congress attempted to rectify the problem in 1909 with the passage of the Enlarged Homestead Act, which allowed homesteaders to claim as much as 320 acres of land. It failed to spur westward migration. Other amendments followed in 1912 and 1916 but they too had little effect. The Homestead Act was repealed for the 48 contiguous states in 1976. Individuals were able to obtain homesteads in Alaska until 1986.

FURTHER READING

Anderson, Hannah L. 2011. "That Settles It: The Debate and Consequences of the Homestead Act of 1862." *The History Teacher* 45, no. 1: 117–137.

Krall, Lisi. 2001. "US Land Policy and the Commodification of Arid Land (1862–1920)." *Journal of Economic Issues* 35, no. 3: 657–674.

Porterfield, Jason. 2005. *The Homestead Act of 1862: A Primary Source History of the Settlement of the American Heartland in the Late 19th Century*. New York: Rosen Publishing Group.

West, Elliott. 1995. *The Way to the West: Essays on the Central Plains*. Albuquerque: University of New Mexico Press.

An Act to Establish a Bureau for the Relief of Freedmen and Refugees

- ***Document:*** Freedmen's Bureau Bill of 1865
- ***Date:*** March 3, 1865
- ***Where:*** Washington, D.C.
- ***Significance:*** The bill created the Bureau of Refugees, Freedmen, and Abandoned Lands, later renamed the Freedmen's Bureau, as a temporary federal agency within the War Department to aid former slaves to transition to life as free men and women.

DOCUMENT

Be it enacted by the Senate and House of Representatives of the United States of America in Congress assembled, That there is hereby established in the War Department, to continue during the present war of rebellion, and for one year thereafter, a bureau of refugees, freedmen, and abandoned lands, to which shall be committed, as hereinafter provided, the supervision and management of all abandoned lands, and the control of all subjects relating to refugees and freedmen from rebel states, or from any district of country within the territory embraced in the operations of the army, under such rules and regulations as may be prescribed by the head of the bureau and approved by the President. The said bureau shall be under the management and control of a commissioner to be appointed by the President, by and with the advice and consent of the Senate, whose compensation shall be three thousand dollars per annum, and such number of clerks as may be assigned to him by the Secretary of War, not exceeding one chief clerk, two of the fourth class, two of the third class, and five of the first class. And the commissioner and all persons appointed under this act, shall, before entering upon their duties, take the oath of office prescribed in an act entitled "An act to prescribe an oath of office, and for other purposes," approved July second, eighteen hundred and sixty-two, and the commissioner and the chief clerk shall, before entering upon their duties, give bonds to the treasurer of the United States, the former in the sum of fifty thousand dollars, and the latter in the sum of ten thousand dollars, conditioned for the faithful discharge of their duties respectively, with securities to be approved as sufficient by the Attorney-General, which bonds shall be filed in the office of the first comptroller of the treasury, to be by him put in suit for the benefit of any injured party upon any breach of the conditions thereof.

SEC. 2. *And be it further enacted*, That the Secretary of War may direct such issues of provisions, clothing, and fuel, as he may deem needful for the immediate and temporary shelter and supply of destitute and suffering refugees and freedmen and their wives and children, under such rules and regulations as he may direct.

SEC. 3. *And be it further enacted*, That the President may, by and with the advice and consent of the Senate, appoint an assistant commissioner for each of the states declared to be in insurrection, not exceeding ten in number, who shall, under the direction of the commissioner, aid in the execution of the provisions of this act; and he shall give a bond to the Treasurer of the United States, in the sum of twenty thousand dollars, in the form and manner prescribed in the first section of this act. Each of said commissioners shall receive an annual salary of two thousand five hundred dollars in full compensation for all his services. And any military officer may be detailed and assigned to duty under this act without increase of pay or allowances. The commissioner shall, before the commencement of each regular session of congress, make full report of his proceedings with exhibits of the state of his accounts to the President, who shall communicate the same to congress, and shall also make special reports whenever required to do so by the President or either house of congress; and the assistant commissioners shall make quarterly reports of their proceedings to the commissioner, and also such other special reports as from time to time may be required.

SEC. 4. *And be it further enacted*, That the commissioner, under the direction of the President, shall have authority to set apart, for the use of loyal refugees and freedmen, such tracts of land within the insurrectionary states as shall have been abandoned, or to which the United States shall have acquired title by confiscation or sale, or otherwise, and to every male citizen, whether refugee or freedman, as aforesaid, there shall be assigned not more than forty acres of such land, and the person to whom it was so assigned shall be protected in the use and enjoyment of the land for the term of three years at an annual rent not exceeding six per centum upon the value of such land, as it was appraised by the state authorities in the year eighteen hundred and sixty, for the purpose of taxation, and in case no such appraisal can be found, then the rental shall be based upon the estimated value of the land in said year, to be ascertained in such manner as the commissioner may by regulation prescribe. At the end of said term, or at any time during said term, the occupants of any parcels so assigned may purchase the land and receive such title thereto as the United States can convey, upon paying therefor the value of the land, as ascertained and fixed for the purpose of determining the annual rent aforesaid.

SEC. 5. *And be it further enacted*, That all acts and parts of acts inconsistent with the provisions of this act, are hereby repealed.

SOURCE: U.S. House of Representatives. 1866. *Executive Documents: Printed by Order of the House of Representatives during the First Session of the Thirty-Ninth Congress, 1865–66.* 16 vols. Washington, D.C.: Government Printing Office.

ANALYSIS

The Bureau of Refugees, Freedmen, and Abandoned Lands, later renamed the Freedmen's Bureau, was headquartered in Washington, D.C., although its responsibilities centered on aiding former slaves and ensuring their equality in the South. Initially headed by General Oliver O. Howard, the agency was involved in a number of initiatives, including overseeing business relations between freed people and their former masters, the operation of some legal institutions, and the education of former slaves of all ages. Although its responsibilities had a wide scope, the agency was chronically underfunded and did not have the political support required to effectively accomplish its work due to conflicts between President Andrew Johnson and the Radical Republicans in Congress.

The initial legislation for the Freedmen's Bureau called for the agency to exist for one year. Howard believed that one of his primary responsibilities was to distribute confiscated or abandoned lands in the South in 40-acre plots to newly freed slaves. This drew the ire of President Johnson, who believed that the lands should be returned to their former white owners. Howard honored Johnson's request to cease the distribution of land but the disagreement over the treatment of whites and freedmen in the South spilled into Congress. The Radical Republicans in February 1866 passed a bill that reauthorized the Freedmen's Bureau's existence for an additional two years but it was vetoed by Johnson. They were able to override the veto in July of that year by inserting language into the legislation that forbade the redistribution of land.

In the field, the Freedmen's Bureau was having mixed success. Great controversy arose over the actions of agency officials in their oversight of business relationships between freedmen and whites. Predictably, white businessmen believed they were being unfairly treated in the transactions as they had been previously able to depend on an unpaid labor force. Despite their feelings, they had little recourse because the Freedmen's Bureau was also overseeing the legality of the contracts in their special courts, whose authority exceeded that of the state courts. They did find champions in the U.S. Congress in the form of northern Democrats, who advocated on their behalf while also expanding their political base into the South. The continued animosity with the white community eventually led agents in the bureau to allow for the development of a sharecropping system that proved a detriment to the freed people achieving economic independence from their former masters.

The bureau was able to achieve great success in the area of education. Over the course of its existence, more than 3,000 schools were established in the South. Many operated long after the Freedmen's Bureau had ceased operation. Some of the bureau's success can be traced to its partners in the endeavor, such as the American

Missionary Society, who helped fund and staff the schools. The Freedmen's Bureau also helped create a number of higher education institutions, including Fisk University in Nashville, Tennessee, and Howard University in Washington, D.C.

Gradually, the former Confederate states began rejoining the Union over the latter half of the 1860 and thus began remaking the composition of Congress. By 1869, the Radical Republicans had lost much of the political power they had wielded earlier in the decade. This allowed for a significant reduction in the funding of the Freedmen's Bureau that year. In response, the bureau was forced to greatly reduce its manpower in the South. The result was the evisceration of the bureau's ability to advocate on behalf of the former slaves. In June 1872, the agency's activities in the South were brought to conclusion.

FURTHER READING

Cimbala, Paul A. 1997. *Under the Guardianship of the Nation: The Freedmen's Bureau and the Reconstruction of Georgia, 1865–1870*. Athens: University of Georgia Press.

Cimbala, Paul A., and Randall M. Miller, eds. 1999. *The Freedmen's Bureau and Reconstruction*. New York: Fordham University Press.

Farmer-Kaiser, Mary. 2010. *Freedwomen and the Freedmen's Bureau: Race, Gender, and Public Policy in the Age of Emancipation*. New York: Fordham University Press.

Faulkner, Carol. 2003. *Women's Radical Reconstruction: The Freedmen's Aid Movement*. Philadelphia: University of Pennsylvania Press.

Foner, Eric. 1988. *Reconstruction 1863–1877: America's Unfinished Revolution*. New York: Harper & Row.

McFeely, William S. 1994. *Yankee Stepfather: General O. O. Howard and the Freedmen*. New Haven, CT: Yale University Press.

Summers, Mark Wahlgren. 2014. *The Ordeal of the Reunion: A New History of Reconstruction*. Chapel Hill: University of North Carolina Press.

"To Defray the Expense of Regulating Immigration under This Act, and for the Care of Immigrants Arriving in the United States"

- ***Document:*** Immigration Act of 1882
- ***Date:*** August 3, 1882
- ***Where:*** Washington, D.C.
- ***Significance:*** The act was designed to generate revenue to fund the examination of immigrants in order to determine if they were fit to enter the United States. Among those not allowed to immigrate were convicts and individuals who were deemed unable to care for themselves without public assistance.

DOCUMENT

CHAP. 376.—An act to regulate Immigration.

Be it enacted by the Senate and House of Representatives of the United States of America in Congress assembled, That there shall be levied, collected, and paid a duty of fifty cents for each and every passenger not a citizen of the United States who shall come by steam or sail vessel from a foreign port to any port within the United States. The said duty shall be paid to the collector of customs of the port to which such passenger shall come, or if there be no collector at such port, then to the collector of customs nearest thereto, by the master, owner, agent, or cosignee of every such vessel, within twenty-four hours after the entry thereof into such port. The money thus collected shall be paid into the United States Treasury, and shall constitute a fund to be called the immigrant fund, and shall be used, under the direction of the

Secretary of the Treasury, to defray the expense of regulating immigration under this act, and for the care of immigrants arriving in the United States, for the relief of such as are in distress, and for the general purposes and expenses of carrying this act into effect. The duty imposed by this section shall be a lien upon the vessels which shall bring such passengers into the United States, and shall be a debt in favor of the United States against the owner or owners of such vessels; and the payment of such duty may be enforced by any legal or equitable remedy. *Provided*, That no greater sum shall be expended for the purposes hereinbefore mentioned, at any port, than shall have been collected at such port.

SEC. 2.—That the Secretary of the Treasury is hereby charged with the duty of executing the provisions of this act and with supervision over the business of immigration to the United States, and for that purpose he shall have power to enter into contracts with such State commission, board, or officers as may be designated for that purpose by the governor of any State to take charge of the local affairs of immigration in the ports within said State, and to provide for the support and relief of such immigrants therein landing as may fall into distress or need public aid, under the rules and regulations to be prescribed by said Secretary; and it shall be the duty of such State commission, board, or officers so designated to examine into the condition of passengers arriving at the ports within such State in any ship or vessel, and for that purpose all or any of such commissioners or officers, or such other person or persons as they shall appoint, shall be authorized to go on board of and through any such ship or vessel; and if on such examination there shall be found among such passengers any convict, lunatic, idiot, or any person unable to take care of himself or herself without becoming a public charge, they shall report the same in writing to the collector of such port, and such persons shall not be permitted to land.

SEC. 3.—That the Secretary of the Treasury shall establish such regulations and rules and issue from time to time such instructions not inconsistent with law as he shall deem best calculated to protect the United States and immigrants into the United States from fraud and loss, and for carrying out the provisions of this act and the immigration laws of the United States; and he shall prescribe all forms of bonds, entries, and other papers to be used under and in the enforcement of the various provisions of this act.

SEC. 4.—That all foreign convicts except those convicted of political offences, upon arrival, shall be sent back to the nations to which they belong and from whence they came. The Secretary of the Treasury may designate the State board of charities of any State in which such board shall exist by law, or any commission in any State, or any person or persons in any State, whose duty it shall be to execute the provisions of this section without compensation. The Secretary of the Treasury shall prescribe regulations for the return of the aforesaid persons to the countries from whence they came, and shall furnish instructions to the board, commission, or persons charged with the execution of the provision of this section as to the mode of procedure in respect thereto, and may change such instructions from time to time. The expense of such return of the aforesaid persons not permitted to land shall be borne by the owners of the vessels in which they came.

SEC. 5.—That this act shall take effect immediately.

SOURCE: U.S. Congress. 1891. *Report of the Select Committee on Immigration and Naturalization: And Testimony Taken by the Committee on Immigration of the Senate and the Select Committee on Immigration and Naturalization of the House of Representatives under Concurrent Resolution of March 12, 1890*. Washington, D.C.: U.S. Government Printing Office, 214–215.

ANALYSIS

During the second half of the nineteenth century, there was a substantial increase in the number of immigrants to the United States. Many individual states attempted to stem the flow of migrants crossing their borders by passing laws welcoming only those who would be law-abiding and productive members of society. On October 1, 1875, the U.S. Supreme Court declared all of the respective state laws unconstitutional through the case *Chy Lung v. Freeman*. The rationale was that the regulation of immigration was a federal responsibility that could not be usurped by the states.

Through the Immigration Act of 1882, the U.S. Congress achieved the same goal that had previously been pursued by the states. People convicted of nonpolitical crimes were not allowed to enter the United States. Also denied entry were individuals identified as having a mental deficiency or those believed to be destined to be dependent on charity to subsist. The inspections necessitated by the restrictions were funded by a levy of 50 cents per foreign passenger arriving in a U.S. port, which was due to be paid by the owner of the vessel, or the owner's designee, within 24 hours of arrival. The revenue resulting from the levy also helped offset other expenses related to the care of newly arrived immigrants.

The Immigration Act of 1891 bolstered the 1882 legislation. It expanded the excluded class to include people infected with disease, polygamists, and those who committed other immoral acts. The inspection process was also formalized through the creation of the position within the Treasury Department of Superintendent of Immigration. This new post was necessitated by an increase in the number of inspectors posted at ports around the country for the purpose of interviewing individuals hoping to enter the United States.

FURTHER READING

Baynton, Douglas C. 2016. "Defectives in the Land: Disability and American Immigration Policy, 1882–1924." *Journal of American Ethnic History* 24, no. 3: 31–44.

Hirota, Hidetaka. 2016. " 'The Great Entrepot for Mendicants': Foreign Poverty and Immigration Control in New York State to 1882." In John J. Bukowczyk, ed. *Immigrant Identity and the Politics of Citizenship*. Champaign: University of Illinois Press, 32–59.

Zolberg, Aristide R. 2006. *A Nation by Design: Immigration Policy in the Fashioning of America*. Cambridge, MA: Harvard University Press.

"The Investigation into the Slums of Cities"

- ***Document:*** *The Slums of Baltimore, Chicago, New York, and Philadelphia* (Excerpts)
- ***Date:*** July 27, 1894
- ***Where:*** Washington, D.C.
- ***Significance:*** *The Slums of Baltimore, Chicago, New York, and Philadelphia* was the first report commissioned by the U.S. Congress to compare how poverty manifested itself in different cities.

DOCUMENT

GENERAL RESULTS OF THE INVESTIGATION.

While the general results of the investigation into the slums of cities are clearly brought out in the text analysis of the various tables, there are a few general results which may with profit he culled from the analysis and set forth in the present place.

LIQUOR SALOONS.—In the city of New York there was, at the time of the investigation, 1 liquor saloon to every 200 persons, but in the slum district canvassed there was 1 saloon to every 129 persons. In Philadelphia, in the city at large, there was 1 liquor saloon to every 870 persons, but in the slum district canvassed there was 1 such saloon to every 502 persons. In Baltimore, in the city at large, there was 1 saloon to every 229 persons, but in the slum district canvassed there was 1 saloon to every 105 persons. In Chicago, in the city at large, there was 1 saloon to every 212 persons, while in the slum district canvassed there was 1 saloon to every 127 persons.

. . .

SEX.—Comparing the sex of the population in the slum districts canvassed with that of the whole city, it is found that in each case the per cent of males is greater in the slum districts. In Baltimore, in the city at large, 47.44 per cent of the population are males, while in the slum district selected the males constitute 49.84 per cent of the population. In Chicago the difference is between 51.68 per cent for the whole city and 53.93 per cent for the slum district. In New York the difference is between 49.34 per cent for the whole city and 54.61 per cent for the slums. In Philadelphia, it is between 48.82 per cent for the city at large and 53.48 per cent for the slum districts.

NATIVE AND FOREIGN BORN.—The total foreign born in the city of Baltimore is 15.88 per cent of the total population, but in the slum district canvassed it is 40.21 per cent; in Chicago the total foreign born in the city at large constitutes 40.98 per cent of the population, while in the slum district it is 57.51 per cent; in New York the foreign born is 42.23 per cent of the total population, while in the slum districts it is 62.58 percent; and in Philadelphia the foreign born constitutes 25.74 per cent of the total population and 60.45 per cent of the slum population. These figures show conclusively that the proportion of foreign born persons in the slums of each city is very largely in excess of the proportion for the whole population. This excess is in Baltimore 24.33 per cent; in Chicago, 16.53 per cent; in New York, 20.35 per cent, and in Philadelphia, 34.71 per cent. The proportions as to nationality are brought out as to each of the cities investigated in the tables and the text analysis preceding them, and particular attention is called thereto. The facts take up too much space to allow them to be brought forward at this point.

ILLITERACY.—In the whole city of Baltimore the illiterates constitute 9.17 per cent of the native born population and 12.40 per cent of the foreign born, the percentage for both being 9.79. In the slum district of that city 8.13 per cent of the native born and 30.62 per cent of the foreign born are illiterate, while the percentage for both is 19.60. In the city of Chicago at large the illiterates constitute 0.81 per cent of the native born population and 8.31 per cent of the foreign born, the percentage for both being 4.63; but in the slum district canvassed 5.64 per cent of the native born persons are illiterate and 33.89 percent of the foreign born, the percentage for both being 25.37. In New York the percentage of illiterates is 1.16 of the entire native born population and 14.00 of the foreign born, the percentage for both being 7.69, while for the slum population the percentage of native born who are illiterate is 7.20 and of the foreign born 57.69, the percentage for both boing 46.65. Philadelphia shows nearly as large a proportion of illiterates in the slum districts as New York, the figures for the whole population showing that 2.18 per cent of all native born persons are illiterate and 11.29 per cent of foreign born, the united percentage being 4.07. In the slum districts of Philadelphia, however, 8.44 per cent of the native born persons and 46.61 per cent of the foreign born are illiterate, the percentage for the two classes being 37.67. The tables and analyses accompanying them show distinctions as to illiteracy by sex, nativity, age periods, etc.

VOTERS.—In the city of Baltimore 20.13 per cent of all the voters of the city are foreign born, but in the slum district canvassed 44.04 per cent of the voters are foreign born. The variation in Chicago is not so great, the foreign born voters of the whole city being 50.62 per cent, and in the slum district canvassed 61.31 per cent. Of the whole number of voters in New York City 49.93 per cent are foreign born, while in the slum districts canvassed 62.44 per cent are foreign born. In Philadelphia the differences are greater, 29.52 per cent of the total voters being foreign born, and 58.94 per cent of the voters in the slum districts belonging to that class.

OCCUPATIONS.—The occupations of the residents of the slum districts in the four cities named are as varied, probably, as in the cities at large, but direct comparisons with the occupations of the whole city in each case cannot be made, as the classification of occupations as shown by the eleventh census is not yet ready for use.

EARNINGS.—The earnings of the people living in the slum districts canvassed are quite up to the average earnings of the people generally and at large, but as there are no data with which to make comparisons of average earnings, the results of this investigation must practically stand alone; yet, from all that can be learned from various sources, the statement made is believed to be correct.

HEALTH.—The agents and experts employed in this investigation were nearly unanimous in the opinions they expressed relative to the health of the people of the slum districts. It should be remembered that this investigation was conducted in the most thorough census manner, each and every house and every tenement in every house being visited and the facts taken down for each and every individual living in the slum districts. The testimony of the agents, therefore, relative to general conditions is most valuable. The statistics drawn from the schedule replies show no greater sickness prevailing in the districts canvassed than in other parts of the cities involved, and while the most wretched conditions were found here and there, the small number of sick people discovered was a surprise to the canvassers. It may be that owing to the time of year (late spring) the people were living with open windows, and thus not subjected to the foul air which might be found in the winter. The report of Dr. Houghton, however, already referred to, the results of which are shown at the end of the chapter on analyses of the tables, will throw much light upon this question.

PERSONS TO EACH DWELLING.—According to the eleventh census, the number of persons to a dwelling in Baltimore was 6.02; in Chicago, 8.60; in New York, 18.52; in Philadelphia, 5.60. The averages for the slum districts are about the same for Baltimore and Philadelphia, there being in the former city 7.71 persons to a dwelling, and in Philadelphia 7.34 persons; but in Chicago the slum population averages 15.51 persons to each dwelling, and in New York 36.79 persons.

These points which have been brought out show the value of the present report, and other features can be studied with nearly, if not quite, as valuable results.

SOURCE: Wright, Carroll D. 1894. *The Slums of Baltimore, Chicago, New York, and Philadelphia.* Washington, D.C.: Government Printing Office, 14–19.

ANALYSIS

At the behest of Congress, the Department of Labor conducted a study of the poorer neighborhoods in four of the nation's largest cities, namely, Baltimore, Maryland; Chicago, Illinois; Philadelphia, Pennsylvania; and New York City, New York.

It marked the first initiative funded by the Congress to document the manifestations of poverty in the United States. Among the conclusions was that immigrant populations were more likely to be found residing in the slums than people whose families had been in the country for at least two generations. In retrospect, the veracity of the data is questionable as in all four cities the poor were generally found to be just as healthy as people in other parts of their respective cities. This was a very different conclusion than what was provided in other contemporary publications, most notably Jacob Riis's *How the Other Half Lives*.

FURTHER READING

Gandal, Keith. 1997. *The Virtues of the Vicious: Jacob Riis, Stephen Crane, and the Spectacle of the Slum*. New York: Oxford University Press.

McCarthy, Michael P. 1989. "Urban Optimism and Reform Thought in the Progressive Era." *The Historian* 51, no. 2: 239–262.

"The Interests of the Nation Are Involved in the Welfare of This Army of Children"

- ***Document:*** Special Message, February 15, 1909
- ***Date:*** February 15, 1909
- ***Where:*** Washington, D.C.
- ***Significance:*** The White House Conference on Dependent Children helped lead to the creation of the U.S. Children's Bureau in 1912.

DOCUMENT

To the Senate and House of Representatives:

On January 25–26, 1909, there assembled in this city, on my invitation, a conference on the care of dependent children. To this conference there came from nearly every State in the Union men and women actively engaged in the care of dependent children, and they represented all the leading religious bodies.

The subject considered is one of high importance to the well-being of the nation. The Census Bureau reported in 1904 that there were in orphanages and children's homes about 93,000 dependent children. There are probably 50,000 more (the precise number never having been ascertained) in private homes, either on board or in adopted homes provided by the generosity of foster parents. In addition to these there were 25,000 children in institutions for juvenile delinquents.

Each of these children represents either a potential addition to the productive capacity and the enlightened citizenship of the nation, or, if allowed to suffer from neglect, a potential addition to the destructive forces of the community. The ranks of criminals and other enemies of society are recruited in an altogether undue proportion from children bereft of their natural homes and left without sufficient care.

The interests of the nation are involved in the welfare of this army of children no less than in our great material affairs.

Notwithstanding a wide diversity of views and methods represented in the conference, and notwithstanding the varying legislative enactments and policies of the States from which the members came, the conference, at the close of its sessions, unanimously adopted a series of declarations expressing the conclusions which they had reached. These constitute a wise, constructive, and progressive programme of child-caring work. If given full effect by the proper agencies, existing methods and practices in almost every community would be profoundly and advantageously modified.

More significant even than the contents of the declarations is the fact that they were adopted without dissenting vote and with every demonstration of hearty approval on the part of all present. They constitute a standard of accepted opinion by which each community should measure the adequacy of its existing methods and to which each community should seek to conform its legislation and its practice.

The keynote of the conference was expressed in these words:

Home life is the highest and finest product of civilization. Children should not be deprived of it except for urgent and compelling reasons.

Surely poverty alone should not disrupt the home. Parents of good character suffering from temporary misfortune, and above all deserving mothers fairly well able to work but deprived of the support of the normal breadwinner, should be given such aid as may be necessary to enable them to maintain suitable homes for the rearing of their children. The widowed or deserted mother, if a good woman, willing to work and to do her best, should ordinarily be helped in such fashion as will enable her to bring up her children herself in their natural home. Children from unfit homes, and children who have no homes, who must be cared for by charitable agencies, should, so far as practicable, be cared for in families.

I transmit herewith for your information a copy of the conclusions reached by the conference, of which the following is a brief summary:

1. *Home care.*—Children of worthy parents or deserving mothers should, as a rule, be kept with their parents at home.
2. *Preventive work.*—The effort should be made to eradicate causes of dependency, such as disease and accident, and to substitute compensation and insurance for relief.
3. *Home finding.*—Homeless and neglected children, if normal, should be cared for in families, when practicable.
4. *Cottage system.*—Institutions should be on the cottage plan with small units, as far as possible.
5. *Incorporation.*—Agencies caring for dependent children should be incorporated, on approval of a suitable state board.
6. *State inspection.*—The State should inspect the work of all agencies which care for dependent children.
7. *Inspection of educational work.*—Educational work of institutions and agencies caring for dependent children should be supervised by state educational authorities.

8. *Facts and records.*—Complete histories of dependent children and their parents, based upon personal investigation and supervision, should be recorded for guidance of child-caring agencies.
9. *Physical care.*—Every needy child should receive the best medical and surgical attention, and be instructed in health and hygiene.
10. *Cooperation.*—Local child-caring agencies should cooperate and establish joint bureaus of information.
11. *Undesirable legislation.*—Prohibitive legislation against transfer of dependent children between States should be repealed.
12. *Permanent organization.*—A permanent organization for work along the lines of these resolutions is desirable.
13. *Federal children's bureau.*—Establishment of a federal children's bureau is desirable, and enactment of pending bill is earnestly recommended.
14. Suggests special message to Congress favoring federal children's bureau and other legislation applying above principles to District of Columbia and other federal territory.

While it is recognized that these conclusions can be given their fullest effect only by the action of the several States or communities concerned, or of their charitable agencies, the conference requested me, in section 14 of the conclusions, to send to you a message recommending federal action.

There are pending in both Houses of Congress bills for the establishment of a children's bureau, i.e., Senate bill No. 8323 and House bill No. 24148. These provide for a children's bureau in the Department of the Interior, which shall investigate and report upon all matters pertaining to the welfare of children and child life, and shall especially investigate the questions of infant mortality, the birth rate, physical degeneracy, orphanage, juvenile delinquency and juvenile courts, desertion and illegitimacy, dangerous occupations, accidents and diseases of children of the working classes, employment, legislation affecting children in the several States and Territories, and such other facts as have a bearing upon the health, efficiency, character, and training of children.

One of the needs felt most acutely by the conference was that of accurate information concerning these questions relating to childhood. The National Government not only has the unquestioned right of research in such vital matters, but is the only agency which can effectively conduct such general inquiries as are needed for the benefit of all our citizens. In accordance with the unanimous request of the conference, I therefore most heartily urge your favorable action on these measures.

It is not only discreditable to us as a people that there is now no recognized and authoritative source of information upon these subjects relating to child life, but in the absence of such information as should be supplied by the Federal Government many abuses have gone unchecked; for public sentiment, with its great corrective power, can only be aroused by full knowledge of the facts. In addition to such information as the Census Bureau and other existing agencies of the Federal Government already provide, there remains much to be ascertained through lines of research not now authorized by law; and there should be correlation and dissemination of the knowledge obtained without any duplication of effort or interference with what is already being done. There are few things more vital to the welfare of the nation than accurate and dependable knowledge of the best methods of dealing with children, especially with those who are in one way or another handicapped by misfortune; and in the absence of such knowledge each community is left to work out its own problem without being able to learn of and profit by the success or failure of other communities along the same lines of endeavor. The bills for the establishment of the children's bureau are advocated not only by this conference, but by a large number of national organizations that are disinterestedly working for the welfare of children, and also by philanthropic, educational, and religious bodies in all parts of the country.

I further urge that such legislation be enacted as may be necessary in order to bring the laws and practices in regard to the care of dependent children in all federal territory into harmony with the other conclusions reached by the conference.

LEGISLATION FOR THE DISTRICT OF COLUMBIA.

Congress took a step in the direction of the conclusions of this conference in 1893, when, on the recommendation of the late Amos G. Warner, then superintendent of charities for the District of Columbia, the Board of Children's Guardians was created, with authority, among other things, to place children in family homes. That board has made commendable progress, and its work should be strengthened and extended.

I recommend legislation for the District of Columbia in accordance with the fifth, sixth, seventh, and eighth sections of the conclusions of the conference, as follows:

1. That the approval of the Board of Charities be required for the incorporation of all child-caring agencies, as well as amendments of the charter of any benevolent corporation which includes child-caring work, and that other than duly incorporated agencies be forbidden to engage in the care of needy children. This legislation is needed in order to insure the fitness and responsibility of those who propose to undertake the care of helpless children. Such laws have long been in satisfactory operation in several of the larger States of the Union.
2. That the Board of Charities, through its duly authorized agents, shall inspect the work of all agencies which care for dependent children, whether by institutional or by home-finding methods, and whether supported by public or private funds. The State has always jealously guarded the interests of children whose parents have been able to leave them property by requiring the appointment of a guardian, under bond, accountable directly to the courts, even though there be a competent surviving parent. Surely the interests of the child who is not only an orphan but penniless ought to be no less sacred than those of the more fortunate orphan who inherits property. If the protection of the Government is necessary in the one case, it is even more necessary in the other. If we are to require that only incorporated institutions shall be allowed to engage in this responsible work, it is necessary to provide for

public inspection, lest the State should become the unconscious partner of those who either from ignorance or inefficiency are unsuited to deal with the problem.

3. That the education of children in orphan asylums and other similar institutions in the District of Columbia be under the supervision of the board of education, in order that these children may enjoy educational advantages equal to those of the other children. Normal school life comes next to normal home life in the process of securing the fullest development of the child.
4. That all agencies engaged in child-caring work in the District of Columbia be required by law to adopt adequate methods of investigation and make permanent records relative to children under their care, and to exercise faithful personal supervision over their wards until legally adopted or otherwise clearly beyond the need of further supervision; the forms and methods of such investigation, records, and supervision to be prescribed and enforced by the Board of Charities.

I deem such legislation as is herein recommended not only important for the welfare of the children immediately concerned, but important as setting an example of a high standard of child protection by the National Government to the several States of the Union, which should be able to look to the nation for leadership in such matters.

I herewith transmit a copy of the full text of the proceedings.

THEODORE ROOSEVELT.

SOURCE: Roosevelt, Theodore. 1909. "Special Message." *Proceedings of the Conference on the Care of Dependent Children, Held at Washington, D.C., January 25, 26, 1909.* Washington, D.C.: Government Printing Office, 5–8.

ANALYSIS

Beginning in the late nineteenth century, female reformers sought to make the care of children a national priority. The so-called maternalists concluded that the reason that the mistreatment of children persisted within the nation was that the general populace was unaware of their plight. They determined that the solution was a federal agency to collect information that could be distributed to policymakers around the nation. Approximately a decade of lobbying bore fruit when President Theodore Roosevelt convened the White House Conference on Dependent Children on January 25–26, 1909. The conferees utilized the event to make the case for the creation of a children's bureau. Senate bill No. 8323 and House bill No. 24148 were introduced in Congress for the purpose of forming the agency. Despite Roosevelt's public lobbying for the bureau, Congress ultimately opted not to pass the legislation.

In 1912, the U.S. Children's Bureau was created as a part of the Department of Labor, thanks in large part to the efforts of Lillian Wald and Florence Kelley. The bureau proved unique as it was not only headed by a woman, Julia Lathrop, but had a staff that was predominantly female. This was a notable achievement considering that women in the United States had not yet achieved suffrage rights.

FURTHER READING

Ladd-Taylor, Molly. 1994. *Mother-Work: Women, Child Welfare, and the State, 1890–1930.* Urbana: University of Illinois Press.

Parker, Jacqueline K., and Edward M. Carpenter. 1981. "Julia Lathrop and the Children's Bureau: The Emergence of an Institution." *Social Service Review* 55, no. 1: 60–77.

Sklar, Kathryn Kish. 1995. *Florence Kelley and the Nation's Work: The Rise of Women's Political Culture, 1830–1900.* New Haven, CT: Yale University Press.

Skocpol, Theda. 1992. *Protecting Soldiers and Mothers: The Politics of Social Provision in the United States, 1870s–1920s.* Cambridge, MA: Harvard University Press.

"To Prevent Interstate Commerce in the Products of Child Labor"

- ***Document:*** Keating-Owen Child Labor Act of 1916
- ***Date:*** September 1, 1916
- ***Where:*** Washington, D.C.
- ***Significance:*** The Keating-Owen Act was intended to discourage the use of child labor by preventing the products they worked on from being shipped across state lines.

DOCUMENT

AN ACT

To prevent interstate commerce in the products of child labor, and for other purposes.

Be it enacted by the Senate and House of Representatives of the United States of America in Congress assembled, That no producer, manufacturer, or dealer shall ship or deliver for shipment in interstate or foreign commerce, any article or commodity the product of any mine or quarry situated in the United States, in which within thirty days prior to the time of the removal of such product therefrom children under the age of sixteen years have been employed or permitted to work, or any article or commodity the product of any mill, cannery, workshop, factory, or manufacturing establishment, situated in the United States, in which within thirty days prior to the removal of such product therefrom children under the age of fourteen years have been employed or permitted to work, or children between the ages of fourteen years and sixteen years have been employed or permitted to work more than eight hours in any day, or more than six days in any week, or after the hour of seven o'clock postmeridian, or before the hour of six o'clock antemeridian: *Provided,* That a prosecution and conviction of a defendant for the shipment or delivery for shipment of any article or commodity under the conditions herein prohibited shall be a bar to any further prosecution against the same defendant for shipments or deliveries for shipment of any such article or commodity before the beginning of said prosecution.

SEC. 2. That the Attorney General, the Secretary of Commerce and the Secretary of Labor shall constitute a board to make and publish from time to time uniform rules and regulations for carrying out the provisions of this Act.

SEC. 3. That for the purpose of securing proper enforcement of this Act the Secretary of Labor, or any person duly authorized by him, shall have authority to enter and inspect at any time mines quarries, mills, canneries, workshops, factories, manufacturing establishments, and other places in which goods are produced or held for interstate commerce; and the Secretary of Labor shall have authority to employ such assistance for the purposes of this Act as may from time to time be authorized by appropriation or other law.

SEC. 4. That it shall be the duty of each district attorney to whom the Secretary of Labor shall report any violation of this Act, or to whom any State factory or mining or quarry inspector, commissioner of labor, State medical inspector or school-attendance officer, or any other person shall present satisfactory evidence of any such violation to cause appropriate proceedings to be commenced and prosecuted in the proper courts of the United States without delay for the enforcement of the penalties in such cases herein provided: *Provided,* That nothing in this Act shall be construed to apply to bona fide boys' and girls' canning clubs recognized by the Agricultural Department of the several States and of the United States.

SEC. 5. That any person who violates any of the provisions of section one of this Act, or who refuses or obstructs entry or inspection authorized by section three of this Act, shall for each offense prior to the first conviction of such person under the provisions of this Act, be punished by a fine of not more than $200, and shall for each offense subsequent to such conviction be punished by a fine of not more than $1,000, nor less than $100, or by imprisonment for not more than three months, or by both such fine and imprisonment, in the discretion of the court: *Provided,* That no dealer shall be prosecuted under the provisions of this Act for a shipment, delivery for shipment, or transportation who establishes a guaranty issued by the person by whom the goods shipped or delivered for shipment or transportation were manufactured or produced, resident in the United States, to the effect that such goods were produced or manufactured in a mine or quarry in which within thirty days prior to their removal therefrom no children under the age of sixteen years were employed or permitted to work, or in a mill, cannery, workshop, factory, or manufacturing establishment in which within thirty days prior to the removal of such goods therefrom no children under the ages of fourteen years were employed or permitted to work, nor children between the ages of fourteen years and sixteen years employed or permitted to work more than eight hours in any day or more than six days in any week or after the hour of seven o'clock postmeridian o before the hour of six o'clock antemeridian; and in such event, if the guaranty contains any false statement or a material fact the guarantor shall be amenable to prosecution and to the fine or imprisonment provided by this section for violation of the provisions of this Act. Said guaranty, to afford the protection above provided, shall contain the name and address of the person giving the same: And provided further, That no producer, manufacturer, or dealer shall be prosecuted under this Act for the shipment, delivery for shipment, or transportation of a product of any mine, quarry, mill, cannery, workshop, factory, or manufacturing establishment, if the only employment therein within thirty days prior to the removal of such product therefrom, of a child under the age of sixteen years has been that of a child as to whom the producer, or manufacturer has in; good faith procured, at the time of employing such child, and has since in good faith relied upon and kept on file a certificate, issued in such form, under such conditions, any by such persons as may be prescribed by the board, showing the child to be of such an age that the shipment, delivery for shipment, or transportation was not prohibited by this Act. Any person who knowingly makes a false statement or presents false evidence in or in relation to any such certificate or application therefor shall be amenable to prosecution and to the fine or imprisonment provided by this section for violations of this Act. In any State designated by the board, an employment certificate or other similar paper as to the age of the child, issued under the laws of that State and not inconsistent with the provisions of this Act, shall have the same force and effect as a certificate herein provided for.

SEC. 6. That the word "person" as used in this Act shall be construed to include any individual or corporation or the members of any partnership or other unincorporated association. The term "ship or deliver for shipment in interstate or foreign commerce" as used in this Act means to transport or to ship or deliver for shipment from any State or Territory or the District of Columbia to or through any other State or Territory or the District of Columbia or to any foreign country; and in the case of a dealer means only to transport or to ship or deliver for shipment from the State, Territory or district of manufacture or production.

SEC. 7. That this Act shall take effect from and after one year from the date of its passage.

SOURCE: An act to prevent interstate commerce in the products of child labor, and for other purposes, September 1, 1916; Enrolled Acts and Resolutions of Congress, 1789–2011; General Records of the U.S. Government; Record Group 11; National Archives.

ANALYSIS

The Keating-Owen Child Labor Act of 1916 (KOCLA) had its ideological origins within the National Child Labor Committee (NCLC). Founded in 1907, the NCLC endeavored to have children removed from the workforce so that they could gain an education and enjoy their respective childhoods. Their mission was a reflection of their membership, which was comprised primarily of white women from the middle and upper classes. Many lower-class families had no desire to send their children to school since the resulting wages were necessary for the family to subsist.

Mutual benefit resulted in impoverished families and employers aligning themselves as opponents of any legislation that would regulate child labor.

With such entrenched opposition, the NCLC opted to embark on a public relations campaign in 1908 that saw photographer Lewis W. Hine taking and publicizing photographs of children working in often dangerous conditions. By illuminating visually the exploitation of children, the NCLC was able to gain the sympathy of the electorate. The NCLC's campaign gained an ally with the creation of the U.S. Children's Bureau in 1912. The resulting alliance between a private organization and a federal agency resulted in the effective lobbying of Congress to enact legislation regarding the labor of children.

The passage of the KOCLA proved a short-term victory. President Woodrow Wilson signed the bill into law but questioned its constitutionality. Predictably, it was challenged before the law ever went into effect. The U.S. Supreme Court declared the law unconstitutional in its majority decision in the 1918 case *Hammer v. Dagenhart*. The reasoning was that the law was not passed to regulate interstate commerce, which would have been constitutional, but was instead designed to govern child labor, which was a power reserved for the respective states.

FURTHER READING

Goldberg, Vicki. 1999. *Lewis W. Hine: Children at Work*. New York: Prestel.

Hindman, Hugh D. 2002. *Child Labor: An American History*. Armonk, NY: M.E. Sharpe.

Lindenmeyer, Kriste. 1997. *"A Right to Childhood": The U.S. Children's Bureau and Child Welfare, 1912–1946*. Urbana: University of Illinois Press.

Schuman, Michael. 2017. "History of Child Labor in the United States—Part 1: Little Children Working." *Monthly Labor Review* January 2017: 1–19.

Schuman, Michael. 2017. "History of Child Labor in the United States—Part 2: The Reform Movement." *Monthly Labor Review* January 2017: 1–23.

Trattner, Walter I. 1970. *Crusade for the Children: A History of the National Child Labor Committee and Child Labor Reform in America*. Chicago: Quadrangle Books.

"Tax on Employment of Child Labor"

- ***Document:*** Child Labor Tax Act of 1919
- ***Date:*** February 24, 1919
- ***Where:*** Washington, D.C.
- ***Significance:*** The purpose of the tax was to discourage employers from hiring children.

DOCUMENT

REVENUE ACT OF 1918
AN ACT TO PROVIDE REVENUE, AND FOR OTHER PURPOSES

. . .

TITLE XII—TAX ON EMPLOYMENT OF CHILD LABOR

Sec. 1200. That every person (other than a bona fide boys' or girls' canning club recognized by the Agricultural Department of a State and of the United States) operating (a) any mine or quarry situated in the United States in which children under the age of sixteen years have been employed or permitted to work during any portion of the taxable year; or (b) any mill, cannery, workshop, factory, or manufacturing establishment situated in the United States in which children under the age of fourteen years have been employed or permitted to work, or children between the ages of fourteen and sixteen have been employed or permitted to work more than eight hours in any day or more than six days in any week, or after the hour of seven o'clock post meridian, or before the hour of six o'clock ante meridian, during any portion of the taxable year, shall pay for each taxable year, in addition to all other taxes imposed by law, an excise tax equivalent to 10 per centum of the entire net profits received or accrued for such year from the sale or disposition of the product of such mine, quarry, mill, cannery, workshop, factory, or manufacturing establishment.

Sec. 1201. That in computing net profits under the provisions of this title, for the purpose of the tax there shall be allowed as deductions from the gross amount received or accrued for the taxable year from the sale or disposition of such products manufactured within the United States the following items:

(a) The cost of raw materials entering into the production;

(b) Running expenses, including rentals, cost of repairs, and maintenance, heat, power, insurance, management, and a reasonable allowance for salaries or other compensations for personal service actually rendered, and for depreciation;

(c) Interest paid within the taxable year on debts or loans contracted to meet the needs of the business, and the proceeds of which have been actually used to meet such needs;

(d) Taxes of all kinds paid during the taxable year with respect to the business or property relating to the production; and

(e) Losses actually sustained within the taxable year in connection with the business of producing such products, including losses from fire, flood, storm, or other casualties, and not compensated for by insurance or otherwise.

Sec. 1202. That if any such person during any taxable year or part thereof, whether under any agreement, arrangement, or understanding or otherwise, sells or disposes of any product of such mine, quarry, mill, cannery, workshop, factory, or manufacturing establishment at less than the fair market price obtainable therefor either (a) in such manner as directly or indirectly to benefit such person or any person directly or indirectly interested in the business of such person; or (b) with intent to cause such benefit; the gross amount received or accrued for such year or part thereof from the sale or disposition of such product shall be taken to be the amount which would have been received or accrued from the sale or disposition of such product if sold at the fair market price.

Sec. 1203. (a) That no person subject to the provisions of this title shall be liable for the tax herein imposed if the only employment or permission to work which but for this section would subject him to the tax, has been of a child as to whom such person has in good faith procured at the time of employing such child or permit ting him to work, and has since in good faith relied upon and kept on file a certificate, issued in such form, under such conditions and by such persons as may be prescribed by a board consisting of the Secretary, the Commissioner, and the Secretary of Labor, showing the child to be of such age as not to subject such person to the tax imposed by this title. Any person who knowingly makes a false statement or presents false evidence in or in relation to any such certificate or application therefor shall be punished by a fine of not less than $100, nor more than $1,000, or by imprisonment for not more than three months, or by both such fine and imprisonment, in the discretion of the court.

In any State designated by such board an employment certificate or other similar paper as to the age of the child, issued under the laws of that State, and not inconsistent with the provisions of this title, shall have the same force and effect as a certificate herein provided for.

(b) The tax imposed by this title shall not be imposed in the case of any person who proves to the satisfaction of the Secretary that the only employment or permission to work which but for this section would subject him to the tax, has been of a child employed or permitted to work under a mistake of fact as to the age of such child, and without intention to evade the tax.

Sec. 1204. That on or before the first day of the third month following the close of each taxable year, a true and accurate return under oath shall be made by each person subject to the provisions of this title to the collector for the district in which such person has his principal office or place of business, in such form as the Commissioner, with the approval of the Secretary, shall prescribe, setting forth specifically the gross amount of income received or accrued during such year from the sale or disposition of the product of any mine, quarry, mill, cannery, workshop, factory, or manufacturing establishment, in which children have been employed subjecting him to the tax imposed by this title, and from the total thereof deducting the aggregate items of allowance authorized by this title, and such other particulars as to the gross receipts and items of allowance as the Commissioner, with the approval of the Secretary may require.

Sec. 1205. That all such returns shall be transmitted forthwith by the collector to the Commissioner, who shall, as soon as practicable, assess the tax found due and notify the person making such return of the amount of tax for which such person is liable, and such person shall pay the tax to the collector on or before thirty days from the date of such notice.

Sec. 1206. That for the purposes of this Act the Commissioner, or any other person duly authorized by him, shall have authority to enter and inspect at any time any mine, quarry, mill, cannery, workshop, factory, or manufacturing establishment. The Secretary of Labor, or any person duly authorized by him, shall, for the purpose of complying with a request of the Commissioner to make such an inspection, have like authority, and shall make report to the Commissioner of inspections made under such authority in such form as may be prescribed by the Commissioner with the approval of the Secretary of the Treasury.

Any person who refuses or obstructs entry or inspection authorized by this section shall be punished by a fine of not more than $1,000, or by imprisonment for not more than one year, or both such fine and imprisonment.

Sec. 1207. That as used in this title the term "taxable year" shall have the same meaning as provided for the purposes of income tax in section 200. The first taxable year for the purposes of this title shall be the period between sixty days after the passage of this Act and December 31, 1919, both inclusive, or such portion of such period as is included within the fiscal year (as defined in section 200) of the taxpayer.

SOURCE: Holmes, George E. 1919. *Federal Income Tax War-Profits and Excess-Profits Taxes Including Stamp Taxes, Capital Stock Tax, Tax on Employment of Child Labor, Tax on Undistributed Profits*. Chicago: Callaghan and Company: 881, 945–948.

ANALYSIS

In the 1918 case *Hammer v. Dagenhart*, the U.S. Supreme Court declared the Keating-Owen Child Labor Act of 1916 unconstitutional because it violated the Fifth and Fourteenth Amendments to the U.S. Constitution. Determined to curb the employment of children, Congress opted to change tactics. An amendment that became Title XII of the Revenue Act of 1919 levied a 10 percent tax on goods made by children. It too proved unconstitutional. In the majority opinion in the 1922 case *Bailey v. Drexel Furniture Company*, Chief Justice William Howard Taft wrote that the measure was not a tax because it was not designed to raise revenue. It was instead an unlawful and punitive attempt to dissuade companies from utilizing child labor.

FURTHER READING

Fisher, Louis. 2016. *Congress: Protecting Individual Rights*. Lawrence: University Press of Kansas.

Hindman, Hugh D. 2002. *Child Labor: An American History*. Armonk, NY: M.E. Sharpe.

Ross, William G. 1994. *A Muted Fury: Populists, Progressives, and the Unions Confront the Courts, 1890–1937*. Princeton, NJ: Princeton University Press.

Schmidt, James D. 2010. *Industrial Violence and the Legal Origins of Child Labor*. New York: Cambridge University Press.

Sealander, Judith. 2003. *The Failed Century of the Child: Governing America's Young in the Twentieth Century*. New York: Cambridge University Press.

"These Studies Have No Class Basis—They Include Every Baby Born in a Given Town in a Given Year"

- ***Document:*** *Public Protection of Maternity and Infancy* (Excerpts)
- ***Date:*** December 20–29, 1920
- ***Where:*** Washington, D.C.
- ***Significance:*** The hearings before the United States House of Representatives' Committee on Interstate and Foreign Commerce led to the passage of the Sheppard-Towner Maternity and Infancy Act of 1921.

DOCUMENT

STATEMENT OF HON. HORACE M. TOWNER, A REPRESENTATIVE IN CONGRESS FROM THE STATE OF IOWA.

Mr. TOWNER. Mr. Chairman and gentlemen of the committee, this bill, as I presume you all know, is a bill for the protection of maternity and infancy. It is built upon the general plan of aid from the National Government to the States for the purpose of stimulating the States to greater activity in these regards and for the purpose as well of aiding them by contributions from the General Government.

Those who will follow me will present the necessity more particularly, and also the reasons why the aid from the General Government and stimulation from the General Government are necessary. I shall only briefly outline the provisions of the bill.

The first section of the bill provides that the amounts to be provided in the bill to be paid from the General Treasury shall be paid to the several States for the purpose of cooperating with the States in promoting the care of maternity and infancy in the several States. That is a general statement of the purposes of the bill.

I should call the attention of the committee to the fact that there are not appropriations provided in the bill; they are merely authorizations. It is hardly necessary for me to tell the members of the committee that an authorization does not necessarily impose any obligation on the General Government; an authorization usually is followed by an appropriation, but not by any means is that always the case. Conditions exist under which it will be practically impossible that all of the authorizations provided shall be followed by appropriations. For instance, only those States that take advantage of the law will have the benefit of the law; it is not probable that all of the States—immediately, at least—will take advantage of the law. . .

The provision in section 2 is that there shall be granted absolute amount, without condition, to each of the States, of $10,000, if they accede to the general condition imposed that they shall organize a department or bureau or commission, or whatever it may be, that shall use it for the particular purposes specified. It does not require, so far as this authorization is concerned, that the States shall meet this expenditure with equal amounts. . .

But I will say to the committee that, after all, the expenditure of this money from the General Government can not under any circumstances meet the requirement of certain of the States. In some of the States they will not only meet the amount which is given by the General Government but may multiply it five times or even ten times, in order to meet particular and peculiar conditions. The States are not alike; the conditions are not alike. The necessity for this legislation is not so great in some of them as it is in others. The States will, after all, have to be the determining factors as to how much money shall be expended with regard for the desired purpose. . .

The only purpose of the bill is to simply provide, if we possibly can, that the amount expended by the General Government shall be used for the purposes for which it is intended; and the purpose is to help in the administration of the law and the expenditure of the amount just as far as it is possible to help the State. . .

We want the States, as far as possible, to take this work in their hands. We want to aid them, because in some of the States they need aid. We want to stimulate them, because in some of the States they need stimulation. In one State already they have appropriated $3,800 for two years, or $1,900 a year, and they found, in trying to administer the law, that they could not get anybody at all to take charge of this work in their State who would be qualified for a less salary than $1,800, so that $1,800 out of the $1,900 was to be used for paying one person for superintending the work. Of course the amount was grossly inadequate and insufficient. They need aid there perhaps; they need stimulation certainly.

So all along the line that is the object and purpose of the bill. It is not to control it; the Government does not want to control it. Why should they? The purpose is to reach the poor individuals who are suffering and who need this aid. The purpose is to save the lives of the 250,000 people who die every year because of need of aid. If it was proposed here in Congress to save the lives of 250,000 from some impending calamity out in California, or in Alaska, or anywhere, there would be no hesitancy on the part of the Government in doing it. But because these mothers and these babies are dying right along from day to day and from year to year, and it does not occur all at once, for that reason we are not shocked. . .

We know that the loss in the United States is shamefully large. We know that we are way down among the list of nations of the world in regard to this. In the year 1914, 14 of the different Governments of the world made a much better showing than this country did with regard to the proportion of these lives that were saved, and in 1918, 23,000 mothers died from these particular causes. We have made great advancement in reducing the mortality in the United States from diphtheria—I believe about 75 per cent—and in cases of typhoid fever we have reduced the mortality by about 50 per cent. . .

With regard to many and, indeed, to most diseases we have had a reduction in almost all without aid from the General Government or the stimulation of the General Government to activity. And the result, of course, has been to reduce, as the years have gone by, very strongly and splendidly the mortality in those cases.

But unfortunately, in this class of cases, involving the mothers and children, the mortality has not been reduced. Unfortunately, owing to the want of stimulation or from some cause in the United States, we are perhaps the most backward among the civilized nations in that regard. We should meet these conditions, because, after all, it is an emergency case. These people who favor this legislation on the part of the General Government are not coming to you with regard to the cases in which progress is being made; but we are saying to you that the States have not met or can not meet these conditions. We are saying to you that England and other nations have met these conditions, because of the necessities which have arisen in those countries, and we are not doing it. We are in the condition in which it almost appears that, for want of activity and aid and encouragement and stimulation on the part of the National Government, we are allowing these thousands and tens of thousands of women and children to die that might be saved. . .

I want to say this, gentlemen: I presume you gentlemen realize, as all of those who have had practical experience in public life do, the inertia that exists, expecially [*sic*] in the State legislature, with regard to this kind of legislation. And you gentlemen understand, I am quite sure, far better than most men could understand, how it will stimulate them to activity, stimulate them to meet the demands of their real duty, if it can be said, when the proposition is presented to the legislature, "You will receive aid from the general Government in this matter." That has been the case in other instances where we have this kind of legislation, with this kind of a proposition of cooperative effort; and I am quite sure it will be made more promptly and more completely with regard to this legislation, if it shall pass, than it had ever been in the case of any other legislation. Because this more appeals to men, if they can really understand its appeal, than anything else I can imagine.

. . .

STATEMENT OF MISS JULIA LATHROP, CHIEF OF THE CHILDREN'S BUREAU, DEPARTMENT OF LABOR.

Miss Lathrop. I think I ought to say how this bill came into existence because I am well aware of the fact that it is not popular for bureaus to create new activities for themselves, nor ask for measures increasing their own powers. The Children's

Bureau was created in 1912, its object provided in the act being "to investigate and report upon all matters pertaining to the welfare of children and child life among all classes of our people, and especially to investigate the questions of infant mortality, the birth rate, orphanage, juvenile courts, desertion, dangerous occupations, accidents and diseases of children, employment, legislation affecting children in the several States and Territories."

This law directed governmental study in a new field, that of child welfare with the broadest definition, and it was hard to know where to begin. However, persons who had been active in urging the creation of the bureau had sent out letters before the bureau was under way, asking opinions as to what it ought first to undertake, and the replies were turned over to the bureau. So many of them urged preparation of information for everyday use of mothers that a series of popular bulletins on prenatal, infant, and child care was under taken.

The bureau also began as promptly as possible field investigations—choosing for the first, the first subject mentioned in the law, infant mortality. Physicians and authorities in the social field have called public attention for years to the needless waste of infant life in foreign countries but the subject had awakened little popular attention in the United States. This subject was not approached as" a medical problem. The plan was originated in the bureau and subjected to searching criticism in advance. In each city studied the history of every baby born in a given year was traced from birth through the first year of life or so long as the child survived in that year. The social, civic, family, and economic conditions surrounding the baby were noted with a view to learning what conditions accompanied varying infant mortality rates.

These investigations have been continued by the bureau since 1912 and have resulted in a body of facts showing the intimate coincidence of ignorance and poverty and civic neglect with high infant mortality rates. Studies of nearly 24,000 infants in 7 industrial cities show that an income earned by the father fairly guaranteeing the possibility of decent family life and permitting the mother to remain at home with her children, accompanies an infant death rate about three times as favorable as is the infant mortality rate in the lowest income group. In families in the lowest group, 1 baby in every 6 failed to survive its first year, while in families in the adequate income group but 1 baby in 17 died within the first year.

These studies have no class basis—they include every baby born in a given town in a given year.

Maternal ignorance is not confined to the low-income group as Sir Arthur Newsholme has pointed out, but the prosperous mother can preserve her child from the results of her ignorance by doctors, nurses, sanitary housing, etc., better than can the poorer mother.

Both among rich and poor mothers there is genuine eagerness for knowledge. This is proved by the millions of publications on child welfare sent out by the Children's Bureau in response to requests largely from individual mothers.

The largest proportion of the total infant deaths occur in the first month of life and are apparently due to conditions preceding the birth of the child. Hence, authorities agree that prenatal instruction and care is of the highest importance, yet the bureau's studies in rural areas of six different States revealed the fact that 80 per cent of the mothers had received no advice or trained care during pregnancy.

Maternal mortality, the deaths of mothers from causes connected with childbirth, can not be ignored in connection with infant mortality. In the Waterbury study it was found that the rate of infant deaths was three times greater among those babies whose mothers died than among those whose mothers lived. In Baltimore the death rate of motherless infants was five times as great as that for those who had mothers.

It was found that we had no assembled body of information on maternal mortality in the United States and consequently a study of all available figures in the United States and foreign countries has been made.

According to the most reliable obtainable data the United States has the highest maternal death rate in a list of 17 civilized countries, and the chances of a child surviving its first year in this country are worse than in 10 other countries.

We found, also, as we studied this matter, that every European country had made some sort of provision for the protection of maternity and infancy, provisions which would seem entirely inadequate, according to our standards; indeed, they were so meager that they had to be greatly increased when the war came on. But the public responsibility for protecting maternity and infancy was recognized, and as we considered the meaning of the reports and statistics secured in the bureau's investigations we felt that it was not for us to say that we had done enough when we had written pamphlets and had them printed and bound and sent them out to libraries for preservation, while the vast body of taxpayers never knew of their existence nor of the facts as to human life which they set forth in costly tabulations.

And therefore we are responsible for this measure which has been placed before you. Some of its provisions are necessarily experimental. We are confident, however, that if administered in good faith, with a sense of educational, social, and economic and hygienic values, enthusiasm and an interest can be created in the States which will make many of them go much further than duplicating the appropriations which we are suggesting from the Federal Government.

The bureau has endeavored in every reasonable way to popularize and candidly to interpret its statistical data. This bill for the protection of maternity and infancy is one result of the social studies of the bureau interpreted into a plan of constructive public action, whose methods of care have been proven sound by many experiments here and abroad.

The bill is designed to avoid an obnoxious governmental authority. It respects the rights and duties of the States and requires" no rigid control of their appropriations. But experience shows that there should be a central source affording to the different States, when they make their plans, the best experience of all of the other States and of the world, and a central body competent to assure taxpayers and the special beneficiaries of the measure that its spirit is effectively carried out and that intelligent use is made of every dollar.

The actual public health nursing anticipated under the bill would be done by local employees, not by the Federal Government. The percentage of the appropriation that may be spent for administrative purposes by the Federal Government can not exceed 5 per cent, and at least 95 per cent must be allotted to the States.

The bill does not contemplate the creation of new machinery in the States. It is its purpose to have the work done in the States by State child-hygiene or child-welfare divisions, and 35 of the 48 States already have such divisions, most of them under the State boards of health. Necessarily, the bill provides for the creation of a suitable agency by States lacking such child-hygiene or child-welfare divisions. But there can be no danger of the creation of duplicating machinery in the States.

SOURCE: Committee on Interstate and Foreign Commerce of the House of Representatives. 1921. *Public Protection of Maternity and Infancy: Hearings before the Committee on Interstate and Foreign Commerce of the House of Representatives, Sixty-Sixth Congress, Third Session on H. R. 10925*. Washington, D.C.: Government Printing Office, 5–18.

ANALYSIS

The hearings before the United States House of Representatives' Committee on Interstate and Foreign Commerce were key to the passage of the Act for the Promotion of the Welfare and Hygiene of Maternity and Infancy, and for other Purposes, better known as the Sheppard-Towner Act of 1921. Congressman Horace Towner set the tone through his statement, which emphasized that most "civilized" (i.e., European) countries had already created programs to improve the health of mothers and children. The programs had obviously been successful because the mortality rates of both groups quickly declined. Since the United States had not enacted such legislation, it had the distinction of having the highest mortality rates for mothers and infants of the countries in its peer group. For the sake of national pride, the United States had to follow the lead of other wealthy countries and enact similar legislation.

Julia Lathrop, who as the head of the U.S. Children's Bureau, used numerous statistics to buttress Towner's presentation. Her support was predictable because it was the Children's Bureau that was in line to oversee the initiatives in the proposed legislation. The most influential part of her statement was that the mortality rates crossed class lines. This distinction meant that women and children of all social classes were at risk should the Promotion of the Welfare and Hygiene of Maternity and Infancy Act not become law. Lathrop misrepresented her data to support that claim because she believed that Congress would not act on a problem that primarily afflicted the impoverished. Her ploy was successful, as it helped galvanize the political support necessary for the passage of the law.

FURTHER READING

Ladd-Taylor, Molly. 1994. *Mother-Work: Women, Child Welfare, and the State, 1890–1930*. Urbana: University of Illinois Press.

Lindenmeyer, Kriste. 1997. *A Right to Childhood: The U.S. Children's Bureau and Child Welfare, 1912–1946*. Urbana: University of Illinois Press.

Skocpol, Theda. 1992. *Protecting Soldiers and Mothers: The Political Origins of Social Policy in the United States*. Cambridge, MA: Harvard University Press.

U.S. Children's Bureau, U.S. Department of Labor. 1921. *Promotion of the Welfare and Hygiene of Maternity and Infancy: Text of Act of November 23, 1921 and Maximum Amounts Available to the States*. Washington, D.C.: Government Printing Office. http://mchlibrary.jhmi.edu/downloads/file-949-1 (accessed February 15, 2017).

Wilson, Jan Doolittle. 2007. *The Women's Joint Congressional Committee and the Politics of Maternalism, 1920–30*. Urbana: University of Illinois Press.

"For the Promotion of the Welfare and Hygiene of Maternity and Infancy"

- ***Document:*** An Act for the Promotion of the Welfare and Hygiene of Maternity and Infancy (also known as the Sheppard-Towner Maternity and Infancy Act) (Excerpts)
- ***Date:*** November 23, 1921
- ***Where:*** Washington, D.C.
- ***Significance:*** The Sheppard-Towner Maternity and Infancy Act of 1921 was one of the first welfare programs initiated by the federal government.

DOCUMENT

CHAP. 135.—An Act For the promotion of the welfare and hygiene of maternity and infancy, and for other purposes.

Be it enacted by the Senate and House of Representatives in the United States of America in Congress assembled, That there is hereby authorized to be appropriated annually, out of any money in the Treasury not otherwise appropriated, the sums specified in section 2 of this Act, to be paid to the several States for the purpose of cooperating with them in promoting the welfare and hygiene of maternity and infancy as hereinafter provided.

SEC. 2. For the purpose of carrying out the provisions of this Act, there is authorized to be appropriated, out of any money in the Treasury not otherwise appropriated, for the current fiscal year $480,000, to be equally apportioned among the several States in the manner hereinafter provided. . .

SEC 3. There is hereby created a Board of Maternity and Infant Hygiene, which shall consist of the Chief of the Children's Bureau, the Surgeon General of the

DID YOU KNOW?

Adkins v. Children's Hospital (1923)

In 1918, a federal law was passed that created a board that was tasked with determining minimum wages to be paid to women and children in the District of Columbia. It was believed that the provision of a minimum wage would improve the health of the workers and prevent them from engaging in immoral behavior. The law was challenged by the District of Columbia's Children's Hospital. Felix Frankfurter maintained that the law served as a police power to address the discrimination against women in the workforce. Lawyers for the hospital maintained that the minimum wage law was actually a price-fixing scheme that violated the freedom of contracts.

The justices ruled 5–3 in favor of the Children's Hospital. Writing for the majority, Justice George Sutherland observed that the use of the federal police power was appropriate for use in protecting individuals, but that its use in this case was not appropriate because the law expressly included the purpose of protecting the morals of women. The protections needed to include all segments of the population. In addition, since the law was intended to elevate women and children from poverty, it was forcing employers to serve a welfare function that was not their responsibility. That responsibility belonged to society at large.

FURTHER READING

Zimmerman, Joan G. 1991. "The Jurisprudence of Equality: The Women's Minimum Wage, the First Equal Rights Amendment, and Adkins v. Children's Hospital, 1905–1923." *Journal of American History* 78, no. 1: 188–225.

United States Public Health Service, and the United States Commissioner of Education, and which is hereafter designated in this Act as the Board. The Board shall elect its own chairman and perform the duties provided for in this Act.

The Children's Bureau of the Department of Labor shall be charged with the administration of this Act, except as herein otherwise provided, and the Chief of the Children's Bureau shall be the executive officer. It shall be the duty of the Children's Bureau to make cause to be made such studies, investigations, and reports as will promote the efficient administration of this Act.

SEC. 4. In order to secure the benefits of the appropriations authorized in section 2 of this Act, any State shall, through the legislative authority thereof, accept the provisions of this Act and designate or authorize the creation of a State agency with which the Children's Bureau shall have all necessary powers to cooperate as herein provided in the administration of the provisions of this Act: *Provided*, That in any State having a child-welfare or child-hygiene division in its State agency of health, the said State agency of health shall administer the provisions of this Act through such divisions. If the legislature of any State has not Made provision for accepting the provisions of this Act the governor of such State may in so far as he is authorized to do so by the laws of such State accept, the provisions of this Act and designate, or create a State agency to cooperate with the Children's Bureau until six months after the adjournment of the first regular session of the legislature in such State following the passage of this Act.

. . .

SEC. 8. Any State desiring to receive the benefits of this Act shall, by its agency described in section 4, submit to the Children's Bureau detailed plans for carrying out the provisions of this Act within such State, which plans shall be subject to the approval of the Board: *Provided*, That the plans of the States under this Act shall provide that no official, or agent, or representative in carrying out the provisions of this Act shall enter any home or take charge of any child over the objection of the parents, or either of them, or the person standing in loco parentis or having custody of such child. If these plans shall be in conformity with the provisions of the Act and reasonably appropriate and adequate to carry out its purposes they shall be approved by the board and due notice of such approval shall be sent to the State agency by the Chief of the Children's Bureau.

SEC. 9. No official, agent, or representative of the Children's Bureau shall by virtue of the Act have any right to enter any home over the objection of the owner thereof, or to take charge of any child over the objection of the parents, or either of them, or the person standing in loco parentis or having custody of such child. Nothing in this Act shall be construed as limiting the power of a parent or guardian or person standing in loco parentis to determine what treatment or correction shall be provided for a child or the agency or agencies to be employed for such purpose.

SEC. 10. Within sixty days after any appropriation authorized by this Act has been made, and as often thereafter while such appropriation remains unexpended as changed conditions my warrant, the Children's Bureau shall ascertain the amounts that have been appropriated by the legislatures of the several States accepting the provisions of this Act and shall certify to the Secretary of the Treasury the amount to which each state is entitled under the provisions of this Act. Such certificate shall state (1) that the State has, through its legislative authority, accepted the provisions of this Act and designated or authorized the creation of an agency to cooperate with the Children's Bureau, or that the State has otherwise accepted this Act as provided in Section 4 hereof; (2) the fact that the proper agency of the State has submitted to the Children's Bureau detailed plans for carrying out the provisions of this Act, and that such plans have been approved by the board; (3) the amount, if any, that has been appropriated by the legislature of the State for the maintenance of the services and facilities of this Act, as provided in section 2 hereof; and (4) the amount to which the State is entitled under the provisions of this Act. Such certificate, when in conformity with the provisions hereof, shall, until revoked as provided in section 12 hereof, be sufficient authority to the Secretary of the Treasury to make payment to the State in accordance therewith.

. . .

SEC. 12. No portion of any moneys apportioned under this Act for the benefit of the States shall be applied, directly or indirectly, to the purchase, erection, preservation, or repair of any building, buildings, or equipment, or for the purchase or rental of any buildings or lands, nor shall any such moneys or moneys required to be appropriated by any State for the purposes and in accordance with the provisions of this Act be used for the payment of any maternity or infancy pension, stipend, or gratuity.

SOURCE: An Act for the Promotion of the Welfare and Hygiene of Maternity and Infancy, and for Other Purposes. 67th Congress, Session 1, Ch. 135, S. 1039. November 23, 1921. *U.S. Statutes at Large.* Washington, D.C.: Government Printing Office.

ANALYSIS

The Act for the Promotion of the Welfare and Hygiene of Maternity and Infancy, better known as the Sheppard-Towner Act of 1921, was signed by President Warren G. Harding on November 23, 1921. It authorized the Department of Labor's

Children's Bureau to distribute up to $1 million in matching funds to each of the states in order to establish programs to help keep women and their children healthy. If the state chose to accept the funding, they had to both match the federal money on a dollar-to-dollar basis and establish an agency to manage the programs that the monies were used to create. The initiatives undertaken at the state level had to address both prenatal care and the needs of mothers and children that were sick and ailing.

The Sheppard-Towner Act was the brainchild of Julia Lathrop, who as the head of the U.S. Children's Bureau had utilized statistics to show that the United States had the highest rate of both maternal and infant mortality of any of the world's wealthiest countries. Being a politician, she slightly misinterpreted her data during the hearings in December 1920 when she commented that the mortality rates crossed class lines. This was a deft decision on her part because if she identified the problem as one only affecting the poor, she believed that Congress would view the issue as a charity problem rather than a national health issue.

The act was sponsored in the House of Representatives by Horace Towner and in the Senate by Morris Sheppard of Texas. Although their names were on the bill, the legislation also bore the strong influence of the Women's Joint Congressional Committee (WJCC). The WJCC was a lobbying group that represented approximately 12 million women at its height. It had the attention of the male membership of Congress since the legislators were unsure of the political strength of women, who had just received the right to vote in 1920. Rather than drawing the ire of the new voting bloc, congressmen opted to strongly support the legislation. Women's groups took their support as a sign of their belief in the legislation rather than an act of political expediency.

The act was a success during the eight years it was authorized. Over that period, there was a continuous decline in the mortality rate of women and infants. Every state accepted the federal funding, which resulted in the construction of more than 2,500 health centers. These clinics, many of which were established in rural areas that had previously been underserved, were staffed by female physicians and nurses. In areas where medical professionals were absent, the Children's Bureau turned to midwives, to whom they provided training and licensing.

Buoyed by the obvious success of the Sheppard-Towner Act, its supporters took it for granted that its sunset date of 1929 would be extended by Congress. They did not lobby for its extension with the same rigor that they had in 1920. Unfortunately for them, the act's primary opponent from the very beginning, the American Medical Association (AMA), had never ceased its activities. It maintained that the act was an unlawful intrusion into medical care by the federal government. Congress was much more receptive to the AMA's entreats in 1926 than it had been in 1921 because there had been enough elections held by that point to gauge the costs of upsetting the women's vote. Enough congressmen who had ardently supported the Sheppard-Towner Act when initially presented switched sides, which made an extension impossible.

FURTHER READING

Ladd-Taylor, Molly. 1994. *Mother-Work: Women, Child Welfare, and the State, 1890–1930.* Urbana: University of Illinois Press.

Lindenmeyer, Kriste. 1997. *A Right to Childhood: The U.S. Children's Bureau and Child Welfare, 1912–1946.* Urbana: University of Illinois Press.

Skocpol, Theda. 1992. *Protecting Soldiers and Mothers: The Political Origins of Social Policy in the United States.* Cambridge, MA: Harvard University Press.

U.S. Children's Bureau, U.S. Department of Labor. 1921. *Promotion of the Welfare and Hygiene of Maternity and Infancy: Text of Act of November 23, 1921, and Maximum Amounts Available to the States.* Washington, D.C.: Government Printing Office. http://mchlibrary.jhmi.edu/downloads/file-949-1 (accessed February 15, 2017).

Wilson, Jan Doolittle. 2007. *The Women's Joint Congressional Committee and the Politics of Maternalism, 1920–30.* Urbana: University of Illinois Press.

"To Limit, Regulate, and Prohibit the Labor of Persons Under 18 Years of Age"

- ***Document:*** Child Labor Amendment of 1924
- ***Date:*** June 2, 1924
- ***Where:*** Washington, D.C.
- ***Significance:*** The amendment was an unsuccessful effort to regulate the labor of children under the age of 18 in the workforce.

DOCUMENT

JOINT RESOLUTION PROPOSING AN AMENDMENT TO THE CONSTITUTION OF THE UNITED STATES

Resolved by the Senate and House of Representatives of the United States of America in Congress assembled (two-thirds of each House concurring therein), That the following article is proposed as an amendment to the Constitution of the United States, which when ratified by the legislatures of three-fourths of the several States, shall be valid to all intents and purposes as a part of the Constitution:

ARTICLE———.

SECTION 1. The Congress shall have power to limit, regulate, and prohibit the labor of persons under 18 years of age.

SECTION 2. The power of the several States is unimpaired by this article except that the operation of State laws shall be suspended to the extent necessary to give effect to legislation enacted by the Congress.

SOURCE: Child Labor Amendment. H.J. Res. 184. *Congressional Record.* 68th Cong., 1st sess., 1924, Vol. 65, pt. 7294–7295.

ANALYSIS

At the dawn of twentieth century, the Progressive movement took an interest in the plight of children in the workforce. Rather than going to school, children were instead working long hours in dangerous mines or factories to help support their families. One organization that formed to advocate for them was the National Child Labor Committee (NCLC). The NCLC initially focused on child labor laws at the state level. Although it brought great attention to child labor by hiring Lewis Hine in 1908 to tour the country taking pictures of working children and writing about their plight, its efforts did not yield the passage of child labor laws in the states where children made up a significant proportion of the workforce. The reformers opted to change tactics by moving to effect change in the halls of the U.S. Congress. The move bore fruit with the passage of the Keating-Owen Child Labor Act of 1916.

The Keating-Owen legislation was designed to discourage the hiring of children under the age of 14 by restricting the transfer of goods that utilized their labor across state lines. It also included labor standards governing the working conditions of children between the ages of 14 and 16. The Keating-Owen Act was declared unconstitutional by the U.S. Supreme Court in a 5–3 decision in the case *Hammer v. Dagenhart*. The justices determined that the law violated both the Fifth and Fourteenth Amendments to the U.S. Constitution. Congress in 1919 responded by amending the Revenue Act of 1919 with a 10 percent tax on goods made by children. The Supreme Court also found that solution unconstitutional in the 1922 case *Bailey v. Drexel Furniture Company*. In an opinion authored by Chief Justice William Howard Taft, it was determined that the tax was a punitive measure designed to punish companies that employed children rather than an instrument designed to raise revenue.

Having seen two laws concerning child labor found unconstitutional, Progressives in Congress determined that the solution was to amend the Constitution through the Child Labor Amendment of 1924. In order to become a part of the Constitution, the amendment had to be ratified by the legislatures of 38 states. To date, only 28 states have ratified the amendment. Technically, the amendment can still become a part of the Constitution if it gains approval of 10 more state legislatures as Congress failed to include an end date in the original legislation. In practical terms, the need for the amendment was eclipsed with the inclusion of child labor provisions in the Fair Labor Standards Act of 1938. The constitutionality of the 1938 law was affirmed by the Supreme Court in the 1941 case *United States v. Darby Lumber Co.*, which saw the Court reject some of the constitutional interpretations that were made in the majority opinion in *Hammer v. Dagenhart.*

FURTHER READING

Aldous, Joan. 1997. "The Political Process and the Failure of the Child Labor Amendment." *Journal of Family Issues* 18, no. 1: 71–91.

Committee on the Judiciary, House of Representatives. 1924. *Proposed Child Labor Amendment to the Constitution of the United States: Hearings before the Committee on the Judiciary House of Representatives*. Washington, D.C.: Government Printing Office.

Schmidt, James D. 2010. *Industrial Violence and the Legal Origins of Child Labor*. New York: Cambridge University Press.

Sealander, Judith. 2003. *The Failed Century of the Child: Governing America's Young in the Twentieth Century*. New York: Cambridge University Press.

4

THE GREAT DEPRESSION AND THE NEW DEAL

"The Economic Consequences of Previous Crashes under a Much Less Secured Financial System Created Unwarranted Pessimism and Fear"

- ***Document:*** Annual Message to Congress on the State of the Union (Excerpts)
- ***Date:*** December 3, 1929
- ***Where:*** Washington, D.C.
- ***Significance:*** Approximately two months after the onset of the Great Depression, President Herbert Hoover used his first State of the Union address to assure the nation's populace that the sudden economic decline was not as significant as many feared. People just needed to study earlier financial crises in U.S. history to see how the issues negatively impacting the economy were always quickly corrected by market forces, leading to extended periods of prosperity.

DOCUMENT

To the Senate and House of Representatives:

The Constitution requires that the President "shall, from time to time, give to the Congress information of the state of the Union, and recommend to their consideration such measures as he shall judge necessary and expedient." In complying with that requirement I wish to emphasize that during the past year the Nation has continued to grow in strength; our people have advanced in comfort; we have gained in knowledge; the education of youth has been more widely spread; moral and spiritual forces have been maintained; peace has become more assured. The problems with which we are confronted are the problems of growth and of progress. In their solution we have to determine the facts, to develop the relative importance to be assigned to such facts, to formulate a common judgment upon them, and to realize solutions in spirit of conciliation.

. . .

FINANCES OF THE GOVERNMENT

The finances of the Government are in sound condition. I shall submit the detailed evidences and the usual recommendations in the special Budget message. I may, however, summarize our position. The public debt on June 30 this year stood at $16,931,000,000, compared to the maximum in August, 1919, of $26,596,000,000. Since June 30 it has been reduced by a further $238,000,000. In the Budget to be submitted the total appropriations recommended for the fiscal year 1931 are $3,830,445,231, as compared to $3,976,141,651 for the present fiscal year. The present fiscal year, however, includes $150,000,000 for the Federal Farm Board, as to which no estimate can as yet be determined for 1931.

Owing to the many necessary burdens assumed by Congress in previous years which now require large outlays, it is with extreme difficulty that we shall be able to keep the expenditures for the next fiscal year within the bounds of the present year. Economies in many directions have permitted some accommodation of pressing needs, the net result being an increase, as shown above, of about one-tenth of 1 per cent above the present fiscal year. We can not fail to recognize the obligations of the Government in support of the public welfare but we must coincidentally bear in mind the burden of taxes and strive to find relief through some tax reduction. Every dollar so returned fertilizes the soil of prosperity.

TAX REDUCTION

The estimate submitted to me by the Secretary of the Treasury and the Budget Director indicates that the Government will close the fiscal year 1930 with a surplus of about $225,000,000 and the fiscal year 1931 with a surplus of about $123,000,000. Owing to unusual circumstances, it has been extremely difficult to estimate future revenues with accuracy.

I believe, however, that the Congress will be fully justified in giving the benefits of the prospective surpluses to the taxpayers, particularly as ample provision for debt reduction has been made in both years through the form of debt retirement from ordinary revenues. In view of the uncertainty in respect of future revenues and the comparatively small size of the indicated surplus in 1931, relief should take the form of a provisional revision of tax rates.

I recommend that the normal income tax rates applicable to the incomes of individuals for the calendar year 1929 be reduced from 5, 3, and 1 ½ per cent, to 4, 2, and ½ per cent, and that the tax on the income of corporations for the calendar year 1929 be reduced from 12 to 11 per cent. It is estimated that this will result in a reduction of $160,000,000 in income taxes to be collected during the calendar year 1930. The loss in revenue will be divided approximately equally between the fiscal years 1930 and 1931. Such a program will give a measure of tax relief to the maximum number of taxpayers, with relatively larger benefits to taxpayers with small or moderate incomes.

. . .

GENERAL ECONOMIC SITUATION

The country has enjoyed a large degree of prosperity and sound progress during the past year with a steady improvement in methods of production and distribution and consequent advancement in standards of living. Progress has, of course, been unequal among industries, and some, such as coal, lumber, leather, and textiles, still lag behind. The long upward trend of fundamental progress, however, gave rise to over-optimism as to profits, which translated itself into a wave of uncontrolled speculation in securities, resulting in the diversion of capital from business to the stock market and the inevitable crash. The natural consequences have been a reduction in the consumption of luxuries and semi-necessities by those who have met with losses, and a number of persons thrown temporarily out of employment. Prices of agricultural products dealt in upon the great markets have been affected in sympathy with the stock crash.

Fortunately, the Federal reserve system had taken measures to strengthen the position against the day when speculation would break, which together with the strong position of the banks has carried the whole credit system through the crisis without impairment. The capital which has been hitherto absorbed in stock-market loans for speculative purposes is now returning to the normal channels of business. There has been no inflation in the prices of commodities; there has been no undue accumulation of goods, and foreign trade has expanded to a magnitude which exerts a steadying influence upon activity in industry and employment.

The sudden threat of unemployment and especially the recollection of the economic consequences of previous crashes under a much less secured financial system created unwarranted pessimism and fear. It was recalled that past storms of similar character had resulted in retrenchment of construction, reduction of wages, and laying off of workers. The natural result was the tendency of business agencies throughout the country to pause in their plans and proposals for continuation and extension of their businesses, and this hesitation unchecked could in itself intensify into a depression with widespread unemployment and suffering.

I have, therefore, instituted systematic, voluntary measures of cooperation with the business institutions and with State and municipal authorities to make certain that fundamental businesses of the country shall continue as usual, that wages and therefore consuming power shall not be reduced, and that a special effort shall be made to expand construction work in order to assist in equalizing other deficits in employment. Due to the enlarged sense of cooperation and responsibility which has grown in the business world during the past few years the response has been remarkable and satisfactory. We have canvassed the Federal Government and instituted measures of prudent expansion in such work that should be helpful, and upon which the different departments will make some early recommendations to Congress.

I am convinced that through these measures we have reestablished confidence. Wages should remain stable. A very large degree of industrial unemployment and suffering which would otherwise have occurred has been prevented. Agricultural prices have reflected the returning confidence. The measures taken must be vigorously pursued until normal conditions are restored.

AGRICULTURE

The agricultural situation is improving. The gross farm income as estimated by the Department of Agriculture for the crop season 1926–27 was $12,100,000,000; for 1927–28 it was $12,300,000,000; for 1928–29 it was $12,500,000,000; and estimated on the basis of prices since the last harvest the value of the 1929–30 crop would be over $12,650,000,000. The slight decline in general commodity prices during the past few years naturally assists the farmers' buying power.

The number of farmer bankruptcies is very materially decreased below previous years. The decline in land values now seems to be arrested and rate of movement from the farm to the city has been reduced. Not all sections of agriculture, of course, have fared equally, and some areas have suffered from drought. Responsible farm leaders have assured me that a large measure of confidence is returning to agriculture and that a feeling of optimism pervades that industry.

The most extensive action for strengthening the agricultural industry ever taken by any government was inaugurated through the farm marketing act of June 15 last. Under its provisions the Federal Farm Board has been established, comprised of men long and widely experienced in agriculture and sponsored by the farm organizations of the country. During its short period of existence the board has taken definite steps toward a more efficient organization of agriculture, toward the elimination of waste in marketing, and toward the upbuilding of farmers' marketing organizations on sounder and more efficient lines. Substantial headway has been made in the organization of four of the basic commodities—grain, cotton, livestock, and wool. Support by the board to cooperative marketing organizations and other board activities undoubtedly have served to steady the farmers' market during the recent crisis and have operated also as a great stimulus to the cooperative organization of agriculture. The problems of the industry are most complex, and the need for sound organization is imperative. Yet the board is moving rapidly along the lines laid out for it in the act, facilitating the creation by farmers of farmer-owned and farmer-controlled organizations and federating them into central institutions, with a view to increasing the bargaining power of agriculture, preventing and controlling surpluses, and mobilizing the economic power of agriculture.

THE TARIFF

The special session of Congress was called to expedite the fulfillment of party pledges of agricultural relief and the tariff. The pledge of farm relief has been carried out. At that time I stated the principles upon which I believed action should be taken in respect to the tariff:

> "An effective tariff upon agricultural products, that will compensate the farmer's higher costs and higher standards of living, has a dual purpose. Such a tariff not only protects the farmer in our domestic market but it also stimulates him to diversify his crops and to grow products that he could not otherwise produce, and thus lessens his dependence upon exports to foreign

markets. The great expansion of production abroad under the conditions I have mentioned renders foreign competition in our export markets increasingly serious. It seems but natural, therefore, that the American farmer, having been greatly handicapped in his foreign market by such competition from the younger expanding countries, should ask that foreign access to our domestic market should be regulated by taking into account the differences in our costs of production.

"In considering the tariff for other industries than agriculture, we find that there have been economic shifts necessitating a readjustment of some of the tariff schedules. Seven years of experience under the tariff bill enacted in 1922 have demonstrated the wisdom of Congress in the enactment of that measure. On the whole it has worked well. In the main our wages have been maintained at high levels; our exports and imports have steadily increased; with some exceptions our manufacturing industries have been prosperous. Nevertheless, economic changes have taken place during that time which have placed certain domestic products at a disadvantage and new industries have come into being, all of which create the necessity for some limited changes in the schedules and in the administrative clauses of the laws as written in 1922.

"It would seem to me that the test of necessity for revision is, in the main, whether there has been a substantial slackening of activity in an industry during the past few years, and a consequent decrease of employment due to insurmountable competition in the products of that industry. It is not as if we were setting up a new basis of protective duties. We did that seven years ago. What we need to remedy now is whatever substantial loss of employment may have resulted from shifts since that time.

"In determining changes in our tariff we must not fail to take into account the broad interests of the country as a whole, and such interests include our trade relations with other countries."

No condition has arisen in my view to change these principles stated at the opening of the special session. I am firmly of the opinion that their application to the pending revision will give the country the kind of a tariff law it both needs and wants. It would be most helpful if action should be taken at an early moment, more especially at a time when business and agriculture are both cooperating to minimize future uncertainties. It is just that they should know what the rates are to be.

Even a limited revision requires the consideration and readjustment of many items. The exhaustive inquiries and valuable debate from men representative of all parts of the country which is needed to determine the detailed rates must necessarily be accomplished in the Congress. However perfectly this rate structure may be framed at any given time, the shifting of economic forces which inevitably occurs will render changes in some items desirable between the necessarily long intervals of congressional revision. Injustices are bound to develop, such as were experienced by the dairymen, the flaxseed producers, the glass industry, and others, under the 1922 rates. For this reason, I have been most anxious that the broad principle of the flexible tariff as provided in the existing law should be preserved and its delays in action avoided by more expeditious methods of determining the costs of production at home and abroad, with executive authority to promulgate such changes upon recommendation of the Tariff Commission after exhaustive investigation. Changes by the Congress in the isolated items such as those to which I have referred would have been most unlikely both because of the concentrations of oppositions in the country, who could see no advantage to their own industry or State, and because of the difficulty of limiting consideration by the Congress to such isolated cases.

There is no fundamental conflict between the interests of the farmer and the worker. Lowering of the standards of living of either tends to destroy the other. The prosperity of one rests upon the well-being of the other. Nor is there any real conflict between the East and the West or the North and the South in the United States. The complete interlocking of economic dependence, the common striving for social and spiritual progress, our common heritage as Americans, and the infinite web of national sentiment, have created a solidarity in a great people unparalleled in all human history. These invisible bonds should not and can not be shattered by differences of opinion growing out of discussion of a tariff.

. . .

THE BANKING SYSTEM

It is desirable that Congress should consider the revision of some portions of the banking law.

The development of "group" and "chain" banking presents many new problems. The question naturally arises as to whether if allowed to expand without restraint these methods would dangerously concentrate control of credit, and whether they would not in any event seriously threaten one of the fundamentals of the American credit system—which is that credit which is based upon banking deposits should be controlled by persons within those areas which furnish these deposits and thus be subject to the restraints of local interest and public opinion in those areas. To some degree, however, this movement of chain or group banking is a groping for stronger support to the banks and a more secure basis for these institutions.

The growth in size and stability of the metropolitan banks is in marked contrast to the trend in the country districts, with its many failures and the losses these failures have imposed upon the agricultural community.

The relinquishment of charters of national banks in great commercial centers in favor of State charters indicates that some conditions surround the national banks which render them unable to compete with State banks; and their withdrawal results in weakening our national banking system.

It has been proposed that permission should be granted to national banks to engage in branch banking of a nature that would preserve within limited regions the local responsibility and the control of such credit institutions.

All these subjects, however, require careful investigation, and it might be found advantageous to create a joint commission embracing Members of the Congress and other appropriate Federal officials for subsequent report.

. . .

SOCIAL SERVICE

The Federal Government provides for an extensive and valuable program of constructive social service, in education, home building, protection to women and children, employment, public health, recreation, and many other directions.

In a broad sense Federal activity in these directions has been confined to research and dissemination of information and experience, and at most to temporary subsidies to the States in order to secure uniform advancement in practice and methods. Any other attitude by the Federal Government will undermine one of the most precious possessions of the American people; that is, local and individual responsibility. We should adhere to this policy.

Federal officials can, however, make a further and most important contribution by leadership in stimulation of the community and voluntary agencies, and by extending Federal assistance in organization of these forces and bringing about cooperation among them.

As an instance of this character, I have recently, in cooperation with the Secretaries of Interior and Labor, laid the foundations of an exhaustive inquiry into the facts precedent to a nation-wide White House conference on child health and protection. This cooperative movement among interested agencies will impose no expense upon the Government. Similar nation-wide conferences will be called in connection with better housing and recreation at a later date.

In view of the considerable difference of opinion as to the policies which should be pursued by the Federal Government with respect to education, I have appointed a committee representative of the important educational associations and others to investigate and present recommendations. In cooperation with the Secretary of the Interior, I have also appointed a voluntary committee of distinguished membership to assist in a nation-wide movement for abolition of illiteracy.

I have recommended additional appropriations for the Federal employment service in order that it may more fully cover its cooperative work with State and local services. I have also recommended additional appropriations for the Women's and Children's Bureaus for much needed research as to facts which I feel will prove most helpful.

. . .

CONCLUSION

The test of the rightfulness of our decisions must be whether we have sustained and advanced the ideals of the American people; self-government in its foundations of local government; justice whether to the individual or to the group; ordered liberty; freedom from domination; open opportunity and equality of opportunity; the initiative and individuality of our people; prosperity and the lessening of poverty; freedom of public opinion; education; advancement of knowledge; the growth of religious spirit; the tolerance of all faiths; the foundations of the home and the advancement of peace.

HERBERT HOOVER
The White House,
December 3, 1929.

SOURCE: *Public Papers of the Presidents of the United States. Herbert Hoover, 1929*. Washington, D.C.: Government Printing Office, 1974, 404–436.

ANALYSIS

President Herbert Hoover took office in 1929. Like many Republicans of his day, he had great faith in the nation's capitalist system and believed that it operated best when allowed to function without interference from the government. This core belief explains how Hoover reacted to the onset of the Great Depression in October 1929. Rather than recognizing that many throughout the country were being financially devastated, he optimistically argued that the American capitalist engine was far stronger than many believed and that time would show that it was more than capable of self-correcting any structural problems that might be manifesting themselves. His faith in American capitalism undergirded his first State of the Union address.

Hoover's belief proved misguided as the Depression deepened. His administration made tentative steps to help the economy through acts like asking employers not to shed jobs during the downturn. What Hoover viewed as examples of his administration showing leadership by advising private interests that influenced capital activity, the populace saw as government inaction. Rising public resentment of Hoover was exemplified through the appearance of "Hoovervilles" across the nation. These were shantytowns that were created by the impoverished and unemployed.

Hoover's administration attempted to repair his political viability as he ran for reelection through the enactment of legislation such as the Reconstruction Finance Corporation Act of 1932. The effort went for naught as Hoover was repudiated at the polls by voters who instead put their faith in Franklin Delano Roosevelt.

FURTHER READING

Jeansonne, Glen. 2012. *The Life of Herbert Hoover: Fighting Quaker, 1928–1933*. New York: Palgrave Macmillan.

Jeansonne, Glen. 2016. *Herbert Hoover: A Life*. New York: New American Library.

Leuchtenburg, William E. 2009. *Herbert Hoover*. New York: Times Books.

Rappleye, Charles. 2016. *Herbert Hoover in the White House: The Ordeal of the Presidency*. New York: Simon & Schuster.

"To Establish and Maintain Such Balance between the Production and Consumption of Agricultural Commodities"

- ***Document:*** Agricultural Adjustment Act of 1933
- ***Date:*** May 12, 1933
- ***Where:*** Washington, D.C.
- ***Significance:*** The Agricultural Adjustment Act set prices for agricultural products and provided for subsidies to be paid to farmers for not producing certain commodities in order to lessen their surplus supply.

DOCUMENT

AN ACT

To relieve the existing national economic emergency by increasing agricultural purchasing power, to raise revenue for extraordinary expenses incurred by reason of such emergency, to provide emergency relief with respect to agricultural indebtedness, to provide for the orderly liquidation of joint-stock land banks, and for other purposes.

Be it enacted by the Senate and House of Representatives of the United States of America in Congress assembled,

TITLE I—AGRICULTURAL ADJUSTMENT DECLARATION OF EMERGENCY

That the present acute economic emergency being in part the consequence of a severe and increasing disparity between the prices of agricultural and other commodities, which disparity has largely destroyed the purchasing power of farmers for industrial products, has broken down the orderly exchange of commodities, and has seriously impaired the agricultural assets supporting the national credit structure, it is hereby declared that these conditions in the basic industry of agriculture have affected transactions in agricultural commodities with a national public interest, have burdened and obstructed the normal currents of commerce in such commodities, and render imperative the immediate enactment of title I of this Act.

DECLARATION OF POLICY

SEC. 2. It is hereby declared to be the policy of Congress—

(1) To establish and maintain such balance between the production and consumption of agricultural commodities, and such marketing conditions therefor, as will reestablish prices to farmers at a level that will give agricultural commodities a purchasing power with respect to articles that farmers buy, equivalent to; the purchasing power of agricultural commodities in the base period. The base period in the case of all agricultural commodities except tobacco shall be the prewar period, August 1909–July 1914. In the case of tobacco, the base period shall be the postwar period, August 1919– July 1929.

(2) To approach such equality of purchasing power by gradual correction of the present inequalities therein at as rapid a rate as is deemed feasible in view of the current consumptive demand in domestic and foreign markets.

(3) To protect the consumers' interest by readjusting farm production at such level as will not increase the percentage of the consumers' retail expenditures for agricultural commodities, or products derived therefrom, which is returned to the farmer, above the percentage which was returned to the farmer in the prewar period, August 1909–July 1914.

PART 1—COTTON OPTION CONTRACTS

SEC. 3. The Federal Farm Board and all departments and other agencies of the Government, not including the Federal intermediate credit banks, are hereby directed—

(a) To sell to the Secretary of Agriculture at such price as may be agreed upon, not in excess of the market price, all cotton now owned by them.

(b) To take such action and to make such settlements as are necessary in order to acquire full legal title to all cotton on which money has been loaned or advanced by any department or agency of the United States, including futures contracts for cotton or which is held as collateral for loans or advances and to make final settlement of such loans and advances as follows:

(1) In making such settlements with regard to cotton, including operations to which such cotton is related, such cotton shall be taken over by all such departments or agencies other than the Secretary of Agriculture at a price or sum equal to the amounts directly or indirectly loaned or advanced thereon and outstanding, including loans by the Government department or agency and any loans senior thereto, plus any sums required to adjust advances to growers to 90 per centum of the value of their cotton at the date of its delivery in the first instance as collateral to the department or agency involved, such sums to be computed by subtracting the total

amount already advanced to growers on account of pools of which such cotton was a part, from 90 per centum of the value of the cotton to be taken over as of the time of such delivery as collateral, plus unpaid accrued carrying charges and operating costs on such cotton, less, however, any existing assets of the borrower derived from net income, earnings^ or profits arising from such cotton, and from operations to which such cotton is related; all as determined by the department or agency making the settlement.

(2) The Secretary of Agriculture shall make settlements with respect to cotton held as collateral for loans or advances made by him on such terms as in his judgment may be deemed advisable, and to carry out the provisions of this section, is authorized to indemnify or furnish bonds to warehousemen tor lost warehouse receipts and to pay the premiums on such bonds.

When full legal title to the cotton referred to in (b) has been acquired, it shall be sold to the Secretary of Agriculture for the purposes of this section, in the same manner as provided in (a).

(c) The Secretary of Agriculture is hereby authorized to purchase the cotton specified m paragraphs (a) and (b).

SEC. 4. The Secretary of Agriculture shall have authority to borrow money upon all cotton in his possession or control and deposit as collateral for such loans the warehouse receipts for such cotton.

SEC. 5. The Reconstruction Finance Corporation is hereby authorized and directed to advance money and to make loans to the Secretary of Agriculture to acquire such cotton and to pay the classing, carrying, and merchandising costs thereon, in such amounts and upon such terms as may be agreed upon by the Secretary and the Reconstruction Finance Corporation, with such warehouse receipts as collateral security: *Provided, however,* That in any instance where it is impossible or impracticable for the Secretary to deliver such warehouse receipts as collateral security for the advances and loans herein provided to be made, the Reconstruction Finance Corporation may accept in lieu of all or any part thereof such other security as it may consider acceptable for the purposes aforesaid, including an assignment or assignments of the equity and interest of the Secretary in warehouse receipts pledged to secure other indebtedness. The amount of notes, bonds, debentures, and other such obligations which the Reconstruction Finance Corporation is authorized and empowered to issue and to have outstanding at any one time under existing law is hereby increased by an amount sufficient to carry out the provisions of this section.

SEC. 6. (a) The Secretary of Agriculture is hereby authorized to enter into option contracts with the producers of cotton to sell to any such producer an amount of cotton to be agreed upon not in excess of the amount of reduction in production of cotton by such producer below the amount produced by him in the preceding crop year, in all cases where such producer agrees in writing to reduce the amount of cotton produced by him in 1933, below his production in the previous year, by not less than 30 per centum, without increase in commercial fertilization per acre.

(b) To any such producer so agreeing to reduce production the Secretary of Agriculture shall deliver a nontransferable-option contract agreeing to sell to said producer an amount, equivalent to the amount of his agreed reduction, of the cotton in the possession and control of the Secretary.

(c) The producer is to have the option to buy said cotton at the average price paid by the Secretary for the cotton procured under section 3, and is to have the right at any time up to January 1, 1934, to exercise his option, upon proof that he has complied with his contract and with all the rules and regulations of the Secretary of Agriculture with respect thereto, by taking said cotton upon payment by him of his option price and all actual carrying charges on such cotton; or the Secretary may sell such cotton for the account of such producer, paying him the excess of the market price at the date of sale over the average price above referred to after deducting all actual and necessary carrying charges: *Provided,* That in no event shall the producer be held responsible or liable for financial loss incurred in the holding of such cotton or on account of the carrying charges therein: *Provided further,* That such agreement to curtail cotton production shall contain a further provision that such cotton producer shall not use the land taken out of cotton production for the production for sale, directly or indirectly, of any other nationally produced agricultural commodity or product.

(d) If any cotton held by the Secretary of Agriculture is not disposed of under subsection (c), the Secretary is authorized to enter into similar option contracts with respect to such cotton, conditioned upon a like reduction of production in 1934, and permitting the producer in each case to exercise his option at any time up to January 1, 1935.

SEC. 7. The Secretary shall sell the cotton held by him at his discretion, but subject to the foregoing provisions: *Provided,* That he shall dispose of all cotton held by him by March 1, 1936: *Provided further,* That the Secretary shall have authority to enter into additional option contracts for so much of such cotton as is not necessary to comply with the provisions of section 6, in combination with benefit payments as provided for in part 2 of this title.

PART 2—COMMODITY BENEFITS GENERAL POWERS

SEC. 8. In order to effecuate the declared policy, the Secretary of Agriculture shall have power—

(1) To provide for reduction in the acreage or reduction in the production for market, or both, of any basic agricultural commodity, through "agreements with producers or by other voluntary methods, and to provide for rental or benefit payments in connection therewith or upon that part of the production of any basic agricultural commodity required for domestic consumption, in such amounts as the Secretary deems fair and reasonable, to be paid out of any moneys available for such payments. Under regulations of the Secretary of Agriculture requiring adequate facilities for the storage of any non-perishable agricultural commodity on the farm, inspection and measurement of any such commodity so stored, and the locking and sealing thereof, and such other regulations as may be prescribed by the Secretary of Agriculture for the protection of such commodity and for the marketing thereof, a reasonable percentage of any benefit payment may be advanced on any such commodity so stored. In any such case, such deduction may be made from the amount of the benefit payment as the Secretary of Agriculture determines will reasonably compensate for the cost of inspection and sealing, but no deduction may be made for interest.

(2) To enter into marketing agreements with processors, associations of producers, and others engaged in the handling, in the current of interstate or foreign commerce of any agricultural commodity or product thereof, after due notice and opportunity for hearing to interested parties. The making of any such agreement shall not be held to be in violation of any of the antitrust laws of the United States, and any such agreement shall be deemed to be lawful: *Provided,* That no such agreement shall remain in force after the termination of this Act. For the purpose of carrying out any such agreement the parties thereto shall-be eligible for loans from the Reconstruction Finance Corporation under section 5 of the Reconstruction Finance Corporation Act. Such loans shall not be in excess of such amounts as may be authorized by the agreements.

(3) To issue licenses permitting processors, associations of producers, and others to engage in the handling, in the current of interstate or foreign commerce, of any agricultural commodity or product thereof, or any competing commodity or product thereof. Such licenses shall be subject to such terms and conditions, not in conflict with existing Acts of Congress or regulations pursuant thereto, as may be necessary to eliminate unfair practices or charges that prevent or tend to prevent the effectuation of the declared policy and the restoration of normal economic conditions in the marketing of such commodities or products and the financing thereof. The Secretary of Agriculture may suspend or revoke any such license, after due notice and opportunity for hearing, for violations of the terms or conditions thereof. Any order of the Secretary suspending or revoking any such license shall be final if in accordance with law. Any such person engaged in such handling without a license as required by the Secretary under this section shall be subject to a fine of not more than $1,000 for each day during which tne violation continues.

(4) To require any licensee under this section to furnish such reports as to quantities of agricultural commodities or products thereof bought and sold and the prices thereof, and as to trade practices and charges, and to keep such systems or accounts, as may be necessary for the purpose of part 2 of this title.

(5) No person engaged in the storage in a public warehouse of any basic agricultural commodity in the current of interstate or foreign commerce, shall deliver any such commodity upon which a warehouse receipt has been issued and is outstanding, without prior surrender and cancellation of such warehouse receipt. Any person violating any of the provisions of this subsection shall, upon conviction, be punished by a fine of not more than $5,000, or by imprisonment for not more than two years, or both. The Secretary of Agriculture may revoke any license issued under subsection (3) of this section, if he finds; after due notice and opportunity for hearing, that the licensee has violated the provisions of this subsection.

SOURCE: 73rd Congress. 1933. Public Law 73-10, 73rd Congress, H.R. 3835, 48 Stat. 31.

ANALYSIS

The agricultural sector of the U.S. economy was in severe decline long before the Great Depression. Although production rose following the conclusion of World War I, farmers were not able to benefit because it was accompanied by a decline in the price they were being given when they sold their agricultural commodities. When the Great Depression struck in 1929, farmers who previously were barely able to make ends meet fell into bankruptcy. To ameliorate the problems, farmers and their professional organizations began pushing farm-state congressmen to call for the federal government to intervene. Although President Herbert Hoover opposed government intervention into the agricultural sector in principle, he signed the Agricultural Marketing Act (AMA) on June 15, 1929, to assist agricultural cooperatives in marketing the wares of their members. In theory, improved marketing would yield higher prices. Since the AMA did not address the problem of overproduction, the effort failed to stem the economic struggles faced by farmers.

Upon assuming the presidency, Franklin Delano Roosevelt made it a priority to enact legislation to address the needs of farm-belt states. The Agricultural Adjustment Act (AAA) of 1933 gave the secretary of agriculture the authority to limit the production of certain crops, farm animals, and dairy commodities. The act also created the Agricultural Adjustment Administration to oversee payments to farmers not to produce certain commodities. By reducing the supply of certain goods, it would ensure an increase in price for the respective commodities. The production controls proved controversial as some farmers were receiving monies from the federal government not to grow crops or raise animals during a time that many people were going hungry.

The AAA made fundamental changes to the agricultural sector nationally. Many of the experts in the AAA came from farm-belt states such as Iowa and Wisconsin and they advocated farming techniques that were successful in those states. The farms in those locales tended to produce a few crops on large farms that were intended to be sold for use elsewhere. It was a different type of farming than could be found in rural areas like those in Appalachian Kentucky. In that region, subsistence farming on small farms was the norm. The farms produced the foodstuffs required for a family to provide for itself with just a small amount of surplus left over to be exchanged in local markets for the goods that the family could not produce on its own. In order to participate in just one AAA program, a farmer had to adhere to all of the AAA's regulations. This meant that subsistence farmers in Eastern Kentucky had to abandon raising a variety of crops and animals in favor of growing one or two crops approved for production in the region, such as tobacco. In the case of tobacco, one could not really opt out of following the AAA's guidelines because if farmers grew tobacco independently, they were assessed a 24 percent marketing tax on each pound produced because of the enactment of the 1934 Kerr-Smith Act. Due to thin soils on mountainous terrain, farmers in Appalachia did not produce as much per acre as their counterparts in other parts of the country. This meant a smaller profit that they had to use to buy everything they and their families required in the market because they could no longer provide all of the corn, meat, and dairy they needed due to AAA rules. The end result was that farmers in the region became dependent on federal agricultural programs for their meager income for decades rather than being able to provide for themselves.

Liberal administrators in the Agricultural Adjustment Administration did severe damage to the political support of the AAA in the South by requiring that monies paid to cotton producers be shared with the tenants they utilized for labor. Many of the tenants were African Americans and the farm owners were white. The farm owners refused and called on their congressmen to ameliorate the situation. They were able to bring enough political pressure to bear that many of the administrators calling for a 50 percent cut of the payments for the tenants lost their jobs. Due to the refusal of the farm owners to share revenue, many of the tenants quit. The owners were not negatively affected as they simply shifted to the program that allowed them to be paid for not growing cotton and leaving their fields fallow.

Opponents of the AAA were not able to get the act repealed politically so they turned to the federal courts. On January 6, 1936, the U.S. Supreme Court in the case *United States v. Butler* declared the AAA unconstitutional. In particular, the justices determined that the processing tax created within the legislation was not really a tax because its purpose was to control production rather than generating revenue. Congress was able to address the concerns of the justices through the Agricultural Adjustment Act of 1938, which did pass constitutional muster.

FURTHER READING

Burch, John R., Jr. 2008. *Owsley County, Kentucky, and the Perpetuation of Poverty*. Jefferson, NC: McFarland & Company.

Domhoff, G. William, and Michael J. Webber. 2011. *Class and Power in the New Deal: Corporate Moderates, Southern Democrats, and the Liberal-Labor Coalition*. Palo Alto, CA: Stanford University Press.

Katznelson, Ira. 2012. *Fear Itself: The New Deal and the Origins of Our Time*. New York: Liveright Publishing.

White, Ann Folino. 2015. *Plowed Under: Food Policy Protests and Performance in New Deal America*. Bloomington: Indiana University Press.

Winders, Bill. 2009. *The Politics of Food Supply: U.S. Agricultural Policy in the World Economy*. New Haven: Yale University Press.

"Relieving the Hardship and Suffering Caused by Unemployment"

- ***Document:*** Federal Emergency Relief Act of 1933
- ***Date:*** May 12, 1933
- ***Where:*** Washington, D.C.
- ***Significance:*** The legislation created the Federal Emergency Relief Administration to manage the disbursement of $500 million to the states for distribution to the impoverished.

DOCUMENT

AN ACT

To provide for cooperation by the Federal Government with the several States and Territories and the District of Columbia in relieving the hardship and suffering caused by unemployment, and for other purposes.

Be it enacted by the Senate and House of Representatives of the United States of America in Congress assembled, That the Congress hereby declares that the present economic depression has created a serious emergency, due to widespread unemployment and increasing inadequacy of State and local relief funds, resulting in the existing or threatened deprivation of a considerable number of families and individuals of the necessities of life, and making it imperative that the Federal Government cooperate more effectively with the several States and Territories and the District of Columbia in furnishing relief to their needy and distressed people.

Sec. 2. (a) The Reconstruction Finance Corporation is authorized and directed to make available out of the funds of the Corporation not to exceed $500,000,000, in addition to the funds authorized under title I of the Emergency Relief and

Construction Act of 1932, for expenditure under the provisions of this Act upon certification by the Federal Emergency Relief Administrative provided for in section 3.

(b) The amount of notes, debentures, bonds, or other such obligations which the Reconstruction Finance Corporation is authorized and empowered under section 9 of the Reconstruction Finance Corporation Act, as amended, to have outstanding at any one time is increased by $500,000,000: Provided, That no such additional notes, debentures, bonds, or other such obligations authorized by this subsection shall be issued except at such times and in such amounts as the President shall approve.

(c) After the expiration of ten days after the date upon which the Federal Emergency Relief Administrator has qualified and has taken office, no application shall be approved by the Reconstruction Finance Corporation under the provisions of title I of the Emergency Relief and Construction Act of 1932, and the Federal Emergency Relief Administrator shall have access to all files and records of the Reconstruction Finance Corporation relating to the administration of funds under title I of such Act. At the expiration of such ten-day period, the unexpended and unobligated balance of the funds authorized under title I of such Act shall be available for the purposes of this Act.

Sec. 3. (a) There is hereby created a Federal Emergency Relief Administration, all the powers of which shall be exercised by a Federal Emergency Relief Administrator (referred to in this Act as the *Administrator*) to be appointed by the President, by and with the advice and consent of the Senate. The Administrator shall receive a salary to be fixed by the President at not to exceed $10,000, and necessary traveling and subsistence expenses within the limitations prescribed by law for civilian employees in the executive branch of the Government. The Federal Emergency Relief Administration and the office of Federal Emergency Relief Administrator shall case to exist upon the expiration of two years after the date of enactment of this Act, and the unexpended balance on such date of any funds made available under the provisions of this Act shall be disposed of as the Congress may by law provide.

(b) The Administrator may appoint and fix the compensation of such experts and their appointment may be made and compensation fixed without regard to the civil service laws, or the Classification Act of 1923, as amended, and the Administrator may, in the same manner, appoint and fix the compensation of such other officers

DID YOU KNOW?

End Poverty in California

Upton Sinclair was a reform-minded journalist whose 1906 book *The Jungle* illuminated issues in the meatpacking industry such as the intentional use of diseased animals for meat. The book was widely read and the horrified public demanded action from federal officials. In response, President Theodore Roosevelt and Congress worked together to craft both the Pure Food and Drug Act and the Meat Inspection Act.

The Great Depression found Sinclair preparing to run for California's governorship. His campaign themes were presented in 1933's *I, Governor of California, and How I Ended Poverty*. It contained an initial version of "End Poverty in California" (EPIC). When he officially declared his candidacy, EPIC became "Immediate EPIC." The name change signaled that the plan was not a proposal for gradual change, but for immediate relief for the poor who were suffering mightily from the Great Depression. Despite a vigorous campaign, Sinclair lost because his Socialist political views allowed his opponent to depict him as a Communist. Nonetheless, Immediate EPIC proved extremely influential as versions of some of its proposals became encapsulated in New Deal legislation advanced by President Franklin Delano Roosevelt.

FURTHER READING

Mitchell, Greg. 1992. *The Campaign of the Century: Upton Sinclair's Race for Governor of California and the Birth of Media Politics*. New York: Random House.

and employees as are necessary to carry out the provisions of this Act, but such compensation shall not exceed in any case the sum of $8,000; and may make such expenditures (including expenditures for personal services and rent at the seat of government and elsewhere and for printing and binding), not to exceed $350,000, as are necessary to carry out the provisions of this Act, to be paid by the Reconstruction Finance Corporation out of funds made available by this Act upon presentation of vouchers approved by the Administrator or by an officer of the Administration designated by him for that purpose. The Administrator may, under rules and regulations prescribed by the President, assume control of the administration in any State or States where, in his judgment, more effective and efficient cooperation between the State and Federal authorities may thereby be secured in carrying out the purposes of this Act.

(c) In executing any of the provisions of this Act, the Administrator, and any person duly authorized or designated by him, may conduct any investigation pertinent or material to the furtherance of the purposes of this Act and, at the request of the President, shall make such further investigations and studies as the President may deem necessary in dealing with problems of unemployment relief.

(d) The Administrator shall print monthly, and shall submit to the President and to the Senate and the House of Representatives (or to the Secretary of the Senate and the Clerk of the House of Representatives, if those bodies are not in session), a report of his activities and expenditures under this Act. Such reports shall, when submitted, be printed as public documents.

Sec. 4. (a) Out of the funds of the Reconstruction Finance Corporation made available by this Act, the Administrator is authorized to make grants to the several States to aid in meeting the costs of furnishing relief and work relief and in relieving the hardship and suffering caused by unemployment in the form of money, service, materials, and/or commodities to provide the necessities of life to persons in need as a result of the present emergency, and/or to their dependents, whether resident, transient, or homeless.

(b) Of the amounts made available by this Act not to exceed $250,000,000 shall be granted to the several States applying therefor, in the following manner: Each State shall be entitled to receive grants equal to one third of the amount expended by such State, including the civil subdivisions thereof, out of public moneys from all sources for the purposes set forth in subsection (a) of this section; and such grants shall be made quarterly, beginning with the second quarter in the calendar year 1933, and shall be made during any quarter upon the basis of such expenditures certified by the States to have been made during the preceding quarter.

(c) The balance of the amounts made available by this Act, except the amount required for administrative expenditures under section 3, shall be used for grants to be made whenever, from an application presented by a State, the Administrator finds that the combined moneys which can be made available within the State from all sources, supplemented by any moneys, available under subsection (b) of this section, will fall below the estimated needs within the State for the purposes specified in subsection (a) of this section: Provided, That the Administrator may certify out of the funds made available by this subsection additional grants to States applying therefor to aid needy persons who have no legal settlement in any one State or community, and to aid in assisting cooperative and self-help associations for the barter of goods and services.

(d) After October 1, 1933, notwithstanding the provisions of subsection (b), the unexpended balance of the amounts available for the purposes of subsection (b) may, in the discretion of the Administrator and with the approval of the President, be available for grants under subsection (c).

(e) The decision of the Administrator as to the purpose of any expenditure shall be final.

(f) The amount available to any one State under subsections (b) and (c) of this section shall not exceed 15 per centum of the total amount made available by such subsections.

Sec. 5. Any State desiring to obtain funds under this Act shall through its Governor make application therefor from time to time to the Administrator. Each application so made shall present in the manner requested by the Administrator information showing (1) the amounts necessary to meet relief needs in the State during the period covered by such application and the amounts available from public or private sources within the State, its political subdivisions, and private agencies, to meet the relief needs of the State, (2) the provision made to assure adequate administrative supervision, (3) the provision made for suitable standards of relief, and (4) the purposes for which the funds requested will be used.

Sec. 6. The Administrator upon approving a grant to any State shall so certify to the Reconstruction Finance Corporation which shall, except upon revocation of a certificate by the Administrator, make payments without delay to the State in such amounts and at such times as may be prescribed in the certificate. The Governor of each State receiving grants under this Act shall file monthly with the Administrator, and in the form required by him, a report of the disbursements made under such grants.

Sec. 7. As used in the foregoing provisions of this Act, the term *State* shall include the District of Columbia, Alaska, Hawaii, the Virgin Islands, and Puerto Rico; and the term *Governor* shall include the Commissioners of the District of Columbia.

Sec. 8. This Act may be cited as the *Federal Emergency Relief Act of 1933*.

SOURCE: U.S. Statutes at Large (73rd Congress, Sess. I, Chp. 30, p. 55–58).

ANALYSIS

The Federal Emergency Relief Act of 1933 was one of the many pieces of New Deal legislation enacted during President Franklin D. Roosevelt's first 100 days in office. The act created the Federal Emergency Relief Administration (FERA) to administer the disbursement of $500 million that was appropriated from the Reconstruction Finance Corporation for relief payments to the unemployed. The money was provided to the states in the form of grants. Harry Hopkins was appointed to lead the new agency. He was uniquely qualified for the task due to his management of the New York Temporary Emergency Relief Association in the administration of the then New York governor Roosevelt.

In order to dissuade state officials from using the federal funds for political patronage, Hopkins only sent half of the $500 million to the respective states for use as local officials saw fit. He retained the remainder of the funds to distribute for initiatives that he believed would provide the maximum amount of benefit, such as the programs of the Civil Works Administration. Predictably, once the politicians in the respective states were given the discretion to determine the distribution of the grants, money began to be utilized in ways not intended by the federal government. Hopkins's efforts to address the corruption led to political battles around the country. In truth, administrators in FERA were also using the money to advance political goals. States that were believed key to Roosevelt's reelection had more projects funded by the agency than their counterparts whose loyalties were firmly established. Political conflagrations, particularly in Colorado, North Dakota, Ohio, had taken a political toll in just two years. In addition, the provision of emergency relief had come to be viewed as a handout that was primarily benefiting people unwilling to work. As a result, FERA officially ceased operations in December 1935.

FURTHER READING

Daniels, Roger. 2015. *Franklin D. Roosevelt: Road to the New Deal, 1882–1939*. Champaign: University of Illinois Press.

Golay, Michael. 2013. *America 1933: The Great Depression, Lorena Hickok, Eleanor Roosevelt, and the Shaping of the New Deal.* New York: Free Press.

Kennedy David M. 1999. *Freedom from Fear: The American People in Depression and War, 1929–1945*. New York: Oxford University Press.

"An Act for the Relief of Unemployment through the Performance of Useful Public Work"

- ***Document:*** Executive Order 6101 Starting the Civilian Conservation Corps
- ***Date:*** April 5, 1933
- ***Where:*** Washington, D.C.
- ***Significance:*** Over the course of its nine-year existence, the Civilian Conservation Corps provided employment to nearly three million young men.

DOCUMENT

By virtue of the authority vested in me by the Act of Congress entitled "An Act for the relief of unemployment through the performance of useful public work, and for other purposes," approved March 31, 1933 (Public No. 5, 73d Congress), it is hereby ordered that:

(1) For the purpose of carrying out the provisions of said Act Robert Fechner is hereby appointed Director of Emergency Conservation Work at an annual rate of compensation of $12,000, less the reduction prescribed in subparagraph (b), Section 2, Title II, of the Act of Congress entitled "An Act to maintain the credit of the United States Government" (Public No. 2, 73d Congress), approved March 20, 1933.

(2) The Secretary of War, the Secretary of Agriculture, the Secretary of the Interior, and the Secretary of Labor each shall appoint a representative, and said representatives shall constitute an Advisory Council to the Director of Emergency Conservation Work.

(3) There is hereby established in the Treasury a fund of $10,000,000 by the transfer of an equal amount from the unobligated balances of the appropriation for emergency construction of public buildings contained in the act approved July 21, 1932, as authorized by Section 4 of the said Act of March 31, 1933, which fund shall be subject to requisition by the said Robert Fechner, as Director of Emergency Conservation Work, on the approval of the President.

(4) Subject to direction by the President, supplies and materials of the several departments or establishments shall be furnished on the requisition of the Director of Emergency Conservation Work, and the departments and establishments furnishing such supplies and materials shall be reimbursed therefor in accordance with instructions of the President.

(5) Reimbursement, if any, to the departments or establishments for other services rendered shall be made in accordance with instructions of the President.

SOURCE: Roosevelt, Franklin D. 1933. "Executive Order 6101 Relief of Unemployment through the Performance of Useful Public Work." *Executive Orders and Presidential Proclamations, 1933–1936*, Franklin D. Roosevelt Presidential Library & Museum.

ANALYSIS

During his campaign for the presidency of the United States during the Great Depression, Franklin Delano Roosevelt pledged to address the poverty and unemployment that was afflicting large segments of the population. One measure he enacted to honor his promise during his first 100 days in office was the creation of the Civilian Conservation Corps (CCC). It was designed as a short-term relief program to provide jobs to unmarried young men between the ages of 18 and 25 who hailed from families receiving some form of federal relief. Each participant in the program received free room and board, clothes, and a salary of $30 a week. The worker received only $5 of that amount, with the remainder being sent to their family members. In exchange, the participant worked 40 hours a week on projects to improve the environment. Between 1933 and 1942, CCC workers planted more than 2 billion trees, constructed approximate 800 state parks, established more than 12,500 miles of hiking trails, and built approximately 97,000 miles of roads.

The CCC began operation in 1933 with 250,000 enrollees who were sent to work in camps operated by one of three federal departments: the Agricultural Department's Forest Service and Soil Conservation Service; the Department of the Interior's National Park Service; and the War Department. Over the course of the CCC's existence, roughly 2,600 corps camps were established in every state and U.S. territory. The program reached its maximum size in 1935, when it had 500,000 men enrolled. Gradually, enrollments declined as the nation's economy began to improve over the course of the late 1930s. Since the CCC had been created as a temporary measure to alleviate unemployment and poverty, Congress in 1942 determined that it was no longer needed and defunded it through the budget process.

FURTHER READING

Cole, Olen. 1999. *The African-American Experience in the Civilian Conservation Corps*. Gainesville: University Press of Florida.

Kennedy, David M. 1999. *Freedom from Fear: The American People in Depression and War, 1929–1945*. New York: Oxford University Press.

Maher, Neil M. 2007. *Nature's New Deal: The Civilian Conservation Corps and the Roots of the American Environmental Movement*. New York: Oxford University Press.

Mielnik, Tara Mitchell. 2011. *New Deal, New Landscape: The Civilian Conservation Corps and South Carolina's State Parks*. Columbia: University of South Carolina Press.

Speakman, Joseph M. 2006. *At Work in Penn's Woods: The Civilian Conservation Corps in Pennsylvania*. University Park, PA: Pennsylvania State University Press.

Taylor, Dorceta E. 2016. *The Rise of the American Conservation Movement: Power, Privilege, and Environmental Protection*. Durham, NC: Duke University Press.

"To Provide for the Agricultural and Industrial Development of Said Valley"

- ***Document:*** Tennessee Valley Authority Act of 1933
- ***Date:*** May 18, 1933
- ***Where:*** Washington, D.C.
- ***Significance:*** The Tennessee Valley Authority was intended to control flooding along the Tennessee River and its tributaries, provide jobs to residents of the Tennessee Valley, and generate electricity. Its primary objective was to provide cheap electrical power to fuel economic growth in the South.

DOCUMENT

AN ACT

to Improve the Navigability and to Provide for the Flood Control of the Tennessee River: To Provide for Reforestation and the Proper Use of Marginal Lands in the Tennessee Valley; to Provide for the Agricultural and Industrial Development of Said Valley; to Provide for the National Defense by the Creation of a Corporation for the Operation of Government Properties at and Near Muscle Shoals in the State of Alabama, and for Other Purposes May 18, 1933.

Be it enacted by the Senate and House of Representatives of the United States of America in Congress assembled, That for the purpose of maintaining and operating the properties now owned by the United States in the vicinity of Muscle Shoals, Alabama, in the interest of the national defense and for agriculture and industrial development, and to improve navigation in the Tennessee River and to control the destructive flood waters in the Tennessee River and Mississippi River Basins, there is hereby created a body corporate by the name of the "Tennessee Valley

Authority" (hereinafter referred to as the "Corporation"). The board of directors first appointed shall be deemed the incorporators and the incorporation shall be held to have been effected from the date of the first meeting of the board. This Act may be cited as the "Tennessee Valley Authority Act of 1933."

Sec. 2. (a) The board of directors of the Corporation (hereinafter referred to as the "board") shall be composed of three members, to be appointed by the President, by and with the advice and consent of the Senate. In appointing the members of the board, the President shall designate the chairman. All other officials, agents, and employees shall be designated and selected by the board.

. . .

Sec. 4. Except as otherwise specifically provided in this Act, the Corporation—

(a) Shall have succession in its corporate name.

(b) May sue and be sued in its corporate name.

(c) May adopt and use a corporate seal, which shall be judicially noticed.

(d) May make contracts, as herein authorized.

(e) May adopt, amend, and repeal bylaws.

(f) May purchase or lease and hold such real and personal property as it deems necessary or convenient in the transaction of its business, and may dispose of any such personal property held by it.

. . .

(g) Shall have such powers as may be necessary or appropriate for the exercise of the powers herein specifically conferred upon the Corporation.

(h) Shall have power in the name of the United States of America to exercise the right of eminent domain, and in the purchase of any real estate or the condemnation of real estate by condemnation proceedings, the title to such real estate shall be taken in the name of the United States of America, and thereupon all such real estate shall be entrusted to the Corporation as the agent of the United States to accomplish the purposes of this Act.

(i) Shall have power to acquire real estate for the construction of dams, reservoirs, transmission lines, power houses, and other structures, and navigation projects at any point along the Tennessee River, or any of its tributaries, and in the event that the owner or owners of such property shall fail and refuse to sell to the Corporation at a price deemed fair and reasonable by the board, then the Corporation may proceed to exercise the right of eminent domain, and to condemn all property that it deems necessary for carrying out the purposes of this Act, and all such condemnation proceedings shall be had pursuant to the provisions and requirements hereinafter specified, with reference to any and all condemnation proceedings.

(i) Shall have power to construct dams, reservoirs, power houses, power structures, transmission lines, navigation projects, and incidental works in the Tennessee River and its tributaries, and to unite the various power installations into one or more systems by transmission lines.

Sec. 5. The board is hereby authorized—

(a) To contract with commercial producers for the production of such fertilizers or fertilizer materials as may be needed in the Government's program of development and introduction in excess of that produced by Government plants. Such contracts may provide either for outright purchase of materials by the board or only for the payment of carrying charges on special materials manufactured at the board's request for its program.

(b) To arrange with farmers and farm organizations for large scale practical use of the new forms of fertilizers under conditions permitting an accurate measure of the economic return they produce.

(c) To cooperate with National, State, district, or county experimental stations or demonstration farms, for the use of new forms of fertilizer or fertilizer practices during the initial or experimental period of their introduction.

(d) The board in order to improve and cheapen the production of fertilizer is authorized to manufacture and sell fixed nitrogen, fertilizer, and fertilizer ingredients at Muscle Shoals by the employment of existing facilities, by modernizing existing plants, or by any other process or processes that in its judgment shall appear wise and profitable for the fixation of atmospheric nitrogen or the cheapening of the production of fertilizer.

(e) Under the authority of this Act the board may make donations or sales of the product of the plant or plants operated by it to be fairly and equitably distributed through the agency of county demonstration agents, agricultural colleges, or otherwise as the board may direct, for experimentation, education, and introduction of the use of such products in cooperation with practical farmers so as to obtain information as to the value, effect, and best methods of their use.

(f) The board is authorized to make alterations, modifications, or improvements in existing plants and facilities, and to construct new plants.

(g) In the event it is not used for the fixation of nitrogen for agricultural purposes or leased, then the board shall maintain in stand-by condition nitrate plant numbered 2, or its equivalent, for the fixation of atmospheric nitrogen, for the production of explosives in the event of war or a national emergency until the Congress shall by joint resolution release the board from this obligation, and if any part thereof be used by the board for the manufacture or phosphoric acid or potash, the balance of nitrate plant numbered 2 shall be kept in stand-by condition.

(h) To establish, maintain, and operate laboratories and experimental plants, and to undertake experiments for the purpose of enabling the Corporation to furnish nitrogen products for military purposes, and nitrogen and other fertilizer products for agricultural purposes in the most economical manner and at the highest standard of efficiency.

(i) To request the assistance and advice of any officer, agent, or employee of any executive department or of any independent office of the United States, to enable the Corporation the better to carry out its powers successfully, and as far as practicable shall utilize the services of such officers, agents, and employees, and the President shall, if in his opinion, the public interest, service, or economy so require, direct that such assistance, advice, and service be rendered to the Corporation, and any individual that may be by the President directed to render such assistance, advice, and service shall be thereafter subject to the orders, rules, and regulations of the board: Provided, That any invention or discovery made by virtue of and incidental to such service by an employee of the Government of the United States serving under this section, or by any employee of the Corporation, together with any patents which may be granted thereon, shall be the sole and exclusive property of the Corporation, which is hereby authorized to grant licenses thereunder as shall be authorized by the board: Provided further, That the board may pay to such inventor such sum from the income from sale of licenses as it may deem proper.

(j) Upon the requisition of the Secretary of War or the Secretary of the Navy to manufacture for and sell at cost to the United States explosives or their nitrogenous content.

(k) Upon the requisition of the Secretary of War the Corporation shall allot and deliver without charge to the War Department so much power as shall be necessary in the judgment of said Department for use in operation of all locks, lifts, or other facilities in aid of navigation.

(l) To produce, distribute, and sell electric power, as herein particularly specified.

(m) No products of the Corporation shall be sold for use outside of the United States, its Territories and possessions, except to the United States Government for the use of its Army and Navy, or to its allies in case of war.

(n) The President is authorized, within twelve months after the passage of this Act, to lease to any responsible farm organization or to any corporation organized by it nitrate plant number 2 and Waco Quarry, together with the railroad connecting said quarry with nitrate plant number 2, for a term not exceeding fifty years at a rental of not less than $1 per year, but such authority shall be subject to the express condition that the lessee shall use said property during the term of said lease exclusively for the manufacture of fertilizer and fertilizer ingredients to be used only in the manufacture of fertilizer by said lessee and sold for use as fertilizer. The said lessee shall covenant to keep said property in first-class condition, but the lessee shall be authorized to modernize said plant numbered 2 by the installation of such machinery as may be necessary, and is authorized to amortize the cost of said machinery and improvements over the term of said lease or any part thereof. Said lease shall also provide that the board shall sell to the lessee power for the operation of said plant at the same schedule of prices that it charges all other customers for power of the same class and quantity. Said lease shall also provide that if the said lessee does not desire to buy power of the publicly owned plant it shall have the right to purchase power for the operation of said plant of the Alabama Power Company or any other publicly or privately owned corporation engaged in the generation and sale of electrical power, and in such case the lease shall provide further that the said lessee shall have a free right of way to build a transmission line over Government property to said plant paying the actual expenses and damages, if any, incurred by the Corporation on account of such line. Said lease shall also provide that the said lessee shall covenant that during the term of said lease the said lessee shall not enter into any illegal monopoly, combination, or trust with any privately owned corporation engaged in the manufacture, production, and sale of fertilizer with the object or effect of increasing the price of fertilizer to the farmer.

. . .

Sec. 10. The board is hereby empowered and authorized to sell the surplus power not used in its operations, and for operation of locks and other works generated by it, to States, counties, municipalities, corporations, partnerships, or individuals, according to the policies hereinafter set forth- and to carry out said authority, the board is authorized to enter into contracts for such sale for a term not exceeding twenty years, and in the sale of such current by the board it shall give preference to States, counties, municipalities, and cooperative organizations of citizens or farmers, not organized or doing business for profit, but primarily for the purpose of supplying electricity to its own citizens or members: Provided, That all contracts made with private companies or individuals for the sale of power, which is to be resold for a profit, shall contain a provision authorizing the board to cancel said contract upon five years' notice in writing, if the board needs said power to supply the demands of States, counties, or municipalities. In order to promote and encourage the fullest possible use of electric light and power on farms within reasonable distance of any of its transmission lines the board in its discretion shall have power to construct transmission lines to farms and small villages that are not otherwise supplied with electricity at reasonable rates, and to make such rules and regulations governing such sale and distribution of such electric power as in its judgment may be just and equitable:. . . .

Sec. 11. It is hereby declared to be the policy of the Government so far as practical to distribute and sell the surplus power generated at Muscle Shoals equitably among the States, counties, and municipalities within transmission distance. This policy is further declared to be that the projects herein provided for shall be considered primarily as for the benefit of the people of the section as a whole and particularly the domestic and rural consumers to whom the power can economically be made available, and accordingly that sale to and use by industry shall be a secondary purpose, to be utilized principally to secure a sufficiently high load factor and revenue returns which will permit domestic and rural use at the lowest possible rates and in such manner as to encourage increased domestic and rural use of electricity. It is further hereby declared to be the policy of the Government to utilize the Muscle Shoals properties so far as may be necessary to improve, increase, and cheapen the production of fertilizer and fertilizer ingredients by carrying out the provisions of this Act.

. . .

Sec. 18. In order to enable and empower the Secretary of War, the Secretary of the Interior, or the board to carry out the authority hereby conferred, in the most economical and efficient manner, he or it is hereby authorized and empowered in the exercise of the powers of national defense in aid of navigation, and in the control of the flood waters of the Tennessee and Mississippi Rivers, constituting channels of interstate commerce, to exercise the right of eminent domain for all purposes of this Act, and to condemn all lands, easements, rights of way, and other area necessary in order to obtain a site for said Cove Creek Dam, and the flowage rights for the reservoir of water above said dam, and to negotiate and conclude contracts with States, counties, municipalities, and all State agencies and with railroads, railroad corporations, common carriers, and all public utility commissions and any other person, firm or corporation, for the relocation of railroad tracks, highways, highway bridges, mills, ferries, electric-light plants, and any and all other properties, enterprises, and projects whose removal may be necessary in order to carry out the provisions of this Act. When said Cove Creek Dam, transmission line, and power house shall have been completed, the possession, use, and control thereof shall be intrusted to the Corporation for use and operation in connection with the general

Tennessee Valley project, and to promote flood control and navigation in the Tennessee River.

. . .

Sec. 22. To aid further the proper use, conservation, and development of the natural resources of the Tennessee River drainage basin and of such adjoining territory as may be related to or materially affected by the development consequent to this Act, and to provide for the general welfare of the citizens of said areas, the President is hereby authorized, by such means or methods as he may deem proper within the limits of appropriations made therefor by Congress, to make such surveys of and general plans for said Tennessee basin and adjoining territory as may be useful to the Congress and to the several States in guiding and controlling the extent, sequence, and nature of development that may be equitably and economically advanced through the expenditure of public funds, or through the guidance or control of public authority, all for the general purpose of fostering an orderly and proper physical, economic, and social development of said areas; and the President is further authorized in making said surveys and plans to cooperate with the States affected thereby, or subdivisions or agencies of such States, or with cooperative or other organizations, and to make such studies, experiments, or demonstrations as may be necessary and suitable to that end.

Sec. 23. The President shall, from time to time, as the work provided for in the preceding section progresses, recommend to Congress such legislation as he deems proper to carry out the general purposes stated in said section, and for the especial purpose of bringing about in said Tennessee drainage basin and adjoining territory in conformity with said general purposes (1) the maximum amount of flood control; (2) the maximum development of said Tennessee River for navigation purposes; (3) the maximum generation of electric power consistent with flood control and navigation; (4) the proper use of marginal lands; (5) the proper method of reforestation of all lands in said drainage basin suitable for reforestation; and (6) the economic and social well-being of the people living in said river basin.

Sec. 24. For the purpose of securing any rights of flowage, or obtaining title to or possession of any property, real or personal, that may be necessary or may become necessary, in the carrying out of any of the provisions of this Act, the President of the United States for a period of three years from the date of the enactment of this Act, is hereby authorized to acquire title in the name of the United States to such rights or such property, and to provide for the payment for same by directing the board to contract to deliver power generated at any of the plants now owned or hereafter owned or constructed by the Government or by said Corporation, such future delivery of power to continue for a period not exceeding thirty years. Likewise, for one year after the enactment of this Act, the President is further authorized to sell or lease any parcel or part of any vacant real estate now owned by the Government in said Tennessee River Basin, to persons, firms, or corporations who shall contract to erect thereon factories or manufacturing establishments, and who shall contract to purchase of said Corporation electric power for the operation of any such factory or manufacturing establishment. No contract shall be made by the President for the sale of any of such real estate as may be necessary for present or future use on the part of the Government for any of the purposes of this Act. Any such contract made by the President of the United States shall be carried out by the board: Provided, That no such contract shall be made that will in any way abridge or take away the preference right to purchase power given in this Act to States, counties, municipalities, or farm organizations: Provided further, That no lease shall be for a term to exceed fifty years: Provided further, That any sale shall be on condition that said land shall be used for industrial purposes only.

Sec. 25. The Corporation may cause proceedings to be instituted for the acquisition by condemnation of any lands, easements, or rights of way which, in the opinion of the Corporation, are necessary to carry out the provisions of this Act. The proceedings shall be instituted in the United States district court for the district in which the land, easement, right of way, or other interest, or any part thereof, is located, and such court shall have full jurisdiction to divest the complete title to the property sought to be acquired out of all persons or claimants and vest the same in the United States in fee simple, and to enter a decree quieting the title thereto in the United States of America.

Upon the filing of a petition for condemnation and for the purpose of ascertaining the value of the property to be acquired, and assessing the compensation to be paid, the court shall appoint three commissioners who shall be disinterested persons and who shall take and subscribe an oath that they do not own any lands, or interest or easement in any lands, which it may be desirable for the United States to acquire in the furtherance of said project and such commissioners shall not be selected from the locality wherein the land sought to be condemned lies. Such commissioners shall receive a per diem of not to exceed $15 for their services, together with an additional amount of $5 per day for subsistence for time actually spent in performing their duties as commissioners.

It shall be the duty of such commissioners to examine into the value of the lands sought to be condemned, to conduct hearings and receive evidence, and generally to take such appropriate steps as may be proper for the determination of the value of the said lands sought to be condemned, and for such purpose the commissioners are authorized to administer oaths and subpoena witnesses, which said witnesses shall receive the same fees as are provided for witnesses in the Federal courts. The said commissioners shall thereupon file a report setting forth their conclusions as to the value of the said property sought to be condemned, making a separate award and valuation in the premises with respect to each separate parcel involved. Upon the filing of such award in court the clerk of said court shall give notice of the filing of such award to the parties to said proceeding, in manner and form as directed by the judge of said court.

Either or both parties may file exceptions to the award of said commissioners within twenty days from the date of the filing of said award in court. Exceptions filed to such award shall be heard before three Federal district judges unless the parties, in writing, in person, or by their attorneys, stipulate that the exceptions may be heard before a lesser number of judges. On such hearing such judges shall pass de novo upon the proceedings had before the commissioners, may view the property, and may take additional evidence. Upon such hearings the said judges shall file their own award, fixing therein the value of the property sought to be condemned, regardless of the award previously made by the said commissioners.

. . .

Sec. 30. The sections of this Act are hereby declared to be separable, and in the event any one or more sections of this Act be held to be unconstitutional, the same shall not affect the validity of other sections of this Act. Approved, May 18, 1933.

SOURCE: Seventy-Third Congress of the United States. 1933. *An Act to Improve the Navigability and to Provide for the Flood Control of the Tennessee River; to Provide for Reforestation and the Proper Use of Marginal Lands in the Tennessee Valley; to Provide for the Agricultural and Industrial Development of Said Valley; to Provide for the National Defense by the Creation of a Corporation for the Operation of Government Properties at and Near Muscle Shoals in the State of Alabama, and for Other Purposes, May 18, 1933.* Enrolled Acts and Resolutions of Congress, 1789–1996; General Records of the U.S. Government; Record Group 11, National Archives.

ANALYSIS

The Tennessee Valley Authority Act of 1933 created the Tennessee Valley Authority (TVA) to oversee flood control projects on the Tennessee River and its tributaries, the nation's fifth largest river system. The corporation was also charged with overseeing economic development projects on the Tennessee River's watershed. If the regional development efforts proved effective in Appalachia, federal officials planned on using it as a model for the development of other regions in the nation.

Federal interest in the Tennessee River had dated to the onset of World War I. The military required a source of nitrate for munitions and explosives. In 1918, two plants were constructed by the government at Muscle Shoals in northern Alabama for the production of the substance. Also constructed was Wilson Dam, which produced the hydroelectric power required for the nitrate production. Although the end of the war saw an end to the need for massive amounts of nitrate, Congress remained enamored with the idea of improving the Tennessee River. In both 1928 and 1931, senator George Norris of Nebraska saw bills he sponsored to construct dams on the river pass Congress only to be vetoed by the president.

The Tennessee Valley Authority Act of 1933 called for the construction of dams along the expanse of the Tennessee River. The project promised to provide jobs in a region desperately in need of them, make fertilizer for farmers, generate electricity where access to that power source had previously not been available, control flooding, and allow for commercial navigation along the river's length to its confluence with the Ohio River. In total, the legislation touched more than 40,000 miles in the states of Alabama, Georgia, Kentucky, Mississippi, North Carolina, Tennessee, and Virginia. Twelve dams were constructed by the 1950s, which brought electricity to approximately 90 percent of the Tennessee Valley's residents. The availability of cheap power also attracted lots of industry, thereby providing jobs for a great number of people.

The arrival of the TVA was not a panacea for everyone. The construction of dams meant the inundation of a significant amount of the best agricultural land in the Tennessee Valley. TVA officials bought land from local farmers at extremely low prices since people desperately needed money due to the Great Depression and thus were not in the position to bargain for a better price. Those that did not want to sell their land were forced to anyway. Thus, the "dispossessed" lost the ability to provide for their families in the manner that their ancestors had for generations. Their compensation was so low that they could not buy comparable land elsewhere. The TVA was ultimately forced to resettle some of those it harmed in model communities such as Norris, Tennessee, named in honor of senator George Norris. Many more out-migrated to northern cities, such as Chicago, Illinois; Cincinnati, Ohio; and Detroit, Michigan; where they found employment in factories.

The problems of African Americans living in the Tennessee Valley were exacerbated by the arrival of the TVA. This was due to the TVA's political needs at both the local and the federal levels. Assisting the African American community in any manner was guaranteed to draw the ire of southern politicians. The TVA not only denied African Americans jobs but also access to their products, like fertilizer.

World War II in many ways changed the focus of the TVA from developing the economic infrastructure of the region to supporting the war effort. Approximately 70 percent of the monies spent by the TVA during the war years were on defense industries, most notably the Oak Ridge, Tennessee, secret city whose workers were heavily involved in the Manhattan Project. After the conclusion of World War II, the TVA continued its work in the development of atomic power. This research culminated in the 1960s with the TVA building nuclear power plants in the Tennessee Valley. By this point in time, the TVA had become the leading producer of public power in the United States.

The TVA proved to be a mixed blessing for the Appalachians residing in the TVA's service area. The availability of power certainly raised the standard of living in the region and improved the local economy. It also fueled the growth of cities such as Knoxville and Chattanooga in Tennessee. The creation of many reservoirs provided recreational opportunities that attracted people from outside the region, thereby stimulating the tourism industry. Unfortunately, it also destroyed tight-knit communities and forced many to leave the region permanently. Although the TVA more than met some of the objectives set forth by the federal government when it enacted the Tennessee Valley Authority Act of 1933, it was not an effort that was duplicated elsewhere in the United States. In retrospect, the environmental and social costs of the TVA outweighed its economic benefits in the eyes of many U.S. citizens.

FURTHER READING

Creese, Walter L. 1990. *TVA's Public Planning: The Vision, the Reality*. Knoxville: University of Tennessee Press.

Foresta, Ronald A. 2013. *The Land between the Lakes: A Geography of a Forgotten Future*. Knoxville: University of Tennessee Press.

Grant, Nancy. 1990. *TVA and Black Americans*. Philadelphia: Temple University Press.

Hargrove, Erwin C. 2001. *Prisoners of Myth: The Leadership of the Tennessee Valley Authority, 1933–1990*. Knoxville: University of Tennessee Press.

Hubbard, Preston J. 1961. *Origins of the TVA: The Muscle Shoals Controversy, 1920–1932*. Nashville: Vanderbilt University Press.

McDonald, Michael J., and John Muldowny. 1981. *TVA and the Dispossessed: The Resettlement of Population in the Norris Dam Area*. Knoxville: University of Tennessee Press.

Purcell, Aaron D. 2009. *White Collar Radicals: TVA's Knoxville Fifteen, the New Deal, and the McCarthy Era*. Knoxville: University of Tennessee Press.

Taylor, Stephen Wallace. 2001. *The New South's New Frontier: A Social History of Economic Development in Southwestern North Carolina*. Gainesville: University Press of Florida.

Wheeler, William Bruce, and Michael J. McDonald. 1986. *TVA and the Tellico Dam: A Bureaucratic Crisis in Post-Industrial America*. Knoxville: University of Tennessee Press.

Whisnant, David E. 1994. *Modernizing the Mountaineer: People, Power, and Planning in Appalachia*, rev. ed. Knoxville: University of Tennessee Press.

"An Act to Provide for the General Welfare"

- ***Document:*** Social Security Act of 1935 (Excerpts)
- ***Date:*** August 14, 1935
- ***Where:*** Washington, D.C.
- ***Significance:*** The Social Security Act is one of the most far-reaching pieces of legislation enacted in the history of the United States. It created the Social Security Board, which was charged with the provision of old-age insurance, payments to the unemployed, assisting with the care of the blind and the homeless, and aid to crippled and delinquent children.

DOCUMENT

An act to provide for the general welfare by establishing a system of Federal old-age benefits, and by enabling the several States to make more adequate provision for aged persons, blind persons, dependent and crippled children, maternal and child welfare, public health, and the administration of their unemployment compensation laws; to establish a Social Security Board; to raise revenue; and for other purposes.

Be it enacted by the Senate and House of Representatives of the United States of America in Congress assembled,

TITLE I—GRANTS TO STATES FOR OLD-AGE ASSISTANCE

APPROPRIATION

SECTION 1. For the purpose of enabling each State to furnish financial assistance, as far as practicable under the conditions in such State, to aged needy individuals, there is hereby authorized to be appropriated for the fiscal year ended June 30, 1936, the sum of $49,750,000, and there is hereby authorized to be appropriated for each fiscal year thereafter a sum sufficient to carry out the purposes of this title. The sums made available under this section shall be used for making payments to States which have submitted, and had approved by the Social Security Board established by Title VII (hereinafter referred to as the Board), State plans for old-age assistance.

STATE OLD-AGE ASSISTANCE PLANS

SEC. 2. (a) A State plan for old-age assistance must

(1) provide that it shall be in effect in all political subdivisions of the State, and, if administered by them, be mandatory upon them;

(2) provide for financial participation by the State;

(3) either provide for the establishment or designation of a single State agency to administer the plan, or provide for the establishment or designation of a single State agency to supervise the administration of the plan;

(4) provide for granting to any individual, whose claim for old-age assistance is denied, an opportunity for a fair hearing before such State agency;

(5) provide such methods of administration (other than those relating to selection, tenure of office, and compensation of personnel) as are found by the Board to be necessary for the efficient operation of the plan;

(6) provide that the State agency will make such reports, in such form and containing such information, as the Board may from time to time require, and comply with such provisions as the Board may from time to time find necessary to assure the correctness and verification of such reports; and

(7) provide that, if the State or any of its political subdivisions collects from the estate of any recipient of old-age assistance any amount with respect to old-age assistance furnished him under the plan, one- half of the net amount so collected shall be promptly paid to the United States. Any payment so made shall be deposited in the Treasury to the credit of the appropriation for the purposes of this title.

(b) The Board shall approve any plan which fulfills the conditions specified in subsection (a), except that it shall not approve any plan which imposes, as a condition of eligibility for old-age assistance under the plan—

(1) An age requirement of more than sixty-five years, except that the plan may impose, effective until January 1, 1940, an age requirement of as much as seventy years; or

(2) Any residence requirement which excludes any resident of the State who has resided therein five years during the nine years immediately preceding the application for old-age assistance and has resided therein continuously for one year immediately preceding the application; or (3) Any citizenship requirement which excludes any citizen of the United States.

. . .

TITLE II—FEDERAL OLD-AGE BENEFITS OLD-AGE RESERVE ACCOUNT

Section 201. (a) There is hereby created an account in the Treasury of the United States to be known as the Old-Age Reserve Account hereinafter in this title called the Account. There is hereby authorized to be appropriated to the Account for each fiscal year, beginning with the fiscal year ending June 30, 1937, an amount sufficient as an annual premium to provide for the payments required under this title, such amount to be determined on a reserve basis in accordance with accepted actuarial principles, and based upon such tables of mortality as the Secretary of the Treasury shall from time to time adopt, and upon an interest rate of 3 per centum per annum compounded annually. The Secretary of the Treasury shall submit annually to the Bureau of the Budget an estimate of the appropriations to be made to the Account.

(b) It shall be the duty of the Secretary of the Treasury to invest such portion of the amounts credited to the Account as is not, in his judgment, required to meet current withdrawals. Such investment may be made only in interest-bearing obligations of the United States or in obligations guaranteed as to both principal and interest by the United States. For such purpose such obligations may be acquired

(1) on original issue at par, or

(2) by purchase of outstanding obligations at the market price. The purposes for which obligations of the United States may be issued under the Second Liberty Bond Act, as amended, are hereby extended to authorize the issuance at par of special obligations exclusively to the Account. Such special obligations shall bear interest at the rate of 3 per centum per annum. Obligations other than such special obligations may be acquired for the Account only on such terms as to provide an investment yield of not less than 3 per centum per annum.

(c) Any obligations acquired by the Account (except special obligations issued exclusively to the Account) may be sold at the market price, and such special obligations may be redeemed at par plus accrued interest.

(d) The interest on, and the proceeds from the sale or redemption of, any obligations held in the Account shall be credited to and form a part of the Account.

(e) All amounts credited to the Account shall be available for making payments required under this title.

(f) The Secretary of the Treasury shall include in his annual report the actuarial status of the Account.

. . .

TITLE III—GRANTS TO STATES FOR UNEMPLOYMENT COMPENSATION ADMINISTRATION APPROPRIATION

SECTION 301. For the purpose of assisting the States in the administration of their unemployment compensation laws, there is hereby authorized to be appropriated, for the fiscal year ending June 30, 1936, the sum of $4,000,000, and for each fiscal year thereafter the sum of $49,000,000, to be used as hereinafter provided.

. . .

TITLE IV—GRANTS TO STATES FOR AID TO DEPENDENT CHILDREN APPROPRIATION

SECTION 401. For the purpose of enabling each State to furnish financial assistance, as far as practicable under the conditions in such State, to needy dependent children, there is hereby authorized to be appropriated for the fiscal year ending June 30, 1936, the sum of $24,750,000, and there is hereby authorized to be appropriated for each fiscal year thereafter a sum sufficient to carry out the purposes of this title. The sums made available under this section shall be used for making payments to States which have submitted, and had approved by the Board, State plans for aid to dependent children.

. . .

TITLE V—GRANTS TO STATES FOR MATERNAL AND CHILD WELFARE

PART 1—MATERNAL AND CHILD HEALTH SERVICES

APPROPRIATION

SECTION 501. For the purpose of enabling each State to extend and improve, as far as practicable under the conditions in such State, services for promoting the health of mothers and children, especially in rural areas and in areas suffering from severe economic distress, there is hereby authorized to be appropriated for each fiscal year, beginning with the fiscal year ending June 30, 1936, the sum of $3,800,000. The sums made available under this section shall be used for making payments to States which have submitted, and had approved by the Chief of the Children s Bureau, State plans for such services.

. . .

PART 2—SERVICES FOR CRIPPLED CHILDREN

APPROPRIATION

SEC. 511. For the purpose of enabling each State to extend and improve (especially in rural areas and in areas suffering from severe economic distress), as far as practicable under the conditions in such State, services for locating crippled children and for providing medical, surgical, corrective, and other services and care, and facilities for diagnosis, hospitalization, and aftercare, for children who are crippled or who are suffering from conditions which lead to crippling, there is hereby authorized to be appropriated for each fiscal year beginning with the fiscal year ending June 30, 1936, the sum of $2,850,000. The sums made available under this section shall be used for making payments to States which have submitted, and had approved by the Chief of the Children s Bureau, State plans for such services.

. . .

PART 3—CHILD WELFARE SERVICES

SEC. 521. (a) For the purpose of enabling the United States, through the Children s Bureau, to cooperate with State public-welfare agencies establishing, extending, and strengthening, especially in predominantly rural areas, public-welfare services (hereinafter in this section referred to as child-welfare services) for the protection and care of homeless, dependent, and neglected children, and children in danger of becoming delinquent, there is hereby authorized to be appropriated for each fiscal year, beginning with the year ending June 30, 1936, the sum of $1,500,000. Such amount shall be allotted by the Secretary of Labor for use by cooperating State public- welfare agencies on the basis of plans developed jointly by the State agency and the Children s Bureau, to each State, $10,000, and the remainder to each State on the basis of such plans, not to exceed such part of the remainder as the rural population of such State bears to the total rural population of the United States. The amount so allotted shall be expended for payment of part of the cost of district, county or other local child- welfare services in areas predominantly rural, and for developing State services for the encouragement and assistance of adequate methods of community child-welfare organization in areas predominantly rural and other areas of special need. The amount of any allotment to a State under this section for any fiscal year remaining unpaid to such State at the end of such fiscal year shall be available for payment to such State under this section until the end of the second succeeding fiscal year. No payment to a State under this section shall be made out of its allotment for any fiscal year until its allotment for the preceding fiscal year has been exhausted or has ceased to be available.

(b) From the sums appropriated therefor and the allotments available under subsection (a) the Secretary of Labor shall from time to time certify to the Secretary of the Treasury the amounts to be paid to the States, and the Secretary of the Treasury shall, through the Division of Disbursement of the Treasury Department and prior to audit or settlement by the General Accounting Office, make payments of such amounts from such allotments at the time or times specified by the Secretary of Labor.

PART 4—VOCATIONAL REHABILITATION

SEC. 531. (a) In order to enable the United States to cooperate with the States and Hawaii in extending and strengthening their programs of vocational rehabilitation of the physically disabled, and to continue to carry out the provisions and purposes of the Act entitled An Act to provide for the promotion of vocational rehabilitation of persons disabled in industry or otherwise and their return to civil employment, approved June 2, 1920, as amended (U.S.C., title 29, ch. 4; U.S.C., Supp. VII title 29, secs. 31, 32, 34, 35, 37, 39, and 40), there is hereby authorized to be appropriated for the fiscal years ending June 30, 1936, and June 30, 1937, the sum of $841,000 for each such fiscal year in addition to the amount of the existing authorization, and for each fiscal year thereafter the sum of $1,938,000. Of the sums appropriated pursuant to such authorization for each fiscal year, $5,000 shall be apportioned to the Territory of Hawaii and the remainder shall be apportioned among the several States in the manner provided in such Act of June 2, 1920, as amended.

(b) For the administration of such Act of June 2, 1920, as amended, by the Federal agency authorized to administer it, there is hereby authorized to be appropriated for the fiscal years ending June 30, 1936, and June 30, 1937, the sum of $22,000 for each such fiscal year in addition to the amount of the existing authorization, and for each fiscal year thereafter the sum of $102,000.

. . .

TITLE VI—PUBLIC HEALTH WORK APPROPRIATION

SECTION 601. For the purpose of assisting States, counties, health districts, and other political subdivisions of the States in establishing and maintaining adequate public-health services, including the training of personnel for State and local health work, there is hereby authorized to be appropriated for each fiscal year, beginning with the fiscal year ending June 30, 1936, the sum of $8,000,000 to be used as hereinafter provided.

. . .

TITLE VII—SOCIAL SECURITY BOARD ESTABLISHMENT

SECTION 701. There is hereby established a Social Security Board (in this Act referred to as the Board) to be composed of three members to be appointed by the President, by and with the advice and consent of the Senate. During his term of membership on the Board, no member shall engage in any other business, vocation, or employment. Not more than two of the members of the Board shall be members of the same political party. Each member shall receive a salary at the rate of $10,000 a year and shall hold office for a term of six years, except that

(1) any member appointed to fill a vacancy occurring prior to the expiration of the term for which his predecessor was appointed, shall be appointed for the remainder of such term; and

(2) the terms of office of the members first taking office after the date of the enactment of this Act shall expire, as designated by the President at the time of appointment, one at the end of two years, one at the end of four years, and one at the end of six years, after the date of the enactment of this Act. The President shall designate one of the members as the chairman of the Board.

DUTIES OF THE SOCIAL SECURITY BOARD

SEC. 702. The Board shall perform the duties imposed upon it by this Act and shall also have the duty of studying and making recommendations as to the most effective methods of providing economic security through social insurance, and as to legislation and matters of administrative policy concerning old-age pensions, unemployment compensation, accident compensation, and related subjects.

. . .

TITLE VIII—TAXES WITH RESPECT TO EMPLOYMENT

INCOME TAX ON EMPLOYEES

SECTION 801. In addition to other taxes, there shall be levied, collected, and paid upon the income of every individual a tax equal to the following percentages of the wages (as defined in section 811) received by him after December 31, 1936, with respect to employment (as defined in section 811) after such date:

(1) With respect to employment during the calendar years 1937, 1938, and 1939, the rate shall be 1 per centum.

(2) With respect to employment during the calendar years 1940, 1941, and 1942, the rate shall 1 per centum.

(3) With respect to employment during the calendar years 1943, 1944, and 1945, the rate shall be 2 per centum.

(4) With respect to employment during the calendar years 1946, 1947, and 1948, the rate shall be 2 per centum.

(5) With respect to employment after December 31, 1948, the rate shall be 3 per centum.

. . .

TITLE IX—TAX ON EMPLOYERS OF EIGHT OR MORE

IMPOSITION OF TAX

SECTION 901. On and after January 1, 1936, every employer (as defined in section 907) shall pay for each calendar year an excise tax, with respect to having individuals in his employ, equal to the following percentages of the total wages (as defined in section 907) payable by him (regardless of the time of payment) with respect to employment (as defined in section 907) during such calendar year:

(1) With respect to employment during the calendar year 1936 the rate shall be 1 per centum;

(2) With respect to employment during the calendar year 1937 the rate shall be 2 per centum;

(3) With respect to employment after December 31, 1937, the rate shall be 3 per centum.

. . .

TITLE X—GRANTS TO STATES FOR AID TO THE BLIND APPROPRIATION

SECTION 1001. For the purpose of enabling each State to furnish financial assistance, as far as practicable under the conditions in such State, to needy individuals who are blind, there is hereby authorized to be appropriated for the fiscal year ending June 30, 1936, the sum of $3,000,000, and there is hereby authorized to be appropriated for each fiscal year thereafter a sum sufficient to carry out the purposes of this title. The sums made available under this section shall be used for making payments to States which have submitted, and had approved by the Social Security Board, State plans for aid to the blind.

. . .

TITLE XI—GENERAL PROVISIONS

SOURCE: Social Security Act of 1935, Public Law 74-271, *U.S. Statutes at Large*, 49 (1935): 620.

ANALYSIS

Reformers throughout the Progressive Era had called for the federal government to create an old-age pension system modeled on programs instituted in Europe but to no avail. The government believed that the responsibility for the care of the elderly, sickly, and homeless was vested in private charities and the states. In 1920, the U.S. Congress took a tentative step toward federal responsibility for public welfare through the creation of pensions for federal employees. That was soon followed in 1921 by the Sheppard-Towner Act (STA), which provided for the care of mothers and infants. The STA required the states that participated in the program to match the federal contribution on a dollar-to-dollar basis. Federal planners did not see the program as a move away from the private charities and state models for welfare since the respective states were responsible for the provision of services within their borders.

It was the Great Depression that demonstrated the inadequacy of the dependence on private charities and the states to provide for those in need. There were simply too many individuals unemployed who could not provide for their families. The economic collapse also exacerbated the financial issues faced by the elderly. Although some states, most notably New York, created programs to help meet the needs of the unemployed and/or the elderly, pressure grew on the federal government to bring its resources to bear.

The ascension of Franklin D. Roosevelt to the presidency gave hope to proponents of old-age pensions since, as governor of New York, his administration had created such a program for the state in 1929. It was not until 1934 that his administration, led by Frances Perkins, began putting together a social welfare program through the Committee on Economic Security to address the needs of not only the elderly, but also the unemployed, and individuals unable to care for themselves. Their work resulted in the Social Security Act of 1935 (SSA).

The SSA provided the states that opted to participate up to $15 in matching funds for each elderly person, which was defined as a person over 65, receiving benefits. Many states that participated did not have enough revenue to match up to the federal maximum, so their elderly received a lesser portion than peers in other parts of the country. A number of southern states refused to participate in the program at all since they did not want to pay benefits to African Americans. Critics assailed the benefit level as far too meager to make a difference. Dr. Francis Townsend, who had campaigned around the nation for a monthly payment of $200, was particularly hostile to the new program. Despite the criticisms, the SSA proved transformational in that it established a right of employees to retire at 65. Furthermore, the retiree was entitled to receive a pension from the "Old-Age Reserve Account." To ensure the solvency for future retirees, most companies were required to contribute 0.5 percent of the first $3,000 an employee earned into the account.

The SSA also addressed other groups that were suffering as a result of the Great Depression. For the unemployed, the SSA created a federal–state initiative to provide unemployment insurance. This measure was also funded by employers through a tax on their payrolls. Title IV provided funding to the states to assist dependent children. Title V provided funding to meet the need of health needs of mothers, their children, and the crippled. In addition, it included funding for the provision of child welfare services, particularly in rural areas, and vocational rehabilitation. Services for the blind were addressed in Title X.

The constitutionality of the SSA was challenged by a shareholder of Edison Electric Illuminating Company. His profits in the company were being reduced because of the taxes employers were being forced to pay to provide for the elderly and unemployed. The U.S. Supreme Court in the 1937 case *Helvering v. Davis* ruled against the shareholder. In a 7–2 vote, the justices determined that the SSA was constitutional because the "general welfare" of the nation, as defined by Congress, outweighed individual interests.

FURTHER READING

Béland, Daniel. 2005. *Social Security: History and Politics from the New Deal to the Privatization Debate*. Lawrence: University Press of Kansas.

Daniels, Roger. 2015. *Franklin D. Roosevelt: Road to the New Deal, 1882–1939*. Champaign: University of Illinois Press.

DeWitt, Larry. 2010. "The Development of Social Security in America." *Social Security Bulletin* 70, no. 1: 1–26.

Domhoff, G. William, and Michael J. Webber. 2011. *Class and Power in the New Deal: Corporate Moderates, Southern Democrats, and the Liberal-Labor Coalition*. Palo Alto: Stanford University Press.

Kennedy, David M. 1999. *Freedom from Fear: The American People in Depression and War, 1929–1945*. New York: Oxford University Press.

Tani, Karen M. 2016. *States of Dependency: Welfare, Rights, and American Governance, 1935–1972*. New York: Cambridge University Press.

"To Provide for the Establishment of Fair Labor Standards in Employments in and Affecting Interstate Commerce"

- ***Document:*** Fair Labor Standards Act of 1938 (Excerpts)
- ***Date:*** June 25, 1938
- ***Where:*** Washington, D.C.
- ***Significance:*** The act required any business involved in interstate commerce to pay a minimum wage and to follow limits on the number of hours an employee could work in a given week.

DOCUMENT

AN ACT

To provide for the establishment of fair labor standards in employments in and affecting interstate commerce and for other purposes.

Be it enacted by the Senate and House of Representatives of the United States of America in Congress assembled, That this Act may be cited as the "Fair Labor Standards Act of 1938."

FINDING AND DECLARATION OF POLICY

SEC. 2. (a) The Congress hereby finds that the existence, in industries engaged in commerce or in the production of goods for commerce, of labor conditions detrimental to the maintenance of the minimum standards of living necessary for health, efficiency, and general well-being of workers (1) causes commerce and the channels and instrumentalities of commerce to be used to spread and perpetuate such labor conditions among the workers of several States; burdens commerce and the free flow of goods in commerce; (3) constitutes an unfair method of competition in commerce; (4) leads to labor disputes burdening and obstructing commerce and the free flow of goods in commerce; and (5) interferes with the orderly and fair marketing of goods in commerce.

(b) It is hereby declared to be the policy of this Act, through the exercise by Congress of its power to regulate commerce among the several States, to correct and as rapidly as practicable to eliminate the conditions above referred to in such industries without substantially curtailing employment or earning power.

. . .

MINIMUM WAGES

SEC. 6. (a) Every employer shall pay to each of his employees who is engaged in commerce or in the production of goods for commerce wages at the following rates—

(1) during the first year from the effective date of this section, not less than 25 cents an hour,

(2) during the next six years from such date, not less than 30 cents an hour,

(3) after the expiration of seven years from such date, not less than 40 cents an hour, or the rate (not less than 30 cents an hour) prescribed in the applicable order of the Administrator issued under section 8, whichever is lower, and

(4) at any time after the effective date of this section, not less than the rate (not in excess of 40 cents an hour) prescribed in the applicable order of the Administrator issued under section 8.

(b) This section shall take effect upon the expiration of one hundred and twenty days from the date of enactment of this Act.

MAXIMUM HOURS

SEC. 7. (a) No employer shall, except as otherwise provided in this section, employ any of his employees who is engaged in commerce or in the production of goods for commerce—

(1) for a workweek longer than forty-four hours during the first year from the effective date of this section,

(2) for a workweek longer than forty-two hours during the second year from such date, or

(3) for a workweek longer than forty hours after the expiration of the second year from such date, unless such employee receives compensation for his employment in excess of the hours above specified at a rate not less than one and one-half times the regular rate at which he is employed.

(b) No employer shall be deemed to have violated subsection (a) by employing any employee for a workweek in excess of that specified in such subsection without paying the compensation for overtime employment prescribed therein if such employee is so employed—

(1) in pursuance of an agreement, made as a result of collective bargaining by representatives of employees certified as bona fide by the National Labor Relations Board, which provides that no employee shall be employed more than one thousand hours during any period of twenty-six consecutive weeks,

(2) on an annual basis in pursuance of an agreement with his employer, made as a result of collective bargaining by representatives of employees certified as bona fide by the . National Labor Relations Board, which provides that the employee shall not be employed more than two thousand hours during any period of fifty-two consecutive weeks, or

(3) for a period or periods of not more than fourteen workweeks in the aggregate in any calendar year in an industry found by the Administrator to be of a seasonal nature, and if such employee receives compensation for employment in excess of 12 hours in any workday, or for employment in excess of 56 hours in any workweek, as the case may be, at a rate not less than one and one-half times the regular rate at which he is employed.

(c) In the case of an employer engaged in the first processing of milk, whey, skimmed milk, or cream into dairy products, or in the ginning and compressing of cotton, or in the processing of cottonseed, or in the processing of sugar beets, sugar beet molasses, sugarcane, or maple sap, into sugar (but not refined sugar) or into syrup, the provisions of subsection (a) shall not apply to his employees in any place of employment where he is so engaged; and in the case of an employer engaged in the first processing of, or in canning or packing, perishable or seasonal fresh fruits or vegetables, or in the first processing, within the area of production (as defined by the Administrator), of any agricultural or horticultural commodity during seasonal operations, or in handling, slaughtering, or dressing poultry or livestock, the provisions of subsection (a) during a period or periods of not more than fourteen workweeks in the aggregate in any calendar year, shall not apply to his employees in any place of employment where he is so engaged.

(d) This section shall take effect upon the expiration of one hundred and twenty days from the date of enactment of this Act.

WAGE ORDERS

SEC. 8. (a) With a view to carrying out the policy of this Act by reaching, as rapidly as is economically feasible without substantially curtailing employment, the objective of a universal minimum wage of 40 cents an hour in each industry engaged in commerce or in the production of goods for commerce, the Administrator shall from time to time convene the industry committee for each such industry, and the industry committee shall from time to time recommend the minimum rate or rates of wages to be paid under section 6 by employers engaged in commerce or in the production of goods for commerce in such industry or classifications therein.

(b) Upon the convening of an industry committee, the Administrator shall refer to it the question of the minimum wage rate or rates to be fixed for such industry. The industry committee shall investigate conditions in the industry and the committee, or any authorized subcommittee thereof, may hear such witnesses and receive such evidence as may be necessary or appropriate to enable the committee to perform its duties and functions under this Act. The committee shall recommend to the Administrator the highest minimum wage rates for the industry which it determines, having due regard to economic and competitive conditions, will not substantially curtail employment in the industry.

(c) The industry committee for any industry shall recommend such reasonable classifications within any industry as it determines to be necessary for the purpose of fixing for each classification within such industry the highest minimum wage rate (not in excess of 40 cents an hour) which (1) will not substantially curtail employment in such classification and (2) will not give a competitive advantage to any group in the industry, and shall recommend for each classification in the industry the highest minimum wage rate which the committee determines will not substantially curtail employment in such classification . In determining whether such classifications should be made in any industry, in making such classifications, and in determining the minimum wage rates for such classifications, no classification shall be made, and no minimum wage rate shall be fixed, solely on a regional basis, but the industry committee and the Administrator shall consider among other relevant factors the following:

(1) competitive conditions as affected by transportation, living, and production costs;

(2) the wages established for work of like or comparable character by collective labor agreements negotiated between employers and employees by representatives of their own choosing; and

(3) the wages paid for work of like or comparable character by employers who voluntarily maintain minimum-wage standards in the industry. No classification shall be made under this section on the basis of age or sex.

(d) The industry committee shall file with the Administrator a report containing its recommendations with respect to the matters referred to it. Upon the filing of such report, the Administrator, after due notice to interested persons, and giving them an opportunity to be heard, shall by order approve and carry into effect the recommendations contained in such report, if he finds that the recommendations are made in accordance with law, are supported by the evidence adduced at the hearing, and, taking into consideration the same factors as are required to be considered by the industry committee, will carry out the purposes of this section; otherwise he shall disapprove such recommendations. If the Administrator disapproves such recommendations, he shall again refer the matter to such committee, or to another industry committee for such industry (which he may appoint for such purpose), for further consideration and recommendations.

(e) No order issued under this section with respect to any industry prior to the expiration of seven years from the effective date of section 6 shall remain in effect after such expiration, and no order shall be issued under this section with respect to any industry on or after such expiration, unless the industry committee by a preponderance of the evidence before it recommends, and the Administrator by a preponderance of the evidence adduced at the hearing finds, that the continued effectiveness or the issuance of the order, as the case may be, is necessary in order to prevent substantial curtailment of employment in the industry.

(f) Orders issued under this section shall define the industries and classifications therein to which they are to apply, and shall contain such terms and conditions as the Administrator finds necessary to carry out the purposes of such orders, to prevent the circumvention or evasion thereof, and to safeguard the minimum wage rates established therein . No such order shall take effect until after due notice is given of the issuance thereof by publication in the Federal Register and by such other means as the Administrator deems reasonably calculated to ire to interested persons general notice of such issuance.

(g) Due notice of any hearing provided for in this section shall be given by publication in the Federal Register and by such other means as the Administrator deems reasonably calculated to give general notice to interested persons.

. . .

CHILD LABOR PROVISIONS

SEC. 12. (a) After the expiration of one hundred and twenty days from the date of enactment of this Act, no producer, manufacturer, or dealer shall ship or deliver for shipment in commerce any goods produced in an establishment situated in the United States in or about which within thirty days prior to the removal of such goods therefrom any oppressive child labor has been employed : Provided, That a prosecution and conviction of a defendant for the shipment or delivery for shipment of any goods under the conditions herein prohibited shall be a bar to any further prosecution against the same defendant for shipments or deliveries for shipment of any such goods before the beginning of said prosecution.

(b) The Chief of the Children's Bureau in the Department of Labor, or any of his authorized representatives, shall make all investigations and inspections under section 11 (a) with respect to the employment of minors, and subject to the direction and control of the Attorney General, shall bring all actions under section 17 to enjoin any act or practice which is unlawful by reason of the existence of oppressive child labor, and shall administer all other provisions of this Act relating to oppressive child labor.

. . .

LEARNERS, APPRENTICES, AND HANDICAPPED WORKERS

SEC. 14. The Administrator, to the extent necessary in order to prevent curtailment of opportunities for employment, shall by regulations or by orders provide for (1) the employment of learners, of apprentices, and of messengers employed exclusively in delivering letters and messages, under special certificates issued pursuant to regulations of the Administrator, at such wages lower than the minimum wage applicable under section 6 and subject to such limitations as to time, number, proportion, and length of service as the Administrator shall prescribe, and (2) the employment of individuals whose earning capacity is impaired by age or physical or mental deficiency or injury, under special certificates issued by the Administrator, at such wages lower than the minimum wage applicable under section 6 and for such period as shall be fixed in such certificates.

. . .

PENALTIES

SEC. 16. (a) Any person who willfully violates any of the provisions of section 15 shall upon conviction thereof be subject to a fine of not more than $10,000, or to imprisonment for not more than six months, or both. No person shall be imprisoned under this subsection except for an offense committed after the conviction of such person for a prior offense under this subsection.

(b) Any employer who violates the provisions of section 6 or section 7 of this Act shall be liable to the employee or employees affected in the amount of their unpaid minimum wages, or their unpaid overtime compensation, as the case may be, and in an additional equal amount as liquidated damages. Action to recover such liability may be maintained in any court of competent jurisdiction by any one or more employees for and in behalf of himself or themselves and other employees similarly situated, or such employee or employees may designate an agent or representative to maintain such action for and in behalf of all employees similarly situated. The court in such action shall, in addition to any judgment awarded to the plaintiff or plaintiffs, allow a reasonable attorney's fee to be paid by the defendant, and costs of the action.

SOURCE: U.S. Congress. 1938. Fair Labor Standards Act of 1938. U.S. Code 29, §§ 201 et seq.

ANALYSIS

The Fair Labor Standards Act of 1938 (FLSA) proved one of the final pieces of legislation from the New Deal era. It established a minimum wage and set the maximum hours that an employee could be forced to work. In addition, it significantly limited the employment of children under the age of 16. Political considerations in the U.S. Congress resulted in agricultural workers being exempted from the legislation. In order to appease southern legislators, the minimum wage was set a level that would not result in pay increases for most African American workers.

Prior to the onset of the Great Depression, each state made decisions that impacted labor within its borders. This piecemeal approach proved disastrous for the poorest workers, who were disproportionately comprised of women, children, and ethnic or racial minorities. States were incentivized to suppress wages since they feared that companies within their borders would relocate to another state where labor costs were more favorable. Unions, most notably the American Federation of Labor (AFL), did not challenge the actions of the respective states because they too benefited from the existing system. Systemic efforts to push down salaries made unionization extremely attractive since it promised more pay and better benefits.

Federal involvement in the regulation of labor began at the onset of the New Deal. The National Recovery Administration, a federal agency, attempted to force specific industries to adopt standards but those efforts went for naught when the U.S. Supreme Court determined in 1935 that their initiatives were unconstitutional in the case *Schechter Poultry Corp. v. United States*. Members of Congress utilized the Supreme Court's decision to help craft legislation that would pass constitutional muster. The end result was the FLSA. It set the minimum wage at 25 cents and included yearly increases that saw the amount grow to 40 cents after seven years.

It also initially set the maximum hours that an employee could labor at 44 hours. That maximum was reduced to 40 hours after two years. A by-product of the legislation was that it essentially eliminated the movement of companies from state to state in order to minimize labor costs, as all manufacturers faced the same minimums.

While the 1938 act was very limited in scope, as it only impacted companies involved in interstate commerce, it did establish the right of the federal government to regulate wages and working conditions. Critics contended that the FLSA smacked of communist influence because it standardized salary norms. With such beliefs prevalent, court challenges were inevitable. The key case proved to be *United States v. Darby Lumber Company*. In a unanimous ruling in 1941, the justices determined that the Constitution's Commerce Clause granted Congress the power to enact legislation to regulate how employees were treated in the workplace. With the constitutional question answered, amendments to the FLSA followed that eventually impacted the labor conditions of a vast majority of workers in the United States.

FURTHER READING

Fleck, Robert K. 2002. "Democratic Opposition to the Fair Labor Standards Act of 1938." *Journal of Economic History* 62, no. 1: 25–54.

Hart, Vivien. 1994. *Bound by Our Constitution: Women, Workers, and the Minimum Wage*. Princeton, NJ: Princeton University Press.

Paulsen, George E. 1996. *A Living Wage for the Forgotten Man: The Quest for Fair Labor Standards 1933–1941*. Selingsgrove, PA: Susquehanna University Press.

Storrs, Landon R. Y. 2000. *Civilizing Capitalism: The National Consumers' League, Women's Activism, and Labor Standards in the New Deal Era*. Chapel Hill: University of North Carolina Press.

Waltman, Jerold. 2006. "Supreme Court Activism in Economic Policy in the Waning Days of the New Deal: Interpreting the Fair Labor Standards Act, 1941–1946." *Journal of Supreme Court History* 31, no. 1: 58–80.

"Interstate Commerce Should Not Be Made the Instrument of Competition in the Distribution of Goods Produced under Substandard Labor Conditions"

- ***Document:*** *United States v. Darby Lumber Company* (Syllabus)
- ***Date:*** February 3, 1941
- ***Where:*** Washington, D.C.
- ***Significance:*** The opinion in *United States v. Darby Lumber Company* established the constitutionality of the minimum wage and the maximum number of hours that an employee could be forced to work per week.

DOCUMENT

1. The Fair Labor Standards Act of 1938 provides for fixing minimum wages and maximum hours for employees engaged in the production of goods for interstate commerce, with increased compensation for overtime, and forbids, under pain of fine and imprisonment: (1) violation by an employer of such wage and hour provisions; (2) shipment by him in interstate commerce of any goods in the production of which any employee was employed in violation of such provisions, and (3) failure of the employer to keep such records of his employees and of their wages and hours, as shall be prescribed by administrative regulation or order. Held within the commerce power and consistent with the Fifth and Tenth Amendments. P. 111.

2. While manufacture is not of itself interstate commerce, the shipment of manufactured goods interstate is such commerce, and the prohibition of such shipment by Congress is a regulation of interstate commerce. P. 113.

3. Congress, following its own conception of public policy concerning the restrictions which may appropriately be imposed on interstate commerce, is free to exclude from it articles whose use in the State for which they are destined it may conceive to be injurious to the public health, morals or welfare, even though the State has not sought to regulate their use. P. 114.

4. Such regulation is not a forbidden invasion of state power merely because either its motive or its consequence is to restrict the use of articles of commerce within the States of destination, and is valid unless prohibited by other Constitutional provisions. P. 114.

5. The motive and purpose of the present regulation are plainly to make effective the Congressional conception of public policy that interstate commerce should not be made the instrument of competition in the distribution of goods produced under substandard labor conditions, which competition is injurious to the commerce and to the States from and to which it flows. P. 115.

6. The motive and purpose of a regulation of interstate commerce are matters for the legislative judgment upon the exercise of which the Constitution places no restriction, and over which the courts are given no control. P. 115.

7. In prohibiting interstate shipment of goods produced under the forbidden substandard labor conditions, the Act is within the authority of Congress, if no Constitutional provision forbids. P. 115.

8. Hammer v. Dagenhart, 247 U.S. 251, overruled; Carter v. Carter Coal Co., 298 U.S. 238, declared to have been limited. Pp. 115, 123.

9. The "production for interstate commerce" intended by the Act includes, at least, production of goods, which, at the time of production, the employer, according to the normal course of his business, intends or expects to move in interstate commerce although, through the exigencies of the business, all of the goods may not thereafter actually enter interstate commerce. P. 117.

10. The power of Congress over interstate commerce extends to those intrastate activities which so affect interstate commerce or the exercise of the power of Congress over it as to make their regulation an appropriate means to the attainment of a legitimate end—the exercise of the granted power of Congress to regulate interstate commerce. P. 118.

11. Congress, having by the present Act adopted the policy of excluding from interstate commerce all goods produced for that commerce which do not conform to the specified labor standards, it may choose the means reasonably adapted to the attainment of the permitted end, even though they involve control of intrastate activities. P. 121.

12. Independently of the prohibition of shipment or transportation of the proscribed goods, the provision of the Act for the suppression of their production for interstate commerce is within the commerce power. P. 122.

13. The Tenth Amendment is not a limitation upon the authority of the National Government to resort to all means for the exercise of a granted power which are appropriate and plainly adapted to the permitted end. P. 123.

14. The requirements of the Act as to the keeping of records are valid as incidental to the wage and hour requirements. P. 124.

15. The wage and hour provisions of the Act do not violate the due process clause of the Fifth Amendment. P. 125.

16. In its criminal aspect, the Act is sufficiently definite to meet constitutional demands. P. 125.

APPEAL, under the Criminal Appeals Act, from a judgment quashing an indictment.

SOURCE: United States v. Darby Lumber Co., 312 U.S. 100 (1941).

ANALYSIS

The onset of the Great Depression saw companies desperate to remain in business slash the wages of their employees. They were allowed to do so by their respective states who believed that employers would leave for another locale if their labor costs grew too high. The end result was that the states with the lowest labor standards essentially forced other states to follow their lead. One of the purposes of the Fair Labor Standards Act of 1938 (FLSA) was to stop the suppression of wages by setting a common minimum wage and a standard workweek for all companies engaged in interstate commerce. It was the minimum wage requirement that led to case *United States v. Darby Lumber Company*.

Although the FLSA set the minimum wage at 25 cents, the Darby Lumber Company continued to pay its workers between 12 and 17 cents an hour. The federal government promptly conducted an investigation and found that the company had intentionally ignored the FLSA's requirements. Fines were levied along with a demand that wages be increased to at least 25 cents an hour. The lumber company's intransigence led the matter to be settled by the courts. The company prevailed within Georgia's court system as its judges relied on the 1918 U.S. Supreme Court case *Hammer v. Dagenhart* to determine that the FLSA was unconstitutional. Since the FLSA impacted interstate commerce, the U.S. Supreme Court agreed to take the case up on appeal.

The Supreme Court issued a unanimous decision that was penned by Justice Harlan Fiske Stone. The Court found that the FSLA was constitutional because interstate commerce had to be regulated and the appropriate body to do so was the Congress. The Constitution provided that authority to Congress through the commerce clause. That interpretation set a new legal standard that set aside the precedents established through the cases *Hammer v. Dagenhart* (1918), *Schechter Poultry Corp. v. United States* (1935), and *Carter v. Carter Coal Company* (1936).

FURTHER READING

Paulsen, George E. 1996. *A Living Wage for the Forgotten Man: The Quest for Fair Labor Standards 1933–1941*. Selingsgrove, PA: Susquehanna University Press.

Waltman, Jerold. 2006. "Supreme Court Activism in Economic Policy in the Waning Days of the New Deal: Interpreting the Fair Labor Standards Act, 1941–1946." *Journal of Supreme Court History* 31, no. 1: 58–80.

"We Have Come to a Clear Realization of the Fact That True Individual Freedom Cannot Exist without Economic Security and Independence"

- ***Document:*** President Franklin Delano Roosevelt's State of the Union Address (Excerpt)
- ***Date:*** January 11, 1944
- ***Where:*** Washington, D.C.
- ***Significance:*** In his State of the Union address to Congress, President Roosevelt proffered his vision for an Economic Bill of Rights.

DOCUMENT

It is our duty now to begin to lay the plans and determine the strategy for the winning of a lasting peace and the establishment of an American standard of living higher than ever before known. We cannot be content, no matter how high that general standard of living may be, if some fraction of our people—whether it be one-third or one-fifth or one-tenth—is ill-fed, ill-clothed, ill housed, and insecure.

This Republic had its beginning, and grew to its present strength, under the protection of certain inalienable political rights—among them the right of free speech, free press, free worship, trial by jury, freedom from unreasonable searches and seizures. They were our rights to life and liberty.

As our Nation has grown in size and stature, however—as our industrial economy expanded—these political rights proved inadequate to assure us equality in the pursuit of happiness.

We have come to a clear realization of the fact that true individual freedom cannot exist without economic security and independence. "Necessitous men are not free men." People who are hungry and out of a job are the stuff of which dictatorships are made.

In our day these economic truths have become accepted as self-evident. We have accepted, so to speak, a second Bill of Rights under which a new basis of security and prosperity can be established for all regardless of station, race, or creed.

Among these are:

The right to a useful and remunerative job in the industries or shops or farms or mines of the Nation;

The right to earn enough to provide adequate food and clothing and recreation;

The right of every farmer to raise and sell his products at a return which will give him and his family a decent living;

The right of every businessman, large and small, to trade in an atmosphere of freedom from unfair competition and domination by monopolies at home or abroad;

The right of every family to a decent home;

The right to adequate medical care and the opportunity to achieve and enjoy good health;

The right to adequate protection from the economic fears of old age, sickness, accident, and unemployment;

The right to a good education.

All of these rights spell security. And after this war is won we must be prepared to move forward, in the implementation of these rights, to new goals of human happiness and well-being.

America's own rightful place in the world depends in large part upon how fully these and similar rights have been carried into practice for our citizens. For unless there is security here at home there cannot be lasting peace in the world.

One of the great American industrialists of our day—a man who has rendered yeoman service to his country in this crisis—recently emphasized the grave dangers of "rightist reaction" in this Nation. All clear-thinking businessmen share his concern. Indeed, if such reaction should develop—if history were to repeat itself and we were to return to the so-called "normalcy" of the 1920's—then it is certain that even though we shall have conquered our enemies on the battlefields abroad, we shall have yielded to the spirit of Fascism here at home.

I ask the Congress to explore the means for implementing this economic bill of rights—for it is definitely the responsibility of the Congress so to do. Many of these problems are already before committees of the Congress in the form of proposed legislation. I shall from time to time communicate with the Congress with respect to these and further proposals. In the event that no adequate program of progress is evolved, I am certain that the Nation will be conscious of the fact.

Our fighting men abroad—and their families at home—expect such a program and have the right to insist upon it. It is to their demands that this Government should pay heed rather than to the whining demands of selfish pressure groups who seek to feather their nests while young Americans are dying.

The foreign policy that we have been following—the policy that guided us at Moscow, Cairo, and Teheran—is based on the common sense principle which was best expressed by Benjamin Franklin on July 4, 1776: "We must all hang together, or assuredly we shall all hang separately."

I have often said that there are no two fronts for America in this war. There is only one front. There is one line of unity which extends from the hearts of the people at home to the men of our attacking forces in our farthest outposts. When we speak of our total effort, we speak of the factory and the field, and the mine as well as of the battleground—we speak of the soldier and the civilian, the citizen and his Government.

Each and every one of us has a solemn obligation under God to serve this Nation in its most critical hour—to keep this Nation great—to make this Nation greater in a better world.

SOURCE: Franklin D. Roosevelt Presidential Library and Museum. Available online at http://www.fdrlibrary.marist.edu/archives/address_text.html.

ANALYSIS

Franklin D. Roosevelt became president after the United States was mired in the Great Depression. He launched the New Deal in order to assist a population that had been economically devastated. By 1944, the country was on much firmer financial footing but the scars on the national psyche were lasting. In his State of the Union address, he proposed an "Economic Bill of Rights," arguing that all Americans deserved to benefit from the nation's prosperity, not just the elite class. He thus proclaimed that everybody had a right to expect, among other things, an education, a job, housing, access to health care, and comfort in their twilight years. Since 1944 was a presidential election year, his address was perceived by many in Congress as a campaign speech to potential voters. In truth, he provided a vision that would be extremely influential within the Democratic Party into the twenty-first century. The Economic Bill of Rights would help shape the policies followed by President John F. Kennedy as he crafted the New Frontier. Roosevelt's call for all Americans to share in the country's prosperity was echoed by President Lyndon Johnson in his Great Society, especially in the War on Poverty. The right to health care shaped President William Clinton's first term in office as First Lady Hillary Clinton pushed unsuccessfully for health care reform. That goal was finally achieved by President Barack Obama in 2010 with the signing of the Patient Protection and Affordable Care Act. The Progressive wing of the Democratic Party is presently endeavoring to protect the political gains inspired by the Economic Bill of Rights from promised challenges by the administration of President Donald Trump.

FURTHER READING

Jordan, David M. 2011. *FDR, Dewey, and the Election of 1944*. Bloomington: Indiana University Press.

Rauchway, Eric. 2015. *The Money Makers: How Roosevelt and Keynes Ended the Depression, Defeated Fascism, and Secured a Prosperous Peace*. New York: Basic Books.

Smith, Rogers M. 2016. "The Progressive Seedbed: Claims of American Political Community in the Twentieth and Twenty-First Centuries." In Stephen Skowronek, Stephen M. Engel, and Bruce Ackerman, eds. *The Progressives' Century: Political Reform, Constitutional Government, and the Modern American State*. New Haven: Yale University Press, 264–268.

"It Gives Servicemen and Women the Opportunity of Resuming Their Education or Technical Training after Discharge"

- ***Document:*** President Franklin D. Roosevelt's Statement on Signing the G.I. Bill
- ***Date:*** June 22, 1944
- ***Where:*** Washington, D.C.
- ***Significance:*** The Servicemen's Readjustment Act of 1944, better known as the G.I. Bill, provided veterans of World War II benefits at government expense that allowed them to attend colleges or universities, gain job skills through vocational schools or on-the-job training, and obtain loan guarantees to purchase a home.

DOCUMENT

This bill, which I have signed today, substantially carries out most of the recommendations made by me in a speech on July 28, 1943, and more specifically in messages to the Congress dated October 27, 1943, and November 23, 1943:

1. It gives servicemen and women the opportunity of resuming their education or technical training after discharge, or of taking a refresher or retrainer course, not only without tuition charge up to $500 per school year, but with the right to receive a monthly living allowance while pursuing their studies.

2. It makes provision for the guarantee by the Federal Government of not to exceed 50 percent of certain loans made to veterans for the purchase or construction of homes, farms, and business properties.

3. It provides for reasonable unemployment allowances payable each week up to a maximum period of one year, to those veterans who are unable to find a job.

4. It establishes improved machinery for effective job counseling for veterans and for finding jobs for returning soldiers and sailors.

5. It authorizes the construction of all necessary additional hospital facilities.

6. It strengthens the authority of the Veterans Administration to enable it to discharge its existing and added responsibilities with promptness and efficiency.

With the signing of this bill a well-rounded program of special veterans' benefits is nearly completed. It gives emphatic notice to the men and women in our armed forces that the American people do not intend to let them down.

By prior legislation, the Federal Government has already provided for the armed forces of this war: adequate dependency allowances; mustering-out pay; generous hospitalization, medical care, and vocational rehabilitation and training; liberal pensions in case of death or disability in military service; substantial war risk life insurance, and guaranty of premiums on commercial policies during service; protection of civil rights and suspension of enforcement of certain civil liabilities during service; emergency maternal care for wives of enlisted men; and reemployment rights for returning veterans.

This bill therefore and the former legislation provide the special benefits which are due to the members of our armed forces—for they "have been compelled to make greater economic sacrifice and every other kind of sacrifice than the rest of us, and are entitled to definite action to help take care of their special problems." While further study and experience may suggest some changes and improvements, the Congress is to be congratulated on the prompt action it has taken.

There still remains one recommendation which I made on November 23, 1943, which I trust that the Congress will soon adopt—the extension of social security credits under the Federal Old-Age and Survivors' Insurance Law to all servicemen and women for the period of their service.

I trust that the Congress will also soon provide similar opportunities for postwar education and unemployment insurance to the members of the merchant marine, who have risked their lives time and again during this war for the welfare of their country.

But apart from these special benefits which fulfill the special needs of veterans, there is still much to be done.

As I stated in my message to the Congress of November 23, 1943,

DID YOU KNOW?

Universal Declaration of Human Rights

After the horrors of World War II, the nations of the world sought to ensure that disputes between them could be negotiated peacefully rather than settled through warfare. To facilitate cooperation, the United Nations was founded. One of the United Nations' first priorities was the creation of the Universal Declaration of Human Rights (UDHR). Article 25 of that document specifically addressed issues relating to poverty, including a right to food, housing, medical care, and security in old age. Federal officials subsequently utilized the UDHR as an international mandate to address domestic issues like the scourges of economic inequality.

FURTHER READING

Glendon, Mary Ann. 2001. *A World Made New: Eleanor Roosevelt and the Universal Declaration of Human Rights.* New York: Random House.

Morsink, Johannes. 1999. *The Universal Declaration of Human Rights: Origins, Drafting, and Intent.* Philadelphia: University of Pennsylvania Press.

"What our servicemen and women want, more than anything else, is the assurance of satisfactory employment upon their return to civil life. The first task after the war is to provide employment for them and for our demobilized workers. . . . The goal after the war should be the maximum utilization of our human and material resources."

As a related problem the Congress has had under consideration the serious problem of economic reconversion and readjustment after the war, so that private industry will be able to provide jobs for the largest possible number. This time we have wisely begun to make plans in advance of the day of peace, in full confidence that our war workers will remain at their essential war jobs as long as necessary until the fighting is over.

The executive branch of the Government has taken, and is taking, whatever steps it can, until legislation is enacted. I am glad to learn that the Congress has agreed on a bill to facilitate the prompt settlement of terminated contracts. I hope that the Congress will also take prompt action, when it reconvenes, on necessary legislation which is now pending to facilitate the development of unified programs for the demobilization of civilian war workers, for their reemployment in peacetime pursuits, and for provision, in cooperation with the States, of appropriate unemployment benefits during the transition from war to peace. I hope also that the Congress, upon its return, will take prompt action on the pending legislation to facilitate the orderly disposition of surplus property.

A sound postwar economy is a major present responsibility.

SOURCE: Samuel I. Rosenman Papers; File: GI Bill (Box 8), Franklin D. Roosevelt Presidential Library & Museum.

ANALYSIS

Prior to the enactment of the Servicemen's Readjustment Act of 1944, also known as the G.I. Bill, the United States had always rewarded its war veterans with bonuses in the form of land and/or pension payments. During the early years of the nation, the land grants were on the frontier. Once the land had been distributed, the federal government felt no further obligation to the beneficiary. Over time, pensions replaced the granting of land. The problem with pensions was that the monies were distributed to veterans long after they had completed their service to the country. Many died of old age before their pension was scheduled to be disbursed.

The G.I. Bill marked a sea change by addressing the economic needs of servicemen immediately after their wartime service had concluded. This benefited the interests of both those transitioning to civilian life and the country at large. For veterans, the provision of an education and improved job skills allowed them to earn far more money over the course of their lives than they would have had they not enlisted in the military. A significant segment of the population that had been in the economic lower class before World War II was thus able to elevate itself to the nation's burgeoning middle class. The economic prosperity enjoyed by many veterans benefited other segments of the population through taxes. The federal government was receiving so much tax revenue that it became interested in using surplus funds to address the needs of those who had been bypassed by the post–World II economic boom. This change could be seen through the nation's political focus. Prior to World War II, the New Deal had been designed to ensure that all citizens received what they required to subsist. By the 1960s, through both John F. Kennedy's "New Frontier" and Lyndon Johnson's "Great Society," the federal government's goal was to improve the quality of life enjoyed by all.

Despite the economic prosperity produced by the first G.I. Bill for both its intended recipients and the nation as a whole, subsequent versions proved to be less generous. This unfortunate trend culminated in the 1967 G.I. Bill, designed for Vietnam War veterans. Not only were its benefits more limited than even the Cold War G.I. Bill enacted just a year earlier, but one did not even qualify for its benefits unless he or she had served at least 18 months in the military. The denial of access to those who did not meet the minimum enlistment was particularly cruel since some of those who fought in the conflict were conscripts rather than volunteers. Later G.I. bills would see improvements in benefits, especially in the area of education. The motivation for the change had to do with the composition of the military. Since the federal government had determined to construct an all-volunteer fighting force, the G.I. Bill became an inducement to encourage individuals to enlist.

FURTHER READING

Boulton, Mark. 2014. *Failing Our Veterans: The G.I. Bill and the Vietnam Generation*. New York: New York University Press.

Frydl, Kathleen J. 2009. *The G.I. Bill*. New York: Cambridge University Press.

Humes, Edward. 2006. *Over Here: How the G.I. Bill Transformed the American Dream*. New York: Harcourt.

Mettler, Suzanne. 2005. *Soldiers to Citizens: The G.I. Bill and the Making of the Greatest Generation*. New York: Oxford University Press.

Olson, Keith W. 1974. *The G.I. Bill, the Veterans, and the Colleges*. Lexington: University Press of Kentucky.

5

THE POST–WORLD WAR II ERA THROUGH THE CARTER ADMINISTRATION

"The Right to Adequate Medical Care and the Opportunity to Achieve and Enjoy Good Health"

- ***Document:*** President Harry S. Truman's Special Message to the Congress Recommending a Comprehensive Health Program (Excerpts)
- ***Date:*** November 19, 1945
- ***Where:*** Washington, D.C.
- ***Significance:*** President Truman's speech helped lead to the passage of the Hospital Survey and Construction Act, which was signed into law on August 13, 1946.

DOCUMENT

To the Congress of the United States:

In my message to the Congress of September 6, 1945, there were enumerated in a proposed Economic Bill of Rights certain rights which ought to be assured to every American citizen. One of them was: "The right to adequate medical care and the opportunity to achieve and enjoy good health." Another was the "right to adequate protection from the economic fears of . . . sickness. . . ."

. . .

There are five basic problems which we must attack vigorously if we would reach the health objectives of our Economic Bill of Rights.

The first has to do with the number and distribution of doctors and hospitals. One of the most important requirements for adequate health service is professional personnel—doctors, dentists, public health and hospital administrators, nurses and other experts.

The United States has been fortunate with respect to physicians. In proportion to population it has more than any large country in the world, and they are well trained for their calling. It is not enough, however, that we have them in sufficient numbers. They should be located where their services are needed. In this respect we are not so fortunate.

The distribution of physicians in the United States has been grossly uneven and unsatisfactory. Some communities have had enough or even too many; others have had too few. Year by year the number in our rural areas has been diminishing. Indeed, in 1940, there were 31 counties in the United States, each with more than a thousand inhabitants, in which there was not a single practicing physician. The situation with respect to dentists was even worse.

One important reason for this disparity is that in some communities there are no adequate facilities for the practice of medicine. Another reason—closely allied with the first—is that the earning capacity of the people in some communities makes it difficult if not impossible for doctors who practice there to make a living.

The demobilization of 60,000 doctors, and of the tens of thousands of other professional personnel in the Armed Forces is now proceeding on a large scale. Unfortunately, unless we act rapidly, we may expect to see them concentrate in the places with greater financial resources and avoid other places, making the inequalities even greater than before the war.

Demobilized doctors cannot be assigned. They must be attracted. In order to be attracted, they must be able to see ahead of them professional opportunities and economic assurances.

Inequalities in the distribution of medical personnel are matched by inequalities in hospitals and other health facilities. Moreover, there are just too few hospitals, clinics and health centers to take proper care of the people of the United States.

About 1,200 counties, 40 percent of the total in the country, with some 15,000,000 people, have either no local hospital, or none that meets even the minimum standards of national professional associations.

The deficiencies are especially severe in rural and semirural areas and in those cities where changes in population have placed great strains on community facilities.

I want to emphasize, however, that the basic problem in this field cannot be solved merely by building facilities. They have to be staffed; and the communities have to be able to pay for the services. Otherwise the new facilities will be little used.

. . .

These then are the five important problems which must be solved, if we hope to attain our objective of adequate medical care, good health, and protection from the economic fears of sickness and disability.

To meet these problems, I recommend that the Congress adopt a comprehensive and modern health program for the Nation, consisting of five major parts—each of which contributes to all the others.

FIRST: CONSTRUCTION OF HOSPITALS AND RELATED FACILITIES

The Federal Government should provide financial and other assistance for the construction of needed hospitals, health centers and other medical, health, and rehabilitation facilities. With the help of Federal funds, it should be possible to meet deficiencies in hospital and health facilities so that modern services—for both prevention and cure—can be accessible to all the people. Federal financial aid should be available not only to build new facilities where needed, but also to enlarge or modernize those we now have.

In carrying out this program, there should be a clear division of responsibilities between the States and the Federal Government. The States, localities and the Federal Government should share in the financial responsibilities. The Federal Government should not construct or operate these hospitals. It should, however, lay down minimum national standards for construction and operation, and should make sure that Federal funds are allocated to those areas and projects where Federal aid is needed most. In approving state plans and individual projects, and in fixing the national standards, the Federal agency should have the help of a strictly advisory body that includes both public and professional members.

Adequate emphasis should be given to facilities that are particularly useful for prevention of diseases—mental as well as physical—and to the coordination of various kinds of facilities. It should be possible to go a long way toward knitting together facilities for prevention with facilities for cure, the large hospitals of medical centers with the smaller institutions of surrounding areas, the facilities for the civilian population with the facilities for veterans.

The general policy of Federal-State partnership which has done so much to provide the magnificent highways of the United States can be adapted to the construction of hospitals in the communities which need them.

SOURCE: Truman, Harry S. 1966. "Special Message to the Congress Recommending a Comprehensive Health Program." November 19, 1945. *Public Papers of the Presidents of the United States, Harry S. Truman, 1945–1953*. Document 192. Washington, D.C.: U.S. Government Printing Office.

ANALYSIS

During his presidency, Harry Truman worked diligently to advance health care initiatives. His advocacy had its origins in World War II, which saw thousands of volunteers turned away from service in the U.S. military because they could not pass physicals. Since national defense was one of his primary responsibilities, he endeavored to create a health care system that would ensure a healthy pool of men available for military service. He ambitiously called for the creation of a national health care program for men who were of age to serve in a branch of the military and their families. The irony is that national defense is what prevented its passage in Congress. Since the nation was in the throes of the Cold War, anything tied to communism was taboo. Opponents of the legislation, led by the American Medical Association, successfully labeled Truman's proposal "socialized medicine." Pieces of his proposal eventually reemerged in later Congress's program, most notably Medicare.

Truman did successfully shepherd the Hospital Survey and Construction Act of 1946 through the legislative process. Also known as the Hill–Burton Act, in honor of senators Harold Burton and Lester Hill, it helped finance the construction of hospitals in rural areas and aided in the modernization of existing medical facilities. In order to receive funding, a community had to pay two-third of the total cost of the project. This requirement effectively ensured that only communities with affluent residents could qualify for the program. In addition, the facility could not discriminate on the basis of race, creed, or place of origin. Between 1946 and 1963, exceptions were made in the South, where the doctrine of "separate but equal" held sway. Another requirement was the provision of free health care for 20 years to a "reasonable volume" of people without the wherewithal to pay for medical services. The final requirement proved particularly controversial as the phrase "reasonable volume" was not defined in the act. Predictably, federal officials had a more expansive view of the term than that of the respective health care facility administrators. The disagreement continued long after the final funds were disbursed in 1977 because, by the 1970s, some of the grants did away with the 20-year requirement and replaced it with "perpetuity." Over time, the Hospital Survey and Construction Act of 1946 has proven to be one of the most transformative medical initiatives ever undertaken by the federal government. Its import is illustrated through its effect in 2017, as 142 facilities in operation within the United States are still required to follow the Hill–Burton regulations (Health Resources and Services Administration).

FURTHER READING

Hamby, Alonzo L. 1995. *Man of the People: A Life of Harry S. Truman*. New York: Oxford University Press.

Health Resources and Services Administration. 2017. *Hill-Burton Facilities Obligated to Provide Free of Reduced-Cost Health Care*. https://www.hrsa.gov/gethealthcare/affordable/hillburton/facilities.html#alternative (accessed June 22, 2017).

Holt, Marilyn Irvin. 2014. *Cold War Kids: Politics and Childhood in Postwar America, 1945–1960*. Lawrence: University Press of Kansas.

McCullough, David. 1992. *Truman*. New York: Simon & Schuster.

Thomas, Karen Kruse. 2006. "The Hill-Burton Act and Civil Rights: Expanding Hospital Care for Black Southerners, 1939–1960." *Journal of Southern History* 72, no. 4: 823–870.

"Strengthening the Nation through Better Nutrition for Our School Children"

- ***Document:*** Statement by the President upon Signing the National School Lunch Act
- ***Date:*** June 4, 1946
- ***Where:*** Washington, D.C.
- ***Significance:*** The National School Lunch Act ensured that all poor children received at least one nutritious meal a day.

DOCUMENT

TODAY, as I sign the National School Lunch Act, I feel that the Congress has acted with great wisdom in providing the basis for strengthening the nation through better nutrition for our school children. In my message to Congress last January, I pointed out that we have the technical knowledge to provide plenty of good food for every man, woman, and child in this country, but that despite our capacity to produce food we have often failed to distribute it as well as we should. This action by the Congress represents a basic forward step toward correcting that failure.

In the long view, no nation is any healthier than its children or more prosperous than its farmers; and in the National School Lunch Act, the Congress has contributed immeasurably both to the welfare of our farmers and the health of our children.

Under previous school lunch programs made possible by year-to-year authorizations we have been able to provide as many as six million children with nutritious lunches at noon. This has laid a good foundation for the permanent program. In the future, increasing numbers will benefit—and on a permanent basis.

I hope that all State and local authorities will cooperate fully with the United States Department of Agriculture in establishing the cooperative school lunch in every possible community.

SOURCE: Truman, Harry S. 1966. "Statement by the President upon Signing the National School Lunch Act." June 4, 1946. *Public Papers of the Presidents of the United States, Harry S. Truman, 1945–1953*. Document 128. Washington, D.C.: U.S. Government Printing Office.

ANALYSIS

Although some schools provided lunch to students as early as the 1930s, it was not until 1946 with the signing of the National School Lunch Act that all public schools were required to feed their pupils. While the act benefited schools, it actually had its origins with the War Department and the Department of Agriculture. Advocates for the meals first began lobbying the War Department during World War II to declare feeding school children an essential part of the war effort since mothers were too busy working in factories to find the time to make nutritious meals. The War Department did not support that effort. Due to the ongoing conflict, the War Department did develop a close relationship with the Department of Agriculture as they worked together to feed the U.S. military overseas. As part of that effort, the two departments also steered surplus agricultural products to schools. As the war neared its end, farmers around the country who had prospered during the war years suddenly saw peace as an obstacle to their prosperity. To ensure that farmers continued to be able to sell their products in the tonnage they had grown accustomed to, the two departments, the administration, and Congress created the school lunch program. It shifted the sale of agricultural commodities from the military to schools. As such, it was instantly popular as it benefited the families of many school children and the nation's farmers.

As was true of most legislation of the day, the lunch program was a shared federal and state initiative. For every federal dollar contributed, the respective states had to provide a match of as much as $3. The states accepted the monies but did not necessarily follow the rules that came with the funding. The act banned discriminating against children by race and also required that students whose families were poor be provided reduced-price or free meals. Since the legislation did not define "poor," it was left to local administrators to determine eligibility for free or reduced meals. In some areas, this meant that white children whose families were not impoverished received free meals while poor African American or Latino children went hungry. These issues began to be addressed with the National School Lunch Act of 1962, which charged the Department of Agriculture with ensuring that all poor children received a nutritious and affordable meal. Unfortunately, Congress did not provide funding for the enforcement initiative until 1966.

FURTHER READING

Fite, Gilbert C. 1991. *Richard B. Russell, Jr., Senator from Georgia*. Chapel Hill: University Press of North Carolina.

Holt, Marilyn Irvin. 2014. *Cold War Kids: Politics and Childhood in Postwar America, 1945–1960*. Lawrence: University Press of Kansas.

Levine, Susan. 2008. *School Lunch Politics: The Surprising History of America's Favorite Welfare Program*. Princeton: Princeton University Press.

"The Goal of a Decent Home and a Suitable Living Environment for Every American Family"

- ***Document:*** Housing Act of 1949 (Excerpts)
- ***Date:*** July 15, 1949
- ***Where:*** Washington, D.C.
- ***Significance:*** The Housing Act of 1949 allowed many people to obtain nice homes. It also succeeded in concentrating impoverished members of minority groups in high-rise slums.

DOCUMENT

AN ACT

To establish a national housing objective and the policy to be followed in the attainment thereof, to provide Federal aid to assist slum-clearance projects and low-rent public housing projects initiated by local agencies, to provide for financial assistance by the Secretary of Agriculture for farm housing, and for other purposes.

Be it enacted by the Senate and House of Representatives of the United States of America in Congress assembled, That this Act may be cited as the "Housing Act of 1949."

DECLARATION OF NATIONAL HOUSING POLICY

SEC. 2. The Congress hereby declares that the general welfare and security of the Nation and the health and living standards of its people require housing production and related community development sufficient to remedy the serious housing shortage, the elimination of substandard and other inadequate housing through the clearance of slums and blighted areas, and the realization as soon as feasible of the goal of a decent home and a suitable living environment for every American family, thus contributing to the development and redevelopment of communities and to the advancement of the growth, wealth, and security of the Nation. The Congress further declares that such production is necessary to enable the housing industry to make its full contribution toward an economy of maximum employment, production, and purchasing power. The policy to be followed in attaining the national housing objective hereby established shall be: (1) private enterprise shall be encouraged to serve as large a part of the total need as it can; (2) governmental assistance shall be utilized where feasible to enable private enterprise to serve more of the total need; (3) appropriate local public bodies shall be encouraged and assisted to undertake positive programs of encouraging and assisting the development of well-planned, integrated residential neighborhoods, the development and redevelopment of communities, and the production, at lower costs, of housing of sound standards of design, construction, livability, and size for adequate family life; (4) governmental assistance to eliminate substandard and other inadequate housing through the clearance of slums and blighted areas, to facilitate community development and redevelopment, and to provide adequatehousing for urban and rural nonfarm families with incomes so low that they are not being decently housed in new or existing housing shall be extended to those localities which estimate their own needs and demonstrate that these needs are not being met through reliance solely upon private enterprise, and without such aid; and (5) governmental assistance for decent, safe, and sanitary farm dwellings and related facilities shall be extended where the farm owner demonstrates that he lacks sufficient resources to provide such housing on his own account and is unable to secure necessary credit for such housing from other sources on terms and conditions which he could reasonably be expected to fulfill. The Housing and Home Finance Agency and its constituent agencies, and any other departments or agencies of the Federal Government having powers, functions, or duties with respect to housing, shall exercise their powers, functions, and duties under this or any other law, consistently with the national housing policy declared by this Act and in such manner as will facilitate sustained progress in attaining the national housing objective hereby established, and in such manner as will encourage and assist (1) the production of housing of sound standards of design, construction, livability, and size for adequate family life; (2) tie reduction of the costs of housing without sacrifice of such sound standards; (3) the use of new designs, materials, techniques, and methods in residential construction, the use of standardized dimensions and methods of assembly of home-building materials and equipment, and the increase of efficiency in residential construction and maintenance; (4) the development of well-planned, integrated, residential neighborhoods and the development and redevelopment of communities; and (5) the stabilization of the housing industry at a high annual volume of residential construction.

TITLE I—SLUM CLEARANCE AND COMMUNITY DEVELOPMENT AND REDEVELOPMENT

SEC. 101. In extending financial assistance under this title, the Administrator shall—

(a) give consideration to the extent to which appropriate local public bodies have undertaken positive programs

(1) for encouraging housing cost reductions through the adoption, improvement, and modernization of building and other local codes and regulations so as to permit the use of appropriate new materials, techniques, and methods in land and residential planning, design, and construction, the increase of efficiency in residential construction, and the elimination of restrictive practices which unnecessarily increase housing costs, and

(2) for preventing the spread or recurrence, in such community, of slums and blighted areas through the adoption, improvement, and modernization of local codes and regulations relating to land use and adequate standards of health, sanitation, and safety for dwelling accommodations; and

(b) encourage the operations of such local public agencies as are established on a State, or regional (within a State), or unified metropolitan basis or as are established on such other basis as permits such agencies to contribute effectively toward the solution of community development or redevelopment problems on a State, or regional (within a State), or unified metropolitan basis.

. . .

TITLE II—AMENDMENTS TO NATIONAL HOUSING ACT

. . .

TITLE III—LOW-RENT PUBLIC HOUSING LOCAL RESPONSIBILITIES AND DETERMINATIONS; TENANCY ONLY BY LOW-INCOME FAMILIES

SEC. 301. The United States Housing Act of 1937, as amended, is hereby amended by adding the following additional subsections to section 15:

"(7) In recognition that there should be local determination of the need for low-rent housing to meet needs not being adequately met by private enterprise—

"(a) The Authority shall not make any contract with a public housing agency for preliminary loans (all of which shall be repaid out of any moneys which become available to such agency for the development of the projects involved) for surveys and planning in respect to any low-rent housing projects initiated after March 1, 1949, (i) unless the governing body of the locality involved has by resolution approved the application of the public housing agency for such preliminary loan; and (ii) unless the public housing agency has demonstrated to the satisfaction of the Authority that there is a need for such low-rent housing which is not being met by private enterprise; and

"(b) the Authority shall not make any contract for loans (other than preliminary loans) or for annual contributions pursuant to this Act with respect to any low-rent housing project initiated after March 1, 1949, (i) unless the governing body of the locality involved has entered into an agreement with the public housing agency providing for the local cooperation required by the Authority pursuant to this Act; and (ii) unless the public housing agency has demonstrated to the satisfaction of the Authority that a gap of at least 20 per centum has been left between the upper rental limits for admission to the proposed low-rent housing and the lowest rents at which private enterprise unaided by public subsidy is providing (through new construction and available existing structures) a substantial supply of decent, safe, and sanitary housing toward meeting the need of an adequate volume, thereof.

"(8) Every contract made pursuant to this Act for annual contributions for any low-rent housing project initiated after March 1, 1949, shall provide that—

"(a) the public housing agency shall fix maximum income limits for the admission and for the continued occupancy of families in such housing, that such maximum income limits and all revisions thereof shall be subject to the prior approval of the Authority, and that the Authority may require the public housing agency to review and to revise such maximum income limits if the Authority determines that changed conditions in the locality make such revisions necessary in achieving the purposes of this Act;

(b) a duly authorized official of the public housing agency involved shall make periodic written statements to the Authority that an investigation has been made of each family admitted to the low-rent housing project involved during the period covered thereby, and that, on the basis of the report of said investigation, he has found that each such family at the time of its admission (i) had a net family income not exceeding the maximum income limits theretofore fixed by the public housing agency (and approved by the Authority) for admission of families of low income to such housing; and (ii) lived in an unsafe, insanitary, or overcrowded dwelling, or was to be displaced by another low-rent housing project or by a public slum-clearance or redevelopment project, or actually was without housing, or was about to be without housing as a result of a court order of eviction, due to causes other than the fault of the tenant: Provided, That the requirement in (ii) shall not be applicable in the case of the family of any veteran or serviceman (or of any deceased veteran or serviceman) where application for admission to such housing is made not later than five years after March 1, 1949;

"(c) in the selection of tenants (i) the public housing agency shall not discriminate against families, otherwise eligible for admission to such housing, because their incomes are derived in whole or in part from public assistance and (ii) in initially selecting families for admission to dwellings of given sizes and at specified rents the public housing agency shall (subject to the preferences prescribed in subsection 10 (g) of this Act) give preference to families having the most urgent housing needs, and thereafter, in selecting families for admission to such dwellings, shall give due consideration to the urgency of the families' housing needs; and

"(d) the public housing agency shall make periodic reexaminations of the net incomes of tenant families living in the low-rent housing project involved; and if it is found, upon such reexamination, that the net incomes of any such families have increased beyond the maximum income limits fixed by the public housing agency (and approved by the Authority) for continued occupancy in such housing, such families shall be required to move from the project."

. . .

TITLE IV—HOUSING RESEARCH

. . .

TITLE V—FARM HOUSING FINANCIAL ASSISTANCE BY TIM SECRETARY OF AGRICULTURE

SEC. 501. (a) The Secretary of Agriculture (hereinafter referred to as the "Secretary") is authorized, subject to the terms and conditions of this title, to extend financial assistance, through the Farmers Home Administration, to owners of farms in the United States and in the Territories of Alaska and Hawaii and in Puerto Rico and the Virgin Islands, to enable them to construct, improve, alter, repair, or replace dwellings and other farm buildings on their farms, to provide them, their tenants, lessees, sharecroppers, and laborers with decent, safe, and sanitary living conditions and adequate farm buildings as specified in this title.

. . .

TITLE VI—MISCELLANEOUS PROVISIONS

SOURCE: Housing Act of 1949. Title V of Public Law 81-171.

ANALYSIS

The Housing Act of 1949 (HA) had its origins in President Franklin Delano Roosevelt's New Deal. In the late 1930s, his administration began a program that tore down old, dilapidated buildings in order to construct public housing in the form of three- or four-story buildings on the newly vacant lots. The homes were available to those who could afford the rental fees that were charged by the local public agency that managed the real estate. Politicians were enthused by the initial results and strengthened the program through the HA.

The act authorized the construction of approximately 810,000 housing units to be built over a six-year period. As part of the urban renewal effort, developers quickly tore down ramshackle buildings, thereby displacing the residents, but did not build new structures rapidly. The end result was a shortage of affordable housing because it took more than 20 years to construct the homes authorized by the HA.

While this effort succeeded in revitalizing inner cities, it also led to the concentration of impoverished members of minority groups as they moved to the remaining slums. To address that issue, the federal government began to construct high-rise buildings, often in the form of towers. These new buildings quickly decayed, partially because of the shoddy workmanship utilized in their construction.

FURTHER READING

Biles, Roger. 2011. *The Fate of Cities: Urban America and the Federal Government, 1945–2000.* Lawrence: University Press of Kansas.

Conn, Steven. 2014. *Americans against the City: Anti-Urbanism in the Twentieth Century*. New York: Oxford University Press.

Hays, R. Allen. 2012. *The Federal Government & Urban Housing*. 3rd ed. Albany, NY: SUNY Press.

Vale, Lawrence J. 2002. *Reclaiming Public Housing: A Half Century of Struggle in Three Public Neighborhoods*. Cambridge, MA: Harvard University Press.

"In Order That the Nation May Meet the Staffing Requirements of the Struggle for Freedom"

- ***Document:*** Manpower Development and Training Act of 1962, as Amended (Excerpts)
- ***Date:*** November 8, 1966
- ***Where:*** Washington, D.C.
- ***Significance:*** The Manpower Development and Training Act was created to retrain workers who had lost their jobs to new technologies in factories.

DOCUMENT

AN ACT

Relating to manpower requirements, resources, development and utilization, and for other purposes.

Be it enacted by the Senate and House of Representatives of the United States of America in Congress assembled, That this Act may be cited as the "Manpower Development Training Act of 1962."

TITLE I—MANPOWER REQUIREMENTS, DEVELOPMENT, AND UTILIZATION

STATEMENT OF FINDINGS AND PURPOSE

SEC. 101. The Congress finds that there is critical need for more and better trained personnel in many vital occupational categories, including professional, scientific, technical, and apprenticeable categories; that even in periods of high unemployment, many employment opportunities remain unfilled because of the shortages of qualified personnel; and that it is in the national interest that current and prospective manpower shortages be identified and that persons who can be qualified for these positions through education and training be sought out and trained, in order that the Nation may meet the staffing requirements of the struggle for freedom. The Congress further finds that the skills of many persons have been rendered obsolete by dislocations in the economy arising from automation or other technological developments, foreign competition, relocation of industry, shifts in market demands, and other changes in the structure of the economy; that Government leadership is necessary to insure that the benefits of automation do not become burdens of widespread unemployment; that the problem of assuring sufficient employment opportunities will be compounded by the extraordinarily rapid growth of the labor force in the next decade, particularly by the entrance of young people into the labor force, that improved planning and expanded efforts will be required to assure that men, women, and young people will be trained and available to meet shifting employment needs; that many persons now unemployed or underemployed, in order to become qualified for reemployment or full employment must be assisted in providing themselves with skills which are or will be in demand in the labor market; that the skills of many persons now employed are inadequate to enable them to make their maximum contribution to the Nation's economy; and that it is in the national interest that the opportunity to acquire new skills be afforded to these people with the least delay in order to alleviate the hardships of unemployment, reduce the costs of unemployment compensation and public assistance, and to increase the Nation's productivity and its capacity to meet the requirements of the space age. The Congress further finds that many professional employees who have become unemployed because of the specialized nature of their previous employment are in need of brief refresher or reorientation educational courses in order to become qualified for other employment in their professions, where such training would further the purpose of this Act. It is therefore the purpose of this Act to require the Federal Government to appraise the manpower requirements and resources of the Nation, and to develop and apply the information and methods needed to deal with the problems of unemployment resulting from automation and technological changes and other types of persistent unemployment.

TITLE II—TRAINING AND SKILL DEVELOPMENT PROGRAMS

PART A—DUTIES OF THE SECRETARY OF LABOR

SEC. 201. In carrying out the purposes of this Act, the Secretary of Labor shall determine the skill requirements of the economy, develop policies for the adequate occupational development and maximum utilization of the skills of the Nation's workers, promote and encourage the development of broad and diversified training programs, including on-the-job training, designed to qualify for employment the many persons who cannot reasonably be expected to secure full-time employment without such training, and to equip the Nation's workers with the new and improved skills that are or will be required. Whenever appropriate, the Secretary of Labor shall coordinate and provide for combinations of programs, to be pursued concurrently or sequentially, under this Act with programs under other Federal Acts, where the purposes of this Act would be accomplished thereby.

. . .

PART B—DUTIES OF THE SECRETARY OF HEALTH, EDUCATION, AND WELFARE

SEC. 231. The Secretary of Health, Education, and Welfare, shall, pursuant to the provisions of this title enter into agreements with States under which the appropriate State education agencies will undertake to provide training needed to equip persons referred to the Secretary of Health, Education, and Welfare by the Secretary of Labor pursuant to section 202, for the occupations specified in the referrals, except that with respect to education to be provided pursuant to referrals under subsection (b) or (i) of section 202, the Secretary of Health, Education, and Welfare may make arrangements for the provision of the education to be provided under such through other appropriate education agencies. Such State agencies shall provide for such training through public educational agencies or institutions or through arrangements with private educational or training institutions where such private institutions can provide equipment or services not available in public institutions, particularly for training in technical and subprofessional occupations, or where such institutions can, at comparable cost, (1) provide substantially equivalent training, or (2) make possible an expanded use of the individual referral method, or (3) aid in reducing more quickly unemployment or current and prospective manpower shortages. . . .

PART C—REDEVELOPMENT AREAS

SEC. 241. The Secretaries of Labor and of Health, Education, and Welfare, in accordance with their respective responsibilities under parts A and B of this title, are authorized to provide a supplementary program of training and training allowances, in consultation with the Secretary of Commerce, for unemployed and underemployed persons residing in areas designated as redevelopment areas by the Secretary of Commerce under the Area Redevelopment Act or any subsequent Act authorizing such designation. . . .

PART D—CORRECTIONAL INSTITUTIONS

SEC. 251. Without regard to any other provision of this title or section 301 of this Act, the Secretary of Labor shall, during the period ending June 30, 1969, develop and carry out experimental and demonstration programs of training and education for persons in correctional institutions who are in need thereof to obtain employment upon release. Arrangements for such education and training shall be made by the Secretary of Health, Education, and Welfare after consultation with the appropriate area manpower development and training advisory committee. . . .

PART E—WORK EXPERIENCE AND TRAINING PROGRAMS

SEC. 261. (a) The Secretary of Labor in cooperation with the Secretary of Health, Education, and Welfare shall provide, under this part, programs for needy persons who require work experience or special family and supportive services, as well as training, in order that they may be assisted to secure and hold regular employment in a competitive labor market. . . .

(b) In developing and approving programs under this part, the Secretary of Labor shall give priority to programs with a high-training potential and which afford the pest prospects for contributing to the upward mobility of participants. . . .

TITLE III—MISCELLANEOUS

. . .

Termination of Authority

SEC. 310. (a) All authority conferred under title II of this Act shall terminate at the close of June 30, 1969.

SOURCE: U.S. Congress. 1966. Manpower Development and Training Act of 1962, as Amended. Public Law 87-415.

ANALYSIS

In 1961, the unemployment rate nationally stood at 7 percent. One of the causes was the automation of numerous factories over the course of the 1950s that resulted in the loss of jobs by workers. They required new job skills in order to find comparable paying jobs like the ones they had lost. Congress responded with the Manpower Development and Training Act of 1962 (MDTA), which was signed into law by President John F. Kennedy.

The Department of Labor was charged with retraining the laborers. Its program combined classroom instruction and on-the-job training. The first trainees tended to be white men who were head of households. They received a stipend to support their families as they enrolled in the program for up to a year. After that group had cycled through, the program was expanded to include women and African American men. What began as a retraining program quickly evolved into a poverty program as the training was shifted from individuals reentering the workforce to those who had difficulty obtaining a job.

The MDTA was under constant criticism during its existence, which ranged from 1963 to 1974. It was alleged that the training that was being offered was only beneficial to the poor as they received payment to gain job skills that were not required in the workforce. Criticisms also included that far too much money was being spent on the program for the number of workers that it produced. Much of the expense was blamed on the creation of a large bureaucracy in Washington, D.C., to administrate the nationwide effort. The MDTA was superseded in 1974 by the Comprehensive Educational and Training Act, which allowed for similar training to continue under the auspices of local communities.

FURTHER READING

Kremen, Gladys Roth. 1974. "MDTA: The Origins of the Manpower Development and Training Act of 1962." https://www.dol.gov/dol/aboutdol/history/mono-mdtatext.htm (accessed February 12, 2017).

Mucciaroni, Gary. 1990. *The Political Failure of Employment Policy, 1945–1982*. Pittsburgh: University of Pittsburgh Press.

Weir, Margaret. 1992. *Politics and Jobs: The Boundaries of Employment Policy in the United States*. Princeton, NJ: Princeton University Press.

"This Economic Distress of the Appalachian Region is a Matter of Serious Concern"

- ***Document:*** Joint Meeting of the Advisory Policy Board to Area Redevelopment Administration and Conference of Appalachian Governors (Excerpt)
- ***Date:*** April 9, 1963
- ***Where:*** Washington, D.C.
- ***Significance:*** President John F. Kennedy outlined how his administration was working to address Appalachian poverty and the reasons that it was yielding mixed results. During his talk, he also proposed the creation of what became the President's Appalachian Research Commission (PARC). That body produced a report entitled *Appalachia: A Report by the President's Appalachian Regional Commission 1964*, which was utilized to craft the Appalachian Regional Development Act of 1965.

DOCUMENT

SECRETARY HODGES: Gentlemen, the President of the United States.

Mr. President, we have already heard from Mr. McDermott on what is being done in the disaster work; we heard a few words from Secretary Wirtz and Secretary Freeman. We have several governors here or their representatives and we have told this group we think this is a wonderful event, to get the people here from the Appalachian region and we are going to continue talking.

We would like very much to have you say how you feel about this and give us any advice you care to.

THE PRESIDENT: Governors, I have a statement here, which is to be distributed. I think this economic distress of the Appalachian region is a matter of serious concern to all of us.

Our primary goal has been to reduce the immediate distress of the Appalachian region is a matter of serious concern to all of us.

The Food Surplus Program was expanded and the Food Stamp Plan in the Appalachian region extended. You are familiar with what the Area Development Act has done in the region, what the accelerated Public Works Program has done, which has amounted to $60 million in the Appalachian region, 100,000 man months of employment.

If we can get the additional $500 million we have requested for this program, we can put many more men to work. I think this program is essential.

I think if we are not able to get this money replaced by Congress, we are not going to get any action in these programs. I don't think we can look with equanimity on this continued concentration of long-term hard core unemployment. I hope, therefore, the Congress, the House of Representatives, will reverse itself, and any action you generally can take—I know you have been in touch with your congressional representatives—I know will be very helpful because this country is in a rather prosperous state now, I think we are all comfortable, but for the fact we are not able to do much for these five million people out of work, particularly in your region, so we have to have a program which will take care of them.

Now our regular programs I think are also some help. The Corps of Engineers has under construction in this region projects costing $167 million. Soil Conservation Service, $28 million. The Virginia's program in the Appalachian counties totals $215 million. Housing and Home Finance Agency has outstanding over $133 million in loans and almost $4 million in planning advances.

The federal portion of highway construction underway in the region is valued at $659 million. Total federal public works therefore amounts to more than a billion dollars.

Now with only five per cent of the labor force, this region has over 11 per cent of the countries unemployment. The current unemployment averages 12 ½ per cent, more than twice the national average.

Of all the nations r edevelopment areas eligible for assistance under the Area Redevelopment Act, the Appalachian region accounts for 35 per cent of the unemployment.

What we are all concerned about is that in spite of these programs, in spite of what you have done in the states and counties, we still have the problem, we still haven't made a dent. I think Mr. Batt told you this morning about some program they got into one of these areas, creating 75 jobs, and that same day they threw 250 people out of coal mines, so we are not making much progress in the sense of really biting into the long-term unemployment.

On the other hand, if we desisted, it would be much worse than it is. So I don't think it is really a good argument to say our actions haven't been successful. I think if we didn't act we would be in worse shape. What we have to do is act more.

I am directing every department head and agency responsible for programs which can properly contribute to the economic development of the Appalachian region to review programs and make appropriate changes under present authorities and budgets in order to give greater assistance to the economic development of the region. An appropriate special consideration should be given to this area in developing proposals for the fiscal year 1965 budget, on which work will begin in the agencies within the next few months. The agency head should designate an individual to be responsible for seeing to it that these things are accomplished and to submit a progress report by May 15, 1963.

I propose the establishment within the Department of Commerce of a Joint Federal-State Committee on the Appalachian Region, under the chairmanship of Under-secretary of Commerce, Mr. Roosevelt. He knows the region. It should consist of members representing each of the federal agencies concerned and each of the states. As its first job I would expect the committee to prepare for this year a comprehensive program for the economic development of the Appalachian region.

I expect that program to consist of plans for improving facilities for all forms of passenger and freight transportation in the region, expansion of facilities for education, research and training, development of water, minerals and forest resources, and establishing expanded opportunities for the attraction of tourists and other visitors to the region.

I have directed the Area Redevelopment Administrator to work closely with state officials and university heads, in the Appalachian region, to establish an Appalachian Institute, as a center for research and training in connection with the long-run needs for economic development of the region.

These programs I think are all moving in the right direction, but of course we still, it seems to me, have to move more intensively.

Our tax proposals will be of assistance, as will the passage of the Administration's proposed Youth Employment Act. None of these acts by themselves can do the job, but altogether if we can maintain prosperity through the rest of the country we can concentrate our resources in attacking this particular region which is our most serious national problem. So that a good many of our programs, which are not directly applicable to the region, such as the tax reduction, still will help the region, if it takes the pressure off of the rest of the country and we can then steer a good deal more of our national effort into this one area. I want to express my appreciation, Governor, for the chance to be here and also to express my thanks to the governors for coming and I hope out of this meeting, you can get some additional suggestions on what action we might take.

SOURCE: The White House. 1963. *Joint Meeting of the Advisory Policy Board to Area Redevelopment Administration and Conference of Appalachian Governors.* Washington, D.C.: ACE-Federal Reporters, Inc., 18–23.

ANALYSIS

In 1960, national attention was brought to Appalachia through senator John F. Kennedy's campaign in West Virginia for the Democratic Party's presidential nomination. West Virginia was a key test for Kennedy to determine whether a Roman Catholic candidate could win an election in a predominantly Protestant state. He won the primary with more than 60 percent of the votes cast after he promised to address West Virginia's obvious poverty if he became president. His administration technically kept his promise by formulating the Area Redevelopment Act of 1961. Although the act was written to address urban poverty, Kennedy encouraged Appalachian leaders to use it to address their needs.

With the help of the governors of the Appalachian states, Kennedy established the President's Appalachian Research Commission (PARC) in 1963. The commission began working on a plan that called for government assistance with tasks such as improving the region's infrastructure through highway construction, installing water delivery and sewage systems, improving the region's educational system, and supporting existing industries through tax breaks. Before Kennedy was able to implement the recommendations coming from PARC as part of his Appalachian program, he was assassinated.

FURTHER READING

Eller, Ronald D. 2008. *Uneven Ground: Appalachia since 1945*. Lexington: University Press of Kentucky.

President's Appalachian Regional Commission. 1964. *Appalachia: A Report by the President's Appalachian Regional Commission 1964*. Washington, D.C.: U.S. Government Printing Office.

Taul, Glen Edward. 2001. "Poverty, Development, and Government in Appalachia: Origins of the Appalachian Regional Commission." PhD dissertation, University of Kentucky.

"This Administration Today, Here and Now, Declares Unconditional War on Poverty"

- ***Document:*** President Lyndon Johnson's State of the Union Address (Excerpt)
- ***Date:*** January 8, 1964
- ***Where:*** Washington, D.C.
- ***Significance:*** President Lyndon Baines Johnson declared unconditional War on Poverty.

DOCUMENT

Unfortunately, many Americans live on the outskirts of hope—some because of their poverty, and some because of their color, and all too many because of both. Our task is to help replace their despair with opportunity.

This administration today, here and now, declares unconditional War on Poverty in America. I urge this Congress and all Americans to join with me in that effort.

It will not be a short or easy struggle, no single weapon or strategy will suffice, but we shall not rest until that war is won. The richest Nation on earth can afford to win it. We cannot afford to lose it. One thousand dollars invested in salvaging an unemployable youth today can return $40,000 or more in his lifetime.

Poverty is a national problem, requiring improved national organization and support. But this attack, to be effective, must also be organized at the State and the local level and must be supported and directed by State and local efforts.

For the war against poverty will not be won here in Washington. It must be won in the field, in every private home, in every public office, from the courthouse to the White House.

The program I shall propose will emphasize this cooperative approach to help that one-fifth of all American families with incomes too small to even meet their basic needs.

Our chief weapons in a more pinpointed attack will be better schools, and better health, and better homes, and better training, and better job opportunities to help more Americans, especially young Americans, escape from squalor and misery and unemployment rolls where other citizens help to carry them.

Very often a lack of jobs and money is not the cause of poverty, but the symptom. The cause may lie deeper in our failure to give our fellow citizens a fair chance to develop their own capacities, in a lack of education and training, in a lack of medical care and housing, in a lack of decent communities in which to live and bring up their children.

But whatever the cause, our joint Federal-local effort must pursue poverty, pursue it wherever it exists—in city slums and small towns, in sharecropper shacks or in migrant worker camps, on Indian Reservations, among whites as well as Negroes, among the young as well as the aged, in the boom towns and in the depressed areas.

Our aim is not only to relieve the symptom of poverty, but to cure it and, above all, to prevent it. No single piece of legislation, however, is going to suffice.

We will launch a special effort in the chronically distressed areas of Appalachia.

We must expand our small but our successful area redevelopment program.

We must enact youth employment legislation to put jobless, aimless, hopeless youngsters to work on useful projects.

We must distribute more food to the needy through a broader food stamp program.

We must create a National Service Corps to help the economically handicapped of our own country as the Peace Corps now helps those abroad.

We must modernize our unemployment insurance and establish a high-level commission on automation. If we have the brain power to invent these machines, we have the brain power to make certain that they are a boon and not a bane to humanity.

We must extend the coverage of our minimum wage laws to more than 2 million workers now lacking this basic protection of purchasing power.

We must, by including special school aid funds as part of our education program, improve the quality of teaching, training, and counseling in our hardest hit areas.

We must build more libraries in every area and more hospitals and nursing homes under the Hill-Burton Act, and train more nurses to staff them.

DID YOU KNOW?

The Other America: Poverty in the United States

In 1962, Michael Harrington's *The Other America* was published. It proved one of the landmark books of the twentieth century because it brought to the public's attention the plight of approximately 40–50 million Americans who were trapped in a "culture-of-poverty." Since the members of that group came from families that had for generations been undereducated, malnourished, and in generally poor health, it was doubtful that they had the means to rise above their present state. Harrington put the onus on financial elites and the government to provide the impoverished the resources and tools required to allow them to share in the American dream. President John F. Kennedy read the book and used it to inform some antipoverty initiatives that were being drafted by his administration. Kennedy was assassinated before the measures could be advanced to Congress. President Lyndon Baines Johnson subsequently adopted Kennedy's proposals and made them components of his 1964 War on Poverty.

FURTHER READING

Isserman, Maurice. 2000. *The Other American: The Life of Michael Harrington*. New York: PublicAffairs.

We must provide hospital insurance for our older citizens financed by every worker and his employer under Social Security, contributing no more than $1 a month during the employee's working career to protect him in his old age in a dignified manner without cost to the Treasury, against the devastating hardship of prolonged or repeated illness.

We must, as a part of a revised housing and urban renewal program, give more help to those displaced by slum clearance, provide more housing for our poor and our elderly, and seek as our ultimate goal in our free enterprise system a decent home for every American family.

We must help obtain more modern mass transit within our communities as well as low-cost transportation between them.

Above all, we must release $11 billion of tax reduction into the private spending stream to create new jobs and new markets in every area of this land.

These programs are obviously not for the poor or the underprivileged alone. Every American will benefit by the extension of social security to cover the hospital costs of their aged parents. Every American community will benefit from the construction or modernization of schools, libraries, hospitals, and nursing homes, from the training of more nurses and from the improvement of urban renewal in public transit. And every individual American taxpayer and every corporate taxpayer will benefit from the earliest possible passage of the pending tax bill from both the new investment it will bring and the new jobs that it will create.

SOURCE: *Public Papers of the Presidents of the United States: Lyndon B. Johnson, 1965*. Vol. 1, entry 91 (Washington, D.C.: Government Printing Office, 1965): 112–118.

ANALYSIS

In his first State of the Union address, President Lyndon Baines Johnson famously declared unconditional War on Poverty. In his address, which is excerpted here, he signaled his intention to address endemic poverty in locales such as rural Appalachia, Native American reservations, and African American ghettos. He envisioned his programs as a partnership between federal, state, and local officials. Also included was the idea of "maximum feasible participation of the poor," which meant that the impoverished themselves were to have a voice in the process. To the poor, this meant that they were finally going to be empowered to address local issues that kept them locked out of economic opportunity. Unfortunately, despite President Johnson's leadership on the issue, local political power brokers were uninterested in input from their poorer constituents. They welcomed the federal money but chose in many cases to apply it in ways that benefited their political and economic interests and those of their constituents. Due to the failure of the federal government to address local cabals, the War on Poverty, which began with so much promise, ultimately failed to substantially benefit the United States' most impoverished citizens.

FURTHER READING

Ashmore, Susan Youngblood. 2008. *Carry It On: The War on Poverty and the Civil Rights Movement in Alabama, 1964–1972*. Athens, GA: University of Georgia Press.

Burch, John Russell, Jr. 2008. *Owsley County, Kentucky, and the Perpetuation of Poverty*. Jefferson, NC: McFarland & Co.

Gillette, Michael L. 2010. *Launching the War on Poverty: An Oral History*. 2nd ed. New York: Oxford University Press.

Goldstein, Alyosha. 2012. *Poverty in Common: The Politics of Community Action during the American Century*. Durham: Duke University Press.

Newman, Katherine S. 2010. *Who Cares?: Public Ambivalence and Government Activism from the New Deal to the Second Gilded Age*. Princeton, NJ: Princeton University Press.

O'Connor, Alice. 2001. *Poverty Knowledge: Social Science, Social Policy, and the Poor in Twentieth-Century U.S. History*. Princeton, NJ: Princeton University Press.

Orleck, Annelise, and Lisa Gayle Hazirjian, eds. 2011. *The War on Poverty: A New Grassroots History, 1964–1980*. Athens: University of Georgia Press.

Quadagno, Jill. 1994. *The Color of Welfare: How Racism Undermined the War on Poverty*. New York: Oxford University Press.

"Conquest of Poverty Is Well within Our Power"

- ***Document:*** The Council of Economic Adviser's Economic Report of 1964 (Excerpts)
- ***Date:*** January 1964
- ***Where:*** Washington, D.C.
- ***Significance:*** The *Economic Report of 1964*, prepared by the Council of Economic Advisers, made the case that poverty could be eradicated by government-stimulated economic growth, which would inevitably result in the full employment of the nation's workforce.

DOCUMENT

ELIMINATING POVERTY—A NATIONAL GOAL

There will always be some Americans who are better off than others. But it need not follow that "the poor are always with us." In the United States today we can see on the horizon a society of abundance, free of much of the misery and degradation that have been the age-old fate of man. Steadily rising productivity, together with an improving network of private and social insurance and assistance, has been eroding mass poverty in America. But the process is far too slow. It is high time to redouble and to concentrate our efforts to eliminate poverty.

Poverty is costly not only to the poor but to the whole society. Its ugly by-products include ignorance, disease, delinquency, crime, irresponsibility, immorality, indifference. None of these social evils and hazards will, of course, wholly disappear with the elimination of poverty. But their severity will be markedly reduced. Poverty is no purely private or local concern. It is a social and national problem.

But the overriding objective is to improve the quality of life of individual human beings. For poverty deprives the individual not only of material comforts but of human dignity and fulfillment. Poverty is rarely a builder of character.

The poor inhabit a world scarcely recognizable, and rarely recognized, by the majority of their fellow Americans. It is a world apart, whose inhabitants are isolated from the mainstream of American life and alienated from its values. It is a world where Americans are literally concerned with day-to-day survival—a roof over their heads, where the next meal is coming from. It is a world where a minor illness is a major tragedy, where pride and privacy must be sacrificed to get help, where honesty can become a luxury and ambition a myth. Worst of all, the poverty of the fathers is visited upon the children.

Equality of opportunity is the American dream, and universal education our noblest pledge to realize it. But, for the children of the poor, education is a handicap race; many are too ill prepared and ill motivated at home to learn at school. And many communities lengthen the handicap by providing the worst schooling for those who need the best.

Although poverty remains a bitter reality for too many Americans, its incidence has been steadily shrinking. The fruits of general economic growth have been widely shared; individuals and families have responded to incentives and opportunities for improvement; government and private programs have raised the educational attainments, housing standards, health, and productivity of the population; private and social insurance has increasingly protected families against loss of earnings due to death, disability, illness, old age, and unemployment. Future headway against poverty will likewise require attacks on many fronts: the active promotion of a full-employment, rapid-growth economy; a continuing assault on discrimination; and a wide range of other measures to strike at specific roots of low income. As in the past, progress will require the combined efforts of all levels of government and of private individuals and groups. All Americans will benefit from this progress. Our Nation's most precious resource is its people. We pay twice for poverty: once in the production lost in wasted human potential, again in the resources diverted to coping with poverty's social by-products. Humanity compels our action,

but it is sound economics as well. . . .

ORGANIZING THE ATTACK ON POVERTY

In this latest phase of the Nation's effort to conquer poverty, we must marshal already developed resources, focus already expressed concerns, and back them with the full strength of an aroused public conscience.

Poverty, as has been shown, has many faces. It is found in the North and in the South; in the East and in the West; on the farm and in the city.

It is found among the young and among the old, among the employed and the unemployed. Its roots are many and its causes complex. To defeat it requires a coordinated and comprehensive attack. No single program can embrace all who are poor, and no single program can strike at all the sources of today's and tomorrow's poverty.

Diverse attacks are needed, but we must not lose sight of their common target—poverty. Many programs are directed against social problems which the poor share with the non-poor—insecurity of income, depressed regional economies, inefficient and unattractive rural and urban environments, disabilities of health and age, inadequate educational opportunities, racial discrimination. These are all to the good. But we must not let poor individuals and families get lost between these programs. Programs must be sufficiently coordinated that, whatever else they individually accomplish, they act together to lift the economic and social status of America's poor. And soon. For war has now been declared on poverty as such.

This coordinated attack must be adapted to local circumstances. The needs of the poor are not the same in East Kentucky and in West Harlem. Coordinated programs of community action will play a critical role in the assault on poverty. Communities will be encouraged and helped to develop individual programs aimed at the special problems of their own poor families. Individual communities thus can participate in a nationwide action, research, and demonstration program, backed by the interest and resources of State and local governments and private organizations, and the coordinated efforts of Federal agencies working in such fields as education, health, housing, welfare, and agriculture.

Conquest of poverty is well within our power. About $11 billion a year would bring all poor families up to the $3,000 income level we have taken to be the minimum for a decent life. The majority of the Nation could simply tax themselves enough to provide the necessary income supplements to their less fortunate citizens. The burden—one-fifth of the annual defense budget, less than 2 percent of GNP—would certainly not be intolerable. But this "solution" would leave untouched most of the roots of poverty. Americans want to *earn* the American standard of living by their own efforts and contributions. It will be far better, even if more difficult, to equip and to permit the poor of the Nation to produce and to earn the additional $11 billion, and more. We can surely afford greater generosity in relief of distress. But the major thrust of our campaign must be against causes rather than symptoms. We can afford the cost of that campaign too.

The Nation's attack on poverty must be based on a change in national attitude. We must open our eyes and minds to the poverty in our midst. Poverty is not the inevitable fate of any man. The condition can be eradicated; and since it can be, it must be. It is time to renew our faith in the worth and capacity of all human beings; to recognize that, whatever their past history or present condition, all kinds of Americans can contribute to their country; and to allow Government to assume its responsibility for action and leadership in promoting the general welfare.

SOURCE: Economic Report of the President: Transmitted to the Congress January 1964: Together with the Annual Report of the Council of Economic Advisers. Washington, D.C.: U.S. Government Printing Office, 1964.

ANALYSIS

On January 4, 1964, President Lyndon Baines Johnson declared War on Poverty in his first State of the Union address. To support Johnson's contention that it was not only possible to wage War on Poverty but also to actually eliminate it, the *Council of Economic Adviser's Economic Report of 1964* provided the outlines of how full employment could be achieved. The report served to strongly influence Congress to enact the Economic Opportunity Act of 1964, which created the Office of Economic Opportunity to oversee many of the administration's War on Poverty initiatives. Unfortunately, for the administration, the impoverished, and the nation at large, the War on Poverty never came close to achieving full employment.

FURTHER READING

Goldstein, Alyosha. 2012. *Poverty in Common: The Politics of Community Action during the American Century*. Durham: Duke University Press.

O'Connor, Alice. 2001. *Poverty Knowledge: Social Science, Social Policy, and the Poor in Twentieth-Century U.S. History*. Princeton, NJ: Princeton University Press.

Orleck, Annelise, and Lisa Gayle Hazirjian, eds. 2011. *The War on Poverty: A New Grassroots History, 1964–1980*. Athens: University of Georgia Press.

Woods, Randall B. 2016. *Prisoners of Hope: Lyndon B. Johnson, the Great Society, and the Limits of Liberalism*. New York: Basic Books.

Zelizer, Julian E. 2015. *The Fierce Urgency of Now: Lyndon Johnson, Congress, and the Battle for the Great Society*. New York: Penguin Press.

"For the First Time in All the History of the Human Race, a Great Nation Is Able to Make and Is Willing to Make a Commitment to Eradicate Poverty among Its People"

- ***Document:*** President Lyndon Johnson's Remarks following the Signing of the Economic Opportunity Act
- ***Date:*** August 20, 1964
- ***Where:*** Washington, D.C.
- ***Significance:*** The Economic Opportunity Act of 1964 created the Office of Economic Opportunity to administer many War on Poverty programs, including Volunteers in Service to America (VISTA), the Job Corps, and the Community Action Program.

DOCUMENT

My fellow Americans:

On this occasion the American people and our American system are making history.

For so long as man has lived on this earth poverty has been his curse.

On every continent in every age men have sought escape from poverty's oppression.

Today for the first time in all the history of the human race, a great nation is able to make and is willing to make a commitment to eradicate poverty among its people.

Whatever our situation in life, whatever our partisan affiliation, we can be grateful and proud that we are able to pledge ourselves this morning to this historic course. We can be especially proud of the nature of the commitments that we are making.

This is not in any sense a cynical proposal to exploit the poor with a promise of a handout or a dole.

We know—we learned long ago—that answer is no answer.

The measure before me this morning for signature offers the answer that its title implies—the answer of opportunity. For the purpose of the Economic Opportunity Act of 1964 is to offer opportunity, not an opiate.

For the million young men and women who are out of school and who are out of work, this program will permit us to take them off the streets, put them into work training programs, to prepare them for productive lives, not wasted lives.

In this same sound, sensible, and responsible way we will reach into all the pockets of poverty and help our people find their footing for a long climb toward a better way of life.

We will work with them through our communities all over the country to develop comprehensive community action programs—with remedial education, with job training, with retraining, with health and employment counseling, with neighborhood improvement. We will strike at poverty's roots.

This is by no means a program confined just to our cities. Rural America is afflicted deeply by rural poverty, and this program will help poor farmers get back on their feet and help poor farmers stay on their farms.

It will help those small businessmen who live on the borderline of poverty. It will help the unemployed heads of families maintain their skills and learn new skills.

In helping others, all of us will really be helping ourselves. For this bill will permit us to give our young people an opportunity to work here at home in constructive ways as volunteers, going to war against poverty instead of going to war against foreign enemies.

All of this will be done through a program which is prudent and practical, which is consistent with our national ideals.

Every dollar authorized in this bill was contained in the budget request that I sent to the Congress last January. Every dollar spent will result in savings to the country and especially to the local taxpayers in the cost of crime, welfare, of health, and of police protection.

We are not content to accept the endless growth of relief rolls or welfare rolls. We want to offer the forgotten fifth of our people opportunity and not doles.

That is what this measure does for our times.

DID YOU KNOW?

Ms. Poverty

Mollie Orshansky earned the moniker "Ms. Poverty" by changing how the federal government determined who was impoverished and who was not. During the Kennedy administration, the Council of Economic Advisers arbitrarily selected $3,000 to mark the poverty line. Orshansky developed a formula that utilized both financial and demographic data to create a more accurate picture of poverty. She published her initial data, which focused on children, at the very time that planners in the midst of creating the Office of Economic Opportunity happened to be seeking a better way of measuring poverty. Intrigued by her work, the planners asked if she could expand her research to include other segments of the population. Those results were published in her article "Counting the Poor: Another Look at the Poverty Profile." Less than six months later, the Office of Economic Opportunity adopted Orshansky's poverty thresholds as the official federal determination of poverty.

FURTHER READING

O'Connor, Alice. 2001. *Poverty Knowledge: Social Science, Social Policy, and the Poor in Twentieth-Century U.S. History.* Princeton: Princeton University Press.

Orshansky, Mollie. 1965. "Counting the Poor: Another Look at the Poverty Profile." *Social Security Bulletin* 28, no. 1: 3–29.

Our American answer to poverty is not to make the poor more secure in their poverty but to reach down and to help them lift themselves out of the ruts of poverty and move with the large majority along the high road of hope and prosperity.

The days of the dole in our country are numbered. I firmly believe that as of this moment a new day of opportunity is dawning and a new era of progress is opening for us all.

And to you men and women in the Congress who fought so long, so hard to help bring about this legislation, to you private citizens in labor and in business who lent us a helping hand, to Sargent Shriver and that band of loyal men and women who made up this task force that brings our dream into a reality today, we say "Thank you" for all the American people. In the days and years to come, those who have an opportunity to participate in this program will vindicate your thinking and vindicate your action.

Thank you very much.

SOURCE: Lyndon B. Johnson: "Remarks upon Signing the Economic Opportunity Act, August 20, 1964." *Public Papers of the Presidents of the United States, Lyndon Johnson, 1963–1964, Book II.* Washington, D.C.: Government Printing Office, 1965, 988–990.

ANALYSIS

Soon after assuming the presidency following the assassination of President John F. Kennedy in November 1963, Lyndon Baines Johnson determined that the eradication of poverty would be the centerpiece of his domestic agenda. In his first State of the Union address, which was delivered on January 8, 1964, he declared "unconditional war" on poverty. The president's rhetoric was supported by the *Economic Report of 1964*, prepared by his Council of Economic Advisers, which made the case that poverty could be eradicated by government-stimulated economic growth, which would inevitably result in the full employment of the nation's workforce. Congress responded by passing the Economic Opportunity Act of 1964, which created the Office of Economic Opportunity (OEO) to administer many War on Poverty (WOP) programs, such as VISTA, the Job Corps, and the Community Action Program. The OEO's first director was Sargent Shriver, who was President Kennedy's brother-in-law.

In the years that followed World War II, the United States was enjoying obvious economic prosperity. The country's boom did not extend to rural areas, where many residents were forced to out-migrate to urban centers where it was believed economic opportunities abounded. The migrants tended to form enclaves inhabited by people with similar backgrounds. Cities, such as Cincinnati, Ohio, and Detroit, Michigan, saw significant growth in poor and working-class communities inhabited by African Americans, Puerto Ricans, Mexican Americans, and white Appalachians. The impact of the internal migration can be illustrated by Akron, Ohio, where so many West

Virginians settled that it became known as "the capital of West Virginia." While many of the migrants found jobs, others did not. The arrival of so many poorer people strained city resources and budgets. Since many cities were unable to serve the needs of the new arrivals, people did what was required to subsist. In many places, crime rates soared. Frustrated local politicians turned to the federal government for the money required to address urban poverty. Their pleas were answered through the WOP, which focused primarily on the needs of urban areas. Even programs aimed at rural areas had an urban justification. If you provided enough economic development in rural America to keep the people from migrating to cities, then progress had been made in alleviating urban poverty.

Although poverty was a national concern, Appalachia was the one area in rural America that became a priority because of race. It was an embarrassment to many around the country that many white people in America were impoverished. Thus, it became a national mission to uplift Appalachians. Appalachians were the one group that all politicians at the national level could support. Southern Dixiecrat politicians supported programs that benefited whites, but worked diligently against WOP and civil rights legislation that would benefit African American communities. A similar dynamic was at play in the Southwest, where severely impoverished minority communities comprised of Mexicans were denied access to WOP programs.

Although Johnson's WOP was launched with great fanfare, the lack of political support was evident from the very beginning. While Congress passed the Economic Opportunity Act, it only provided initial funding of $970 million, which represented approximately 1 percent of the federal budget. This was a pittance for an effort underpinned by a theory that poverty could be eradicated by government-stimulated economic growth.

A key component of the OEO's charge was the idea of "maximum feasible participation of the poor." The impoverished were to be given a voice because they had a unique perspective that was essential to decision making at the local level. Johnson's administration hoped that the participation of the poor at the local level would show that the poverty programs were a hand-up instead of a handout. This proved a catastrophic mistake that undercut political support for the WOP. In Appalachia, entrenched elites welcomed the federal money but were not interested in any interference from outsiders in how to utilize the money locally. Much of the money that made it into the region was siphoned off by local political machines and never made it to the poor.

Similarly in cities, the ruling politicians were opposed to all nonelected decision makers and were angered by the flow of money to nongovernmental organizations. The politicians, including such powerful national figures like Chicago's mayor Richard M. Daley, argued that they could better address local poverty and thus should be able to control how all of the funding was utilized. In order to protect themselves from the politicians, many urban community action programs (CAPs) began participating in the electoral process by supporting candidates opposed to incumbent politicians. This political activity caused the Johnson administration to begin distancing itself from its creation.

By 1966, there were efforts underfoot in Congress to eradicate the CAP. The program was saved in 1967 through the efforts of Representative Edith Green of

Oregon, who shepherded several amendments through Congress that transferred oversight of the respective CAAs to local or state governments. During the same period, Congress changed how it funded the WOP, moving from approving large pieces of legislation that created or funded numerous programs under one umbrella to only funding specific programs, like Head Start, that were popular.

Another controversial WOP program was the Job Corps. Modeled after the New Deal's Civilian Conservation Corps, the Job Corps was intended to first provide vocational training to young people and then move them into a job. It was believed that providing people jobs would result in a drop in crime. The program attracted far too many enrollees than it could realistically help. By 1965, there were approximately 10,000 people in the program. Unfortunately, the Job Corps' administrators could not find meaningful employment, especially in urban areas where many of the workers lived. The inability of the Job Corps to place people in jobs drew many criticisms in Congress. The complaints escalated after a riot erupted at a Job Corps Center in Morganfield, Kentucky, in August 1965. The OEO was able to assuage the congressmen by making some structural changes in 1966 that allowed the Job Corps to continue to the present day.

Johnson's administration was unable to force Congress to provide the needed fiscal support for the WOP due to the escalating Vietnam War, which eroded Johnson's popularity, authority, and the federal Treasury. The WOP effectively ended at the close of Johnson's presidency. President Richard Nixon's administration had no interest in continuing most of his predecessor's "liberal policies." During the 1968 campaign, Nixon had actually articulated his intent to address Johnson's expansion of the country's welfare system. The Nixon administration, led by OEO director Donald Rumsfeld, took several years to dismantle many of the WOP programs. Those initiatives that the administration favored were gradually moved out from under the OEO's umbrella. During his second term, Nixon formally disbanded the OEO and replaced it with the Community Services Administration, which was politically far weaker than its predecessor. When President Ronald Reagan took office, he continued the Republican assault on the vestiges of the WOP by dismantling the Community Services Administration.

FURTHER READING

Ashmore, Susan Youngblood. 2008. *Carry It On: The War on Poverty and the Civil Rights Movement in Alabama, 1964–1972*. Athens, GA: University of Georgia Press.

Burch, John Russell, Jr. 2008. *Owsley County, Kentucky, and the Perpetuation of Poverty*. Jefferson, NC: McFarland & Co.

Council of Economic Advisors. 1964. *Economic Report of 1964*. Washington, D.C.: Government Printing Office.

Gillette, Michael L. 2010. *Launching the War on Poverty: An Oral History*. 2nd ed. New York: Oxford University Press.

Goldstein, Alyosha. 2012. *Poverty in Common: The Politics of Community Action during the American Century*. Durham: Duke University Press.

Newman, Katherine S. 2010. *Who Cares?: Public Ambivalence and Government Activism from the New Deal to the Second Gilded Age*. Princeton, NJ: Princeton University Press.

O'Connor, Alice. 2001. *Poverty Knowledge: Social Science, Social Policy, and the Poor in Twentieth-Century U.S. History*. Princeton, NJ: Princeton University Press.

Orleck, Annelise, and Lisa Gayle Hazirjian, eds. 2011. *The War on Poverty: A New Grassroots History, 1964–1980*. Athens: University of Georgia Press.

Quadagno, Jill. 1994. *The Color of Welfare: How Racism Undermined the War on Poverty*. New York: Oxford University Press.

Woods, Randall B. 2016. *Prisoners of Hope: Lyndon B. Johnson, the Great Society, and the Limits of Liberalism*. New York: Basic Books.

Zelizer, Julian E. 2015. *The Fierce Urgency of Now: Lyndon Johnson, Congress, and the Battle for the Great Society*. New York: Penguin Press.

"To Insure Equal Employment Opportunities for Federal Employees without Discrimination because of Race, Color, Religion, Sex or National Origin"

- ***Document:*** Civil Rights Act of 1964, Title VII (Excerpts)
- ***Date:*** July 2, 1964
- ***Where:*** Washington, D.C.
- ***Significance:*** Title VII of the Civil Rights Act of 1964 banned discrimination against individuals seeking employment regardless of sex or race. The title's language invoked the Commerce Clause of the Constitution, thereby making it applicable to both the public and private sectors.

DOCUMENT

TITLE VII—EQUAL EMPLOYMENT OPPORTUNITY
DEFINITIONS

SEC. 701. For the purposes of this title—

(a) The term "person" includes one or more individuals, labor unions, partnerships, associations, corporations, legal representatives, mutual companies, joint-stock companies, trusts, unincorporated organizations, trustees, trustees in bankruptcy, or receivers.

(b) The term "employer" means a person engaged in an industry affecting commerce who has twenty-five or more employees for each working day in each of twenty or more calendar weeks in the current or preceding calendar year, and any agent of such a person, but such term does not include (1) the United States, a corporation wholly owned by the Government of the United States, an Indian tribe, or a State or political subdivision thereof, (2) a bona fide private membership club (other than a labor organization) which is exempt from taxation under section 501(c) of the Internal Revenue Code of 1954: . . . That it shall be the policy of the United States to insure equal employment opportunities for Federal employees without discrimination because of race, color, religion, sex or national origin and the President shall utilize his existing authority to effectuate this policy.

(c) The term "employment agency" means any person regularly undertaking with or without compensation to procure employees for an employer or to procure for employees opportunities to work for an employer . . .

(d) The term "labor organization" means a labor organization engaged in an industry affecting commerce, and any agent of such an organization, and includes any organization of any kind, any agency, or employee representation committee, group, association, or plan so engaged in which employees participate and which exists for the purpose, in whole or in part, of dealing with employers concerning grievances, labor disputes, wages, rates of pay, hours, or other terms or conditions of employment, and any conference, general committee, joint or system board, or joint council so engaged which is subordinate to a national or international labor organization . . .

EXEMPTION

SEC. 702. This title shall not apply to an employer with respect to the employment of aliens outside any State, or to a religious corporation, association, or society with respect to the employment of individuals of a particular religion to perform work connected with the carrying on by such corporation, association, or society of its religious activities or to an educational institution with respect to the employment of individuals to perform work connected with the educational activities of such institution.

DISCRIMINATION BECAUSE OF RACE, COLOR, RELIGION, SEX, OR NATIONAL ORIGIN

SEC. 703. (a) It shall be an unlawful employment practice for an employer—

(1) to fail or refuse to hire or to discharge any individual, or otherwise to discriminate against any individual with respect to his compensation, terms, conditions, or privileges of employment, because of such individual's race, color, religion, sex, or national origin; or

(2) to limit, segregate, or classify his employees in any way which would deprive or tend to deprive any individual of employment opportunities or otherwise adversely affect his status as an employee, because of such individual's race, color, religion, sex, or national origin.

(b) It shall be an unlawful employment practice for an employment agency to fail or refuse to refer for employment, or otherwise to discriminate against, any individual because of his race, color, religion, sex, or national origin, or to classify or refer for employment any individual on the basis of his race, color, religion, sex, or national origin.

(c) It shall be an unlawful employment practice for a labor organization—

(1) to exclude or to expel from its membership, or otherwise to discriminate against, any individual because of his race, color, religion, sex, or national origin;

(2) to limit, segregate, or classify its membership, or to classify or fail or refuse to refer for employment any individual, in any way which would deprive or tend to deprive any individual of employment opportunities, or would limit such employment opportunities or otherwise adversely affect his status as an employee or as an applicant for employment, because of such individual's race, color, religion, sex, or national origin; or

(3) to cause or attempt to cause an employer to discriminate against an individual in violation of this section.

(d) It shall be an unlawful employment practice for any employer, labor organization, or joint labor-management committee controlling apprenticeship or other training or retraining, including on-the-job training programs to discriminate against any individual because of his race, color, religion, sex, or national origin in admission to, or employment in, any program established to provide apprenticeship or other training. . . .

OTHER UNLAWFUL EMPLOYMENT PRACTICES

SEC. 704. (a) It shall be an unlawful employment practice for an employer to discriminate against any of his employees or applicants for employment, for an employment agency to discriminate against any individual, or for a labor organization to discriminate against any member thereof or applicant for membership, because he has opposed, any practice made an unlawful employment practice by this title, or because he has made a charge, testified, assisted, or participated in any manner in an investigation, proceeding, or hearing under this title.

(b) It shall be an unlawful employment practice for an employer, labor organization, or employment agency to print or publish or cause to be printed or published any notice or advertisement relating to employment by such an employer or membership in or any classification or referral for employment by such a labor organization, or relating to any classification or referral for employment by such an employment agency, indicating any preference, limitation, specification, or discrimination, based on race, color, religion, sex, or national origin, except that such a notice or advertisement may indicate a preference, limitation, specification, or discrimination based on religion, sex, or national origin when religion, sex, or national origin is a bona fide occupational qualification for employment.

EQUAL EMPLOYMENT OPPORTUNITY COMMISSION

SEC. 705. (a) There is hereby created a Commission to be known as the Equal Employment Opportunity Commission, which shall be composed of five members, not more than three of whom shall be members of the same political party, who shall be appointed by the President by and with the advice and consent of the Senate. . . .

PREVENTION OF UNLAWFUL EMPLOYMENT PRACTICES

SEC. 706. (a) Whenever it is charged in writing under oath by a person claiming to be aggrieved, or a written charge has been filed by a member of the Commission where he has reasonable cause to believe a violation of this title has occurred (and such charge sets forth the facts upon which it is based) that an employer, employment agency, or labor organization has engaged in an unlawful employment practice, the Commission shall furnish such employer, employment agency, or labor organization (hereinafter referred to as the "respondent") with a copy of such charge and shall make an investigation of such charge, provided that such charge shall not be made public by the Commission. If the Commission shall determine, after such investigation, that there is reasonable cause to believe that the charge is true, the Commission shall endeavor to eliminate any such alleged unlawful employment practice by informal methods of conference, conciliation, and persuasion. . . .

SEC. 707. (a) Whenever the Attorney General has reasonable cause to believe that any person or group of persons is engaged in a pattern or practice of resistance to the full enjoyment of any of the rights secured by this title, and that the pattern or practice is of such a nature and is intended to deny the full exercise of the rights herein described, the Attorney General may bring a civil action in the appropriate district court of the United States by filing with it a complaint (1) signed by him (or in his absence the Acting Attorney General), (2) setting forth facts pertaining to such pattern or practice, and (3) requesting such relief, including an application for a permanent or temporary injunction, restraining order or other order against the person or persons responsible for such pattern or practice, as he deems necessary to insure the full enjoyment of the rights herein described. . . .

EFFECT ON STATE LAWS

SEC. 708. Nothing in this title shall be deemed to exempt or relieve any person from any liability, duty, penalty, or punishment provided by any present or future law of any State or political subdivision of a State, other than any such law which purports to require or permit the doing of any act which would be an unlawful employment practice under this title.

INVESTIGATIONS, INSPECTIONS, RECORDS, STATE AGENCIES

SEC. 709. (a) In connection with any investigation of a charge filed under section 706, the Commission or its designated representative shall at all reasonable times have access to, for the purposes of examination, and the right to copy any evidence of any person being investigated or proceeded against that relates to unlawful employment practices covered by this title and is relevant to the charge under investigation.

(b) The Commission may cooperate with State and local agencies charged with the administration of State fair employment practices laws and, with the consent of such agencies, may for the purpose of carrying out its functions and duties under this title and within the limitation of funds appropriated specifically for such purpose, utilize the services of such agencies and their employees and, notwithstanding any other provision of law, may reimburse such agencies and their employees for services rendered to assist the Commission in carrying out this title. . . .

INVESTIGATORY POWERS

SEC. 710. (a) For the purposes of any investigation of a charge filed under the authority contained in section 706, the Commission shall have authority to examine witnesses under oath and to require the production of documentary evidence relevant or material to the charge under investigation. . . .

SEC. 711. (a) Every employer, employment agency, and labor organization, as the case may be, shall post and keep posted in conspicuous places upon its premises where notices to employees, applicants for employment, and members are customarily posted a notice to be prepared or approved by the Commission setting forth excerpts from or, summaries of, the pertinent provisions of this title and information pertinent to the filing of a complaint.

(b) A willful violation of this section shall be punishable by a fine of not more than $100 for each separate offense.

VETERANS' PREFERENCE

SEC. 712. Nothing contained in this title shall be construed to repeal or modify any Federal, State, territorial, or local law creating special rights or preference for veterans.

RULES AND REGULATIONS

SEC. 713. (a) The Commission shall have authority from time to time to issue, amend, or rescind suitable procedural regulations to carry out the provisions of this title. Regulations issued under this section shall be in conformity with the standards and limitations of the Administrative Procedure Act.

(b) In any action or proceeding based on any alleged unlawful employment practice, no person shall be subject to any liability or punishment for or on account of (1) the commission by such person of an unlawful employment practice if he pleads and proves that the act or omission complained of was in good faith, in conformity with, and in reliance on any written interpretation or opinion of the Commission, or (2) the failure of such person to publish and file any information required by any provision of this title if he pleads and proves that he failed to publish and file such information in good faith, in conformity with the instructions of the Commission issued under this title regarding the filing of such information. . . .

FORCIBLY RESISTING THE COMMISSION OR ITS REPRESENTATIVES

SEC. 714. The provisions of section 111, title 18, United States Code, shall apply to officers, agents, and employees of the Commission in the performance of their official duties.

SPECIAL STUDY BY SECRETARY OF LABOR

SEC. 715. The Secretary of Labor shall make a full and complete study of the factors which might tend to result in discrimination in employment because of age and of the consequences of such discrimination on the economy and individuals affected. The Secretary of Labor shall make a report to the Congress not later than June 30, 1965, containing the results of such study and shall include in such report such recommendations for legislation to prevent arbitrary discrimination in employment because of age as he determines advisable.

EFFECTIVE DATE

SEC. 716. (a) This title shall become effective one year after the date of its enactment.

(b) Notwithstanding subsection (a), sections of this title other than sections 703, 704, 706, and 707 shall become effective immediately.

(c) The President shall, as soon as feasible after the enactment of this title, convene one or more conferences for the purpose of enabling the leaders of groups whose members will be affected by this title to become familiar with the rights afforded and obligations imposed by its provisions, and for the purpose of making plans which will result in the fair and effective administration of this title when all of its provisions become effective. The President shall invite the participation in such conference or conferences of (1) the members of the President's Committee on Equal Employment Opportunity, (2) the members of the Commission on Civil Rights, (3) representatives of State and local agencies engaged in furthering equal employment opportunity, (4) representatives of private agencies engaged in furthering equal employment opportunity, and (5) representatives of employers, labor organizations, and employment agencies who will be subject to this title.

SOURCE: Civil Rights Act of 1964. Public Law 88-352. *U.S. Statutes at Large*, 78 (1964): 241.

ANALYSIS

The Civil Rights Act of 1964 (CRA) was one of the most important pieces of legislation to emerge from President Lyndon Baines Johnson's Great Society. In many ways, it hearkened back to the Civil Rights Act of 1875, which was intended by its framers to guarantee equality to all citizens of the United States regardless of race. Unfortunately, the 1875 act was under siege soon after its passage. In 1883, it was declared unconstitutional when the U.S. Supreme Court justices determined it violated the Fourteenth Amendment of the Constitution because the act required "state action" for the law to be applicable in private areas.

It was not until 1957 that another civil rights act would emerge from the U.S. Congress. It was a compromise bill that was shepherded through the Senate by its majority leader, Lyndon Johnson. Southern legislators complained vociferously because the act did not require jury trials to be convened against individuals who violated the civil rights of African Americans. Their desire for such a penalty was not an effort to strengthen the legislation but rather a cynical ploy, as they knew that the chances of a white citizen being convicted of civil rights violations was a near impossibility in cases tried before all-white juries.

The Civil Rights Act of 1960 represented the culmination of several years of lobbying President Dwight David Eisenhower's administration by the National Association for the Advancement of Colored People (NAACP) to pass a civil rights act that would be used by the federal government to arrest and prosecute those who violated civil rights laws in the South. Unfortunately, since it was an election year, the legislation that was drafted was little more than an acknowledgment that further work needed to be done in order to allow African Americans to have the same rights as other Americans. The legislation was for all practical purposes passed to ensure that African American civil rights would not be a campaign issue that might impact Democrats or Republicans.

Momentum for the creation of an effective civil rights bill emerged soon after the 1960 elections were concluded due to the efforts of African Americans, including Martin Luther King and the many leaders of the NAACP, and the election of John F. Kennedy to the presidency. Although Kennedy campaigned to get the desired legislation drafted and passed by Congress, he was unable to accomplish the goal before he was assassinated in 1963. Declaring Kennedy a martyr to the cause, newly inaugurated President Lyndon Johnson was able to use his knowledge of the workings of Congress to ensure that the CRA was passed.

The CRA was a far-reaching piece of legislation that included among its many achievements the end of the Jim Crow South by making it illegal to discriminate against the nation's citizenry in public places. Language was included in the legislation to ensure that the new law would not be found unconstitutional through a violation the Fourteenth Amendment. The constitutionality of the CRA was quickly challenged through two 1964 cases on the Supreme Court's docket. This was a key test because the Supreme Court was the body that had declared the Civil Rights Act of 1875 unconstitutional. *Heart of Atlanta Motel v. United States* focused on whether a hotel located on an interstate highway could discriminate against African Americans. *Katzenbach v. McClung* questioned whether Ollie's Barbecue, a local establishment, could legally discriminate. In both cases, a majority of the justices concluded that the federal commerce clause made it illegal for both the motel and restaurant to discriminate against African Americans.

Curiously, Title VII of the CRA exempted state and local governments from its dictates, meaning that they could continue to discriminate against jobseekers on the basis of sex or race. Although the exemption applied to state and local governments around the country, it was actually a concession to congressmen from the South, who argued that their home states would need years in order to gradually make the changes required by the legislation. The CRA's initial success, combined with the reticence of southern states and communities to make a legitimate effort to diversify their labor forces, led to a 1972 amendment, known as "The Equal Opportunity Act," which extended the original legislation's reach to encompass all levels of government.

FURTHER READING

Ackerman, Bruce. 2014. *We the People: Volume 3: The Civil Rights Revolution*. Cambridge: Belknap Press of Harvard University Press.

Finley, Keith M. 2008. *Delaying the Dream: Southern Senators and the Fight against Civil Rights, 1938–1965*. Baton Rouge: Louisiana State University Press.

Purdum, Todd S. 2014. *An Idea Whose Time Has Come: Two Presidents, Two Parties, and the Battle for the Civil Rights Act of 1964*. New York: Henry Holt & Company.

Risen, Clay. 2014. *The Bill of the Century: The Epic Battle for the Civil Rights Act*. New York: Bloomsbury USA.

"The Appalachian Region of the United States, while Abundant in Natural Resources and Rich in Potential, Lags behind the Rest of the Nation in Its Economic Growth"

- ***Document:*** Appalachian Regional Development Act of 1965 (Excerpts)
- ***Date:*** March 9, 1965
- ***Where:*** Washington, D.C.
- ***Significance:*** The Appalachian Regional Development Act created the Appalachian Regional Commission to construct the infrastructure required for the economic development of Appalachia.

DOCUMENT

An Act

To provide public works and economic development programs and the planning and coordination needed to assist in development of the Appalachian region.

Be it enacted by the Senate and House of Representatives of the United States of America in Congress assembled, That this Act be cited as the "Appalachian Regional Development Act of 1965."

FINDINGS AND STATEMENT OF PURPOSE

SEC. 2 The Congress hereby finds and declares that the Appalachian region of the United States, while abundant in natural resources and rich in potential, lags behind the rest of the Nation in its economic growth and that its people have not shared properly in the Nation's prosperity. The region's uneven past development, with its historical reliance on a few basic industries and a marginal agriculture, has failed to provide the economic base that is a vital prerequisite for vigorous, self-sustaining growth. The state and local governments and the people of the region understand their problems and have been working and will continue to work purposely toward their solution. The Congress recognizes the comprehensive report of the President's Appalachian Regional Commission documenting these findings and concludes that regionwide development is feasible, desirable, and urgently needed. It is, therefore, the purpose of the Act to assist the region in meeting its special problems, to promote its economic development, and to establish a framework for joint Federal and State efforts toward providing the basic facilities essential to its growth and attacking its common problems and meeting its common needs on a coordinated and concerted regional basis. The public investments made in the region under this Act shall be concentrated in areas where there is a significant potential for future growth, and where the expected return on public dollars will be the greatest. The States will be responsible for recommending local and State projects, within their borders, which will receive assistance under this Act. As the region obtains the needed physical and transportation facilities and develops its human resources, the Congress expects that the region will then be able to support itself, through the workings of a strengthened free enterprise economy.

TITLE I—THE APPALACHIAN REGIONAL COMMISSION

MEMBERSHIP AND VOTING

SEC. 101. (a) There is hereby established an Appalachian Regional Commission (hereinafter referred to as the "Commission") which shall be composed of one Federal member, hereinafter referred to as the "Federal Cochairman," appointed by the President by and with the advice and consent of the Senate, and one member from each participating State in the Appalachian region. The Federal Cochairman shall be one of the two Cochairmen of the Commission. Each State member may be the Governor, or his designee, or such other person as may be provided by the law of the State which he represents. The State members of the Commission shall elect a Cochairman from among their number.

(b) Except as provided in section 105, decisions by the Commission shall require the affirmative vote of the Federal Chairman and of a majority of the State members (exclusive of members representing States delinquent under section 105). In matters coming before the Commission, the Federal Cochairman shall, to the extent practicable, consult with the Federal departments and agencies having an interest in the subject matter.

. . .

FUNCTIONS OF THE COMMISSION

SEC. 102. In carrying out the purposes of this Act, the Commission shall—

(1) develop, on a continuing basis, comprehensive and coordinated plans and programs and establish priorities thereunder, giving due consideration to other Federal, State, and local planning in the region;

(2) conduct and sponsor investigations, research, and studies, including an inventory and analysis of the resources of the region, and, in cooperation with Federal, State, and local agencies, sponsor demonstration projects designed to foster regional productivity and growth.

(3) review and study, in cooperation with the agency involved, Federal, State, and local public and private programs and, where appropriate, recommend modifications or additions which will increase their effectiveness in the region;

(4) formulate and recommend, where appropriate, interstate compacts and other forms of interstate cooperation, and work with State and local agencies in developing appropriate model legislation;

(5) encourage the formation of local development districts;

(6) encourage private investment in industrial, commercial, and recreational projects;

(7) serve as a focal point and coordinating unit for Appalachian programs;

(8) provide a forum for consideration of problems of the region and proposed solutions and establish and utilize, as appropriate, citizens and special advisory councils and public conferences; and

(9) advise the Secretary of Commerce on applications for grants for administrative expenses to local development districts.

RECOMMENDATIONS

SEC. 103. The Commission may, from time to time, make recommendations to the President and to the State Governors and appropriate local officials with respect to—

(1) the expenditure of funds by Federal, State, and local departments and agencies in the region in the fields of natural resources, agriculture, education, training, health and welfare, and other fields related to the purposes of the Act; and

(2) such additional Federal, State, and local legislation or administrative actions as the Commission deems necessary to further the purposes of this Act.

. . .

TITLE II—SPECIAL APPALACHIAN PROGRAMS

Part A—New Programs

APPALACHIAN DEVELOPMENT HIGHWAY SYSTEM

SEC. 201. (a) The Secretary of Commerce (hereafter in this section referred to as the "Secretary") is authorized to assist in the construction of an Appalachian development highway system serving the Appalachian region (the length of which shall not exceed to thousand three hundred and fifty miles. In addition thereto, there are authorized to be constructed not in excess of one thousand miles of local access roads, that will serve specific recreational, residential, commercial, industrial, or other like facilities or will facilitate a school consolidation program). The system, in conjunction with the Interstate System and other Federal-aid highways in the region will provide a highway system which will open up an area or areas with developmental potential where commerce and communication have been inhibited by lack of adequate access. The provisions of title 23, United States Code, that are applicable to Federal-aid primary highways, and which the Secretary determines are not inconsistent with this Act, shall apply to the Appalachian development highway system, and the local access roads.

(b) As soon as feasible, the Commission shall submit to the Secretary its recommendations with respect to (1) the general corridor location and termini of the development highways, (2) the designation of local access roads to be constructed, (3) priorities for construction of the local access roads and of the major segments of the development highways, and (4) other criteria for the program authorized by this section. Before any State member participates in or votes on such recommendations, he shall have the recommendations of the State highway department of the State which he represents.

(c) The Secretary shall have authority to approve in whole or in part such recommendations or to require modifications or revisions thereof. In no event shall the Secretary approve any recommendations for any construction which would require for its completion the expenditure of Federal funds (other than funds available under title 23, United States Code) in excess of the appropriation authorizations in subsection (g). On its completion each development highway not already on the Federal-aid primary system shall be added to such system and shall be required to be maintained by the State.

(d) In the construction of highways and roads authorized under this section, the States may give special preference to the use of mineral resource materials indigenous to the Appalachian region.

(e) For the purposes of research and development in the use of coal and coal products in highway construction and maintenance, the Secretary is authorized to require each participating State, to the maximum extent possible, to use coal derivatives in the construction of not to exceed 10 per centum of the roads authorized under this Act.

(f) Federal assistance to any construction project under this section shall not exceed 50 per centum of the costs of such project, unless the Secretary determines, pursuant to the recommendation of the Commission, that assistance in excess of such percentage is required in furtherance of the purposes of this Act, but in no event shall such Federal assistance exceed 70 per centum of such costs.

(g) To carry out this section, there is hereby authorized to be appropriated $840,000,000.

DEMONSTRATION HEALTH FACILITIES

SEC. 202. (a) In order to demonstrate the value of adequate health and medical facilities to the economic development of the region, the Secretary of Health, Education, and Welfare is authorized to make grants for the construction, equipment, and operation of multicounty demonstration health facilities, including hospitals, regional health diagnostic and treatment centers, and other facilities necessary to health. Grants for such construction (including initial equipment) shall be made in accordance with the applicable provisions of title VI of the Public Health Services Act (42 U.S.C. 291-291z) and the Mental Retardation Facilities and Community Mental Health Centers Construction Act of 1963 (77 Stat. 282), without regard to any provisions therein relating to appropriation ceiling or to allotments among the States. Grants under this section shall be made solely out of funds specifically appropriated for the purpose of carrying out this Act and shall not be taken into account in the computation of the allotments among the States made pursuant to any other provision of law.

. . .

LAND STABILIZATION, CONSERVATION, AND EROSION CONTROL

SEC. 203. (a) In order to provide for the control and prevention of erosion and sediment damages in the Appalachian region and to promote the conservation and development of the soil and water resources of the region, the Secretary of Agriculture is authorized to enter into agreements of not more than ten years with landowners, operators, and occupiers, individually or collectively, in the Appalachian region determined by him to have control for the period of the agreement of the lands described therein, providing for land stabilization, erosion and sediment control, and reclamation through changes in land use, and conservation treatment including the establishment of practices and measure for the conservation and development of soil, water, woodland, wildlife, and recreation resources.

. . .

TIMBER DEVELOPMENT ORGANIZATIONS

SEC. 204. (a) In order that the region shall more fully benefit from the timber stands that are one of its prime assets, the Secretary of Agriculture is authorized to—

(1) provide technical assistance in the organization and operation, under State law, of private timber development organizations having as their objective the carrying out of timber development programs to improve timber productivity and quality, and increase returns to landowners through establishment of private nonprofit corporations, which on a self-supporting basis may provide (A) continuity of management, good cutting practices, and marketing practices, (B) physical consolidation of small holdings or administrative consolidation for efficient management under long-term agreement, (C) management of forest lands, donated to the timber development organizations for demonstrating good forest management, on a profitable and taxpaying basis, and (D) establishment of a permanent fund for perpetuation of the work of the corporations to be composed of donations, real or personal, for educational purposes.

. . .

MINING AREA RESTORATION

SEC. 205. (a) In order to further the economic development of the region by rehabilitating areas presently damaged by deleterious mining practices, the Secretary of the Interior is authorized to—

(1) make financial contributions to States in the region to seal and fill voids in abandoned coal mines, and to reclaim and rehabilitate existing strip and surface mine areas, in accordance with provisions of the Act of July 15, 1955 (30 U.S.C. 571 et seq.), to the extent applicable, without regard to section 2(b) thereof (30 U.S.C. 572(b)) or to any provisions therein limiting assistance to anthracite coal formation, or to the Commonwealth of Pennsylvania. Grants under this paragraph

shall be made wholly out of funds specifically appropriated for the purposes of carrying out this Act.

(2) plan and execute projects for extinguishing underground and outcrop mine fires in the region in accordance with the provisions of the Act of August 31, 1954 (30 U.S.C. 551 et seq.), without regard to any provisions therein relating to annual appropriation authorization ceilings. Grants under this paragraph shall be made solely out of funds specifically appropriated for the purpose of carrying out this Act.

(3) expand and accelerate fish and wildlife restoration projects in the region in accordance with the provisions of the Act of September 2, 1937 (16 U.S.C. 669 et seq.), and the Act of August 9, 1950 (16 U.S.C. 777 et seq.), without regard to any provisions therein relating to apportionments among the States and to limitations on the availability of funds. The expenses of projects under this paragraph shall be paid solely out of funds specifically appropriated for the purpose of carrying out this Act, and shall not be taken into account in the computation of the apportionments among the States pursuant to any other provisions of law.

. . .

(c) The Congress hereby declares its intent to provide for a study of a comprehensive, long-range program for the purpose of reclaiming and rehabilitating strip and surface mining areas in the United States. To this end, the Secretary of the Interior shall, in full cooperation with the Secretary of Agriculture, the Tennessee Valley Authority, and other appropriate Federal, State, and local departments and agencies, and with the Commission, make a survey and study of strip and surface mining operations and their effects in the United States. The Secretary of the Interior shall submit to the President his recommendations for a long-range comprehensive program for reclamation and rehabilitation of strip and surface mining areas in the United States and for the policies under which the program should be conducted, and the President shall submit these to the Congress, together with his recommendations, not later than July 1, 1967. By July 1, 1966, the Secretary shall make an interim report to the Commission summarizing his findings to that date on those aspects of strip and surface mining operations in the region that are most urgently in need of attention. Such study and recommendations shall include, but not be limited to, a consideration of the following matters–

(1) the nature and extent of strip and surface mining operations in the United States and the conditions resulting therefrom;

(2) the ownership of the real property involved in strip and surface mining operations;

(3) the effectiveness of past action by States or local units of government to remedy the adverse effects of strip and surface mining operation by financial or regulatory measures, and requirements for appropriate State legislation, including adequate enforcement thereof, to provide for proper reclamation and rehabilitation of areas which may be strip and surface mined in the future;

(4) the public interest in and public benefits which may result from reclamation, rehabilitation, and appropriate development and use of areas subjected to strip and surface mining operations, including (A) economic development growth, (B) public recreation, (C) public health and safety, (D) water pollution, stream sedimentation,

erosion control, and flood control, (E) highway programs, (F) fish and wildlife protection and restoration, (G) scenic values, and (H) forestry and agriculture;

(5) the appropriate roles of Federal, State, and private interests in the reclamation and rehabilitation of strip and surface mining areas and the relative costs to be borne by each, including specific consideration of (A) the extent, if any, to which strip and surface mine operators are unable to bear the cost of remedial action within the limits imposed by the economics of such mining activity, and (B) the extent to which the prospective value of lands and other natural resources, after remedial work has been completed, would be inadequate to justify the landowners doing the remedial work at their expense; and

(6) the objectives and the total overall costs of a program for accomplishing the reclamation and rehabilitation of existing strip and surface mining areas in the United States, giving adequate consideration to (A) the economic benefits in relation to costs, (B) the prevention of future devastation of reclaimed and rehabilitated areas, (C) the avoidance of unwarranted financial gain to private owners of such improved property, and (D) the types of aid required to accomplish such reclamation and rehabilitation.

. . .

WATER RESOURCE SURVEY

SEC. 206. (a) The Secretary of the Army is hereby authorized and directed to prepare a comprehensive plan for the development and efficient utilization of the water and related resources of the Appalachian region, giving special attention to the need for an increase in the production of economic goods and services within the region as a means of expanding economic opportunities and thus enhancing the welfare of its people, which plan shall constitute and integral and harmonious component of the regional economic development program authorized by this Act.

(b) This plan may recommend measures for the control of floods, the regulation of the rivers to enhance their value as sources of water supply for industrial and municipal development, the generation of hydroelectric power, the prevention of water pollution by drainage from mines, the development and enhancement of the recreational potentials of the region, the improvement of rivers for navigation where this would further industrial development at less cost than would the improvement of other modes of transportation, the conservation and efficient utilization of the land resource, and such other measures as may be found necessary to achieve the objectives of this section.

(c) To insure that the plan prepared by the Secretary of the Army shall constitute a harmonious component of the regional plan, he shall consult with the Commission and the following: the Secretary of Agriculture, the Secretary of Commerce, the Secretary of Health, Education, and Welfare, the Secretary of the Interior, the Tennessee Valley Authority, and the Federal Power Commission.

SOURCE: 89th Congress of the United States. 1965. Public Law 89-4. 89th Congress, S. 3, March 9, 1965. Washington, D.C.: Government Printing Office.

ANALYSIS

In 1963, President John F. Kennedy, with the assistance of the governors from the states in the Appalachian region, created the President's Appalachian Research Commission (PARC). He charged the body with writing a report on how to address the economic challenges facing the region. Kennedy planned to use the document to inform a major initiative that he planned to launch during his second term in office. Due to his assassination, it was left to his successor's administration to determine how best to address poverty in Appalachia.

President Lyndon B. Johnson's administration utilized the recommendations made by PARC in *Appalachia: A Report by the President's Appalachian Regional Commission 1964* to draft the Appalachian Regional Development Act of 1965 (ARDA). Criticisms of the legislation soon emerged. Some congressmen believed that the legislation gave federal agencies too much power at the expense of the states. Others thought that it was unfair to provide economic benefits to the nine Appalachian states, namely Alabama, Georgia, Kentucky, Maryland, North Carolina, Pennsylvania, Tennessee, Virginia, and West Virginia, when other parts of the country were also confronting similar challenges. It became obvious that the proposal was not going to pass without gerrymandering Appalachia's borders. The first states to be added were Ohio and South Carolina. Despite the addition of two states, the ARDA still lacked enough votes to pass. The legislation received the needed backing from New York senator Robert F. Kennedy after 14 counties from his state were added. Congress passed the ARDA and it was signed into law by President Johnson on March 9, 1965. The political concessions made to secure votes in Congress had significant consequences. Much of the federal money spent in Appalachia during the War on Poverty went to urban areas such as Birmingham, Alabama; Buffalo, New York; and Greenville, South Carolina, which were represented by politically powerful congressmen. Much less federal largesse flowed into the truly impoverished mountain communities in states like Kentucky, Tennessee, and West Virginia.

The greatest accomplishment of the ARDA was the creation of the Appalachian Regional Commission (ARC). It was designed as a state–federal partnership to coordinate the development of economic infrastructure such as roads and water projects. Since Appalachia had been largely bypassed when the nation's interstate system was established due to the high cost of building roads in mountainous terrain, the ARC prioritized the construction of the Appalachian Development Highway System, which connected areas that were deemed growth centers, such as urban areas and county seats. The improvements in transportation infrastructure did result in significant economic development in much of Appalachia, with the exception of many of the distressed counties located in Eastern Kentucky and West Virginia. Although highways were built in those areas, the locales were not appealing to companies due to factors like a poorly educated workforce and corrupt local officials.

FURTHER READING

Eller, Ronald D. 2008. *Uneven Ground: Appalachia since 1945*. Lexington: University Press of Kentucky.

President's Appalachian Regional Commission. 1964. *Appalachia: A Report by the President's Appalachian Regional Commission 1964*. Washington, D.C.: U.S. Government Printing Office.

Taul, Glen Edward. 2001. "Poverty, Development, and Government in Appalachia: Origins of the Appalachian Regional Commission." PhD dissertation, University of Kentucky.

Williams, John Alexander. 2002. *Appalachia: A History*. Chapel Hill: University of North Carolina Press.

"To Assist in the Provision of Housing for Low- and Moderate-Income Families"

- ***Document:*** Housing and Urban Development Act of 1965
- ***Date:*** August 10, 1965
- ***Where:*** Washington, D.C.
- ***Significance:*** The Housing and Urban Development Act created the Department of Housing and Urban Development.

DOCUMENT

AN ACT

To assist in the provision of housing for low- and moderate-income families, to promote orderly urban development, to improve living environment in urban areas, and to extend and amend laws relating to housing, urban renewal, and community facilities.

Be it enacted by the Senate and House of Representatives of the United States of America in Congress assembled, That this Act may be cited as the "Housing and Urban Development Act of 1965."

TITLE I—SPECIAL PROVISIONS FOR DISADVANTAGED PERSONS

FINANCIAL ASSISTANCE TO ENABLE CERTAIN PRIVATE HOUSING TO BE AVAILABLE FOR LOWER INCOME FAMILIES WHO ARE ELDERLY, HANDICAPPED, DISPLACED, VICTIMS OF A NATURAL DISASTER, OR OCCUPANTS OF SUBSTANDARD HOUSING

SEC. 101. (a) The Secretary of Housing and Urban Development (hereinafter referred to as the "Secretary") is authorized to make, and contract to make, annual payments to a "housing owner" on behalf of "qualified tenants," as those terms are defined herein, in such amounts and under such circumstances as are prescribed in or pursuant to this section. In no case shall a contract provide for such payments with respect to any housing for a period exceeding forty years. The aggregate amount of the contracts to make such payments shall not exceed amounts approved in appropriation Acts, and payments pursuant to such contract shall not exceed $30,000,000 per annum prior to July 1, 1966, which maximum dollar amount shall be increased by $35,000,000, on July 1, 1966, by $40,000,000 on July 1, 1967, and by $45,000,000 on July 1, 1968.

(b) As used in this section, the term "housing owner" means a private nonprofit corporation or other private nonprofit legal entity, a limited dividend corporation or other limited dividend legal entity, or a cooperative housing corporation, which is a mortgagor under section 221(d) (3) of the National Housing Act and which, after the enactment of this section, has been approved for mortgage insurance thereunder and has been approved for receiving the benefits of this section: *Provided*, That, except as provided in subsection (j), no payments under this section may be made with respect to any property financed with a mortgage receiving the benefits of the interest rate provided for in the proviso in section 221(d) (5) of that Act. Subject to the limitations provided in subsection (j), the term "housing owner" also has the meaning prescribed in such subsection.

(c) As used in this section, the term "qualified tenant" means any individual or family who has, pursuant to criteria and procedures established by the Administrator, been determined—

(1) to have an income below the maximum amount which can be established in the area, pursuant to the limitations prescribed in sections 2(2) and 15(7) (b) (ii) of the United States Housing Act of 1937, for occupancy in public housing dwellings; and

(2) to be one of the following—

(A) displaced by governmental action;

(B) sixty-two years of age or older (or, in the case of a family to have a head who is, or whose spouse is, sixty-two years of age or over);

(C) physically handicapped (or, in the case of a family, to have a head who is, or whose spouse is, physically handicapped);

(D) occupying substandard housing; or

(E) an occupant or former occupant of a dwelling which is (or was) situated in an area determined by the Small Business Administration, subsequent to April 1,1965, to have been affected by a natural disaster, and which has been extensively damaged or destroyed as the result of such disaster.

. . .

TITLE II—FHA INSURANCE OPERATIONS

. . .

TITLE III—URBAN RENEWAL

STUDY OF HOUSING AND BUILDING CODES, ZONING, TAX POLICIES, AND DEVELOPMENT STANDARDS

SEC. 301. (a) The Congress finds that the general welfare of the Nation requires that local authorities be encouraged and aided to prevent slums, blight, and sprawl, preserve natural beauty, and provide for decent, durable housing so that the goal of a decent home and a suitable living environment for every American family may be realized as soon as feasible. The Congress further finds that there is a need to study housing and building codes, zoning, tax policies, and development standards in order to determine how (1) local property owners and private enterprise can be encouraged to serve as large a part as they can of the total housing and building need, and (2) Federal, State, and local governmental assistance can be so directed as to place greater reliance on local property owners and private enterprise and enable them to serve a greater share of the total housing and building need. The Housing and Home Finance Administrator is therefore directed to study the structure of (1) State and local urban and suburban housing and building laws, standards, codes, and regulations and their impact on housing and building costs, how they can be simplified, improved, and enforced, at the local level, and what methods might be adopted to promote more uniform building codes and the acceptance of technical innovations including new building practices and materials; (2) State and local zoning and land use laws, codes, and regulations, to find ways by which States and localities may improve and utilize them in order to obtain further growth and development; and (3) Federal, State, and local tax policies with respect to their effect on land and property cost and on incentives to build housing and make improvements in existing structures.

(b) Administrator shall submit a report based on such study to the President and to the Congress within 18 months after the date of the enactment of the Housing and Urban Development Act of 1965 or the appropriation of funds for the study, whichever is later.

(c) There are authorized to be appropriated such funds as may be necessary to carry out the purposes of this section. Any funds so appropriated shall remain available until expended.

. . .

TITLE IV—LEASE GUARANTEES

AUTHORITY OF THE ADMINISTRATION

SEC. 401. (a) The Administration may, whenever it determines such action to be necessary or desirable, and upon such terms and conditions as it may prescribe, guarantee the payment of rentals under leases of commercial and industrial property entered into by small business concerns that are (1) eligible for loans under section 7(b) (3) of the Small Business Act, or (2) eligible for loans under title IV of the Economic Opportunity Act of 1964, to enable such concerns to obtain such leases. Any such guarantee may be made or effected either directly or in cooperation with any qualified surety company or other qualified company through a participation agreement with such company. . . .

TITLE V—LOW-RENT PUBLIC HOUSING

. . .

TITLE VI—COLLEGE HOUSING

. . .

TITLE VII—COMMUNITY FACILITIES

. . .

TITLE VIII—FEDERAL NATIONAL MORTGAGE ASSOCIATION

. . .

TITLE IX—OPEN-SPACE LAND AND URBAN BEAUTIFICATION AND IMPROVEMENT

. . .

TITLE X—RURAL HOUSING

. . .

TITLE XI—MISCELLANEOUS

SOURCE: U.S. Congress. 1965. Public Law 89-117.

ANALYSIS

As early as 1961, President John F. Kennedy proposed the creation of the Department of Urban Affairs and Housing. His proposal failed to gain traction during his presidency due to opposition within both the private sector and Congress. Upon assuming the presidency, Lyndon Johnson reworked his predecessor's idea and made it part of his Great Society initiative. The initial salvo in the public campaign was launched during his State of the Union address on January 4, 1965, when he called for the creation of the newly dubbed Department of Housing and Urban Development. Over the following months, Johnson took his proposal to the nation's urban areas. In March 1965, President Lyndon Johnson made the case that legislation focused on housing was vitally important to the future of the nation. Johnson argued that a cabinet-level department was a necessity as urban areas were where a majority of Americans were living, and that the trend promised to escalate in future decades. The president made it clear that his proposal was not about the cities themselves, but their occupants:

> The problem is people, and the quality of the lives they lead. We want to build not just housing units, but neighborhoods; not just to construct schools, but to educate children; not just to raise income but to create beauty and end the poisoning of our environment. We must extend the range of choices available to

> all our people so that all, and not just the fortunate, can have access to decent homes and schools, to recreation and to culture. We must work to overcome the forces which divide our people and erode the vitality which comes from the partnership of those with diverse incomes and interests and backgrounds. (Message to Congress: Johnson Requests New Housing Department, Federal Rent Subsidy Program for the Poor)

Johnson's proposal marked a stark departure from housing legislation enacted by Congress in previous decades due to its determination that low-income individuals had a place in the nation's urban centers. Although Johnson's request was honored by Congress through the passage of the Housing and Urban Development Act of 1965 (HUDA), its implementation proved extremely controversial.

Like many Great Society programs, the housing initiative was an extension of an effort begun by President Franklin Delano Roosevelt's New Deal. In the late 1930s, the federal government began a program that tore down old, dilapidated buildings in order to construct public housing, in the form of three- or four-story buildings, on the newly vacant lots. The homes were available to individuals who could afford the rental fees that were charged by the local public agency managing the real estate. Key politicians were so pleased by the initial success of the efforts that they strengthened the program through the Housing Act of 1949. It authorized the construction of 810,000 housing units to be built over a six-year period. The units were to be located in high-rise buildings, often in the form of towers. The unintended effect was to concentrate poor, minority groups into what quickly became slum housing, partially because of the shoddy workmanship utilized in their construction. Unfortunately for advocates of what became known as the Urban Renewal program, it took approximately 20 years to construct all of the housing. Within the influential halls of Congress, the entire initiative was ultimately deemed a failure. Despite the disappointment over the Housing Act of 1949, the HUDA continued its effort to improve urban areas by providing funding for cities to revitalize run-down locales. As part of the renewal effort, the federal government established building codes that set the minimum standards that all housing units constructed with federal funds had to meet.

The signing of the HUDA on September 9, 1965, created the Department of Housing and Urban Development (HUD). Selected to lead the department was Robert C. Weaver, the former head of the Housing and Home Finance Agency. Notably, upon assuming the post, Weaver also became the first African American cabinet member in U.S. history. The new department was charged with oversight of four agencies already administering housing programs: the Federal Housing Administration, the Federal National Mortgage Association (now known as Fannie Mae), the Public Housing Administration, and the Urban Renewal Authority. Although provided the mandate of effectively administering federal efforts focused on housing and urban development, the department was not given the tools to accomplish its task. For example, the Department of Veterans Affairs retained oversight of the Veterans Home Loan program. The Internal Revenue Service continued its management of the Low-Income Housing Tax Credit program. In addition, like most Great Society initiatives, HUD was underfunded. It is a problem that has continued to plague the department to the present day.

The most controversial portion of the HUDA concerned the creation of a rent subsidy program. It required tenants to pay 25 percent of their rent, with the remainder provided directly by the federal government to the property owner. In order to be eligible for the program, individuals had to be deemed impoverished using federal measures and had to meet additional criteria such as being elderly, being handicapped, or residing in dilapidated housing. While the program had the dual purpose of helping the poor find adequate housing and diversifying neighborhoods, its goals were not shared in many communities. Despite the fact that renters had the ability to pay for housing due to the assistance of the federal government, the owners of rental housing often refused access to housing, especially to people of color. This form of discrimination was specifically mentioned in the *Report of the National Advisory Commission on Civil Disorders*, better known as the "Kerner Commission Report," as one of the causes of the urban rioting that exploded in cities around the country from 1965 to 1968.

FURTHER READING

Ackerman, Bruce. 2014. *We the People: Volume 3: The Civil Rights Revolution*. Cambridge: Belknap Press of Harvard University Press.

Conn, Steven. 2014. *Americans against the City: Anti-Urbanism in the Twentieth Century*. New York: Oxford University Press.

Hays, R. Allen. 2012. *The Federal Government & Urban Housing*. 3rd ed. Albany, NY: SUNY Press.

"Message to Congress: Johnson Requests New Housing Department, Federal Rent Subsidy Program for the Poor." 1966. In *CQ Almanac 1965*. Washington, D.C.: Congressional Quarterly.

Pritchett, Wendell E. 2008. *Robert Clifton Weaver and the American City: The Life and Times of an Urban Reformer*. Chicago: University of Chicago Press.

U.S. Department of Housing and Urban Development, Office of Policy Development and Research. 2015. *HUD at 50: Creating Pathways to Opportunity*. Washington, D.C.: U.S. Department of Housing and Urban Development, Office of Policy Development and Research.

"It Is Imperative That We Give First Attention to Our Opportunities—and Our Obligations—for Advancing the Nation's Health"

- ***Document:*** "Message from the President of the United States Transmitting Advancing the Nation's Health," by President Lyndon B. Johnson
- ***Date:*** January 7, 1965
- ***Where:*** Washington, D.C.
- ***Significance:*** President Johnson's message outlined the medical coverages that eventually became encapsulated in the Social Security Amendments of 1965 through Medicare and Medicaid.

DOCUMENT

To the Congress of the United States:

In 1787, Thomas Jefferson wrote that, "Without health there is no happiness. An attention to health, then, should take the place of every other object."

That priority has remained fixed in both the private and public values of our society through generations of Americans since.

Our rewards have been immeasurably bountiful. "An attention to health"—of the individual, the family, the community and the Nation—has contributed to the vitality and efficiency of our system as well as to the happiness and prosperity of our people.

Today, at this point in our history, we are privileged to contemplate new horizons of national advance and achievement in many sectors. But it is imperative that we give first attention to our opportunities—and our obligations—for advancing the Nation's health. For the health of our people is, inescapably, the foundation for fulfillment of all our aspirations.

In these years of the 1960's, we live as beneficiaries of this century's great—and continuing—revolution of medical knowledge and capabilities. Smallpox, malaria, yellow fever, and typhus are conquered in this country. Infant deaths have been reduced by half every two decades. Poliomyelitis, which took 3,154 lives so recently as 1952, cost only 5 lives in 1964. Over the brief span of the past two decades, death rates have been reduced for influenza by 88 percent, tuberculosis by 87 percent, rheumatic fever by 90 percent.

A baby born in America today has a life expectancy half again as long as those born in the year the 20th century began.

The successes of the century are many.

The pace of medical progress is rapid.

The potential for the future is unlimited.

But we must not allow the modern miracles of medicine to mesmerize us. The work most needed to advance the Nation's health will not be done for us by miracles. We must undertake that work ourselves through practical, prudent, and patient programs—to put more firmly in place the foundation for the healthiest, happiest, and most hopeful society in the history of man.

Our first concern must be to assure that the advance of medical knowledge leaves none behind. We can—and we must—strive now to assure the availability of and accessibility to the best health care for all Americans, regardless of age or geography or economic status.

With this as our goal, we must strengthen our Nation's health facilities and services, assure the adequacy and quality of our health manpower, continue to assist our States and communities in meeting their health responsibilities, and respond alertly to the new hazards of our new and complex environment.

We must, certainly, continue and intensify our health research and research facilities. Despite all that has been done, we cannot be complacent before the facts that—

> Forty-eight million people now living will become victims of cancer.
>
> Nearly 15 million people suffer from heart disease and this, together with strokes, accounts for more than half the deaths in the United States each year.
>
> Twelve million people suffer arthritis and rheumatic disease and 10 million are burdened with neurological disorders.
>
> Five and one-half million Americans are afflicted by mental retardation and the number increases by 126,000 new cases each year.

In our struggle against disease, great advances have been made, but the battle is far from won. While that battle will not end in our lifetime—or any time to come—we have the high privilege and high promise of making longer strides forward now than any other generation of Americans.

The measures I am outlining today will carry us forward in the oldest tradition of our society—to give "an attention to health" for all our people. Our advances, thus far, have been most dramatic in the field of health knowledge. We are challenged now to give attention to advances in the field of health care—and this is the emphasis of the recommendations I am placing before you at this time.

I. REMOVING BARRIERS TO HEALTH CARE

In this century, medical scientists have done much to improve human health and prolong human life. Yet as these advances come, vital segments of our populace are being left behind—behind barriers of age, economics, geography, or community resources. Today the political community is challenged to help all our people surmount these needless barriers to the enjoyment of the promise and reality of better health.

A. HOSPITAL INSURANCE FOR THE AGED

Thirty years ago, the American people made a basic decision that the later years of life should not be years of despondency and drift. The result was enactment of our social security program, a program now fixed as a valued part; of our national life. Since World War 11, there has been increasing awareness of the fact that the full value of social security would not be realized unless provision were made to deal with the problem of costs of illnesses am Ong our older citizens.

I believe this year is the year when, with the sure knowledge of public support, the Congress should enact a hospital insurance program for the aged.

The facts of the need are well and widely known:

Four out of five persons 65 or older have a disability or chronic disease.

People over 65 go to the hospital more frequently and stay twice as long as younger people. Health costs for them are twice as high as for the young.

Where health insurance is available it is usually associated with an employer-employee plan. However, since most of our older people are not employed they are usually not eligible under these plans.

Almost half of the elderly have no health insurance at all.

The average retired couple cannot afford the cost of adequate health protection under private health insurance.

I ask that our social security system—proved and tested by three decades of successful operation—be extended to finance the cost of basic health services. In this way, the specter of catastrophic hospital bills can be lifted from the lives of our older citizens. *I again strongly urge the Congress to enact a hospital insurance program for the aged.*

Such a program should—

Be financed under social security by regular, modest contributions during working years; Provide protection against the costs of hospital and posthospital extended care, home nursing services, and outpatient diagnostic services;

Provide similar protection to those who are not now covered by social security, with the costs being paid from the administrative budget;

Clearly indicate that the plan in no way interferes with the patient's complete freedom to select his doctor or hospital.

Like our existing social security cash retirement benefits, this hospital insurance plan will be a basic protection plan. It should cover the heaviest cost elements in serious illnesses. In addition, we should encourage private insurance to provide supplementary protection.

I consider this measure to be of utmost urgency. Compassion and reason dictate that this logical extension of our proven social security system will supply the prudent, feasible, and dignified way to free the aged from the fear of financial hardship in the event of illness.

Also, I urge all States to provide adequate medical assistance under the existing Kerr-Mills program for the aged who cannot afford to meet the noninsured costs.

B. BETTER HEALTH SERVICES FOR CHILDREN AND YOUTH

America's tradition of compassion for the aged is matched by our traditional devotion to our most priceless resource of all-our young. Today far more than many realize, there are great and growing needs, among our children for better health services.

> Acute illness strikes children under 15 nearly twice as frequently as it does adults.
>
> One in five children under age 17 is afflicted with a chronic ailment.
>
> Three out of every 100 children suffer some form of paralysis or orthopedic impairment.
>
> At least 2 million children are mentally retarded, with a higher concentration of them from poor families. Four million children are emotionally disturbed.
>
> At age 15, the average child has more than 10 decayed teeth.

If the health of our Nation is to be substantially improved in the years to come, we must improve the care of the health of our 75 million preschool and school-age children and youth.

There is much to do if we are to make available the medical and dental services our rising generation needs. Nowhere are the needs greater than for the 15 million children of families who live in poverty

> Children in families with incomes of less than $2,000 are able to visit a doctor only half as frequently as those in families with incomes of more than $7,000.
>
> Public assistance payments for medical services to the 3 million needy children receiving dependent children's benefits throughout the Nation average only $2.80 a month, and in some States such medical benefits are not provided at all.
>
> Poor families increasingly are forced to turn to overcrowded hospital emergency rooms and to overburdened city clinics as their only resource to meet their routine health needs.

Military entrance examinations reveal the consequences. Half of those rejected cannot pass the medical tests. Three-fourths of them would benefit from treatment, and earlier treatment would greatly increase recovery and decrease lifelong disability.

The States and localities bear the major responsibility for providing modern medical care to our children and youth. But the Federal Government can help. *I recommend legislation to—*

Increase the authorizations for maternal and child health and crippled children's services, earmarking funds for project grants to provide health screening and diagnosis for children of preschool and school age, as well as treatment and followup care services for disabled children and youth. This should include funds to help defray the operational costs of university-affiliated mental retardation clinical centers. Provisions should also be made for the training of personnel who will operate medical facilities for children.

Broaden the public assistance program to permit specific Federal participation in paying costs of medical and dental care for children in medically needy families, similar to the Kerr-Mills program for the aged.

Extend the grant programs for (a) family health services and clinics for domestic agricultural migratory workers and their children and (b) community vaccination assistance.

C. IMPROVED COMMUNITY MENTAL HEALTH SERVICES

Mental illness afflicts 1 out of 10 Americans, fills nearly one-hall of all the hospital beds in the Nation, and costs $3 billion annually. Fortunately, we are entering a new era in the prevention, treatment, and care of mental illness. Mere custodial care of patients in large, isolated asylums is clearly no longer appropriate. Most patients can be cared for and cured in their own communities.

An important beginning toward community preparation has been made through the legislation enacted by the 88th Congress authorizing aid for constructing community mental health centers. But facilities alone cannot assure services.

It has been estimated that at least 10,000 more psychiatrists are needed.

Few communities have the funds to support adequate programs, particularly during the first years.

Communities with the greatest needs hesitate to build centers without being able to identify the source of operating funds. Most of the people in need are children, the aged, or patients with low incomes.

I therefore recommend legislation to authorize a 5-year program of grants for the initial costs of personnel to man community mental health centers which offer comprehensive services.

D. A NEW LIFE FOR THE DISABLED

Today, we are rehabilitating about 120,000 disabled persons each year. I recommend a stepped-up program to overcome this costly waste of human resources. My 1966 budget will propose increased funds to rehabilitate an additional 25,000.

Our goal should be at least 200,000 a year. I recommend legislation to authorize—

Project grants to help States expand their services.

Special Federal matching so that rehabilitative services can be provided to a greater number of the mentally retarded and other seriously disabled individuals.

Construction and modernization of workshops and rehabilitation centers.

II. STRENGTHENING THE NATION'S HEALTH FACILITIES AND SERVICES

In our urbanized society today, the availability of health care depends uniquely upon the availability and accessibility of modern facilities, located in convenient and efficient places, and on well-organized and adequately supported services. The lack of such facilities and services is, of itself, a barrier to good health care.

A. MULTIPURPOSE REGIONAL MEDICAL COMPLEXES

In this century, we have made more advance than in all other centuries toward overcoming diseases which have taken the heaviest toll of human life. Today we are challenged to meet and master the 3 killers which alone account for 7 out of 10 deaths in the United States each year—heart disease, cancer, and stroke. The Commission on Heart Disease, Cancer, and Stroke has pointed the way for us toward that goal.

The newest and most effective diagnostic methods and the most recent and most promising methods of treatment often require equipment or skills of great scarcity and expense such as—

open heart surgery;
advanced and very high voltage radiation therapy;
advanced disease detection methods.

It is not necessary for each hospital or clinic to have such facilities, equipment, or services, but it is essential that every patient requiring such specialized and expensive procedures and services have access to them. Multipurpose medical complexes can meet these needs. They would—

speed the application of research knowledge to patient care, so as to turn otherwise hollow laboratory triumphs into health victories;

save thousands of lives now needlessly taken annually by the three great killers—heart disease, cancer, and stroke—and by other major diseases.

A plan to improve our attack upon these major causes of death and disability should become a part of the fabric of our regional and community health services. The services provided under this plan will help the practicing physician keep in touch with the latest medical knowledge and by making available to him the latest techniques, specialized knowledge, and the most efficient methods. To meet these objectives, such complexes should—

Be regional in scope.

Provide services for a variety of diseases—heart disease, cancer, stroke, and other major illnesses.

Be affiliated with medical schools, teaching hospitals, and medical centers.

Be supported by diagnostic services in community hospitals. Provide diagnosis and treatment of patients, together with research and teaching in a coordinated system.

Permit clinical trial of advanced techniques and drugs.

Medical complexes—consisting of regional organizations of medical schools, teaching hospitals, and treatment centers tied into community diagnostic and treatment facilities—represent a new kind of organization for providing coordinated teaching, research, and patient care. When we consider that the economic cost of heart disease alone amounts to 540,000 lost man-years annually—worth some $2.5 billion—the urgency and value of effective action is unmistakable. Action on this new approach, stemming from recommendations of the Commission on Heart Disease, Cancer, and Stroke, will provide significant improvements in many fields of medicine.

I recommend legislation to authorize a 5-year program of project grants to develop multipurpose regional medical complexes for an all-out attack on heart disease, cancer, stroke, and other major diseases.

B. IMPROVED SERVICES FOR THE MENTALLY RETARDED

Mental retardation in any individual is a lifelong problem of the most serious nature for the family and for the community. But we know today that the problem need not and must not lead to tragic hopelessness. Much is being done to provide a decent, dignified, place in society for these unfortunate individuals.

The 88th Congress provided a substantial foundation for building an effective national program for the prevention of mental retardation and care of the mentally retarded. Under this authority, grants are authorized—

For construction of mental retardation research centers, community mental retardation centers, and university-affiliated mental retardation centers.

For planning by all the States of comprehensive action to combat mental retardation at the State and community levels.

The 1966 budget includes $282 million—a $40 million increase—for these programs and other mental retardation services, including preventive activities and the training of teachers of the retarded. I urge that this full amount be appropriated.

Extensive resources and programs need to be developed in the States and communities to prevent mental retardation and to care for the mentally retarded. The existing authority for planning grants will end on June 30, 1965. The developmental needs and effective utilization of the construction grants require follow-up action.

I recommend the enactment of mental retardation program development grants for 2 additional years to help the States continue this essential work.

C. MODERNIZATION OF HEALTH FACILITIES

Great progress has been made throughout the Nation in the provision of new general hospitals under the Hill-Burton program. But relatively little assistance has been available for modernization of the older hospitals, found particularly in our large cities. Without aid, deterioration threatens and rapid scientific and technical change is passing by these essential links to health care for millions of our people. The 1966 budget will include funds for a greatly increased hospital modernization effort as well as for expansion in the number and quality of nursing homes. *I urge the Congress to approve the full amount requested for each of these purposes.*

D. AID FOR GROUP PRACTICE FACILITIES

New approaches are needed to stretch the supply of medical specialists and to provide a wider range of medical services in the communities. The growth of voluntary, comprehensive group practice programs has demonstrated the feasibility of grouping health services for the mutual benefit of physicians and patients by—

Integrating the burgeoning medical specialties into an efficient and economical system of patient care.

Reducing the incidence of hospitalization which may now occur because there are few alternative centers for specialized care.

The initial capital requirements for group practice are substantial, and the funds are not now sufficiently available to stimulate the expansion and establishment of group practice. To facilitate and encourage this desirable trend, *I recommend legislation to authorize a program of direct construction loans and loan guarantees of facilities to assist voluntary association in the construction and equipping of facilities for comprehensive group practice.*

III. MANPOWER FOR THE HEALTH SERVICES

The advance of our Nation's health in this century has, in the final measure, been possible because of the unique quality and fortunate quantity of men and women serving in our health professions. Americans respect and are grateful for our doctors, dentists, nurses, and others who serve our Nation's health. But it is clear that the future requires our support now to increase the quantity and assure the continuing high quality of such vital personnel.

In all sectors of health care, the need for trained personnel continues to outstrip the supply:

> At present, the United States has 290,000 physicians. In a decade, we shall need 346,000.
>
> Today we are keeping pace with our needs largely because of the influx of numbers of foreign-trained doctors. Last year 1,600 came into the United States, the equivalent of the output from 16 medical schools and 21 percent of our medical school graduates.

Population growth has badly outpaced the increase in dentists and the shortage of dentists is now acute.

To begin to meet the Nation's health needs, the number of new physicians graduated each year must increase at least 50 percent by 1975, and the output of new dentists by 100 percent. The Health Professions Educational Assistance Act of 1963, authorizing grants to schools for construction of medical and other health education schools and loans to students, will help meet this problem. The magnitude of the need is demonstrated by the response:

Ninety applications have been received from medical and dental schools, requesting $247 million in Federal aid for construction.

Only $100 million is available in 1965; and the full authorization for 1966, which I will shortly request in the budget I am submitting, will provide $75 million more.

In the light of these needs, *I urge the Congress to appropriate the full amount authorized and requested for the Health Professions Educational Assistance Act program.*

While we must build new medical and dental schools, we must also retain and sustain the ones we have. To be neglectful of such schools would be wasteful folly.

We must face the fact that high operating costs and shortages of operating funds are jeopardizing our health professions educational system. Tuition and fees paid by medical and dental students meet less than half the institutional costs of their education. Several underfinanced medical and dental schools are threatened with failure to meet educational standards. New schools are slow to start, even when construction funds are available due to lack of operating funds. *I therefore recommend legislation to authorize—*

formula grants to help cover basic operating costs of our health profession schools in order that they may significantly expand both their capacity and the quality of their educational programs;

project grants to enable health profession schools to experiment and demonstrate new and improved educational methods.

Traditionally, our medical profession has attracted outstanding young talent, and we must be certain that this tradition is not compromised. We must draw the best available talent into the medical profession. Half of last June's medical school graduates came from families with incomes of over $10,000 a year. The high costs of medical school must not deny access to the medical profession for able youths from low- and middle-income families.

I therefore recommend legislation to authorize scholarships for medical and dental students who would otherwise not be able to enter or complete such training.

Looking to the future.

We must also look to the future in planning to meet the health manpower requirements of the Nation.

Unmet health needs are already large. American families are demanding and expecting more and better health services. In the past decades the proportion of our gross national product devoted to health has increased by more than 50 percent. The trend is still upward. If we are to meet our future needs and raise the health of the Nation, we must—

improve utilization of available professional health personnel;

expand the use and training of technicians and ancillary health workers through special schools and under the Vocational Education Act and Manpower Development and Training Act programs;

expand and improve training programs for professional and for supporting health personnel;

plan ahead to meet requirements for which the lead time is often 10 years or more.

With these objectives in mind, I have asked the Secretary of Health, Education, and Welfare to develop a long-range health manpower program for the Nation and to recommend to me the steps which should be taken to put it into effect.

IV. HEALTH RESEARCH AND RESEARCH FACILITIES

Two decades ago this Nation decided that its Government should be a strong supporter of the health research to advance the well-being of its people. This year that support amounts to more than two-thirds of the total national expenditure of $1.5 billion for health research.

Continued growth of this research is necessary and the 1966 budget includes:

Ten-percent growth in expenditures for health research and for the related training.

Funds to begin an automated system for processing the exploding volume of information on drugs and other chemicals related to health.

Health research, no less than patient care, requires adequate facilities. Over the past 8 years the Health Research Facilities Act has been highly successful in helping provide research facilities to universities and other nonprofit institutions. Federal grants of $320 million to 990 construction projects have generated over $500 million in matching institutional dollars. This authority expires on June 30, 1966, and *I recommend that it be extended for 5 years with an increased authorization and with a larger Federal share for specialized research facilities of a national or regional character.*

V. HEALTH GRANTS AND PROTECTION MEASURES

Our complex modem society is creating health hazards never before encountered. The pollution of our environment is assuming such important proportion I shall shortly send to the Congress a special message dealing with this challenge.

But the protection of the public health also requires action on other fronts.

A. HEALTH GRANTS TO COMMUNITIES AND STATES

In safeguarding and advancing the Nation's health, States and communities have long had special responsibilities. General and special-purpose health grants have proved an effective means of strengthening the Federal Government's partnership with them in improving the public health.

I have directed the Secretary of Health, Education, and Welfare to study these programs thoroughly and to recommend to me necessary legislation to increase their usefulness.

Authorizations for many of these programs expire at the close of fiscal mend year that the 1966. So that a thorough review made be made, *I recommend that the Congress extend the authorizations through June 80, 1967.*

B. CONSUMERS HEALTH PROTECTION

Modernization of the Federal Food, Drug, and Cosmetic Act is imperative if our health protection program is to keep pace with the technological and industrial advances of recent years.

The health of all Americans depends on the reliability and safety of the products of the food industry which alone generates nearly $100 billion in retail sales each year;

drug industry with sales reaching $6 billion;

cosmetic industry which markets $2.5 billion of products.

All must be operated under the highest standards of purity and safety.

Yet, despite recent improvements in food and drug legislation, serious gaps in our ability to protect the consumer still exist. The law should be strengthened to provide adequate authority in the regulation of nonprescription drugs, medical devices, cosmetics, and food.

Narcotics are not alone among the hazardous, habit-forming drugs subject to improper use. Barbiturates, amphetamines, and other drugs have harmful effects when improperly used. Widespread traffic resulting from inadequate controls over the manufacture, distribution, and sale of these drugs is creating a growing problem which must be met. We must also counter the threat from counterfeit drugs. *I recommend legislation to bring the production and distribution of barbiturates, amphetamines, and other psychotoxic drugs under more effective control.* For the fuller protection of our families, *I recommend legislation to require—*

Adequate labeling of hazardous substances.

Safety regulation of cosmetics and therapeutic devices by premarketing examination by the Food and Drug Administration.

Authority to seize counterfeit drugs at their source.

CONCLUSION

I believe we have come to a rare moment of opportunity and challenge in the evolution of our society. In the message I have presented to you—and in other messages I shall be sending—my purpose is to outline the attainable horizons of a greater society which a confident and prudent people can begin to build for the future.

Whatever we aspire to do together, our success in those enterprises—and our enjoyment of the fruits that result—will rest finally upon the health of our people. We cannot and we will not overcome all the barriers—or surmount all the obstacles—in one effort, no matter how intensive. But in all the sectors I have mentioned we are already behind our capability and our potential. Further delay will only compound our problems and deny our people the health and happiness that could be theirs.

The Eighty-eighth Congress wrote a proud and significant record of accomplishment in the field of health legislation. I have every confidence that this Congress will write an even finer record that will be remembered with honor by generations of Americans to come.

SOURCE: Public Papers of the Presidents of the United States, Lyndon Johnson, 1965, Book I. Washington, D.C.: Government Printing Office, 1966, 12–21.

ANALYSIS

As acknowledged by President Lyndon Johnson when he signed the Social Security Amendments of 1965 into law with President Harry S. Truman at his side on July 30, 1965, Medicare had its origin in Truman's administration. Truman's interest in public health grew out of his astonishment that many of the men who had volunteered to serve in the armed forces during World War II had failed the physicals required for enlistment. He perceived that as evidence that Americans did not have access to the basic medical care required to be healthy. Since the defense of the country required men to be healthy, Truman proposed to Congress that a national health insurance program be created that provided coverage to working-age men and their families. Since the plan also called for the U.S. surgeon general to establish health boards to ensure that costs were controlled, doctors had the option to determine their participation in the program. Capitalizing on public fears of Communism, the American Medical Association (AMA) and its supporters successfully defeated Truman's proposal by alleging that it was "socialized medicine." Their success with that phrase ensured that it would be reused in future years whenever health care emerged as a policy issue.

President John F. Kennedy's administration tried a smaller scale approach in that it pursued the enactment of insurance for citizens over the age of 65 that would cover limited hospitalization expenses, skilled nursing costs in nursing homes, and home health care charges. Wilbur Cohen, the architect of the proposal, intentionally excluded any payments to doctors in the hope that the AMA would not oppose the legislation. His dream was dashed when the AMA in 1961 launched a

$50 million campaign which, at the time, was the most expensive lobbying effort ever undertaken against a bill. The legislation's opponents were aided by congressman Wilbur Mills, a Democrat representing Arkansas, who served as the chairman of the Ways and Means Committee. Mills believed that creating the new program would result in the bankrupting of Social Security, so he personally ensured that the legislation never emerged from his committee to the floor of the House of Representatives to be voted upon.

By the time Johnson had assumed the presidency, the political climate had begun to shift in a direction more favorable to health care reform. This was due to the perceived failings of the Social Security Act of 1935, which had been designed to ensure that the elderly would be able to retire comfortably. Instead, due to the spiraling costs of health care, retirees were seeing the savings they accumulated over a lifetime quickly depleted. In his State of the Union address in 1964, Johnson asked Congress for legislation that would add hospitalization insurance protection for the elderly to the Social Security program. The Senate was prepared to answer his call with the King-Anderson bill. Modeled on the Cohen proposal put forth by Kennedy's administration, King-Anderson would have created a version of Medicare that fell far short of what Johnson truly desired. Even in that form, the legislation was unacceptable to Wilbur Mills. Recognizing that Mills was the key to advancing Medicare, Johnson had Cohen begin working with Mills to ascertain what he required to allow a Medicare bill to emerge from his committee.

As the presidential election of 1964 approached, it became apparent that Johnson was going to gain a mandate from the voters to advance his Great Society proposals, most notably Medicare. The AMA, recognizing that some form of Medicare was inevitable, decided to back another health care proposal that had been languishing in the House of Representatives known as the Kerr-Mills bill. It called for the elderly to be allowed to purchase some type of insurance, such as Blue Cross/Blue Shield, to help cover catastrophic health care costs. Johnson's administration, believing that it could actually enact legislation on the scale originally envisioned by Truman, worked with its allies in Congress to block the effort.

The election of 1964 saw three representatives who had opposed Medicare in the Ways and Means Committee lose their reelection bids. Recognizing the will of the voters, Mills publicly stated that his committee was willing to consider a Medicare bill. Johnson subsequently made getting medical insurance for the elderly his initial legislative priority of 1965. Mills took the lead in shepherding Medicare through Congress. With Cohen, Mills drew up legislation that he described as a "three-layer cake." One part paid for the medical expenses incurred by those who were too impoverished to pay for medical care, while another section addressed the hospitalization costs of people on Social Security. Much to the horror of the AMA, the third layer made provisions to allow individuals to acquire insurance to pay physicians for their services. The language in that section included a limitation on the amount that could be paid to physicians for their services. In order to honor Truman for his inspiration, Johnson used the Harry S. Truman Library for the signing ceremony.

Created at the same time as Medicare was Medicaid. It was intended as a federal–state initiative to provide health coverage to the poor. The federal government was responsible for establishing the minimum level of health services to be provided to citizens and helping fund those basic provisions. The states that chose to participate in the program had to help fund the basic services plus were given the option of extending additional benefits. As an incentive for the states to expand the initiative locally, they were given broad leeway into how they would fund the extra offerings. Due to decisions made at the state level, Medicaid offerings varied widely from state to state.

FURTHER READING

Altman, Stuart H., and David Shactman. 2011. *Power, Politics, and Universal Health Care: The Inside Story of a Century-Long Battle*. New York: Prometheus Books.

Cohen, Alan B., et al., eds. 2015. *Medicare and Medicaid at 50: America's Entitlement Programs in the Age of Affordable Care*. New York: Oxford University Press.

Cohen, Richard. 2016. *Poverty and the Myths of Health Care Reform*. Baltimore: Johns Hopkins University Press.

David, Sheri I. 1985. *With Dignity: The Search for Medicare and Medicaid*. Westport, CT: Greenwood Press.

Dawes, Daniel E. 2016. *150 Years of Obamacare*. Baltimore: Johns Hopkins University Press.

Woods, Randall B. 2016. *Prisoners of Hope: Lyndon B. Johnson, the Great Society, and the Limits of Liberalism*. New York: Basic Books.

"This Child Nutrition Act of 1966 Will Make It Possible to Close the Nutrition Gap among Children in School"

- ***Document:*** President Lyndon B. Johnson's Remarks at the Signing of the Child Nutrition Act of 1966
- ***Date:*** October 11, 1966
- ***Where:*** Washington, D.C.
- ***Significance:*** The act expanded the school lunch program by providing direct funding for free school lunches. It also piloted the school breakfast program.

DOCUMENT

Secretary Freeman, Senator Ellender, Members of the Congress:

This is a memorable day for the children of America
—for the child who arrives at school hungry, because there was no breakfast for him to eat at home.
—for the child who goes to school where no lunches are served, because there were no facilities to serve him with.
—for the preschool child who is enrolled in school-related activities. This legislation which I shall shortly sign is their program, the children's program—the Child Nutrition Act of 1966.

This Child Nutrition Act of 1966 will make it possible to close the nutrition gap among children in school.

I know what it is to teach children who are listless and tired because they are hungry—and realize the difference a decent meal can make in the lives and attitudes of school children. It can be a heartbreaking and a frustrating experience, if there is nowhere to turn for help when your child is hungry.

This was just one more situation that I saw when I was a very young man, and that I have been trying to do something about, and have determined to do something about ever since.

It is fitting that this landmark legislation becomes law during National School Lunch Week, October 9 to 15. Twenty years ago Congress enacted and President Truman signed the National School Lunch Act. They recognized that good nutrition is essential to good learning. So today, lunch at school is available to almost three-fourths of all children enrolled in elementary and secondary schools.

But major gaps still remain. The Child Nutrition Act is designed to help close those major gaps:

—Thousands of children go to schools that simply cannot afford to finance the basic equipment for food service. This act will help finance such equipment.

—Thousands of children arrive at school hungry because they have no breakfast. This act provides for breakfasts at school.

—Thousands of very young children are now enrolled in preschool activities. They have not been eligible to take part in the national school lunch program. This act provides assistance for them, too.

—The States have always borne the full administrative costs of school services. This act provides for administrative funds to help the States meet the challenge of reaching out to those children who have already been bypassed.

—Authority for the special milk program was to expire next June 30. This act continues this useful supplement to child nutrition for another 3 years.

The Child Nutrition Act of 1966 will help enable us to bring a food service within the reach of every child in school. With its programs and the programs now available under the national school lunch program, we can continue to close the nutrition gap among schoolchildren in the next 5 years.

I am today instructing the Secretary of Agriculture to set this target as his goal.

This legislation was the work of many people.

I want to especially mention Reverend C. B. Woodrich, whose pioneering efforts with poor children in the Denver, Colorado, area has shown how important this program can be to our future. To Senator Ellender, Congressmen Cooley and Harlan Hagen, and to all the other Members of Congress here with us today and all the Members who helped enact this measure, on behalf of all the children of America we say—thank you, and the children say thank you, too.

SOURCE: Johnson, Lyndon Baines. "Remarks at the Signing of the Child Nutrition Act of 1966." *Public Papers of the Presidents of the United States, Lyndon Johnson, 1966, Book II.* Washington, D.C.: Government Printing Office, 1967, 1140–1141.

ANALYSIS

The school lunch program for elementary and secondary schools was created by the National School Lunch Act of 1946 (NCLA). Over the NCLA's first 20 years, it became evident that students who received a nutritious lunch performed better than their peers who were hungry. President Lyndon Baines Johnson, who had once been a teacher in an impoverished school district, was motivated by that finding to make the passage of the Child Nutrition Act of 1966 (CNA), a component of the Great Society's War on Poverty.

The NCLA had required each state accepting funding from the U.S. Department of Agriculture to contribute $3 for each federal dollar received. This requirement resulted in less than one-third of the schools in the nation opting to offer school lunches since installing the facilities required to feed children was an expensive undertaking. In general, it was schools serving minority or rural populations that did not offer school lunches. To ensure that those children received at least one nutritious meal a day, the CNA provided funding to the states to provide for free lunches. Problems quickly arose because the CNA did not provide monies to construct the facilities required to store, prepare, and distribute meals in schools. The burden fell on school districts to bear the associated expenses. The unfunded mandate also did not take into account all of the new personnel that were going to be needed to operate a lunchroom.

Although the money distributed to the states was supposed to be funneled to all schools, state officials often opted to route the monies as they saw fit. In the South, most schools serving African American students were denied funding. Many of the nation's most impoverished communities, such as those in Appalachia, were likewise forgotten. Since Johnson's administration and Congress did not want to alienate local politicians, the CNA did not prescribe who should receive free lunches. By allowing state and local officials to determine who should benefit from the lunch program, the federal officials allowed the program to be used for patronage. Supporters and others favored by the decision makers benefited regardless of need, while many of the poor students that the act was supposed to assist went without food. Movements, such as the Poor People's March, brought attention to the inequities evident in federal initiatives like the CNA. Amendments in 1968 eliminated much of the local discretion that had plagued the CNA's early years. Ironically, criticisms arose from some who had misused the CNA for their benefit that the amendments had turned the CNA into another welfare benefit.

Over time, the CNA emerged as one of the most beneficial nutrition programs benefiting children. In addition to school lunches, the CNA also created a pilot program on the provision of breakfast in schools. The pilot's success resulted in the program becoming permanent. The 1966 legislation proved to be a landmark, as most children in the United States today have both breakfast and lunch available to them. Many receive them for a reduced cost, if not free.

FURTHER READING

Gundersen, Craig, and James P. Ziliak. 2014. "Childhood Food Insecurity in the U.S.: Trends, Causes, and Policy Options." *The Future of Children* 24, Research Report, Fall: 1–19.

Kerr, Norwood Allen. 1990. "Drafted into the War on Poverty: USDA Food and Nutrition Programs, 1961–1969." *Agricultural History* 64, no. 2: 154–166.

Levine, Susan. 2008. *School Lunch Politics: The Surprising History of America's Favorite Welfare Program*. Princeton: Princeton University Press.

"Income Guarantees and Supplements Are Feasible and Compatible with Our Economic System"

- ***Document:*** Economists' Statement on Guaranteed Annual Income
- ***Date:*** May 27, 1968
- ***Where:*** It was circulated throughout the United States to prospective signatories.
- ***Significance:*** Prominent economists, including John Kenneth Galbraith, created this document to pressure the federal government to guarantee all Americans a minimum income. The income level was to be set at a level to ensure that all recipients were elevated to the middle class. Elements of the proposal were included in President Richard Nixon's Family Assistance Plan.

DOCUMENT

The undersigned economists urge the Congress to adopt this year a national system of income guarantees and supplements.

The Poor People's Campaign in Washington is demanding a guaranteed minimum income for all Americans. The Kerner Commission on Civil Disorders called for a national system of income supplements. A group of business leaders recently advocated a "negative income tax." These proposals are all similar in design and purpose.

Like all civilized nations in the twentieth century, this country has long recognized a public responsibility for the living standards of its citizens. Yet our present programs of public assistance and social insurance exclude millions who are in need and meet inadequately the needs of millions more. All too often these programs unnecessarily penalize work and thrift and discourage the building of stable families.

The country will not have met its responsibility until everyone in the nation is assured an income no less than the officially recognized definition of poverty. A workable and equitable plan on income guarantees and supplements must have the following features. (1) Need, as objectively measured by income and family size, should be the sole basis of determining payment to which and individual and/or family is entitled. (2) To provide incentive to work, save and train for better jobs, payments to families who earn income should be reduced by only a fraction of their earnings.

Practical and detailed proposals meeting these requirements have been suggested by individual sponsors of this statement and by others. The costs of such plans are substantial but well within the nation's economic and fiscal capacity.

As economists we offer the professional opinion that income guarantees and supplements are feasible and compatible with our economic system. As citizens we feel strongly that the time for action is now.

SOURCE: "Economists' Statement on Guaranteed Annual Income," 1/15/1968-4/18/1969 folder, General Correspondence Series, Papers of John Kenneth Galbraith, John F. Kennedy Presidential Library.

ANALYSIS

During the 1960s, there were a number of proposals made to alleviate poverty through a guaranteed annual income. This was a minimum income level that would be provided to every eligible citizen by the government. One way of determining the government's contribution was through a "negative income tax." The negative tax amount reflected the difference between one's actual earnings and the minimum income threshold.

Many economists and federal bureaucrats believed that the guaranteed annual income was a far superior, and easier to manage, way of alleviating poverty than creating a multitude of separate programs. The guaranteed annual income idea was even supported in the 1968 *Report of the National Advisory Commission on Civil Disorders*, also known as the Kerner Report, as a way to stop rioting in the nation's urban areas. The idea did not have universal support, as many U.S. congressmen feared that guaranteeing anyone a salary would serve as a disincentive to actually working.

The Poor People's Campaign demanded that the guaranteed minimum income be instituted by the federal government. Their desire was supported in May 1968 by the release of the "Economists' Statement on Guaranteed Annual Income," which was the brainchild of five prominent economists: John Kenneth Galbraith, Robert Lampman, Paul Samuelson, James Tobin, and Harold Watts. It was signed by more than 1,000 economists from institutions of higher education from around the United States.

President Richard Nixon proposed a version of the negative income tax in his Family Assistance Plan, which included work requirements for recipients. The proposal failed to pass through Congress in both 1970 and 1972 because opponents claimed that the guaranteed income level was set too low.

FURTHER READING

Chappell, Marisa. 2010. *The War on Welfare: Family, Poverty, and Politics in Modern America.* Philadelphia: University of Pennsylvania Press.

Mantler, Gordon K. 2013. *Power to the Poor: Black-Brown Coalition and the Fight for Economic Justice, 1960–1974.* Chapel Hill: University of North Carolina Press.

Parker, Richard. 2005. *John Kenneth Galbraith: His Life, His Politics, His Economics.* New York: Farrar, Straus and Giroux.

Steensland, Brian. 2008. *The Failed Welfare Revolution: America's Struggle over Guaranteed Income Policy.* Princeton, NJ: Princeton University Press.

"Our Nation Is Moving toward Two Societies, One Black, One White—Separate and Unequal"

- ***Document:*** Report of the National Advisory Commission on Civil Disorders (Excerpts)
- ***Date:*** February 1968
- ***Where:*** Washington, D.C.
- ***Significance:*** Reflecting the sociological theory of the time, the Kerner Commission utilized culture-of-poverty theory to blame African Americans living in urban ghettos for creating many of the problems that plagued their communities. By blaming the victim, the report largely absolved white society and the federal government for their role in creating the conditions, such as rampant unemployment in African American communities, which led to the riots in many of the nation's cities in the first place.

DOCUMENT

REPORT OF THE NATIONAL ADVISORY COMMISSION ON CIVIL DISORDERS

SUMMARY OF REPORT

INTRODUCTION

The summer of 1967 again brought racial disorders to American cities, and with them shock, fear and bewilderment to the nation.

The worst came during a two-week period in July, first in Newark and then in Detroit.

Each set off a chain reaction in neighboring communities.

On July 28, 1967, the President of the United States established this Commission and directed us to answer three basic questions:

What happened?

Why did it happen?

What can be done to prevent it from happening again?

To respond to these questions, we have undertaken a broad range of studies and investigations. We have visited the riot cities; we have heard many witnesses; we have sought the counsel of experts across the country.

This is our basic conclusion: Our nation is moving toward two societies, one black, and one white—separate and unequal.

Reaction to last summer's disorders has quickened the movement and deepened the division. Discrimination and segregation have long permeated much of American life; they now threaten the future of every American.

This deepening racial division is not inevitable. The movement apart can be reversed.

Choice is still possible. Our principal task is to define that choice and to press for a national resolution.

To pursue our present course will involve the continuing polarization of the American community and, ultimately, the destruction of basic democratic values.

The alternative is not blind repression or capitulation to lawlessness. It is the realization of common opportunities for all within a single society.

This alternative will require a commitment to national action—compassionate, massive and sustained, backed by the resources of the most powerful and the richest nation on this earth. From every American it will require new attitudes, new understanding, and, above all, new will.

The vital needs of the nation must be met; hard choices must be made, and, if necessary, new taxes enacted.

Violence cannot build a better society. Disruption and disorder nourish repression, not justice. They strike at the freedom of every citizen. The community cannot—it will not—tolerate coercion and mob rule.

Violence and destruction must be ended—in the streets of the ghetto and in the lives of people.

Segregation and poverty have created in the racial ghetto a destructive environment totally unknown to most white Americans.

What white Americans have never fully understood but what the Negro can never forget is that white society is deeply implicated in the ghetto. White institutions created it, white institutions maintain it, and white society condones it.

It is time now to turn with all the purpose at our command to the major unfinished business of this nation. It is time to adopt strategies for action that will produce quick and visible progress. It is time to make good the promises of American democracy to all citizens—urban and rural, white and black, Spanish-surname, American Indian, and every minority group.

Our recommendations embrace three basic principles:

- To mount programs on a scale equal to the dimension of the problems:
- To aim these programs for high impact in the immediate future in order to close the gap between promise and performance;
- To undertake new initiatives and experiments that can change the system of failure and frustration that now dominates the ghetto and weakens our society.

* * *

Chapter 4—The Basic Causes

In addressing the question "Why did it happen?" we shift our focus from the local to the national scene, from the particular events of the summer of 1967 to the factors within the society at large that created a mood of violence among many urban Negroes.

These factors are complex and interacting; they vary significantly in their effect from city to city and from year to year; and the consequences of one disorder, generating new grievances and new demands, become the causes of the next. Thus was created the "thicket of tension, conflicting evidence and extreme opinions" cited by the President.

Despite these complexities, certain fundamental matters are clear. Of these, the most fundamental is the racial attitude and behavior of white Americans toward black Americans.

Race prejudice has shaped our history decisively; it now threatens to affect our future.

White racism is essentially responsible for the explosive mixture which has been accumulating in our cities since the end of World War II. Among the ingredients of this mixture are:

- Pervasive discrimination and segregation in employment, education and housing, which have resulted in the continuing exclusion of great numbers of Negroes from the benefits of economic progress.
- Black in-migration and white exodus, which have produced the massive and growing concentrations of impoverished Negroes in our major cities, creating a growing crisis of deteriorating facilities and services and unmet human needs.
- The black ghettos where segregation and poverty converge on the young to destroy opportunity and enforce failure. Crime, drug addiction, dependency on welfare, and bitterness and resentment against society in general and white society in particular are the result.

At the same time, most whites and some Negroes outside the ghetto have prospered to a degree unparalleled in the history of civilization. Through television and other media, this affluence has been flaunted before the eyes of the Negro poor and the jobless ghetto youth.

Yet these facts alone cannot be said to have caused the disorders. Recently, other powerful ingredients have begun to catalyze the mixture:

- Frustrated hopes are the residue of the unfulfilled expectations aroused by the great judicial and legislative victories of the Civil Rights Movement and the dramatic struggle for equal rights in the South.
- A climate that tends toward approval and encouragement of violence as a form of protest has been created by white terrorism directed against nonviolent protest; by the open defiance of law and federal authority by state and local officials resisting desegregation; and by some protest groups engaging in civil disobedience who turn their backs on nonviolence, go beyond the constitutionally protected rights of petition and free assembly, and resort to violence to attempt to compel alteration of laws and policies with which they disagree.
- The frustrations of powerlessness have led some Negroes to the conviction that there is no effective alternative to violence as a means of achieving redress of grievances, and of "moving the system." These frustrations are reflected in alienation and hostility toward the institutions of law and government and the white society which controls them, and in the reach toward racial consciousness and solidarity reflected in the slogan "Black Power."
- A new mood has sprung up among Negroes, particularly among the young, in which self-esteem and enhanced racial pride are replacing apathy and submission to "the system."
- The police are not merely a "spark" factor. To some Negroes police have come to symbolize white power, white racism and white repression. And the fact is that many police do reflect and express these white attitudes. The atmosphere of hostility and cynicism is reinforced by a widespread belief among Negroes in the existence of police brutality and in a "double standard" of justice and protection—one for Negroes and one for whites.

To this point, we have attempted to identify the prime components of the "explosive mixture." In the chapters that follow we seek to analyze them in the perspective of history. Their meaning, however, is clear:

In the summer of 1967, we have seen in our cities a chain reaction of racial violence. If we are heedless, none of us shall escape the consequences.

* * *

Chapter 7—Unemployment, Family Structure, and Social Disorganization

Although there have been gains in Negro income nationally, and a decline in the number of Negroes below the "poverty level," the condition of Negroes ill the central city remains in a state of crisis. Between 2 and 2.5 million Negroes—16 to 20 percent of the total Negro population of all central cities—live in squalor and deprivation in ghetto neighborhoods.

Employment is a key problem. It not only controls the present for the Negro American but, in a most profound way, it is creating the future as well. Yet, despite continuing economic growth and declining national unemployment rates, the unemployment rate for Negroes in 1967 was more than double that for whites.

Equally important is the undesirable nature of many jobs open to Negroes and other minorities. Negro men are more than three times as likely as white men to be in low paying, unskilled or service jobs. This concentration of male Negro employment at the lowest end of the occupational scale is the single most important cause of poverty among Negroes.

In one study of low-income neighborhoods, the "subemployment rate," including both unemployment and underemployment, was about 33 percent or 8.8 times greater than the overall unemployment rate for all United States workers.

Employment problems, aggravated by the constant arrival of new unemployed migrants, many of them from depressed rural areas, create persistent poverty in the ghetto. In 1966, about 11.9 percent of the nation's whites and 40.6 percent of its non-whites were below the "poverty level" defined by the Social Security Administration (currently $3,335 per year for an urban family of four). Over 40 percent of the non-whites below the poverty level live in the central cities.

Employment problems have drastic social impact in the ghetto. Men who are chronically unemployed or employed in the lowest status jobs are often unable or unwilling to remain with their families. The handicap imposed on children growing up without fathers in an atmosphere of poverty and deprivation is increased as mothers are forced to work to provide support.

The culture of poverty that results from unemployment and family breakup generates a system of ruthless, exploitative relationships within the ghetto. Prostitution, dope addiction, and crime create an environmental "jungle" characterized by personal insecurity and tension. Children growing up under such conditions are likely participants in civil disorder.

* * *

CONCLUSION

One of the first witnesses to be invited to appear before this Commission was Dr. Kenneth B. Clark, a distinguished and perceptive scholar. Referring to the reports of earlier riot commissions, he said:

I read that report . . . of the 1919 riot in Chicago, and it is as if I were reading the report of the investigating committee on the Harlem riot of '35, the report of the investigating committee on the Harlem riot of '43, the report of the McCone Commission on the Watts riot.

I must again in candor say to you members of this Commission—it is a kind of Alice in Wonderland—with the same moving picture re-shown over and over again, the same analysis, the same recommendations, and the same inaction.

These words come to our minds as we conclude this report.

We have provided an honest beginning. We have learned much. But we have uncovered no startling truths, no unique insights, no simple solutions. The destruction and the bitterness of racial disorder, the harsh polemics of black revolt and white repression have been seen and heard before in this country.

It is time now to end the destruction and the violence, not only in the streets of the ghetto but in the lives of people.

SOURCE: U.S. National Advisory Commission on Civil Disorders. 1968. *Report of the National Advisory Commission on Civil Disorders*. Washington, D.C.: Government Printing Office.

ANALYSIS

Between 1965 and 1967, more than 160 riots roiled American cities. Some happened because of incidents that occurred within the community, while others began in support of rioters protesting in other cities. In 1967, the prevalence of rioting led President Johnson to appoint a commission to investigate both the causes of the urban rioting and how legal authorities responded to the respective incidents. He appointed Illinois governor Otto Kerner to head the National Advisory Commission on Civil Disorders.

In February 1968, the National Advisory Commission on Civil Disorders issued the *Report of the National Advisory Commission on Civil Disorders*, which became better known as the "Kerner Commission Report." The report famously concluded that the United States was "moving toward two societies, one black, one white—separate and unequal." The commission in its report succeeded in enraging all constituencies by spreading the blame for urban unrest on all parties. Utilizing culture-of-poverty theory, the commission noted that generations of fatherless families and unemployment had resulted in the propensity of young African Americans to disrespect authority and property rights. By blaming the victim, the commission put much of the blame for the rioting on the African American community.

One recommendation in the report that was acted upon quickly was a suggestion that the U.S. Department of Defense recruit African Americans into the very military units that were being utilized to stop urban rioting. The effort was deemed necessary because the military units in question were comprised of mostly white soldiers. The thinking behind the proposal was that people were less prone to act violently if they were engaged by members of their own race and community. Toward the expressed goal, Secretary of Defense Robert McNamara authorized recruiters to exceed their quota per unit by 10 percent as long as the extra recruits were African American. Although this effort began after most of the urban rioting had concluded, it was an early form of the community policing program that is prevalent in many U.S. cities today.

The commission enraged the Johnson administration by also noting that police brutality, housing discrimination, and a lack of economic opportunity had an impact on the hopelessness felt by many in the affected African American communities. These were issues that the War on Poverty had attempted to address through both the Community Action Program and the Model Cities initiative, yet four years into the effort there was nothing to show for it in these urban communities except burned-out buildings. To combat these problems, the commission recommended that the federal government fund programs to employ African Americans and address housing discrimination that kept people trapped in ghettos. Johnson responded to the report by getting the Fair Housing Act of 1968 passed by Congress. He did take the commission's report as a rebuke of his policies, as he refused to send the members of the commission congratulatory notes for their work, which was customary.

FURTHER READING

Abu-Lughod, Janet L. 2007. *Race, Space, and Riots in Chicago, New York, and Los Angeles.* New York: Oxford University Press.

Barnhart, Bill, and Gene Schlickman. 1999. *Kerner: The Conflict of Intangible Rights.* Champaign: University of Illinois Press.

Flamm, Michael W. 2005. *Law and Order: Street Crime, Civil Unrest, and the Crisis of Liberalism in the 1960s.* New York: Columbia University Press.

Horne, Gerald. 1995. *Fire This Time: The Watts Uprising and the 1960s.* Charlottesville: University of Virginia Press.

Hrach, Thomas J. 2016. *The Riot Report and the News: How the Kerner Commission Changed Media Coverage of Black America.* Amherst: University of Massachusetts Press.

Matlin, Daniel. 2013. *On the Corner: African American Intellectuals and the Urban Crisis.* Cambridge: Harvard University Press.

Sugrue, Thomas J. 1996. *The Origins of the Urban Crisis: Race and Inequality in Postwar Detroit.* Princeton: Princeton University Press.

"To Protect the Consumer against Inaccurate and Unfair Credit Billing and Credit Card Practices"

- *Document:* Truth in Lending Act of 1968 (including 2010 amendments)
- *Date:* May 29, 1968
- *Where:* Washington, D.C.
- *Significance:* The purpose of the act was to ensure that the consumer was aware of the total cost of the credit that was being offered.

DOCUMENT

CONSUMER CREDIT PROTECTION ACT

. . .

TITLE I—CONSUMER CREDIT COST DISCLOSURE

. . .

CHAPTER 1—GENERAL PROVISIONS

Sec.

. . .

§ 101. Short title

This title may be cited as the Truth in Lending Act.

. . .

§ 102. Congressional findings and declaration of purpose

(a) INFORMED USE OF CREDIT.—The Congress finds that economic stabilization would be enhanced and the competition among the various financial institutions and other firms engaged in the extension of consumer credit would be strengthened by the informed use of credit. The informed use of credit results from an awareness of the cost thereof by consumers. It is the purpose of this title to assure a meaningful disclosure of credit terms so that the consumer will be able to compare more readily the various credit terms available to him and avoid the uninformed use of credit, and to protect the consumer against inaccurate and unfair credit billing and credit card practices.

(b) TERMS OF PERSONAL PROPERTY LEASES.—The Congress also finds that there has been a recent trend toward leasing automobiles and other durable goods for consumer use as an alternative to installment credit sales and that these leases have been offered without adequate cost disclosures. It is the purpose of this title to assure a meaningful disclosure of the terms of leases of personal property for personal, family, or household purposes so as to enable the lessee to compare more readily the various lease terms available to him, limit balloon payments in consumer leasing, enable comparison of lease terms with credit terms where appropriate, and to assure meaningful and accurate disclosures of lease terms in advertisements.

. . .

§ 106. Determination of finance charge

(a) "FINANCE CHARGE" DEFINED.—Except as otherwise provided in this section, the amount of the finance charge in connection with any consumer credit transaction shall be determined as the sum of all charges, payable directly or indirectly by the person to whom the credit is extended, and imposed directly or indirectly by the creditor as an incident to the extension of credit. The finance charge does not include charges of a type payable in a comparable cash transaction. The finance charge shall not include fees and amounts imposed by third party closing agents (including settlement agents, attorneys, and escrow and title companies) if the creditor does not require the imposition of the charges or the services provided and does not retain the charges. Examples of charges which are included in the finance charge include any of the following types of charges which are applicable:

(1) Interest, time price differential, and any amount payable under a point, discount, or other system of additional charges.

(2) Service or carrying charge.

(3) Loan fee, finder's fee, or similar charge.

(4) Fee for an investigation or credit report.

(5) Premium or other charge for any guarantee or insurance protecting the creditor against the obligor's default or other credit loss.

(6) Borrower-paid mortgage broker fees, including fees paid directly to the broker or the lender (for delivery to the broker) whether such fees are paid in cash or financed.

(b) LIFE, ACCIDENT, OR HEALTH INSURANCE PREMIUMS INCLUDED IN FINANCE CHARGE.—Charges or premiums for credit life, accident, or health insurance written in connection with any consumer credit transaction shall be included in the finance charges unless

(1) the coverage of the debtor by the insurance is not a factor in the approval by the creditor of the extension of credit, and this fact is clearly disclosed in writing to the person applying for or obtaining the extension of credit; and

(2) in order to obtain the insurance in connection with the extension of credit, the person to whom the credit is extended must give specific affirmative written indication of his desire to do so after written disclosure to him of the cost thereof.

(c) PROPERTY DAMAGE AND LIABILITY INSURANCE PREMIUMS INCLUDED IN FINANCE CHARGE.—Charges or premiums for insurance, written in connection with any consumer credit transaction, against loss of or damage to property or against liability arising out of the ownership or use of property, shall be included in the finance charge unless a clear and specific statement in writing is furnished by the creditor to the person to whom the credit is extended, setting forth the cost of the insurance if obtained from or through the creditor, and stating that the person to whom the credit is extended may choose the person through which the insurance is to be obtained.

. . .

§ 107. Determination of annual percentage rate

(a) "ANNUAL PERCENTAGE RATE" DEFINED.—The annual percentage rate applicable to any extension of consumer credit shall be determined, in accordance with the regulations of the Bureau,

(1) in the case of any extension of credit other than under an open end credit plan, as

(A) that nominal annual percentage rate which will yield a sum equal to the amount of the finance charge when it is applied to the unpaid balances of the amount financed, calculated according to the actuarial method of allocating payments made on a debt between the amount financed and the amount of the finance charge, pursuant to which a payment is applied first to the accumulated finance charge and the balance is applied to the unpaid amount financed; or

(B) the rate determined by any method prescribed by the Bureau as a method which materially simplifies computation while retaining reasonable accuracy as compared with the rate determined under subparagraph (A).

(2) in the case of any extension of credit under an open end credit plan, as the quotient (expressed as a percentage) of the total finance charge for the period to which it relates divided by the amount upon which the finance charge for that period is based, multiplied by the number of such periods in a year.

. . .

§ 108. Administrative enforcement

(a) ENFORCING AGENCIES.—Subject to subtitle B of the Consumer Financial Protection Act of 2010, compliance with the requirements imposed under this title shall be enforced under—

(1) section 8 of the Federal Deposit Insurance Act, by the appropriate Federal banking agency, as defined in section 3(q) of the Federal Deposit Insurance Act (12 U.S.C. 1813(q)), with respect to—
  (A) national banks, Federal savings associations, and Federal branches and Federal agencies of foreign banks;
  (B) member banks of the Federal Reserve System (other than national banks), branches and agencies of foreign banks (other than Federal branches, Federal agencies, and insured State branches of foreign banks), commercial lending companies owned or controlled by foreign banks, and organizations operating under section 25 or 25A of the Federal Reserve Act; and
  (C) banks and State savings associations insured by the Federal Deposit Insurance Corporation (other than members of the Federal Reserve System), and insured State branches of foreign banks;

(2) the Federal Credit Union Act, by the Director of the National Credit Union Administration, with respect to any Federal credit union;

(3) the Federal Aviation Act of 1958, by the Secretary of Transportation, with respect to any air carrier or foreign air carrier subject to that Act;

(4) the Packers and Stockyards Act, 1921 (except as provided in section 406 of that Act), by the Secretary of Agriculture, with respect to any activities subject to that Act;

(5) the Farm Credit Act of 1971, by the Farm Credit Administration with respect to any Federal land bank, Federal land bank association, Federal intermediate credit bank, or production credit association; and

(6) subtitle E of the Consumer Financial Protection Act of 2010, by the Bureau, with respect to any person subject to this title.

(7) sections 21B and 21C of the Securities Exchange Act of 1934, in the case of a broker or dealer, other than a depository institution, by the Securities Exchange Commission.

SOURCE: Federal Deposit Insurance Corporation. 2016. *FDIC Law, Regulations, Related Acts: 6000—Consumer Protection*. Washington, D.C.: Federal Deposit Insurance Corporation. https://www.fdic.gov/regulations/laws/rules/6000-200.html.

ANALYSIS

The Truth in Lending Act was Title I of the Consumer Protection Act of 1968. It was enacted to address predatory lending, which included such tactics as advertising low-interest loans and then extending loans with far higher interest rates or hiding fees that had the effect of raising the cost of the credit that was being extended. To curb the opaque lending practices that most severely harmed individuals in the lower economic classes, Congress put the onus on lenders to fully explain to their customers the total cost of the debt that was being offered to them. In order to limit the discretion of lenders, the legislation included language that prescribed how interest rates and fees were to be determined. In addition, lenders were not allowed to advertise "deals" that were only available to a small segment of the population. In order to ensure that lenders did not try to skirt the regulations by calling loans by other terms like "installment plans," Congress extended the regulations to goods that took more than four months to pay off. Since 1968, the Truth in Lending Act has been amended many times to address issues related to financial instruments like credit cards. Major changes to the Truth in Lending Act, as it related to mortgages, were made in Title XIV of the Dodd-Frank Wall Street Reform and Consumer Protection Act of 2010.

FURTHER READING

Caulder, Jonathan L. 2014. "Avoiding the Nuclear Option: Balancing Borrower and Lender Rights under the Truth in Lending Act's Right of Recission." *Washington & Lee Law Review* 71, no. 3: 1925–1977.

Engel, Kathleen C., and Patricia A. McCoy. 2007. "Predatory Lending and Community Development at Loggerheads." In Julia Sass Rubin, ed. *Financing Low Income Communities*. New York: Russell Sage Foundation, 227–262.

Retsinas, Nicolas P., and Eric S. Belsky, eds. 2008. *Borrowing to Live: Consumer and Mortgage Credit Revisited*. Washington, D.C.: Brookings Institution Press.

"Aid to Families with Dependent Children Shall Be Furnished with Reasonable Promptness to All Eligible Individuals"

- ***Document:*** *Reuben K. King, Commissioner of the State Department of Pensions and Security, State of Alabama, et al. v. Sylvester Smith et al.*, 392 U.S. 309 (1968) (Syllabus)
- ***Date:*** Argued April 23, 1968, decided June 17, 1968
- ***Where:*** Washington, D.C.
- ***Significance:*** In their majority decision, the U.S. Supreme Court justices determined that children eligible for benefits under the Aid to Families with Dependent Children program could not have it denied to them due to the activities of their parents.

DOCUMENT

SYLLABUS

Under the Aid to Families with Dependent Children Program (AFDC) established by the Social Security Act of 1935 funds are made available for a "dependent child" largely by the Federal Government, on a matching fund basis, with the participating State administering the program in conformity with the Act and regulations of the Department of Health, Education, and Welfare (HEW). Section 406(a) of the Act defines a "dependent child" as one who has been deprived of "parental" support or care by reason of the death, continued absence, or incapacity of a "parent," and, insofar as relevant in this case, aid can be granted under the provision only if a "parent" of the needy child is continually absent from the home. The Act requires that "aid to families with dependent children shall be furnished with reasonable promptness to all eligible individuals. . . ." 42 U.S.C. § 602(a)(9). Alabama, which, like all other States, participates in the AFDC program, in 1964 promulgated its "substitute father" regulation under which AFDC payments are denied to the children of a mother who "cohabits" in or outside her home with an able-bodied man, a "substitute father" being considered a nonabsent parent within the federal statute. The regulation applies regardless of whether the man is the children's father, is obliged to contribute to their support, or in fact does so. The AFDC aid which appellee Mrs. Smith and her four children, who reside in Alabama, for several years had received was terminated in October, 1966, solely because of the substitute father regulation on the ground that a Mr. Williams came to her home on weekends and had sexual relations with her. Mr. Williams is not the father of any of her children, is not obliged by state law to support them, and does not do so. Appellees thereupon brought this class action in the District Court against appellants, officers, and members of the Alabama Board of Pensions and Security for declaratory and injunctive relief against the substitute father regulation. The State contended that the regulation simply defines who is a nonabsent "parent" under the Act, is a legitimate way of allocating its limited resources available for AFDC assistance, discourages illicit sexual relationships and illegitimate births, and treats informal "married" couples like ordinary married couples who are ineligible for AFDC aid so long as their father is in the home. The District Court found the regulation inconsistent with the Act and the Equal Protection Clause.

Held: Alabama's substitute father regulation is invalid because it defines "parent" in a manner that is inconsistent with § 406(a) of the Social Security Act, and, in denying AFDC assistance to appellees on the basis of the invalid regulation, Alabama has breached its federally imposed obligation to furnish aid to families with dependent children with reasonable promptness to all eligible individuals.

(a) Insofar as Alabama's substitute father regulation (which has no relation to the need of the dependent child) is based on the State's asserted interest in discouraging illicit sexual behavior and illegitimacy, it plainly conflicts with federal law and policy. Under HEW's "Flemming Ruling," as modified by amendments to the Social Security Act, Congress has determined that immorality and illegitimacy should be dealt with through rehabilitative measures, rather than measures punishing dependent children, whose protection is AFDC's paramount goal.

(b) Congress meant by the term "parent" in § 406(a) of the Act an individual who owed the child a state-imposed duty of support, and Alabama may not therefore disqualify a child from AFDC aid on the basis of a substitute father who has no such duty.

277 F.Supp. 31, affirmed.

SOURCE: King v. Smith, 392 U.S. 309 (1968).

ANALYSIS

The Social Security Act of 1935 created the Aid to Dependent Children program, later renamed Aid to Families with Dependent Children (AFDC), to ensure that women without spousal support could adequately provide for their children. It was a joint federal and state initiative that allowed the respective states to add their own eligibility requirements to those created by the federal government. Some states, such as Alabama, included morality clauses designed to pressure women, mainly from minority groups, to act in a manner defined by the state.

Alabama's morality views came into question in 1966 when Ms. Smith, who had four children but no spouse, had her family's AFDC benefits taken away. The reason was that she was involved in a sexual relationship with a man who visited her home on weekends. He was not the father of any of the children and did not provide for them in any way. Although he had no legal responsibility to the children, under Alabama law he was the "man-in-the-house," meaning that the state decided that he was responsible for the care of the entire family. Since other states had similar statutes to the one in Alabama, the civil rights case was litigated through the federal courts. Ms. Smith was able to regain her family's AFDC benefits because the Supreme Court determined that children could not be denied their benefits regardless of whether their mother was involved in immoral acts because none of the males in question had a legal responsibility to the children. By extension, a state could not create an artificial responsibility for an individual who was not a biological relative.

FURTHER READING

Davis, Martha F. 1993. *Brutal Need: Lawyers and the Welfare Rights Movement, 1960–1973.* New Haven, CT: Yale University Press.

Lefkovitz, Alison. 2011. "Men in the House: Race, Welfare, and the Regulation of Men's Sexuality in the United States, 1961–1972." *Journal of the History of Sexuality* 20, no. 3: 594–614.

Ward, Deborah E. 2005. *The White Welfare State: The Racialization of U.S. Welfare Policy.* Ann Arbor: University of Michigan Press.

"The OEO Has Been a Valuable Fount of Ideas and Enthusiasm, but It Has Suffered from a Confusion of Roles"

- ***Document:*** President Richard Nixon's Special Message to the Congress on the Nation's Antipoverty Programs
- ***Date:*** February 19, 1969
- ***Where:*** Washington, D.C.
- ***Significance:*** Dismantling President Lyndon Johnson's Great Society was a major theme for Richard Milhous Nixon as he campaigned for the presidency in 1968. Upon assuming office, Nixon pledged to reform the Office of Economic Opportunity, which was originally created to oversee many of his predecessor's War on Poverty initiatives.

DOCUMENT

To the Congress of the United States:

The blight of poverty requires priority attention. It engages our hearts and challenges our intelligence. It cannot and will not be treated lightly or indifferently, or without the most searching examination of how best to marshal the resources available to the Federal Government for combatting it.

At my direction, the Urban Affairs Council has been conducting an intensive study of the nation's anti-poverty programs, of the way the anti-poverty effort is organized and administered, and of ways in which it might be made more effective.

That study is continuing. However, I can now announce a number of steps I intend to take, as well as spelling out some of the considerations that will guide my future recommendations.

The Economic Opportunity Act of 1964 is now scheduled to expire on June 30, 1970. The present authorization for appropriations for the Office of Economic Opportunity runs only until June 30, 1969.

I will ask Congress that this authorization for appropriations be extended for another year. Prior to the end of the Fiscal Year, I will send Congress a comprehensive proposal for the future of the poverty program, including recommendations for revising and extending the Act itself beyond its scheduled 1970 expiration.

How the work begun by OEO can best be carried forward is a subject on which many views deserve to be heard—both from within Congress, and among those many others who are interested or affected, including especially the poor themselves. By sending my proposals well before the Act's 1970 expiration, I intend to provide time for full debate and discussion.

In the maze of anti-poverty efforts, precedents are weak and knowledge uncertain. These past years of increasing Federal involvement have begun to make clear how vast is the range of what we do not yet know, and how fragile are projections based on partial understanding. But we have learned some lessons about what works and what does not. The changes I propose will be based on those lessons and those discoveries, and rooted in a determination to press ahead with anti-poverty efforts even though individual experiments have ended in disappointment.

From the experience of OEO, we have learned the value of having in the Federal Government an agency whose special concern is the poor. We have learned the need for flexibility, responsiveness, and continuing innovation. We have learned the need for management effectiveness. Even those most thoroughly committed to the goals of the anti-poverty effort recognize now that much that has been tried has not worked.

The OEO has been a valuable fount of ideas and enthusiasm, but it has suffered from a confusion of roles.

OEO's greatest value is as an initiating agency—devising new programs to help the poor, and serving as an "incubator" for these programs during their initial, experimental phases. One of my aims is to free OEO itself to perform these functions more effectively, by providing for a greater concentration of its energies on its innovative role.

Last year, Congress directed that special studies be made by the Executive Branch of whether Head Start and the Job Corps should continue to be administered directly by OEO, or whether responsibility should be otherwise assigned.

Section 309 of the Vocational Education Amendments of 1968 provides:

"The President shall make a special study of whether the responsibility for administering the Head Start program established under the Economic Opportunity Act of 1964 should continue to be vested in the Director of the Office of Economic Opportunity, should be transferred to another agency of the Government, or should be delegated to another such agency pursuant to the provisions of section 602(d) of the aforementioned Economic Opportunity Act of 1964, and shall submit the findings of this study to the Congress not later than March 1, 1969."

I have today submitted this study to the Congress. Meanwhile, under the Executive authority provided by the Economic Opportunity Act, I have directed that preparations be made for the delegation of Head Start to the Department of Health, Education, and Welfare. Whether it should be actually transferred is a question I will take up in my later, comprehensive message, along with my proposals for a permanent status and organizational structure for OEO. Pending a final decision by the Secretary of HEW on where within the department responsibility for Head Start would be lodged, it will be located directly within the Office of the Secretary.

In order to provide for orderly preparation, and to ensure that there is no interruption of programs, I have directed that this delegation be made effective July 1, 1969. By then the summer programs for 1969 will all have been funded, and a new cycle will be beginning.

I see this delegation as an important element in a new national commitment to the crucial early years of life.

Head Start is still experimental. Its effects are simply not known—save of course where medical care and similar services are involved. The results of a major national evaluation of the program will be available this Spring. It must be said, however, that preliminary reports on this study confirm what many have feared: the long term effect of Head Start appears to be extremely weak. This must not discourage us. To the contrary it only demonstrates the immense contribution the Head Start program has made simply by having raised to prominence on the national agenda the fact—known for some time, but never widely recognized—that the children of the poor mostly arrive at school age seriously deficient in the ability to profit from formal education, and already significantly behind their contemporaries. It also has been made abundantly clear that our schools as they now exist are unable to overcome this deficiency.

In this context, the Head Start Follow-Through Program already delegated to HEW by OEO, assumes an even greater importance.

In recent years, enormous advances have been made in the understanding of human development. We have learned that intelligence is not fixed at birth, but is largely formed by the environmental influences of the early formative years. It develops rapidly at first, and then more slowly; as much of that development takes place in the first four years as in the next thirteen. We have learned further that environment has its greatest impact on the development of intelligence when that development is proceeding most rapidly—that is, in those earliest years.

This means that many of the problems of poverty are traceable directly to early childhood experience—and that if we are to make genuine, long-range progress, we must focus our efforts much more than heretofore on those few years which may determine how far, throughout his later life, the child can reach.

Recent scientific developments have shown that this process of early childhood development poses more difficult problems than had earlier been recognized—but they also promise a real possibility of major breakthroughs soon in our understanding of this process. By placing Head Start in the Department of HEW, it will be possible to strengthen it by association with a wide range of other early development programs within the department, and also with the research programs of the National

Institutes of Health, the National Institute of Mental Health, and the National Institute of Child Health and Human Development.

Much of our knowledge is new. But we are not on that ground absolved from the responsibility to respond to it. So crucial is the matter of early growth that we must make a national commitment to providing all American children an opportunity for healthful and stimulating development during the first five years of life. In delegating Head Start to the Department of HEW, I pledge myself to that commitment.

The Vocational Education Amendments of 1968 directed the Commissioner of Education to study the Job Corps in relation to state vocational education programs. I have directed the Secretaries of Labor and of Health, Education, and Welfare, and the Assistant Secretary of Labor for Manpower, to work with the Acting Commissioner of Education in preparing such a report for submission to Congress at the earliest opportunity.

One of the priority aims of the new Administration is the development by the Department of Labor of a comprehensive manpower program, designed to make centrally available to the unemployed and the underemployed a full range of Federal job training and placement services. Toward this end, it is essential that the many Federal manpower programs be integrated and coordinated.

Therefore, as a first step toward better program management, the Job Corps will be delegated to the Department of Labor.

For the Department, this will add another important manpower service component. For the Job Corpsmen, it will make available additional training and service opportunities. From the standpoint of program management, it makes it possible to coordinate the Job Corps with other manpower services, especially vocational education, at the point of delivery.

The Department of Labor already is deeply involved in the recruitment, counseling and placement of Job Corpsmen. It refers 80 percent of all male and 45 percent of all female enrollees; it provides job market information, and helps locate Job Corpsmen in the areas of greatest opportunity.

This delegation will also be made effective on July 1, 1969; and the Departments of Interior and Agriculture will continue to have operating responsibility for the Job Corps centers concerned primarily with conservation.

I have directed that preparations be made for the transfer of two other programs from OEO to the Department of Health, Education, and Welfare: Comprehensive Health Centers, which provide health service to the residents of poor neighborhoods, and Foster Grandparents program. In my judgment, these can be better administered at present, or in the near future, within the structure of the Department.

In making these changes, I recognize that innovation costs money—and that if OEO is to continue its effectiveness as an innovating agency, adequate funds must be made available on a continuing basis. Moreover, it is my intent that Community Action Agencies can continue to be involved in the operation of programs such as Head Start at the local level, even though an agency other than OEO has received such programs, by delegation, at the national level. It also is my intent that the vital Community Action Programs will be pressed forward, and that in the area of economic development OEO will have an important role to play, in cooperation with other agencies, in fostering community-based business development.

One of the principal aims of the Administration's continuing study of the anti-poverty effort will be to improve its management effectiveness. When poverty fund monies are stolen, those hurt most are the poor—whom the monies were meant to help. When programs are inefficiently administered, those hurt most again are the poor. The public generally, and the poor especially, have a right to demand effective and efficient management. I intend to provide it.

I expect that important economies will result from the delegation of the Job Corps to the Department of Labor, and we shall continue to strive for greater efficiency, and especially for greater effectiveness in Head Start.

A Concentrated Management Improvement Program initiated in OEO will be intensified. Under this program, selected Community Action Agencies will be required to take steps to devise improvements in such areas as organizational structure, financial and accounting systems, personnel training and work scheduling. Standards will be applied under the "management improvement program" to evaluate the operations of Community Action Agencies. We intend to monitor these programs actively in order to insure that they are achieving high-level effectiveness and that they are being administered on an orderly basis.

In the past, problems have often arisen over the relationship of State, county and local governments to programs administered by OEO. This has particularly been the case where the State and local officials have wanted to assume greater responsibility for the implementation of the programs but for various reasons have been prevented from doing so. I have assigned special responsibility for working out these problems to the newly-created Office of Intergovernmental Relations, under the supervision of the Vice President.

I have directed the Urban Affairs Council to keep the anti-poverty effort under constant review and evaluation, seeking new ways in which the various departments can help and better ways in which their efforts can be coordinated.

My comprehensive recommendations for the future of the poverty program will be made after the Urban Affairs Council's own initial study is completed, and after I have reviewed the Comptroller General's study of OEO ordered by Congress in 1967 and due for submission next month.

Meanwhile, I would stress this final thought: If we are to make the most of experimental programs, we must frankly recognize their experimental nature and frankly acknowledge whatever shortcomings they develop. To do so is not to belittle the experiment, but to advance its essential purpose: that of finding new ways, better ways, of making progress in areas still inadequately understood.

We often can learn more from a program that fails to achieve its purpose than from one that succeeds. If we apply those lessons, then even the "failure" will have made a significant contribution to our larger purposes.

I urge all those involved in these experimental programs to bear this in mind—and to remember that one of the primary goals of this Administration is to expand our knowledge of how best to make real progress against those social ills that have so stubbornly defied solution. We do not pretend to have all the answers. We are determined to find as many as we can.

The men and women who will be valued most in this administration will be those who understand that not every experiment succeeds, who do not cover up failures but rather lay open problems, frankly and constructively, so that next time we will know how to do better.

In this spirit, I am confident that we can place our anti-poverty efforts on a secure footing—and that as we continue to gain in understanding of how to master the difficulties, we can move forward at an accelerating pace.

SOURCE: Nixon, Richard M. 1971. *Public Papers of the Presidents of the United States: Richard Nixon, 1969*. Washington, D.C.: Government Printing Office, 112–117.

ANALYSIS

Dismantling President Lyndon Johnson's Great Society was a major theme for Richard Milhous Nixon as he campaigned for the presidency in 1968. This was most evident in his speech to the Republican National Convention when he accepted the party's nomination for the presidency.

> [T]his brings me to the clearest choice among the great issues of this campaign. For the past five years we have been deluged by government programs for the unemployed; programs for the cities; programs for the poor. And we have reaped from these programs an ugly harvest of frustration, violence and failure across the land.
>
> And now our opponents will be offering more of the same—more billions for government jobs, government housing, government welfare. I say it is time to quit pouring billions of dollars into programs that have failed in the United States of America. To put it bluntly, we are on the wrong road—and it's time to take a new road, to progress. (Nixon)

Nixon continued the rhetoric into his presidency, but to the chagrin of his fellow Republicans, he followed Johnson's lead in growing the size and influence of the federal government.

When Nixon came into office, the federal budget allocated $55 billion for social welfare programs. The year that he resigned the presidency due to the Watergate scandal, social welfare spending had ballooned to more than $130 billion. Contributing to that increase was the tripling of the number of students receiving free or reduced meals at school and more than quadrupling the number of food stamp recipients. The expansion of welfare spending by Nixon resulted in his repudiation by conservative Republicans, most notably Ronald Reagan. Like Johnson before him, Nixon's domestic agenda was overshadowed by the Vietnam War. Due to budget overruns from both the war and Johnson's Great Society, Nixon was forced to rely on deficit spending during his terms in office. The inflation that this financing method spurred over the course of the 1970s had the net effect of seriously eroding the value of the benefits provided to the impoverished by the administrations of Johnson and Nixon.

FURTHER READING

Ambrose, Stephen E. 1989. *Nixon: The Triumph of a Politician 1962–1972*. New York: Simon & Schuster.

Chappell, Marisa. 2010. *The War on Welfare: Family, Poverty, and Politics in Modern America*. Philadelphia: University of Pennsylvania Press.

Milkis, Sidney M., and Jerome M. Mileur, eds. 2005. *The Great Society and the High Tide of Liberalism*. Amherst: University of Massachusetts Press.

Nixon, Richard. 1968. "Address Accepting the Presidential Nomination at the Republican National Convention in Miami Beach, Florida, August 8, 1968." In Gerhard Peters and John T. Woolley, eds. *The American Presidency Project*. http://www.presidency.ucsb.edu/ws/?pid=25968 (accessed January 29, 2017).

Stricker, Frank. 2007. *Why America Lost the War on Poverty—And How to Win It*. Chapel Hill: University of North Carolina Press.

"Nowhere Has the Failure of Government Been More Tragically Apparent in Past Years than in Its Efforts to Help the Poor"

- ***Document:*** President Richard M. Nixon's Statement Announcing Extension of Welfare Reform Proposals
- ***Date:*** June 10, 1970
- ***Where:*** Washington, D.C.
- ***Significance:*** President Richard Nixon illuminated the manner in which the welfare programs initiated by President Lyndon Baines Johnson during the War on Poverty should be reformed.

DOCUMENT

PAST PROGRAMS to aid the poor have failed. They have degraded the poor and defrauded the taxpayer. The family assistance plan represents the most comprehensive and far-reaching effort to reform social welfare in nearly four decades. Today, I am announcing significant extensions of the administration's welfare reform proposals.

BASIC PRINCIPLES

The family assistance plan is based on four fundamental principles:

—Strong incentives to encourage work and training;
—Equity to provide assistance to working poor families;
—Respect for individual choice and family responsibility; and
—Administrative efficiency to earn the trust of the taxpayer.

Administration officials have worked recently to identify ways to extend the principles of this income strategy to other domestic programs such as Medicaid, food stamps, and public housing.

On the basis of this review, I have made my decision to propose basic amendments to the Family Assistance Act of 1970.

HEALTH INSURANCE FOR POOR FAMILIES

The most important proposal I make today is to reform the Medicaid program.

Medicaid is plagued by serious faults. Costs are mounting beyond reason. Services vary considerably from State to State. Benefits are only remotely related to family resources. Eligibility may terminate abruptly as a family moves off often losing more in medical benefits than it gains in income.

In short—just like the existing welfare system—Medicaid is inefficient, inequitably excludes the working poor, and often provides an incentive for people to stay on welfare.

I will propose legislation at the beginning of the next Congress to establish a family health insurance program for all poor families with children. This insurance would provide a comprehensive package of health services, including both hospital and outpatient care.

Final decisions on the specifications of the family health insurance proposal must await further review by the new Domestic Council. We are satisfied that the basic principles will work. This proposal will constitute the second legislative stage of the administration's income strategy against poverty.

UNIFIED ADMINISTRATION OF FOOD
STAMPS AND FAMILY ASSISTANCE

The administration has already made extensive changes in the food stamp program to improve benefits, make them more equitable, and help even the very poorest families to receive assistance. We will propose that the Congress build on these executive reforms to integrate food stamps with family assistance and other income support programs.

Therefore, I plan to:

—Submit a reorganization plan at the beginning of the next Congress to transfer the food stamp program from the Department of Agriculture to the Department of Health, Education, and Welfare;

—Make it possible for a family to "check off" its food stamp purchase and receive its stamp allotment automatically with its family assistance check; and

—Revise the food stamp price schedule to make it rise evenly with increases in income.

ASSISTED HOUSING

Present subsidized housing programs are marked by inconsistencies and inequities. Many families pay the same rent despite wide differences in income. A small increase in earnings may force the family to move, losing much more housing assistance than is gained in income.

We have proposed a solution to many of these problems in the Housing Act of 1970. Rents would vary directly with income. A family would not be forced to move at some arbitrary income limit. We will offer this provision of the Housing Act to the Senate Finance Committee for its consideration.

REFORM OF INDIVIDUAL AND FAMILY SERVICES

In other amendments, we are proposing significant changes in social services for the poor. This proposal has been developed in recent months and will be ready for submission to the Congress next week. These amendments will:

—Encourage accountability and program results;

—Strengthen the role of Governors, mayors, and county executives;

—Seek to eliminate duplication and overlap.

OTHER MAJOR CHANGES

Other administration amendments to the Family Assistance Act make important changes. For example:

—Phasing out the special program for unemployed fathers, thus eliminating one of the most serious disincentives noted by the Senate Finance Committee;

—Limiting the welfare burden of the States by placing a ceiling on their financial obligations under the program;

—Strengthening the work requirement; and

—Reducing areas of administrative discretion.

Nowhere has the failure of government been more tragically apparent in past years than in its efforts to help the poor. The 91st Congress has an historic but rapidly vanishing opportunity to reverse that record by enacting the Family Assistance Act of 1970. Let there be no mistake about this administration's total commitment to passage of this legislative milestone this year.

SOURCE: Richard Nixon. 1971. *Public Papers of the Presidents of the United States: Richard Nixon*, 1970. Washington, D.C.: Government Printing Office, 490–492.

ANALYSIS

President Richard Nixon proffered a vision in this statement of the manner that the welfare programs initiated by President Lyndon Baines Johnson during the War on Poverty should be reformed. Central to his proposal was the Family Assistance Plan (FAP), which was a major overhaul of the Aid to Families with Dependent Children program. The FAP was essentially Nixon's version of the guaranteed minimum income idea that had been advanced by numerous academics and economists of the day. It promised an income of $1,600 a month for a family of four and an additional $800 in food stamps.

Nixon's proposal was initially embraced by many Democrats in Congress, and widely derided by his fellow Republicans who were opposed to the premise of direct payments to the poor. Robert Finch, Secretary of Health, Education, and Welfare in Nixon's administration, testified in Congress before the Senate Finance Committee and was publicly savaged by Republican senators. He was forced to resign soon thereafter. In response to his party's concerns, Nixon amended his proposal to make it more palatable to Republicans. In doing so, he alienated most of the people in Congress who had earlier voiced support for his initiative.

Congressmen from the Democratic Party came to believe that Nixon's proposed minimum income was an insufficient sum to allow a family to subsist. Their belief was supported by the fact that some states already provided welfare recipients with a higher income than would have been delivered under Nixon's programs. In order to satisfy their demands, Nixon was going to have to at least raise the minimum income to match what was already being distributed by the states with the most generous welfare plan. Predictably, with opponents on all sides of the political spectrum, Nixon's proposed reforms were never enacted.

The demise of FAP made it possible for Nixon to get related forms of legislation passed, such as the Social Security Amendments of 1972, which expanded benefits for the elderly and the disabled. Among the benefits received were a guaranteed annual income and expanded Medicare and Medicaid coverage. It also contained language that provided Medicare coverage to people under the age of 65 who were recipients of Social Security disability payments.

FURTHER READING

Ambrose, Stephen E. 1989. *Nixon: The Triumph of a Politician 1962–1972*. New York: Simon & Schuster.

Chappell, Marisa. 2010. *The War on Welfare: Family, Poverty, and Politics in Modern America*. Philadelphia: University of Pennsylvania Press.

Milkis, Sidney M., and Jerome M. Mileur, eds. 2005. *The Great Society and the High Tide of Liberalism*. Amherst: University of Massachusetts Press.

Stricker, Frank. 2007. *Why America Lost the War on Poverty—And How to Win It*. Chapel Hill: University of North Carolina Press.

"This Is a New and Undesirable Welfare Type Program"

- ***Document:*** White House Memorandum Concerning the Tax Reduction Act of 1975 (Excerpt)
- ***Date:*** The act was signed on March 29, 1975. The memorandum is undated but predates the signing ceremony as it weighs the pros and cons of vetoing the act.
- ***Where:*** Washington, D.C.
- ***Significance:*** The 1975 Tax Reduction Act created the earned income tax credit.

DOCUMENT

MEMORANDUM FOR THE PRESIDENT
SUBJECT: TAX CUT BILL

A Summary of the tax cut bill enacted yesterday is attached. It would reduce 1975 tax liabilities by approximately $23 billion, which is about $6 ½ billion more than you requested.

Undesirable Items

(1) Changes of a permanent nature in individual liabilities.

The bill increases the standard deduction and provides a new $30 per taxpayer credit in addition to the personal exemption. Together those items lose about $8 billion of revenues. Technically they have been written to apply only to 1975. While the necessity for reenactment may possibly provide an occasion to raise revenues or cut expenditures, past experience does not provide much hope in that connection. In the business area, there are an additional $4.8 billion of changes, also of a permanent nature, part of which are effective for one year and part for two years.

(2) Social security distribution.

A $50 distribution will be made to each person on the social security rolls, for a total revenue loss of $1.7 billion. This is a bad precedent in so far as general revenues are used to make payments to social security recipients. The relief provided will be duplicated later on when the cost of living increase goes into effect. While this does not seem likely to become a permanent program, we can expect strong pressures for such payments in the future whenever tax reductions are enacted.

(3) Earned income credit.

This is a new and undesirable welfare type program, which tends to undercut the insurance concept of social security. Since both the House and Senate bills contained an earned income provision (with differences of detail), we are unlikely to get rid of it unless something worse is put in its place. A redeeming aspect of the earned income credit is that it makes other, worse approaches somewhat less likely.

Payroll taxes are virtually certain to become a major political issue in the next two years. There has been much debate on whether they are too high and too regressive, and the debate is part of the larger issue of whether we can really afford the kind of social security system we have. Something along the lines of the earned income credit may be the best defense to a much more radical change, such as the other proposed funding of a part of social security from the general revenues. It reduces the impact of the payroll taxes, but confines the reduction to a relatively small amount and a relatively small group of persons. At the same time, it operates indirectly through the income tax system, and permits us to keep intact the principle that social security is an insurance scheme under which people get what they pay for.

(4) Housing credit.

This credit is self liquidating because it is confined to new housing built or in progress on March 26. It is a waste of money and will probably serve largely to permit builders to move existing houses without cutting prices. However, in its present form there is a good chance it will disappear completely, although Congress often becomes enamored of such provisions once adopted.

Permanence of the Tax Provisions

As noted, the changes in the standard deduction, the $30 credit, the earned income credit and the business changes are very likely to become permanent. They add up to about $15 billion.

The quasi-permanent nature of these changes has disturbing implications as we consider (1) how to turn off the stimulus later on and (2) how to prevent large inflation-inducing deficits in later years. The latter question is solved only if lesser revenues cause expenditures to be held down. Even if that should be the case, however, there would likely be a lag of several years before the reduction effect on the deficit is fully accomplished. Thus it seems inevitable that in the next couple of years we will have extraordinary large deficits and probably excessive stimulus a little later.

Your original proposals called for a one shot stimulus, and, to that extent, did not need to be "turned off." In order to turn off the stimulus from these "permanent provisions," however, Congress will have to refrain from reenacting them for 1976. Since the economy will undoubtedly still be operating below par when that issue arises later this year, and since V.ie will be even closer to November 1976, the prospects do not seem auspicious.

While this aspect is possibly the most compelling ground for vetoing the bill, it would be difficult to complain to the public about "permanent" changes when Congress expressly made the provisions applicable for only one year (except in the case of the investment credit, which is for two years).

Chances of a Better Bill

It is not clear that we could expect a substantially better bill even if a veto were sustained. It seems unlikely that Congress would give up the "permanent" changes for individuals. The social security provisions and the earned income credit are attractive to more voters than the business provisions, and there would be considerable pressure to do any cutting in the investment credit area. We might get rid of the housing credit. At best we are likely to get a bill $2 or $3 billion less than the current bill. In the face of projected deficits in the neighborhood of $100 billion, it will be hard to convince Congress and the electorate that it is worth holding up a needed stimulus for that small difference.

Grounds for a Veto

(1) Total Revenue Loss. This is probably the only issue that the man in the street would understand. However, we are in the position of having proposed $16 ½ billion of it ourselves.

(2) Undesirable Provisions. The reasons for our objections to specific undesirable items are more sophisticated than the ordinary voter will comprehend, but, in combination, would perhaps be saleable.

(3) Permanent Aspects. This is possibly the most important ground for a veto, but it is hard to make it convincing when the provisions are technically effective only for 1975.

(4) A Major Obstacle to Real Tax and Welfare Reform. Difficult to explain but a sound substantive reason for veto.

(5) Eliminates 6 million from the Tax Rolls. Our own proposals in the energy package would eliminate a number of these taxpayers.

(6) Eliminates Oil Depletion Except for Independent Producers. It thus reduces capital available for energy program. Elimination with independent produces exemption substantially complicates law.

Grounds for Signing.

(1) Fastest way to achieve fiscal stimulus.

(2) Provides opportunity to draw the line on *any new spending programs*.

(3) Some of the most objectionable provisions can be attacked when law is reconsidered at end of its one year term.

(4) Provides a tax cut as requested in State of the Union tho not of the type requested.

(5) New unemployment figures are expected to be adverse and may give impetus to a worse bill.

SUMMARY OF FACTS ON TAX CUT BILL

1. Rebate of 1974 taxes
   - —rebate generally equals 10% of 1974 tax liability
   - —minimum rebate equals lesser of actual tax liability or $100
   - —maximum rebate equals $200, phased down to $100 between AGI $20,000 and $30,000
   - —for married persons filing separately, $50 minimum, $100 maximum and phase down between $10,000 and $15,000
   - —rebates disregarded for purposes of other benefit programs

COST: $8.1 billion

2. Standard deduction changes
   - —minimum standard deduction (low income allowance) increased from $1,300 per return ($650 for married persons filing separately) to $1,900 for a joint return or surviving spouse, $1,600 for single persons, and $950 for married persons filing separately
   - —maximum standard deduction increased from 15% of AGI (with a maximum of $2,000, or $1,000 for a married person filing separately) to 16% of AGI (with a maximum of $2,600 for a joint return or surviving spouse, $2,300 for a single person, and $1,300 for married persons filing separately—effective for one year (generally 1975 calendar year)

COST: $2.5 billion

3. Personal exemption tax credit
   - —new $30 per exemption tax credit (except blind and aged exemptions) in addition to present law personal exemptions
   - —effective for one year (generally 1975 calendar year)

COST: $5.3 billion

4. Earned income credit
   - —refundable credit equal to 10% of earned income of an eligible individual with maximum of $400—to be eligible, must maintain a household within the United States that includes a dependent child
   - —maximum credit phased down to zero between AGI $4,000 and AGI $8,000
   - —under AFDC provisions, the earned income credit is taken into account in determining AFDC eligibility—effective for one year (generally 1975 calendar year)

COST: $1.5 billion

5. Child care deduction

—increases the income level at which the phase out of the maximum allowable deduction ($4,800) begins. The old phase out began at $18,000, phasing down to zero at $27,600. The new phase out begins at $35,000, phasing down to zero at $44,600

—permanent change.

COST: $0.1 billion annually

6. Sale of principal residence

—increases from 12 to 18 months the period during which the seller of an old principal residence must purchase a new principal residence, if he wishes to apply section 1034 to avoid recognition of gain. When construction of the new principal residence is begun by the taxpayer himself, the period is increased from 18 to 24 months.

—permanent change—COST: Nominal

7. House purchase credit

—new tax credit for purchases of a principal residence equal to 5% of the taxpayer's tax basis, with maximum credit of $2,000. A taxpayer's tax basis in a new principal residence may be less than cost if, for example, he sold an old principal residence, avoided recognition of gain through the application of section 1034, and was required to reduce his basis in the new principal residence by the amount of gain not recognized.

—applies only to purchases of new houses (including mobile homes and residential units in condominiums or cooperative housing projects). That is, the taxpayer must be the first occupant.

—applies only to new houses, etc., the construction of which was commenced prior to March 26, 1975.

—purchaser must attach to his tax return a certification by the seller that the purchase price is the lowest price at which the residence was ever offered for sale. If the certification is false, the purchaser may recover, in a civil action, three times the difference between the purchase price and the lowest offered price (plus a reasonable attorney's fee) and the seller may be prosecuted.

—effective for acquisitions after March 12, 1975, and before January 1, 1977, but applies to 1976 acquisitions only if constructed by the taxpayer or acquired by the taxpayer under a binding contract entered into before January 1, 1976.

COST: $0.6 billion

8. Withholding

—new withholding tables reflecting standard deduction changes, personal exemption tax credit, and earned income credit to take effect May 1, 1975. IRS advises that employers may be unable to meet that deadline even if new tables made available by IRS in record time.

9. Investment credit
   —two year increase in investment credit from 7% (4% in the case of public utilities) to 10%. Upon lapse of the temporary increase, public utilities would again be eligible for a 4% credit only.
   —additional 1% credit (for total 11% credit) during the two year temporary period for corporate—for public utilities, increase in the portion of tax liability that may be offset by the investment credit from 50% to: 100% in 1975 and 1976, 90% in 1977, 80% in 1978, 70% in 1979, 60% in 1980, and back to 50% in subsequent years
   —increase from $25,000 to $100,000 in amount of used property that may qualify for investment credit
   —provision for credit to be allowed as progress payments are made, a permanent change

COST: $3.3 billion

10. Corporate tax rate changes
    —surtax exemption (which determines amount taxable at rates below 48%) increased from $25,000 to $50,000 of taxable income
    —rate on first $25,000 of taxable income reduced from 22% to 20% (second $25,000 of taxable income will be taxable at 22% rate, balance of income at 48% rate)
    —effective for taxable years ending in 1975

COST: $1.5 billion

11. Accumulated earnings tax
    —minimum accumulated earnings tax credit increased from $100,000 to $150,000—permanent change—COST: Nominal
12. Work Incentive (WIN) Program Tax Credit
    —win credit of 20% of wages paid to a new employee during first 12 months of employment extended to employment of welfare recipients if employment lasts at least one month. Under present law, the new employee must be a participant in the WIN program administered by the Departments of Labor and Health, Education and Welfare and must be employed for at least 24 months
    —as under present law, the new employee may not displace another employee taxpayers only and on condition that stock of the taxpayer (or a parent corporation) having a value equal to the tax savings generated by the additional 1% credit is transferred to an employee stock ownership plan (ESOP). No deduction is allowed to the employer for the transferred stock, and the employees are not taxed until they receive distributions from the plan. The plan may be a qualified or a nonqualified plan.
    —unlike present law, the expanded credit would apply to nonbusiness employees (e.g., domestics), but the maximum credit with respect to each such nonbusiness employee would be $200
    —employment of migrant workers not covered

—effective with respect to wages paid to employees hired after the date of enactment for services rendered between the date of enactment and July 1, 1976.

COST: Nominal

13. Certain Pension Plan Contributions

—for H.R. 10 plans, advanced by one year (to 1976 contribution for 1975 plan years) a provision permitting cash basis taxpayers to treat contributions made before April 15 as having been made in the preceding year.

14. Unemployment compensation

—extends the maximum period of benefits from 52 to 65 weeks, for weeks of unemployment ending before July 1, 1975.

COST: $0.2 billion

15. Payment to Social Security Recipients

—provides $50 payment to each individual who for the month of March, 1975, was entitled (without regard to sections 202(j)(l) and 223(b) of title II of the Social Security Act and without the application of section S(a)(ii) of the Railroad Retirement Act of 1974) to (1) a monthly insurance benefit under title II of the Social Security Act, (2) a monthly annuity or pension payment under one of the Railroad Retirement Acts, or (3) a benefit under SSI

—payments to be made no later than August 31, 1975

—any individual entitled to only one such payment

—only United States residents are eligible

—payments to be disregarded for purposes of other programs

COST: $1.7 billion

Note respecting permanence of changes

As noted above, virtually all of the tax changes and increased benefits are drafted as temporary changes and benefits effective for only one year or at most two years. The only permanent changes are: (1) the provision for the investment credit to be allowed on progress payments, (2) the raising of the phase-out level for the child care expense deduction, (3) the expansion of the tax-free rollover period for sales of a principal residence, and (4) the increase in the accumulated earnings tax credit.

SOURCE: *Memorandum for the President*. 1975. Ron Nessen Papers, Box 29, "Tax Reduction Act of 1975—General Folder," Gerald R. Ford Presidential Library. Available online at https://www.fordlibrarymuseum.gov/library/document/0204/1511983.pdf.

ANALYSIS

President Gerald Ford assumed office at a time when the nation's economy was in decline. An increase in inflation was accompanied by a rise in unemployment. Although the administration was loath to admit the nation's economy was in recession, it was obvious that it had to address the problem. Toward that end, Ford sent Congress a proposal for a stimulus package. His request was honored in the form of the Tax Reduction Act of 1975. As the presidential memorandum that preceded this analysis shows, the administration asked for measures that would provide tax breaks and incentives for the 1975 tax year only.

The bill that emerged from Congress contained much more costly benefits for taxpayers than intended, and many were framed in a manner that showed the intent to make them permanent features of the tax code. One of these was the earned income tax credit (EITC), which is discussed in the memorandum under the heading "undesirable items." It was politically embraceable because it rewarded the working poor. By boosting the wages of those trying to improve their lot, members of Congress hoped to incentivize the unemployed to get off the public dole.

FURTHER READING

Halpern-Meekin, Sarah, et al. 2015. *It's Not Like I'm Poor: How Working Families Make Ends Meet in a Post-Welfare World.* Berkeley: University of California Press.

Hoffman, Saul D., and Laurence S. Seidman. 2002. *Helping Working Families: The Earned Income Tax Credit.* Kalamazoo, MI: W.E. Upjohn Institute for Employment Research.

Meyer, Bruce D., and Douglas Holtz-Eakin, eds. 2001. *Making Work Pay: The Earned Income Tax Credit and Its Impact on America's Families.* New York: Russell Sage Foundation.

Mieczkowski, Yanek. 2005. *Gerald Ford and the Challenges of the 1970s.* Lexington: University Press of Kentucky.

"To Eliminate the Requirement that Households Buy Their Food Stamps"

- ***Document:*** President Jimmy Carter's statement after signing amendments to the Food Stamp Act of 1977
- ***Date:*** August 15, 1979
- ***Where:*** Washington, D.C.
- ***Significance:*** The act put an end to the requirement that the poor pay for food stamps.

DOCUMENT

I have signed into law amendments to the Food Stamp Act of 1977 which will allow us to continue program operations without cutting benefits for needy food stamp families and also will provide a series of new measures to reduce error and fraud. These amendments are needed chiefly because inflation in food prices has boosted program costs well above the ceiling on program spending contained in the 1977 act. The Congress has acted swiftly to raise the spending cap for this fiscal year and to appropriate the additional funding we need to avoid closing the program down entirely for the month of September. The legislation also includes measures to provide additional benefits for elderly and disabled households with high medical or shelter costs. I am also pleased that the Congress has included several antifraud provisions the administration has recommended.

The need for additional funding for the food stamp program is yet another signal that inflation of the price of food is increasing at an unacceptably high rate. When the Food Stamp Act of 1977 was passed, food prices were projected to increase at an annual rate of between 3 and 4 percent a year, and the ceiling on program expenditures was based on this assumption. But in the last 2 years, food prices have risen nearly 20 percent. This rate of inflation in so basic a sector of our economy not only boosts the entire cost of the food stamp program, but it also adds to the inflationary spiral that erodes the purchasing power of all consumers.

Recently, we have learned that while farm prices have fallen, the food industry may not be passing those savings on to consumers. I have met with representatives of the food industry to deal with this matter and will do everything I can to see that consumers benefit from lower farm prices in terms of lower prices in the supermarket.

Recent increases in the number of Americans participating in the food stamp program have raised costs as well. In recent years, the program has undergone sweeping reforms. Administration proposals enacted by Congress have tightened and simplified administration, imposed tough penalties for fraud, and reduced or terminated benefits for higher income households. At the same time the administration's proposal to eliminate the requirement that households buy their food stamps has brought several million new participants into the program who had previously been eligible for food stamps, but had simply been unable to afford them. Many of these people are the elderly and rural poor, whose participation rate has historically been very low.

It would be callous and shortsighted to cut food stamp benefits, which now average a modest 33¢ per person per meal, because the program is reaching larger numbers of the poorest households and because food prices have risen so alarmingly. While this administration is committed to controlling Federal expenditures, we will do so within a budget of compassion that recognizes the fundamental importance of food assistance to our Nation's poorest families.

There can be no question that these families are poor. More than half of the households receiving food stamps have gross annual incomes under $3,600. Because of the critical importance of continued food assistance to these households, I have asked Congress to lift the spending cap for future fiscal years, and to provide the funding that will be needed to avoid cutting benefits in fiscal years 1980 and 1981.

In the interest of tighter program administration, I have also asked the Congress to enact a number of measures to save food stamp funds by reducing error rates. Some of the most important of these provisions are still pending before Congress. I ask Congress to enact these provisions along with provisions to authorize adequate funding for 1980 and 1981.

Recently, teams of doctors sponsored by the Field Foundation revisited the poverty-stricken areas where they had found serious hunger and malnutrition 10 years ago. They reported the presence of "fewer grossly malnourished people in this country today than there were 10 years ago." The doctors concluded that the food stamp program "is making the most crucial difference in improving the quality of the lives of many poor people."

I intend to give this valuable program my full support, and I call upon Congress to do the same.

SOURCE: Carter, Jimmy. 1980. "Food Stamp Act Amendments: Statement on Signing H.R. 4057 into Law. August 15, 1979." *Public Papers of the Presidents of the United States. Jimmy Carter, 1979, Book II.* Washington, D.C.: Government Printing Office, 1432–1433.

ANALYSIS

Between 1971 and 1975, the cost of the food stamp program for the federal government tripled. The growth was spurred by both the inflation of food prices and an increase in the number of people enrolled in the program. In an effort to curb the increasing costs, President Gerald Ford's administration in 1974 announced its intent to raise the price that recipients payed for food stamps. It was believed that the increase in prices would price some people out of the market and cause others to purchase fewer stamps. Throughout his presidency, Ford repeatedly proposed ideas to improve the "scandal-ridden" program. The rhetoric was a political necessity as it was widely assumed that Ronald Reagan would be challenging him in the forthcoming Republican Party primaries for the presidency. To earn another term, Ford had to play to the far-right of the party. As Reagan observed, the food stamp program actually expanded during Ford's presidency. Although Ford may have wanted to reduce the impact of the food stamp program on the federal budget, there was enough congressional support to thwart the administration. Predictably, food stamps became a major issue during the 1975–1976 primaries. Although Ford was able to earn the Republican Party's nomination for the presidency, politically he had been damaged. He was defeated in the presidential election by Jimmy Carter.

Since many people believed that the food stamp program continued to be rife with problems, such as fraud, the Carter administration launched a campaign to reform it. His administration's proposal was built around the idea that many of the alleged financial improprieties would disappear if food stamps were proffered for free. Republicans in Congress immediately opposed as they believed that giving away food stamps would result in the accelerated expansion of the program. Despite the objections, the Food Stamp Act became law on April 15, 1979. As predicted, enrollments soared in subsequent years. Part of that expansion was due to the number of people who were truly poor being able to acquire the stamps. Before the stamps were free, it was the neediest segment of the population that benefited the least since they did not have the money necessary to buy stamps.

FURTHER READING

Epstein, William M. 2017. *The Masses Are the Ruling Classes: Policy Romanticism, Democratic Populism, and American Social Welfare*. New York: Oxford University Press.

King, Ronald F. 2000. *Budgeting Entitlements: The Politics of Food Stamps*. Washington, D.C.: Georgetown University Press.

Rosenfeld, Sam. 2010. "Fed by Reform: Congressional Politics, Partisan Change, and the Food Stamp Program, 1961–1981." *Journal of Policy History* 22, no. 4: 474–507.

6

THE REAGAN REVOLUTION THROUGH THE CLINTON ADMINISTRATION

"America Is Coming Back and Is More Confident than Ever about the Future"

- ***Document:*** Ronald Reagan's Remarks Accepting the Presidential Nomination at the Republican National Convention (Excerpts)
- ***Date:*** August 23, 1984
- ***Where:*** Dallas, Texas
- ***Significance:*** Through his speech, President Reagan effectively linked Walter Mondale, the Democratic Party's nominee for the presidency, to the growth of welfare programs and the accompanying expansion of the federal bureaucracy of the Great Society era. This allowed Reagan to shape the election as a referendum between the Democratic Party's promises of a return to an expanded welfare state versus his economic policies that he argued improved the lives of hardworking Americans. This tactic allowed Reagan to claim a mandate after securing a second term to continue his "reforms" of federal programs designed to help the nation's poorer citizens.

DOCUMENT

Tonight, with a full heart and deep gratitude for your trust, I accept your nomination for the Presidency of the United States. I will campaign on behalf of the principles of our party which lift America confidently into the future.

America is presented with the clearest political choice of half a century. The distinction between our two parties and the different philosophy of our political opponents are at the heart of this campaign and America's future.

. . .

The choices this year are not just between two different personalities or between two political parties. They're between two different visions of the future, two fundamentally different ways of governing—their government of pessimism, fear, and limits, or ours of hope, confidence, and growth.

Their government sees people only as members of groups; ours serves all the people of America as individuals. Theirs lives in the past, seeking to apply the old and failed policies to an era that has passed them by. Ours learns from the past and strives to change by boldly charting a new course for the future. Theirs lives by promises, the bigger, the better. We offer proven, workable answers.

Our opponents began this campaign hoping that America has a poor memory. Well, let's take them on a little stroll down memory lane. Let's remind them of how a 4.8-percent inflation rate in 1976 became back-to-back years of double-digit inflation—the worst since World War I—punishing the poor and the elderly, young couples striving to start their new lives, and working people struggling to make ends meet.

Inflation was not some plague borne on the wind; it was a deliberate part of their official economic policy, needed, they said, to maintain prosperity. They didn't tell us that with it would come the highest interest rates since the Civil War. As average monthly mortgage payments more than doubled, home building nearly ground to a halt; tens of thousands of carpenters and others were thrown out of work. And who controlled both Houses of the Congress and the executive branch at that time? Not us, not us.

Campaigning across America in 1980, we saw evidence everywhere of industrial decline. And in rural America, farmers' costs were driven up by inflation. They were devastated by a wrongheaded grain embargo and were forced to borrow money at exorbitant interest rates just to get by. And many of them didn't get by. Farmers have to fight insects, weather, and the marketplace; they shouldn't have to fight their own government.

The high interest rates of 1980 were not talked about in San Francisco. But how about taxes? They were talked about in San Francisco. Will Rogers once said he never met a man he didn't like. Well, if I could paraphrase Will, our friends in the other party have never met a tax they didn't like or hike.

Under their policies, tax rates have gone up three times as much for families with children as they have for everyone else over these past three decades. In just the 5 years before we came into office, taxes roughly doubled.

DID YOU KNOW?

The Welfare Queen

Over the course of his political career, Ronald Reagan periodically utilized the "welfare queen" to illustrate how federal welfare programs were destroying families, public morals, and allowing the impoverished to benefit themselves at the expense of those who were employed.

> Not too long ago, a judge . . . told me of a young woman who'd come before him for a divorce. She had six children, was pregnant with her seventh. Under his questioning, she revealed her husband was a laborer earning 250 dollars a month. She wanted a divorce to get an eighty dollar raise. She's eligible for 330 dollars a month in the Aid to Dependent Children Program. She got the idea from two women in her neighborhood who'd already done that very thing. (Quoted in Orleck, 447–448)

By exploiting class and racial divisions, Reagan was able to convince a significant number of white- and blue-collar Democrats to cross party lines and join the "Reagan Revolution."

FURTHER READING

Orleck, Annelise. 2011. "Conclusion: The War on the War on Poverty and American Politics since the 1960s." In Annelise Orleck and Lisa Gayle Hazirjian, eds. *The War on Poverty: A New Grassroots History, 1964–1980.* Athens: University of Georgia Press, 437–461.

Some who spoke so loudly in San Francisco of fairness were among those who brought about the biggest single, individual tax increase in our history in 1977, calling for a series of increases in the Social Security payroll tax and in the amount of pay subject to that tax. The bill they passed called for two additional increases between now and 1990, increases that bear down hardest on those at the lower income levels. The Census Bureau confirms that, because of the tax laws we inherited, the number of households at or below the poverty level paying Federal income tax more than doubled between 1980 and 1982. Well, they received some relief in 1983, when our across-the-board tax cut was fully in place. And they'll get more help when indexing goes into effect this January.

Our opponents have repeatedly advocated eliminating indexing. Would that really hurt the rich? No, because the rich are already in the top brackets. But those working men and women who depend on a cost-of-living adjustment just to keep abreast of inflation would find themselves pushed into higher tax brackets and wouldn't even be able to keep even with inflation because they'd be paying a higher income tax. That's bracket creep; and our opponents are for it, and we're against it.

It's up to us to see that all our fellow citizens understand that confiscatory taxes, costly social experiments, and economic tinkering were not just the policies of a single administration. For the 26 years prior to January of 1981, the opposition party controlled both Houses of Congress. Every spending bill and every tax for more than a quarter of a century has been of their doing.

About a decade ago, they said Federal spending was out of control, so they passed a budget control act and, in the next 5 years, ran up deficits of $260 billion. Some control.

In 1981 we gained control of the Senate and the executive branch. With the help of some concerned Democrats in the House we started a policy of tightening the Federal budget instead of the family budget.

A task force chaired by Vice President George Bush—the finest Vice President this country has ever had—it eliminated unnecessary regulations that had been strangling business and industry.

And while we have our friends down memory lane, maybe they'd like to recall a gimmick they designed for their 1976 campaign. As President Ford told us the night before last, adding the unemployment and inflation rates, they got what they called a misery index. In '76 it came to 12 1/2 percent. They declared the incumbent had no right to seek reelection with that kind of a misery index. Well, 4 years ago, in the 1980 election, they didn't mention the misery index, possibly because it was then over 20 percent. And do you know something? They won't mention it in this election either. It's down to 11.6 and dropping.

By nearly every measure, the position of poor Americans worsened under the leadership of our opponents. Teenage drug use, out-of-wedlock births, and crime increased dramatically. Urban neighborhoods and schools deteriorated. Those whom government intended to help discovered a cycle of dependency that could not be broken. Government became a drug, providing temporary relief, but addiction as well.

And let's get some facts on the table that our opponents don't want to hear. The biggest annual increase in poverty took place between 1978 and 1981—over 9 percent each year, in the first 2 years of our administration. Well, I should—pardon me—I didn't put a period in there. In the first 2 years of our administration, that annual increase fell to 5.3 percent. And 1983 was the first year since 1978 that there was no appreciable increase in poverty at all.

Pouring hundreds of billions of dollars into programs in order to make people worse off was irrational and unfair. It was time we ended this reliance on the government process and renewed our faith in the human process.

In 1980 the people decided with us that the economic crisis was not caused by the fact that they lived too well. Government lived too well. It was time for tax increases to be an act of last resort, not of first resort.

The people told the liberal leadership in Washington, "Try shrinking the size of government before you shrink the size of our paychecks."

Our government was also in serious trouble abroad. We had aircraft that couldn't fly and ships that couldn't leave port. Many of our military were on food stamps because of meager earnings, and reenlistments were down. Ammunition was low, and spare parts were in short supply.

. . .

But worst of all, Americans were losing the confidence and optimism about the future that has made us unique in the world. Parents were beginning to doubt that their children would have the better life that has been the dream of every American generation.

We can all be proud that pessimism is ended. America is coming back and is more confident than ever about the future. Tonight, we thank the citizens of the United States whose faith and unwillingness to give up on themselves or this country saved us all.

Together, we began the task of controlling the size and activities of the government by reducing the growth of its spending while passing a tax program to provide incentives to increase productivity for both workers and industry. Today, a working family earning $25,000 has about $2,900 more in purchasing power than if tax and inflation rates were still at the 1980 level.

Today, of all the major industrial nations of the world, America has the strongest economic growth; one of the lowest inflation rates; the fastest rate of job creations—6 1/2 million jobs in the last year and a half—a record 600,000 business incorporations in 1983; and the largest increase in real, after-tax personal income since World War II. We're enjoying the highest level of business investment in history, and America has renewed its leadership in developing the vast new opportunities in science and high technology. America is on the move again and expanding toward new eras of opportunity for everyone.

Now, we're accused of having a secret. Well, if we have, it is that we're going to keep the mighty engine of this nation revved up. And that means a future of sustained economic growth without inflation that's going to create for our children and grandchildren a prosperity that finally will last.

. . .

We've heard a lot about deficits this year from those on the other side of the aisle. Well, they should be experts on budget deficits. They've spent most of their political careers creating deficits. For 42 of the last 50 years, they have controlled both Houses of the Congress.

And for almost all of those 50 years, deficit spending has been their deliberate policy. Now, however, they call for an end to deficits. They call them ours. Yet, at the same time, the leadership of their party resists our every effort to bring Federal spending under control. For 3 years straight, they have prevented us from adopting a balanced budget amendment to the Constitution. We will continue to fight for that amendment, mandating that government spend no more than government takes in.

. . .

Now, their candidate, it would appear, has only recently found deficits alarming. Nearly 10 years ago he insisted that a $52 billion deficit should be allowed to get much bigger in order to lower unemployment, and he said that sometimes "we need a deficit in order to stimulate the economy."

. . .

When we talk of the plight of our cities, what would help more than our enterprise zones bill, which provides tax incentives for private industry to help rebuild and restore decayed areas in 75 sites all across America? If they really wanted a future of boundless new opportunities for our citizens, why have they buried enterprise zones over the years in committee?

Our opponents are openly committed to increasing our tax burden.

. . .

They call their policy the new realism, but their new realism is just the old liberalism. They will place higher and higher taxes on small businesses, on family farms, and on other working families so that government may once again grow at the people's expense. You know, we could say they spend money like drunken sailors, but that would be unfair to drunken sailors—[laughter]—

. . .

The President. I was going to say, it would be unfair, because the sailors are spending their own money. [Laughter]

Our tax policies are and will remain prowork, progrowth, and profamily. We intend to simplify the entire tax system—to make taxes more fair, easier to understand, and, most important, to bring the tax rates of every American further down, not up. Now, if we bring them down far enough, growth will continue strong; the underground economy will shrink; the world will beat a path to our door; and no one will be able to hold America back; and the future will be ours.

. . .

We promised that we'd reduce the growth of the Federal Government, and we have. We said we intended to reduce interest rates and inflation, and we have. We said we would reduce taxes to provide incentives for individuals and business to get our economy moving again, and we have. We said there must be jobs with a future for our people, not government make-work programs, and, in the last 19 months, as I've said, 6 1/2 million new jobs in the private sector have been created. We said we would once again be respected throughout the world, and we are. We said we would restore our ability to protect our freedom on land, sea, and in the air, and we have.

We bring to the American citizens in this election year a record of accomplishment and the promise of continuation.

SOURCE: Reagan, Ronald. "Remarks Accepting the Presidential Nomination at the Republican National Convention in Dallas, Texas, August 23, 1984." *The Public Papers of President Ronald W. Reagan.* Ronald Reagan Presidential Library.

ANALYSIS

In 1962, Ronald Reagan joined the Republican Party. He did so because he believed that the Democratic Party was using the expansion of welfare benefits to justify the accompanying growth of the federal government. Reagan feared that "big government" was a form of socialism and thus posed a threat to the freedoms enjoyed by the nation's citizens. This view was articulated publicly in 1964 as he campaigned on behalf of Republican Party presidential nominee Barry Goldwater. Reagan's advocacy brought him acclaim and ultimately vaulted him to California's governorship in 1966. After two terms as governor, Reagan opted not to seek reelection and instead began writing a syndicated newspaper column and joining the lecture circuit.

These venues gave him the opportunity to not only build the political coalition necessary to win the presidency of the United States but also sharpen his attacks on the evils of big government. He charged that the welfare state robbed people of their freedom by making them dependent on the government. It rewarded the poor and slovenly over those who worked hard to advance their lot in life. Over the course of the 1970s, the appeal of his critique grew among the white, working class. A significant reason for the change was how poverty was perceived. When the War on Poverty was launched, a significant portion of the poor were the elderly. By the time that Reagan was campaigning for the presidency in the 1970s, single mothers of color had become the face of the impoverished. Reagan used that change in demography to exploit emerging divisions within the voting public by class, gender, and race. The electoral tactic proved extremely effective, as Reagan was elected president in 1980 by a coalition that included southern whites, religious conservatives, and both union and nonunion working-class households. His overwhelming victory over President Jimmy Carter in the Electoral College, by a vote of 489–49, provided Reagan a mandate to roll back the nation's social safety net.

The Reagan administration quickly proposed cutting social security for individuals who had retired between the ages of 62 and 64. The proposal was soundly rejected by both Democrats and Republicans in the U.S. Congress. Executive branch representatives subsequently began working with congressional leaders to craft welfare reductions that would be palatable to the bodies of the respective houses. The plan that was enacted made significant cuts to programs benefiting individuals retiring before age 65. This change benefited social security in two ways. It encouraged individuals to stay in the workforce longer and kept workers paying into the social security system for several years longer than they would have if they had chosen early retirement.

While the reductions in early retirement benefits primarily impacted the upper and middle classes, the savings for the federal government paled in comparison to the revenue gained by the reduction in welfare benefits to the poor. Many of the impoverished lost their benefits because federal regulations made it more difficult to qualify for aid. The amount of aid that one could receive was also capped, with the amount including a monetary value placed on noncash benefits such as food stamps. In the eyes of the administration, the programs provided for the basic needs of those who qualified, but the benefits were minimal enough to encourage citizens to seek employment in order to gain a higher income.

Reagan's administration not only targeted benefits for individuals, but also sought to reduce the federal bureaucracy that had expanded exponentially during the 1960s. This was accomplished through the Omnibus Budget Reconciliation Act of 1981. In that legislation, what had been 55 separate programs, each with its own budget and administrative staffs, were lumped together through nine block grants. The funding for the grant programs was approximately 75 percent of what had been appropriated to the respective programs by President Jimmy Carter's administration.

Politically, the Reagan administration's attacks on social security caused a divide among Republican congressmen. This came to the fore in 1985 when Senate Majority Leader Robert Dole, Republican from Kansas, proposed balancing the budget by freezing the social security cost-of-living adjustment (COLA) for one year and also cutting some welfare programs. Republicans from the House of Representatives refused to back Dole's proposals. In order to secure the passage of the budget, President Reagan negotiated with Speaker of the House Tip O'Neill a compromise that excluded the COLA cut. This bathed the Republican senators in a negative political light.

As a politician, Ronald Reagan proved a pragmatist. Although he professed a desire to undercut the advances of the Great Society, his success was muted. While he desired to cut Medicare extensively, he was ultimately prevented from doing so by members of his own party. The American people desired cuts as long as it did not affect them. During the 1980 election cycle, citizens wanted welfare cuts impacting "welfare queens." When Reagan assaulted early retirement benefits, which impacted higher income groups, the views of voters quickly changed. Reagan adapted to the views of the electorate and was able to secure reelection. The Republican Senate, under Dole, did not and saw its majority status disappear as a result of the 1986 election.

FURTHER READING

Bertram, Eva. 2015. *The Workfare State: Public Assistance Politics from the New Deal to the New Democrats*. Philadelphia: University of Pennsylvania Press.

Bothmer, Bernard von. 2010. *Framing the Sixties: The Use and Abuse of a Decade from Ronald Reagan to George W. Bush.* Amherst: University of Massachusetts Press.

Brands, H. W. 2015. *Reagan: The Life*. New York: Doubleday.

Chappell, Marisa. 2010. *The War of Welfare: Family, Poverty, and Politics in Modern America.* Philadelphia: University of Pennsylvania Press.

Crafton, William. 2014. "The Incremental Revolution: Ronald Reagan and Welfare Reform in the 1970s." *Journal of Policy History* 26: 27–47.

Cunningham, Sean P. 2014. *American Politics in the Postwar Sunbelt: Conservative Growth in a Battleground Region*. New York: Cambridge University Press.

Medhurst, Martin J. 2016. "LBJ, Reagan, and the American Dream: Competing Visions of Liberty." *Presidential Studies Quarterly* 46: 98–124.

Orleck, Annelise. 2011. "Conclusion: The War on the War on Poverty and American Politics since the 1960s." In Annelise Orleck and Lisa Gayle Hazirjian, eds. *The War on*

Poverty: A New Grassroots History, 1964–1980. Athens: University of Georgia Press: 437–461.

Schaller, Michael. 2011. *Ronald Reagan*. New York: Oxford University Press.

Stricker, Frank. 2007. *Why America Lost the War on Poverty—And How to Win It*. Chapel Hill: University of North Carolina Press.

Wilentz, Sean. 2008. *The Age of Reagan: A History, 1974–2008*. New York: Harper.

"The Hospital Must Provide for an Appropriate Medical Screening Examination within the Capability of the Hospital's Emergency Department"

- ***Document:*** Emergency Medical Treatment and Active Labor Act of 1986
- ***Date:*** April 7, 1986
- ***Where:*** Washington, D.C.
- ***Significance:*** The act requires all hospitals that receive monies from Medicare to treat patients in need of emergency care regardless of their ability to pay.

DOCUMENT

SEC. 9121. RESPONSIBILITIES OF MEDICARE HOSPITALS IN EMERGENCY CASES.

(a) REQUIREMENT OF MEDICARE HOSPITAL PROVIDER AGREEMENTS.—Section 1866(a)(1) of the Social Security Act (42 U.S.C. 1395cc(a)(l)) is amended—

(1) by striking out "and" at the end of subparagraph (G),

(2) by striking out the period at the end of subparagraph (H) and inserting in lieu thereof, "and," and

(3) by inserting after subparagraph (H) the following new subparagraph:

"(I) in the case of a hospital, to comply with the requirements of section 1867 to the extent applicable."

(b) REQUIREMENTS.—Title XVIII of such Act is amended by inserting after section 1866 the following new section:

"EXAMINATION AND TREATMENT FOR EMERGENCY MEDICAL CONDITIONS AND WOMEN IN ACTIVE LABOR

"SEC. 1867. (a) MEDICAL SCREENING REQUIREMENT.—In the case of a hospital that has a hospital emergency department, if any individual (whether or not eligible for benefits under this title) comes to the emergency department and a request is made on the individual's behalf for examination or treatment for a medical condition, the hospital must provide for an appropriate medical screening examination within the capability of the hospital's emergency department to determine whether or not an emergency medical condition (within the meaning of subsection (e)(1)) exists or to determine if the individual is in active labor (within the meaning of subsection (e)(2)).

"(b) NECESSARY STABILIZING TREATMENT FOR EMERGENCY MEDICAL CONDITIONS AND ACTIVE LABOR.—

"(1) IN GENERAL.—If any individual (whether or not eligible for benefits under this title) comes to a hospital and the hospital determines that the individual has an emergency medical condition or is in active labor, the hospital must provide either—

"(A) within the staff and facilities available at the hospital, for such further medical examination and such treatment as may be required to stabilize the medical condition or to provide for treatment of the labor, or

"(B) for transfer of the individual to another medical facility in accordance with subsection (c).

"(2) REFUSAL TO CONSENT TO TREATMENT.—A hospital is deemed to meet the requirement of paragraph (1)(A) with respect to an individual if the hospital offers the individual the further medical examination and treatment described in that paragraph but the individual (or a legally responsible person, acting on the individual's behalf) refuses to consent to the examination or treatment.

"(3) REFUSAL TO CONSENT TO TRANSFER.—A hospital is deemed to meet the requirement of paragraph (1) with respect to an individual if the hospital offers to transfer the individual to another medical facility in accordance with subsection (c) but the individual (or a legally responsible person acting on the individual's behalf) refuses to consent to the transfer.

"(c) RESTRICTING TRANSFERS UNTIL PATIENT STABILIZED.—

"(1) RULE.—If a patient at a hospital has an emergency medical condition which has not been stabilized (within the meaning of subsection (e)(4)(B)) or is in active labor, the hospital may not transfer the patient unless—

"(A)(i) the patient (or a legally responsible person acting on the patient's behalf) requests that the transfer be effected, or "(ii) a physician (within the meaning of section 1861(r)(l)), or other qualified medical personnel when a physician is not readily available in the emergency department, has signed a certification that, based upon the reasonable risks and benefits to the patient, and based upon the information available at the time, the medical benefits reasonably expected from the provision of appropriate medical treatment at another medical facility outweigh the increased risks to the individual's medical condition from effecting the transfer; and

"(B) the transfer is an appropriate transfer (within the meaning of paragraph (2)) to that facility.

"(2) APPROPRIATE TRANSFER.—An appropriate transfer to a medical facility is a transfer—

"(A) in which the receiving facility—

"(i) has available space and qualified personnel for the treatment of the patient, and

"(ii) has agreed to accept transfer of the patient and to provide appropriate medical treatment;

"(B) in which the transferring hospital provides the receiving facility with appropriate medical records (or copies thereof) of the examination and treatment effected at the transferring hospital;

"(C) in which the transfer is effected through qualified personnel and transportation equipment, as required including the use of necessary and medically appropriate life support measures during the transfer; and

"(D) which meets such other requirements as the Secretary may find necessary in the interest of the health and safety of patients transferred.

"(d) ENFORCEMENT.—

"(1) As REQUIREMENT OF MEDICARE PROVIDER AGREEMENT.—If a hospital knowingly and willfully, or negligently, fails to meet the requirements of this section, such hospital is subject to—

"(A) termination of its provider agreement under this title in accordance with section 1866(b), or

"(B) at the option of the Secretary, suspension of such agreement for such period of time as the Secretary determines to be appropriate, upon reasonable notice to the hospital and to the public.

"(2) CIVIL MONETARY PENALTIES.—In addition to the other grounds for imposition of a civil money penalty under section 1128A(a), a participating hospital that knowingly violates a requirement of this section and the responsible physician in the hospital with respect to such a violation are each subject, under that section, to a civil money penalty of not more than $25,000 for each such violation. As used in the previous sentence, the term 'responsible physician' means, with respect to a hospital's violation of a requirement of this section, a physician who—

"(A) is employed by, or under contract with, the participating hospital, and

"(B) acting as such an employee or under such a contract, has professional responsibility for the provision of examinations or treatments for the individual, or transfers of the individual, with respect to which the violation occurred.

"(3) CIVIL ENFORCEMENT.—

"(A) PERSONAL HARM.—Any individual who suffers personal harm as a direct result of a participating hospital's violation of a requirement of this section may, in a civil action against the participating hospital, obtain those damages available for personal injury under the law of the State in which the hospital is located, and such equitable relief as is appropriate.

"(B) FINANCIAL LOSS TO OTHER MEDICAL FACILITY.—Any medical facility that suffers a financial loss as a direct result of a participating hospital's violation of a requirement of this section may, in a civil action against the participating hospital, obtain those damages available for financial loss, under the law of the State in which the hospital is located, and such equitable relief as is appropriate.

"(C) LIMITATIONS ON ACTIONS.—No action may be brought under this paragraph more than two years after the date of the violation with respect to which the action is brought.

"(e) DEFINITIONS.—In this section:

"(1) The term 'emergency medical condition' means a medical condition manifesting itself by acute symptoms of sufficient severity (including severe pain) such that the absence of immediate medical attention could reasonably be expected to result in—

"(A) placing the patient's health in serious jeopardy,

"(B) serious impairment to bodily functions, or

"(C) serious dysfunction of any bodily organ or part.

"(2) The term 'active labor' means labor at a time at which—

"(A) delivery is imminent,

"(B) there is inadequate time to effect safe transfer to another hospital prior to delivery, or

"(C) a transfer may pose a threat of the health and safety of the patient or the unborn child.

"(3) The term 'participating hospital' means hospital that has entered into a provider agreement under section 1866 and has, under the agreement, obligated itself to comply with the requirements of this section.

"(4) (A) The term 'to stabilize' means, with respect to an emergency medical condition, to provide such medical treatment of the condition as may be necessary to assure, within reasonable medical probability, that no material deterioration of the condition is likely to result from the transfer of the individual from a facility.

"(B) The term 'stabilized' means, with respect to an emergency medical condition, that no material deterioration of the condition is likely, within reasonable medical probability, to result from the transfer of the individual from a facility.

"(5) The term 'transfer' means the movement (including the discharge) of a patient outside a hospital's facilities at the direction of any person employed by (or affiliated or associated, directly or indirectly, with) the hospital, but does not include such a movement of a patient who (A) has been declared dead, or (B) leaves the facility without the permission of any such person.

"(f) PREEMPTION.—The provisions of this section do not preempt any State or local law requirement, except to the extent that the requirement directly conflicts with a requirement of this section."

(c) EFFECTIVE DATE.—The amendments made by this section shall take effect on the first day of the first month that begins at least 90 days after the date of the enactment of this Act.

(d) REPORT.—The Secretary of Health and Human Services shall, not later than 6 months after the effective date described in subsection (c), report to Congress on the methods to be used for monitoring and enforcing compliance with section 1867 of the Social Security Act.

SOURCE: U.S. Congress. 1986. Public Law 99-272. April 7, 1986.

ANALYSIS

The Emergency Medical Treatment and Active Labor Act of 1986 (EMTALA) was enacted in response to the problem of "patient dumping." The term described the common practice of hospitals refusing to offer emergency services to individuals who did not have medical insurance or other means to pay for services. Instead, the hospital would transfer the patient to another hospital that was known to serve a lower income clientele. Unfortunately, the delay in treatment sometimes resulted in severe consequences, including fatalities, which could have been allayed if the respective patients had received the needed treatment when it was first sought.

EMTALA applies to any hospital that receives reimbursements from Medicare. It requires that patients who present themselves in an Emergency Room receive as much treatment as necessary to stabilize them before they can be transferred to another facility. The law specifically requires that women in active labor be provided the appropriate care to ensure the well-being of both mother and child. Even if the person does not appear to need care, emergency personnel are legally bound to medically evaluate the patient. Both hospitals and individual care providers are subject to severe penalties for noncompliance. In the case of hospitals, they can potentially lose access to reimbursements from Medicare. Doctors bear the threat of malpractice suits and/or the loss of medical licensing. Although EMTALA continues to be controversial, since hospitals and physicians are required to provide emergency medical services without Medicare having a corresponding directive to pay for the care, the threat of liability helps ensure that the impoverished are not discriminated against on the basis of their ability to pay in a vast majority of the hospitals across the nation.

FURTHER READING

Johnston, Valerie, and Yuhua Bao. 2011. "Race/Ethnicity-Related and Payer-Related Disparities in the Timeliness of Emergency Care in U.S. Emergency Departments." *Journal of Health Care for the Poor and Underserved* 22, no. 2: 606–620.

Koeninger, W. David. 2013. "Statute Whose Name We Dare Not Speak: EMTALA and the Affordable Care Act." *Journal of Gender, Race, and Justice* 16, no. 1: 139–186.

Rosenbaum, Sara, and Brian Kamoie. 2003. "Finding a Way through the Hospital Door: The Role of EMTALA in Public Health Emergencies." *Journal of Law, Medicine, and Ethics* 31, no. 4: 590–601.

Zuabi, Nadia, Larry D. Weiss, and Mark I. Langdorf. 2016. "Emergency Medical Treatment and Labor Act (EMTALA) 2002–15: Review of Office of Inspector General Patient Dumping Settlements." *Western Journal of Emergency Medicine: Integrating Emergency Care with Population Health* 17, no. 3: 245–251.

"To Engender Respect for the Human Dignity of the Homeless"

- ***Document:*** Stewart B. McKinney Homeless Assistance Act (Excerpts)
- ***Date:*** July 22, 1987
- ***Where:*** Washington, D.C.
- ***Significance:*** The act provided much needed federal funding for nonprofit organizations and government agencies at the state or local level to assist the homeless.

DOCUMENT

An Act

To provide urgently needed assistance to protect and improve the lives and safety of the homeless, with special emphasis on elderly persons, handicapped persons, and families with children.

Be it enacted by the Senate and House of Representatives of the United States of America in Congress assembled,

TITLE I—GENERAL PROVISIONS

SECTION 101. SHORT TITLE AND TABLE OF CONTENTS.

(a) SHORT TITLE.—This Act may be cited as the "Stewart B. McKinney Homeless Assistance Act."

. . .

SECTION 102. FINDINGS AND PURPOSE.

(a) FINDINGS.—The Congress finds that—

(1) the Nation faces an immediate and unprecedented crisis due to the lack of shelter for a growing number of individuals and families, including elderly persons, handicapped persons, families with children, Native Americans, and veterans;

(2) the problem of homelessness has become more severe and, in the absence of more effective efforts, is expected to become dramatically worse, endangering the lives and safety of the homeless;

(3) the causes of homelessness are many and complex, and homeless individuals have diverse needs;

(4) there is no single, simple solution to the problem of homelessness because of the different subpopulations of the homeless, the different causes of and reasons for homelessness, and the different needs of homeless individuals;

(5) due to the record increase in homelessness, States, units of local government, and private voluntary organizations have been unable to meet the basic human needs of all the homeless and, in the absence of greater Federal assistance, will be unable to protect the lives and safety of all the homeless in need of assistance; and

(6) the Federal Government has a clear responsibility and an existing capacity to fulfill a more effective and responsible role to meet the basic human needs and to engender respect for the human dignity of the homeless.

(b) PURPOSE.—It is the purpose of this Act—

(1) to establish an Interagency Council on the Homeless;

(2) to use public resources and programs in a more coordinated manner to meet the critically urgent needs of the homeless of the Nation; and

(3) to provide funds for programs to assist the homeless, with special emphasis on elderly persons, handicapped persons, families with children, Native Americans, and veterans.

. . .

TITLE IV—HOUSING ASSISTANCE

Subtitle A—Comprehensive Homeless Assistance Plan

SECTION 401. REQUIREMENT FOR COMPREHENSIVE HOMELESS ASSISTANCE PLAN.

(a) PLAN REQUIRED.—Assistance authorized by this title may be provided to, or within the jurisdiction of, a State or a metropolitan city or urban county that is eligible to receive a grant under the emergency shelter grants program in an amount in excess of the minimum allocation requirement applicable under section 413(b) only if—

(1) it submits to the Secretary of Housing and Urban Development (in this subtitle referred to as the "Secretary") a comprehensive homeless assistance plan (in this subtitle referred to as the "comprehensive plan"); and

(2) the comprehensive plan is approved by or in accordance with procedures established by the Secretary; except that a private nonprofit organization

may apply for and receive assistance under subtitle C or D without regard to such comprehensive plan approval if the applicable State comprehensive plan has been approved.

. . .

Subtitle B—Emergency Shelter Grants Program

. . .

SEC. 414. ELIGIBLE ACTIVITIES.

(a) IN GENERAL.—Assistance provided under this subtitle may be used for the following activities relating to emergency shelter for homeless individuals:

(1) The renovation, major rehabilitation, or conversion of buildings to be used as emergency shelters.

(2) The provision of essential services, including services concerned with employment, health, drug abuse, or education, if—

(A) such services have not been provided by the local government during any part of the immediately preceding 12-month period; and

(B) not more than 15 percent of the amount of any assistance to a local government under this subtitle is used for activities under this paragraph.

(3) Maintenance, operation (other than staff), insurance, utilities, and furnishings.

(b) WAIVER AUTHORITY.—The Secretary may waive the 15 percent limitation on the use of assistance for essential services contained in subsection (a)(2)(B), if the local government receiving the assistance demonstrates that the other eligible activities under the program are already being carried out in the locality with other resources.

SOURCE: U.S. Congress. 1987. Public Law 100-77.

ANALYSIS

During the 1980s, the homeless population began to grow significantly in many of the nation's urban areas. Local government agencies, churches, and nonprofit were initially able to address the needs of the homeless but their resources were quickly sapped. Concerned constituents began lobbying federal officials to secure funding for cities to address the growing scourge. Their efforts resulted in $140 million being provided in 1983 for the emergency provision of food and shelter. Another $70 million followed a year later. Since the funding in both years was for emergency use, beneficiaries could only be fed and housed for a short period.

Recognizing that the problem of homelessness required a more sophisticated response, many members of Congress began submitting bills in 1985 and 1986 to provide more support for local initiatives. For instance, the requirement that individuals have a permanent address was dropped for the Aid to Families with Dependent Children, food stamp, and Supplemental Security Income programs, thereby allowing for the first time participation by the homeless.

The Stewart B. McKinney Homeless Assistance Act of 1987 soon followed. Its namesake was the Republican sponsor of the legislation who had that year succumbed to Acquired Immune Deficiency Syndrome (AIDS). The law provided a federal commitment of $1 billion for both 1987 and 1988 to combat homelessness. Although the McKinney Act contained provisions to renovate old dilapidated buildings or refurbish studio apartments, that was not what much of the money was used for. Local officials instead continued to emphasize emergency measures, such as providing meals and temporary shelter. In doing so, they treated the symptom of the problem but did not significantly reverse the growth of the homeless population. Many allege that the money should have been used to assist families on the verge of becoming homeless to ensure that they remained in their domicile. Once families became homeless, it became much more difficult to get them back into a stable home.

In 2000, the name of the legislation was changed to the McKinney-Vento Act in order to recognize Congressman Bruce Vento, a supporter of homelessness legislation in the House of Representatives who had recently died. That year also saw an emphasis on ensuring that homeless children were able to attend public schools. Funding for the education initiative has since stayed fairly constant since it has been prioritized over other McKinney–Vento initiatives. Early efforts, such as job training, have been abandoned due to budget reductions over the course of numerous presidential administrations.

FURTHER READING

Ellen, Ingrid Gould, and Brendan O'Flaherty, eds. 2010. *How to House the Homeless*. New York: Russell Sage Foundation.

Miller, Peter M. 2011. "A Critical Analysis of the Research on Student Homelessness." *Review of Educational Research* 81, no. 3: 308–337.

Willse, Craig. 2015. *The Value of Homelessness: Managing Surplus Life in the United States*. Minneapolis: University of Minnesota Press.

"To Encourage and Assist Needy Children and Parents under the New Program to Obtain the Education, Training, and Employment Needed to Avoid Long-Term Welfare Dependence"

- ***Document:*** Family Support Act of 1988 (Excerpts)
- ***Date:*** October 13, 1988
- ***Where:*** Washington, D.C.
- ***Significance:*** The Family Support Act was an unsuccessful attempt to encourage adult recipients of Aid to Families with Dependent Children to join the workforce.

DOCUMENT

To revise the AFDC program to emphasize work, child support, and family benefits, to amend Title IV of the Social Security Act to encourage and assist needy children and parents under the new program to obtain the education, training, and employment needed to avoid long-term welfare dependence, and to make other necessary improvements to assure that the new program will be more effective in achieving its objectives.

Be it enacted by the Senate and the House of Representatives of the United States of America in Congress assembled,

(a) SHORT TITLE.—This Act may be cited as the "Family Support Act of 1988."

. . .

TITLE I—CHILD SUPPORT AND ESTABLISHMENT OF PATERNITY

Subtitle A—Child Support

SEC 101. IMMEDIATE INCOME WITHHOLDING.

(a) IN GENERAL.—Section 466(bX3) of the Social Security Act is amended to read as follows:

(3)(A) The wages of an absent parent shall be subject to such withholding, regardless of whether support payments by such parent are in arrears, in the case of a support order being enforced under this part that is issued or modified on or after the first day of the 25th month banning after the date of the enactment of this paragraph, on the effective date of the order; except that such wages shall not be subject to such withholding under this subparagraph in any case where (i) one of the parties demonstrates, and the court (or administrative process) finds, that there is good cause not to require immediate income withholding, or (ii) a written agreement is reached between both parties which provides for an alternative arrangement.

"(B) The wages of an absent parent shall become subject to such withholding, in the case of wages not subject to withholding under subparagraph (A), on the date on which the payments which the absent parent has failed to make under a support order are at least equal to the support payable for one month or, if earlier, and without regard to whether there is an arrearage, the earliest of—

"(i) the date as of which the absent parent requests that such withholding begin,

"(ii) the date as of which the custodial parent requests that such withholding begin, if the State determines, in accordance with such procedures and standards as it may establish, that the request should be approved, or

"(iii) such earlier date as the State may select."

(b) APPLICATION TO ALL CHILD SUPPORT ORDERS.—Section 466 (aX8) of such Act is amended—

(1) by inserting "(A)" before "Procedures";

(2) by striking "which are issued or modified in the State" and inserting in lieu thereof "not described in subparagraph (B)"; and

(3) by adding at the end the following new subparagraph:

"(B) Procedures under which all child support orders which are initially issued in the State on or after January 1,1994, and are not being enforced under this part will include the following requirements:

"(i) The wages of an absent parent shall be subject to withholding, regardless of whether support payments by such parent are in arrears, on the effective date of the order; except that such wages shall not be subject to withholding under this clause in any case where (I) one of the parties demonstrates, and the court (or administrative process) finds, that there is good cause not to require immediate income withholding, or (II) a written agreement is reached between both parties which provides for an alternative arrangement.

"(ii) The requirements of subsection (b)(1) (which shall apply in the case of each absent parent against whom a support order is or has been issued or modified in the State, without regard to whether the order is being enforced under the State plan).

"(iii) The requirements of paragraphs (2), (5), (6), (7), (8), (9), and (10) of subsection (b), where applicable.

"(iv) Withholding from income of amounts payable as support must be carried out in full compliance with all procedural due process requirements of the State."

(c) STUDY ON MAKING IMMEDIATE INCOME WITHHOLDING MANDATORY IN ALL CASES.—The Secretary of Health and Human Services shall conduct a study of the administrative feasibility, cost implications, and other effects of requiring immediate income withholding with respect to all child support awards in a State and shall report on the results of such study not later than 3 years after the date of the enactment of this Act.

. . .

TITLE III—SUPPORTIVE SERVICES FOR FAMILIES

SEC. 301. CHILD CARE DURING PARTICIPATION IN EMPLOYMENT, EDUCATION, AND TRAINING.

Section 402 of the Social Security Act is amended by adding at the end the following new subsection:

"(g)(1)(A) Each State agency must guarantee child care in accordance with subparagraph (B)—

"(i) for each family with a dependent child requiring such care, to the extent that such care is determined by the State agency to be necessary for an individual in the family to accept employment or remain employed; and

"(ii) for each individual participating in an education and training activity (including participation in a program that meets the requirements of subsection (a)(19) and part F) if the State agency approves the activity and determines that the individual is satisfactorily participating in the activity.

"(B) The State agency may guarantee child care by—

"(i) providing such care directly; Contracts.

"(ii) arranging the care through providers by use of purchase of service contracts, or vouchers;

"(iii) providing cash or vouchers in advance to the caretaker relative in the family;

"(iv) reimbursing the caretaker relative in the family; or

"(v) adopting such other arrangements as the agency deems appropriate.

When the State agency arranges for child care, the agency shall take into account the individual needs of the child.

SOURCE: U.S. Congress. 1988. Public Law 100-485.

ANALYSIS

Throughout his political career, President Ronald Reagan had been a harsh critic of public welfare. He believed that the nation's safety net, as it had been constituted since Franklin Delano Roosevelt's New Deal, robbed individuals of their motivation to work, thereby resulting in their dependence on government largesse. Through the Family Support Act of 1988 (FSA), Reagan endeavored to encourage people to get the education and training that would allow them to find jobs that paid more than they received from the Aid to Families with Dependent Children (AFDC) program. In theory, the return of individuals to the workforce would lessen the cost of AFDC to the federal government while, at the same time, increasing revenue received from payroll taxes.

Reagan tasked the White House Domestic Council with drafting recommendations on how best to reform AFDC. Its recommendation provided the outline for what became the FSA. The new law required welfare recipients to provide 16 hours of community service in exchange for their continued participation in AFDC. Another provision required that single mothers identify the father of each of their children. The name was necessary so that the government could force the employer of the absentee father to garnish their salaries in order to help financially support their offspring.

The FSA was doomed to failure from the very beginning due to its insufficient funding. It was designed as a joint federal and state initiative. Sixty percent of the job training costs were the responsibility of federal authorities with the remainder being paid by the respective states. The problem was that many states failed to pay their share. Also underfunded was the bureaucracy necessary to confirm that the act's edicts were being followed. For example, without government employees available to confirm that AFDC recipients were completing the required community service, individuals continued to receive benefits while ignoring the job requirement.

The FSA proved so ineffective that the number of AFDC recipients grew in the years that it was in force. It was replaced in 1996 by the Personal Responsibility and Work Opportunity Reconciliation Act, which discarded AFDC. Its replacement, Temporary Assistance to Needy Families (TANF), proved much more efficient in shifting individuals from aid programs to the workforce.

FURTHER READING

Cammisa, Anne Marie. 1995. *Governments as Interest Groups: Intergovernmental Lobbying and the Federal System*. Westport, CT: Praeger.

Chilman, Catherine S. 1992. "Welfare Reform or Revision? The Family Support Act of 1988." *Social Service Review* 66, no. 3: 349–377.

"To Assess the Dietary and Nutritional Status of the United States Population"

- ***Document:*** National Nutrition Monitoring and Related Research Act of 1990 (Excerpt)
- ***Date:*** January 23, 1990
- ***Where:*** Washington, D.C.
- ***Significance:*** The act called for the creation of a national nutrition monitoring system to provide research data on food insecurity and its resulting impact on the health of the general populace.

DOCUMENT

An Act

To strengthen national nutrition monitoring by requiring the Secretary of Agriculture and the Secretary of Health and Human Services to prepare and implement a ten-year plan to assess the dietary and nutritional status of the United States population, to support research on, and development of, nutrition monitoring, to foster national nutrition education, to establish dietary guidelines, and for other purposes.

Be it enacted by the Senate and House of Representatives of the United States of America in Congress assembled,

SECTION 1. SHORT TITLE.

This Act may be cited as the "National Nutrition Monitoring and Related Research Act of 1990."

SEC. 2. PURPOSES.

The purposes of this Act are to—

(1) make more effective use of Federal and State expenditures for nutrition monitoring, and enhance the performance and benefits of current Federal nutrition monitoring and related research activities;

(2) establish and facilitate the timely implementation of a coordinated National Nutrition Monitoring and Related Research Program, and thereby provide a scientific basis for the maintenance and improvement of the nutritional status of the people of the United States and the nutritional quality (including, but not limited to, nutritive and nonnutritive content) of food consumed in the United States;

(3) establish and implement a comprehensive plan for the National Nutrition Monitoring and Related Research Program to assess, on a continuing basis, the dietary and nutritional status of the people of the United States and the trends with respect to such status, the state of the art with respect to nutrition monitoring and related research, future monitoring and related research priorities, and the relevant policy implications;

(4) establish and improve the quality of national nutritional and health status data and related data bases and networks, and stimulate research necessary to develop uniform indicators, standards, methodologies, technologies, and procedures for nutrition monitoring;

(5) establish a central Federal focus for the coordination, management, and direction of Federal nutrition monitoring activities;

(6) establish mechanisms for addressing the nutrition monitoring needs of Federal, State, and local governments, the private sector, scientific and engineering communities, health care professionals, and the public in support of the foregoing purposes; and

(7) provide for the conduct of such scientific research and development as may be necessary or appropriate in support of such purposes.

SEC. 3 DEFINITIONS.

As used in this Act—

(1) the term "comprehensive plan" means the comprehensive plan prepared under section 103;

(2) the term "coordinated program" means the National Nutrition Monitoring and Related Research Program established by section 101(a);

(3) the terms "Interagency Board for Nutrition Monitoring and Related Research" and "Board" mean the Federal coordinating body established by section 101(c);

(4) the term "Joint Implementation Plan for a Comprehensive National Nutrition Monitoring System" means the plan of that title dated August 18, 1981 and submitted by the Department of Agriculture and the Department of Health and Human Services under section 1428 of the Food and Agriculture Act of 1977 (7 U.S.C. 3178);

(5) the term "local government" means a local general unit of government or local educational unit;

(6) the terms "National Nutrition Monitoring Advisory Council" and "Council" mean the advisory body established under section 201;

(7) the term "nutrition monitoring and related research" means the set of activities necessary to provide timely information about the role and status of factors that bear on the contribution that nutrition makes to the health of the people of the United States, including—

(A) dietary, nutritional, and health status measurements;

(B) food consumption measurements;

(C) food composition measurements and nutrient data banks;

(D) dietary knowledge and attitude measurements; and

(E) food supply and demand determinations;

(8) the term "nutritional quality" means—

(A) the appropriate levels of individual nutrients in the diet;

(B) the appropriate levels between nutrients in the diet;

(C) the bioavailability of nutrients such as absorption, digestion, and utilization; and

(D) the nutritional importance of nonnutrient substances such as fiber, phytate, and such substances that are naturally found in the food supply; and

(9) the term "Secretaries" means the Secretary of Agriculture and the Secretary of Health and Human Services, acting jointly.

TITLE I—NUTRITION MONITORING AND RELATED RESEARCH

SEC. 101. ESTABLISHMENT OF THE COORDINATED PROGRAM.

(a) IN GENERAL—There is established a ten-year coordinated program, to be known as the National Nutrition Monitoring and Related Research Program, to carry out the purposes of this Act.

(b) IMPLEMENTATION RESPONSIBILITY—The Secretaries shall be responsible for the implementation of the coordinated program.

(c) ESTABLISHMENT OF BOARD—To assist in implementing the coordinated program, there is established an Interagency Board for Nutrition Monitoring and Related Research, of which an Assistant Secretary in the Department of Agriculture (designated by the Secretary of Agriculture) and an Assistant Secretary in the Department of Health and Human Services (designated by the Secretary of Health and Human Services) shall be joint chairpersons. The remaining membership of the Board shall consist of additional representatives of Federal agencies, as determined appropriate by the joint chairpersons of the Board. The Board shall meet no less often than once every three months for the two-year period following the date of the enactment of this Act, and when appropriate thereafter.

(d) ADMINISTRATOR—To establish a central focus and coordinator for the coordinated program, the Secretaries may appoint an Administrator of Nutrition Monitoring and Related Research. The Administrator shall—

(1) be an individual who is eminent in the field of nutrition monitoring and related areas and be selected on the basis of the established record of expertise and distinguished service of such individual; and

(2) administer the coordinated program with the advice and counsel of the joint chairpersons of the Board, serve as the focal point for the coordinated program, and serve as the Executive Secretary for the National Nutrition Monitoring Advisory Council.

SEC. 102. FUNCTIONS OF THE SECRETARIES.

(a) IN GENERAL—The Secretaries, with the advice of the Board, shall—

(1) establish the goals of the coordinated program, identify the activities required to meet such goals, and identify the responsible agencies with respect to the coordinated program;

(2) update the Joint Implementation Plan for a Comprehensive National Nutrition Monitoring System, and integrate it into the coordinated program;

(3) ensure the timely implementation of the coordinated program and the comprehensive plan prepared under section 103;

(4) include in the coordinated program and the comprehensive plan a competitive grants program, to be implemented to the extent funds are available, in accordance with the provisions of this Act to encourage and assist the conduct, by Federal entities, and by non-Federal entities on an appropriate matching funds basis, of research (including research described in section 103(a)(3)) that will accelerate the development of uniform and cost-effective standards and indicators for the assessment and monitoring of nutritional and dietary status and for relating food consumption patterns to nutritional and health status;

(5) include in the coordinated program and the comprehensive plan a grants program, in accordance with the provisions of this Act, to encourage and assist State and local governments in developing the capacity to conduct monitoring and surveillance of nutritional status, food consumption, and nutrition knowledge and in using such capacity to enhance nutrition services (including activities described in section 103(a)(5) and 103(b)(9));

(6) include in the coordinated program each fiscal year an annual interagency budget for each fiscal year of the program;

(7) foster productive interaction, with respect to nutrition monitoring and related research, among Federal efforts, State and local governments, the private sector, scientific communities, health professionals, and the public;

(8)(A) contract with a scientific body, such as the National Academy of Sciences or the Federation of American Societies for Experimental Biology, to interpret available data analyses, and publish every two years, or more frequently if appropriate, except as provided in subparagraph (B), a report on the dietary, nutritional, and health-related status of the people of the United States and the nutritional quality (including the nutritive and nonnutritive content) of food consumed in the United States; or (B) if the Secretaries determine that sufficient data analyses are not available to warrant interpretation of such data analyses, inform Congress of such fact at the time a report required in subparagraph (A) would have been published, and publish such report at least once every five years; and

(9)(A) foster cost recovery management techniques in the coordinated program; and (B) impose appropriate charges and fees for publications of the coordinated program, including print and electronic forms of data and analysis, and use the proceeds of such charges and fees for purposes of the coordinated program (except that no such charge or fee imposed on an educational or other nonprofit organization shall exceed the actual costs incurred by the coordinated program in providing the publications involved).

(b) BIENNIAL REPORT—The Secretaries shall submit to the President for transmittal to Congress by January 15 of each alternate year, beginning with January 15 following the date of the enactment of this Act, a biennial report that shall—

(1) evaluate the progress of the coordinated program;

(2) summarize the results of such coordinated program components as are developed under section 103;

(3) describe and evaluate any policy implications of the analytical findings in the scientific reports required under subsection (a)(8), and future priorities for nutrition monitoring and related research;

(4) include in full the annual reports of the Council provided for in section 202; and

(5) include an executive summary of the report most recently published by the scientific body, as provided for in subsection (a)(8).

SEC. 103. DEVELOPMENT OF THE COMPREHENSIVE PLAN FOR THE NATIONAL NUTRITION MONITORING AND RELATED RESEARCH PROGRAM.

(a) COMPREHENSIVE PLAN—The Secretaries, with the advice of the Board, shall prepare and implement a comprehensive plan for the coordinated program which shall be designed to—

(1) assess, collate data with respect to, analyze, and report, on a continuous basis, the dietary and nutritional status of the people of the United States, and the trends with respect to such status (dealing with such status and trends separately in the case of preschool and school-age children, pregnant and lactating women, elderly individuals, low-income populations, blacks, Hispanics, and other groups, at the discretion of the Secretaries), the state of the art with respect to nutrition monitoring and related research, future monitoring and related research priorities, and relevant policy implications of findings with respect to such status, trends, and research;

(2) sample representative subsets of identifiable low-income populations (such as Native Americans, Hispanics, or the homeless), and assess, analyze, and report, on a continuous basis, for a representative sample of the low-income population, food and household expenditures, participation in food assistance programs, and periods experienced when nutrition benefits are not sufficient to provide an adequate diet;

(3) sponsor or conduct research necessary to develop uniform indicators, standards, methodologies, technologies, and procedures for conducting and reporting nutrition monitoring and surveillance;

(4) develop and keep updated a national dietary and nutritional status data bank, a nutrient data bank, and other data resources as required;

(5) assist State and local government agencies in developing procedures and networks for nutrition monitoring and surveillance; and
(6) focus the nutrition monitoring activities of Federal agencies.

SOURCE: U.S. Congress. H.R.1608, 101st Congress (1989–1990).

ANALYSIS

The National Nutrition Monitoring and Related Research Act of 1990 (NNMRRA) became Public Law 101-445. It called for the U.S. Departments of Agriculture and Health and Human Services to create a survey on food consumption, food insecurity, and the health of the citizenry. The resulting data was then to be made available to both public and private interests to inform ongoing research initiatives and governmental programs at the local, state, and federal levels.

The first survey initiated by the NNMRRA was the Food Security Supplement, which was offered as part of the U.S. Census Bureau's 1995 Current Population Survey. The questionnaire was distributed to approximately 50,000 households with questions focusing on such topics as to whether the family had the wherewithal to ensure that all members had a steady supply of food and whether the nutritional value of the foods consumed were adequate to ensure good health. The survey results provided the federal government its first comprehensive picture of food insecurity, defined as a household that had issues with access to food, in the country. The data from the first survey and the second a year later produced a startling picture of hunger in America. Approximately 10 percent of the population ranged from having to subsist on foods that did not meet their nutritional requirement to not even knowing where their next meal was coming from. The information gleaned from the surveys helped inform the types of foods that were provided through federal food programs such as school lunches and the Special Supplemental Nutrition Program for Women, Infants, and Children, better known as WIC.

Although the NNMRRA was initially authorized for 10 years, the research program it initiated continues. One of the more notable publications to emerge from the NNMRRA was the *Dietary Guidelines for Americans*, which is now in its eighth edition. Issued every five years, it provides the nutrition guidelines that are followed by all federal agencies or departments that oversee food programs.

FURTHER READING

Lewis, Richard D., Emma M. Laing, and Stephanie M. Foss. 2015. "From the War on Hunger to the Fight against Obesity." In Sharon Y. Nickols and Gwen Kay, eds. *Remaking Home Economics: Resourcefulness and Innovation in Changing Times*. Athens: University of Georgia Press: 109–127.

U.S. Department of Agriculture and Department of Health and Human Services. 2015. *Dietary Guidelines for Americans 2015–2020*. 8th ed. Washington, D.C.: U.S. Department of Agriculture and Department of Health and Human Services. https://health.gov/dietaryguidelines/2015/resources/2015-2020_Dietary_Guidelines.pdf (accessed July 17, 2017).

"To Increase the Flexibility of States in Operating a Program"

- ***Document:*** Personal Responsibility and Work Opportunity Reconciliation Act of 1996
- ***Date:*** August 22, 1996
- ***Where:*** Washington, D.C.
- ***Significance:*** The Personal Responsibility and Work Opportunity Reconciliation Act restricted access to federal entitlements. It fixed the maximum amount of welfare benefits that a family could receive over a five-year period as well as requiring able-bodied adults within those families to gain employment or job training within the first two years of obtaining federal aid.

DOCUMENT

TITLE I—BLOCK GRANTS FOR TEMPORARY ASSISTANCE FOR NEEDY FAMILIES

SEC. 101. FINDINGS.

The Congress makes the following findings:

(1) Marriage is the foundation of a successful society.

(2) Marriage is an essential institution of a successful society which promotes the interests of children.

(3) Promotion of responsible fatherhood and motherhood is integral to successful child rearing and the well-being of children.

(4) In 1992, only 54 percent of single-parent families with children had a child support order established and, of that 54 percent, only about one-half

received the full amount due. Of the cases enforced through the public child support enforcement system, only 18 percent of the caseload has a collection.

(5) The number of individuals receiving aid to families with dependent children (in this section referred to as "AFDC") has more than tripled since 1965. More than two-thirds of these recipients are children. Eighty-nine percent of children receiving AFDC benefits now live in homes in which no father is present.

(A)(i) The average monthly number of children receiving AFDC benefits—

(I) was 3,300,000 in 1965;

(II) was 6,200,000 in 1970;

(III) was 7,400,000 in 1980; and

(IV) was 9,300,000 in 1992.

(ii) While the number of children receiving AFDC benefits increased nearly threefold between 1965 and 1992, the total number of children in the United States aged 0 to 18 has declined by 5.5 percent.

(B) The Department of Health and Human Services has estimated that 12,000,000 children will receive AFDC benefits within 10 years.

(C) The increase in the number of children receiving public assistance is closely related to the increase in births to unmarried women. Between 1970 and 1991, the percentage of live births to unmarried women increased nearly threefold, from 10.7 percent to 29.5 percent.

(6) The increase of out-of-wedlock pregnancies and births is well documented as follows:

(A) It is estimated that the rate of nonmarital teen pregnancy rose 23 percent from 54 pregnancies per 1,000 unmarried teenagers in 1976 to 66.7 pregnancies in 1991. The overall rate of nonmarital pregnancy rose 14 percent from 90.8 pregnancies per 1,000 unmarried women in 1980 to 103 in both 1991 and 1992. In contrast, the overall pregnancy rate for married couples decreased 7.3 percent between 1980 and 1991, from 126.9 pregnancies per 1,000 married women in 1980 to 117.6 pregnancies in 1991.

(B) The total of all out-of-wedlock births between 1970 and 1991 has risen from 10.7 percent to 29.5 percent and if the current trend continues, 50 percent of all births by the year 2015 will be out-of-wedlock.

(7) An effective strategy to combat teenage pregnancy must address the issue of male responsibility, including statutory rape culpability and prevention. The increase of teenage pregnancies among the youngest girls is particularly severe and is linked to predatory sexual practices by men who are significantly older. (A) It is estimated that in the late 1980's, the rate for girls age 14 and under giving birth increased 26 percent. (B) Data indicates that at least half of the children born to teenage mothers are fathered by adult men. Available data suggests that almost 70 percent of births to teenage girls are fathered by men over age 20. (C) Surveys of teen mothers have revealed that a majority of such mothers have histories of sexual and physical abuse, primarily with older adult men.

(8) The negative consequences of an out-of-wedlock birth on the mother, the child, the family, and society are well documented as follows: (A) Young

women 17 and under who give birth outside of marriage are more likely to go on public assistance and to spend more years on welfare once enrolled. These combined effects of "younger and longer" increase total AFDC costs per household by 25 percent to 30 percent for 17-year-olds. (B) Children born out-of-wedlock have a substantially higher risk of being born at a very low or moderately low birth weight. (C) Children born out-of-wedlock are more likely to experience low verbal cognitive attainment, as well as more child abuse, and neglect. (D) Children born out-of-wedlock were more likely to have lower cognitive scores, lower educational aspirations, and a greater likelihood of becoming teenage parents themselves. (E) Being born out-of-wedlock significantly reduces the chances of the child growing up to have an intact marriage. (F) Children born out-of-wedlock are 3 times more likely to be on welfare when they grow up.

(9) Currently 35 percent of children in single-parent homes were born out-of-wedlock, nearly the same percentage as that of children in single-parent homes whose parents are divorced (37 percent). While many parents find themselves, through divorce or tragic circumstances beyond their control, facing the difficult task of raising children alone, nevertheless, the negative consequences of raising children in single-parent homes are well documented as follows: (A) Only 9 percent of married-couple families with children under 18 years of age have income below the national poverty level. In contrast, 46 percent of female headed households with children under 18 years of age are below the national poverty level. (B) Among single-parent families, nearly 1/2 of the mothers who never married received AFDC while only 1/5 of divorced mothers received AFDC. (C) Children born into families receiving welfare assistance are 3 times more likely to be on welfare when they reach adulthood than children not born into families receiving welfare. (D) Mothers under 20 years of age are at the greatest risk of bearing low birth weight babies. (E) The younger the single-parent mother, the less likely she is to finish high school. (F) Young women who have children before finishing high school are more likely to receive welfare assistance for a longer period of time. (G) Between 1985 and 1990, the public cost of births to teenage mothers under the aid to families with dependent children program, the food stamp program, and the medicaid program has been estimated at $120,000,000,000. (H) The absence of a father in the life of a child has a negative effect on school performance and peer adjustment. (I) Children of teenage single parents have lower cognitive scores, lower educational aspirations, and a greater likelihood of becoming teenage parents themselves. (J) Children of single-parent homes are 3 times more likely to fail and repeat a year in grade school than are children from intact 2-parent families. (K) Children from single-parent homes are almost 4 times more likely to be expelled or suspended from school. (L) Neighborhoods with larger percentages of youth aged 12 through 20 and areas with higher percentages of single-parent households have higher rates of violent crime. (M) Of those youth held for criminal offenses within the State juvenile justice system, only 29.8 percent lived primarily in a home with both parents. In contrast to these incarcerated youth,

73.9 percent of the 62,800,000 children in the Nation's resident population were living with both parents.

(10) Therefore, in light of this demonstration of the crisis in our Nation, it is the sense of the Congress that prevention of out-of-wedlock pregnancy and reduction in out-of-wedlock birth are very important Government interests and the policy contained in part A of title IV of the Social Security Act (as amended by section 103(a) of this Act) is intended to address the crisis.

. . .

"PART A—BLOCK GRANTS TO STATES FOR TEMPORARY ASSISTANCE FOR NEEDY FAMILIES

"SEC. 401. PURPOSE.

"(a) IN GENERAL.—The purpose of this part is to increase the flexibility of States in operating a program designed to—

"(1) provide assistance to needy families so that children may be cared for in their own homes or in the homes of relatives;

"(2) end the dependence of needy parents on government benefits by promoting job preparation, work, and marriage;

"(3) prevent and reduce the incidence of out-of-wedlock pregnancies and establish annual numerical goals for preventing and reducing the incidence of these pregnancies; and

"(4) encourage the formation and maintenance of two-parent families.

"(b) NO INDIVIDUAL ENTITLEMENT.—This part shall not be interpreted to entitle any individual or family to assistance under any State program funded under this part.

. . .

TITLE II—SUPPLEMENTAL SECURITY INCOME

. . .

Subtitle A—Eligibility Restrictions

SEC. 201. DENIAL OF SSI BENEFITS FOR 10 YEARS TO INDIVIDUALS FOUND TO HAVE FRAUDULENTLY MISREPRESENTED RESIDENCE IN ORDER TO OBTAIN BENEFITS SIMULTANEOUSLY IN 2 OR MORE STATES.

IN GENERAL.—Section 1611(e) (42 U.S.C. 1382(e)), as amended by section 105 (b)(4)(A) of the Contract with America Advancement Act of 1996, is amended by redesignating paragraph (5) as paragraph (3) and by adding at the end the following new paragraph:

"(4)(A) No person shall be considered an eligible individual or eligible spouse for purposes of this title during the 10-year period that begins on the date the person is convicted in Federal or State court of having made a fraudulent statement or representation with respect to the place of residence of the person in order to receive assistance simultaneously from 2 or more States under programs that are funded under title IV, title XIX, or the Food Stamp Act of 1977, or benefits in 2 or more States under the supplemental security income program under this title.

"(B) As soon as practicable after the conviction of a person in a Federal or State court as described in subparagraph (A), an official of such court shall notify the Commissioner of such conviction."

(b) EFFECTIVE DATE.—The amendment made by this section shall take effect on the date of the enactment of this Act.

...

TITLE III—CHILD SUPPORT

...

TITLE IV—RESTRICTING WELFARE AND PUBLIC BENEFITS FOR ALIENS

SEC. 400. STATEMENTS OF NATIONAL POLICY CONCERNING WELFARE AND IMMIGRATION.

The Congress makes the following statements concerning national policy with respect to welfare and immigration:

(1) Self-sufficiency has been a basic principle of United States immigration law since this country's earliest immigration statutes.

(2) It continues to be the immigration policy of the United States that—

(A) aliens within the Nation's borders not depend on public resources to meet their needs, but rather rely on their own capabilities and the resources of their families, their sponsors, and private organizations, and

(B) the availability of public benefits not constitute an incentive for immigration to the United States.

(3) Despite the principle of self-sufficiency, aliens have been applying for and receiving public benefits from Federal, State, and local governments at increasing rates.

(4) Current eligibility rules for public assistance and unenforceable financial support agreements have proved wholly incapable of assuring that individual aliens not burden the public benefits system.

(5) It is a compelling government interest to enact new rules for eligibility and sponsorship agreements in order to assure that aliens be self-reliant in accordance with national immigration policy.

(6) It is a compelling government interest to remove the incentive for illegal immigration provided by the availability of public benefits.

(7) With respect to the State authority to make determinations concerning the eligibility of qualified aliens for public benefits in this title, a State that chooses to follow the Federal classification in determining the eligibility of such aliens for public assistance shall be considered to have chosen the least restrictive means available for achieving the compelling governmental interest of assuring that aliens be self-reliant in accordance with national immigration policy.

...

TITLE V—CHILD PROTECTION

. . .

TITLE VI—CHILD CARE

. . .

TITLE VII—CHILD NUTRITION PROGRAMS

. . .

TITLE VIII—FOOD STAMPS AND COMMODITY DISTRIBUTION

. . .

TITLE IX—MISCELLANEOUS

SOURCE: 104th Congress. 1996. Public Law 104-193.

ANALYSIS

From the end of President Lyndon Johnson's time in office to 1993, the Republican Party held the presidency for all but the four years of Jimmy Carter's term. This period saw the nation's electorate move toward the political right, which had largely been shaped during President Ronald Reagan's presidency. Recognizing that embracing the liberalism of the Great Society era would result in political defeat, five-term Arkansas governor William "Bill" Clinton ran in 1992 for the presidency as a "New Democrat." During the primaries this allowed him to differentiate himself from other Democratic Party contenders by taking a much more conservative stance on issues related to crime and welfare. This was exemplified through his campaign promise to "end welfare as we know it." Clinton's victory in the general election over President George H.W. Bush and Ross Perot marked a sea change in Democratic Party politics as New Democrat centrism came to dominate the party's platform. Although Clinton's administration briefly dallied with Great Society–style liberalism in the area of health care reform, the administration ultimately repudiated a key part of President Johnson's legacy through the passage of the Personal Responsibility and Work Opportunity Reconciliation Act of 1996 (PRWORA).

Although he reiterated in his 1993 State of the Union address to "end welfare as we know it," Clinton proved reticent early in his presidency to honor his pledge. Republicans in Congress had attempted on two occasions to get Clinton to follow through on this stated intent by sending him legislation with welfare cuts only to see him issue a veto. With his presidential approval numbers in the doldrums due to his health care initiative, Clinton opted to sign the Republican-sponsored PRWORA. This was a pragmatic move as his administration had become convinced that some form of welfare reform was inevitable. If they did not agree to the PRWORA, the next bill from the majority Republican Congress might include even more onerous reductions in benefits.

The Clinton administration's influence on the PRWORA was evident in a handful of measures that represented the expansion of certain programs, namely those involving children and education. The bill included an increase in the funding of Head Start, a signature Great Society program, as well as the establishment of job training programs for the impoverished so that they could find gainful employment. To help single mothers entering the workforce, funding was also put in place to help pay for child care. In exchange for those measures, the Clinton administration conceded to a number of measures desired by Republicans in Congress. These included denying welfare benefits to noncitizens of the United States, the establishment of a fixed maximum amount of welfare benefits that a family could receive over a five-year period, and a requirement that any able-bodied adults in those families had to begin working inside of the first two years. The only individuals who would be provided long-term access to welfare were those who had documented medical conditions that made them unable to work. The manner in which many received welfare benefits also changed. Aid to Families with Dependent Children (AFDC) program, the nation's largest welfare program, was supplanted by Temporary Assistance for Needy Families (TANF). This change meant that the states received more control over how welfare funds were used within their borders. AFDC, which was a state-government partnership, had numerous regulations that restricted how states could utilize federal funding. With the TANF, the federal government was providing block grants to the states with few guidelines. From the federal perspective, this allowed the respective states to experiment on how to best serve the poorer segments of their population. The unintended consequence was that, since the states had the discretion on how the funding was utilized, the poor were sometimes not the beneficiaries of the monies.

The Democratic Party's base wanted the legislation vetoed, especially since welfare reform had been a plank of the "Contract with America," which had helped lead to the Republicans gaining control of both houses of Congress. Democratic Party opposition in Congress was led by senator Daniel Moynihan of New York, who claimed that the passage of the PRWORA would lead to homeless children in cities sleeping on grates. Although Clinton signed the PRWORA, he attempted to assuage his political party by claiming it had serious flaws. This allowed him to assert that he had met his campaign promise since the legislation was designed to address poverty by encouraging welfare recipients to find employment, while also giving him an issue for his reelection campaign. His political instincts proved correct as his centrist position in relation to welfare reform helped secure his election to a second term.

Many of Clinton's critics in the Democratic Party were correct in their assessment of the PRWORA, although it was not evident during his presidency. Over much of Clinton's terms in office, the nation's economy grew at an impressive rate. Since jobs were relatively plentiful during that period, the impoverished were often able to gain decent employment. When the tide inevitably turned and the country fell into a recession, employment became scarce. This resulted in many families losing access to benefits after the five-year window was eclipsed.

FURTHER READING

Berkowitz, Edward D., and Larry DeWitt. 2013. *The Other Welfare: Supplemental Security Income and U.S. Social Policy*. Ithaca, NY: Cornell University Press.

Bertram, Eva. 2015. *The Workfare State: Public Assistance Politics from the New Deal to the New Democrats*. Philadelphia: University of Pennsylvania Press.

Chappell, Marisa. 2010. *The War on Welfare: Family, Poverty, and Politics in Modern America*. Philadelphia: University of Pennsylvania Press.

Clinton, William J. 1993. "Address before a Joint Session of Congress on Administration Goals February 17, 1993." In Gerhard Peters and John T. Woolley. *The American Presidency Project*. http://www.presidency.ucsb.edu/ws/?pid=47232 (accessed January 14, 2017).

Lehman, Jeffrey, and Sheldon Danzinger. 2004. "Turning Our Backs on the New Deal: The End of Welfare in 1996." In C. Michael Henry, ed. *Race, Poverty, and Domestic Policy*. New Haven: Yale University Press.

Nelson, Michael, Barbara A. Perry, and Russell L. Riley, eds. 2016. *42: Inside the Presidency of Bill Clinton*. Ithaca: Cornell University Press.

Stricker, Frank. 2007. *Why America Lost the War on Poverty—And How to Win It*. Chapel Hill: University of North Carolina Press.

7

THE NEW MILLENNIUM

"An Act to Close the Achievement Gap with Accountability, Flexibility, and Choice, So that No Child Is Left Behind"

- ***Document:*** No Child Left Behind Act of 2001
- ***Date:*** January 8, 2002
- ***Where:*** Washington, D.C.
- ***Significance:*** The act required schools receiving federal funding to adopt standards-based education. In order to assess whether schools were making progress toward meeting the standards, they were required to administer tests to their students and make publicly available the results.

DOCUMENT

Public Law 107-110
107th Congress

An Act

To close the achievement gap with accountability, flexibility, and choice, so that no child is left behind.

Be it enacted by the Senate and House of Representatives of the United States of America in Congress assembled,

SECTION 1. SHORT TITLE.

This title may be cited as the "No Child Left Behind Act of 2001."

. . .

"TITLE I—IMPROVING THE ACADEMIC ACHIEVEMENT OF THE DISADVANTAGED

"SEC. 1001. STATEMENT OF PURPOSE.

"The purpose of this title is to ensure that all children have a fair, equal, and significant opportunity to obtain a high-quality education and reach, at a minimum, proficiency on challenging State academic achievement standards and state academic assessments. This purpose can be accomplished by—

"(1) ensuring that high-quality academic assessments, accountability systems, teacher preparation and training, curriculum, and instructional materials are aligned with challenging State academic standards so that students, teachers, parents, and administrators can measure progress against common expectations for student academic achievement;

"(2) meeting the educational needs of low-achieving children in our Nation's highest-poverty schools, limited English proficient children, migratory children, children with disabilities, Indian children, neglected or delinquent children, and young children in need of reading assistance;

"(3) closing the achievement gap between high- and lowperforming children, especially the achievement gaps between minority and nonminority students, and between disadvantaged children and their more advantaged peers;

"(4) holding schools, local educational agencies, and States accountable for improving the academic achievement of all students, and identifying and turning around low-performing schools that have failed to provide a high-quality education to their students, while providing alternatives to students in such schools to enable the students to receive a high-quality education;

"(5) distributing and targeting resources sufficiently to make a difference to local educational agencies and schools where needs are greatest;

"(6) improving and strengthening accountability, teaching, and learning by using State assessment systems designed to ensure that students are meeting challenging State academic achievement and content standards and increasing achievement overall, but especially for the disadvantaged;

"(7) providing greater decisionmaking authority and flexibility to schools and teachers in exchange for greater responsibility for student performance;

"(8) providing children an enriched and accelerated educational program, including the use of schoolwide programs or additional services that increase the amount and quality of instructional time;

"(9) promoting schoolwide reform and ensuring the access of children to effective, scientifically based instructional strategies and challenging academic content;

"(10) significantly elevating the quality of instruction by providing staff in participating schools with substantial opportunities for professional development;

"(11) coordinating services under all parts of this title with each other, with other educational services, and, to the extent feasible, with other agencies providing services to youth, children, and families; and

"(12) affording parents substantial and meaningful opportunities to participate in the education of their children.

. . .

"TITLE II—PREPARING, TRAINING, AND RECRUITING HIGH QUALITY TEACHERS AND PRINCIPALS

"PART A—TEACHER AND PRINCIPAL TRAINING AND RECRUITING FUND

"SEC. 2101. PURPOSE.

"The purpose of this part is to provide grants to State educational agencies, local educational agencies, State agencies for higher education, and eligible partnerships in order to—

"(1) increase student academic achievement through strategies such as improving teacher and principal quality and increasing the number of highly qualified teachers in the classroom and highly qualified principals and assistant principals in schools; and

"(2) hold local educational agencies and schools accountable for improvements in student academic achievement.

. . .

"PART B—MATHEMATICS AND SCIENCE PARTNERSHIPS

"SEC. 2201. PURPOSE; DEFINITIONS.

"(a) PURPOSE.—The purpose of this part is to improve the academic achievement of students in the areas of mathematics and science by encouraging State educational agencies, institutions of higher education, local educational agencies, elementary schools, and secondary schools to participate in programs that—

"(1) improve and upgrade the status and stature of mathematics and science teaching by encouraging institutions of higher education to assume greater responsibility for improving mathematics and science teacher education through the establishment of a comprehensive, integrated system of recruiting, training, and advising mathematics and science teachers;

"(2) focus on the education of mathematics and science teachers as a career-long process that continuously stimulates teachers' intellectual growth and upgrades teachers' knowledge and skills;

"(3) bring mathematics and science teachers in elementary schools and secondary schools together with scientists, mathematicians, and engineers to increase the subject matter knowledge of mathematics and science teachers and improve such teachers' teaching skills through the use of sophisticated laboratory equipment and work space, computing facilities, libraries, and other resources that institutions of higher education are better able to provide than the elementary schools and secondary schools;

"(4) develop more rigorous mathematics and science curricula that are aligned with challenging State and local academic content standards and with the standards expected for postsecondary study in engineering, mathematics, and science; and

"(5) improve and expand training of mathematics and science teachers, including training such teachers in the effective integration of technology into curricula and instruction.

"(b) DEFINITIONS.—In this part:

"(1) ELIGIBLE PARTNERSHIP.—The term 'eligible partnership' means a partnership that—

"(A) shall include—

"(i) if grants are awarded under section 2202(a)(1), a State educational agency;

"(ii) an engineering, mathematics, or science department of an institution of higher education; and

"(iii) a high-need local educational agency; and

"(B) may include—

"(i) another engineering, mathematics, science, or teacher training department of an institution of higher education;

"(ii) additional local educational agencies, public charter schools, public or private elementary schools or secondary schools, or a consortium of such schools;

"(iii) a business; or

"(iv) a nonprofit or for-profit organization of demonstrated effectiveness in improving the quality of mathematics and science teachers.

"(2) SUMMER WORKSHOP OR INSTITUTE.—The term 'summer workshop or institute' means a workshop or institute, conducted during the summer, that—

"(A) is conducted for a period of not less than 2 weeks;

"(B) includes, as a component, a program that provides direct interaction between students and faculty; and

"(C) provides for followup training during the academic year that is conducted in the classroom for a period of not less than three consecutive or nonconsecutive days, except that—

"(i) if the workshop or institute is conducted during a 2-week period, the followup training shall be conducted for a period of not less than 4 days; and

"(ii) if the followup training is for teachers in rural school districts, the followup training may be conducted through distance learning.

. . .

"TITLE III—LANGUAGE INSTRUCTION FOR LIMITED ENGLISH PROFICIENT AND IMMIGRANT STUDENTS

. . .

"TITLE IV—21ST CENTURY SCHOOLS

"PART A—SAFE AND DRUG-FREE SCHOOLS AND COMMUNITIES

"SEC. 4001. SHORT TITLE.

"This part may be cited as the 'Safe and Drug-Free Schools and Communities Act.'

"SEC. 4002. PURPOSE.

"The purpose of this part is to support programs that prevent violence in and around schools; that prevent the illegal use of alcohol, tobacco, and drugs; that involve parents and communities; and that are coordinated with related Federal, State, school, and community efforts and resources to foster a safe and drug-free learning environment that supports student academic achievement, through the provision of Federal assistance to—

"(1) States for grants to local educational agencies and consortia of such agencies to establish, operate, and improve local programs of school drug and violence prevention and early intervention;

"(2) States for grants to, and contracts with, community based organizations and public and private entities for programs of drug and violence prevention and early intervention, including community-wide drug and violence prevention planning and organizing activities;

"(3) States for development, training, technical assistance, and coordination activities; and

"(4) public and private entities to provide technical assistance; conduct training, demonstrations, and evaluation; and to provide supplementary services and community-wide drug and violence prevention planning and organizing activities for the prevention of drug use and violence among students and youth.

. . .

"PART B—21ST CENTURY COMMUNITY LEARNING CENTERS

"SEC. 4201. PURPOSE; DEFINITIONS.

"(a) PURPOSE.—The purpose of this part is to provide opportunities for communities to establish or expand activities in community learning centers that—

"(1) provide opportunities for academic enrichment, including providing tutorial services to help students, particularly students who attend low-performing schools, to meet State and local student academic achievement standards in core academic subjects, such as reading and mathematics;

"(2) offer students a broad array of additional services, programs, and activities, such as youth development activities, drug and violence prevention programs, counseling programs, art, music, and recreation programs, technology education programs, and character education programs, that are designed to reinforce and complement the regular academic program of participating students; and

"(3) offer families of students served by community learning centers opportunities for literacy and related educational development.

. . .

"PART C—ENVIRONMENTAL TOBACCO SMOKE

. . .

"TITLE V—PROMOTING INFORMED PARENTAL CHOICE AND INNOVATIVE PROGRAMS

"PART A—INNOVATIVE PROGRAMS

"SEC. 5101. PURPOSES, STATE AND LOCAL RESPONSIBILITY.

"(a) PURPOSES.—The purposes of this part are the following:

"(1) To support local education reform efforts that are consistent with and support statewide education reform efforts.

"(2) To provide funding to enable State educational agencies and local educational agencies to implement promising educational reform programs and school improvement programs based on scientifically based research.

"(3) To provide a continuing source of innovation and educational improvement, including support programs to provide library services and instructional and media materials.

"(4) To meet the educational needs of all students, including at-risk youth.

"(5) To develop and implement education programs to improve school, student, and teacher performance, including professional development activities and class size reduction programs.

"(b) STATE AND LOCAL RESPONSIBILITY.—The State educational agency shall bear the basic responsibility for the administration of funds made available under this part, but it is the intent of Congress that the responsibility be carried out with a minimum of paperwork and that the responsibility for the design and implementation of programs assisted under this part be mainly that of local educational agencies, school superintendents and principals, and classroom teachers and supporting personnel, because local educational agencies and individuals have the most direct contact with students and are most likely to be able to design programs to meet the educational needs of students in their own school districts.

. . .

"PART B—PUBLIC CHARTER SCHOOLS

"Subpart 1—Charter School Programs

"SEC. 5201. PURPOSE.

"It is the purpose of this subpart to increase national understanding of the charter schools model by—

"(1) providing financial assistance for the planning, program design, and initial implementation of charter schools;

"(2) evaluating the effects of such schools, including the effects on students, student academic achievement, staff, and parents;

"(3) expanding the number of high-quality charter schools available to students across the Nation; and

"(4) encouraging the States to provide support to charter schools for facilities financing in an amount more nearly commensurate to the amount the States have typically provided for traditional public schools.

. . .

"Subpart 2—Credit Enhancement Initiatives To Assist Charter School Facility Acquisition, Construction, and Renovation

"SEC. 5221. PURPOSE.

"The purpose of this subpart is to provide grants to eligible entities to permit the eligible entities to demonstrate innovative credit enhancement initiatives that assist charter schools to address the cost of acquiring, constructing, and renovating facilities.

. . .

"Subpart 3—Voluntary Public School Choice Programs

. . .

"PART C—MAGNET SCHOOLS ASSISTANCE

"SEC. 5301. FINDINGS AND PURPOSE.

"(a) FINDINGS.—Congress makes the following findings:

"(1) Magnet schools are a significant part of the Nation's effort to achieve voluntary desegregation in our Nation's schools.

"(2) The use of magnet schools has increased dramatically since the inception of the magnet schools assistance program under this Act, with approximately 2,000,000 students nationwide attending such schools, of whom more than 65 percent are non-white.

"(3) Magnet schools offer a wide range of distinctive programs that have served as models for school improvement efforts.

"(4) It is in the best interests of the United States—

"(A) to continue the Federal Government's support of local educational agencies that are implementing court ordered desegregation plans and local educational agencies that are voluntarily seeking to foster meaningful interaction among students of different racial and ethnic backgrounds, beginning at the earliest stage of such students' education;

"(B) to ensure that all students have equitable access to a high quality education that will prepare all students to function well in a technologically oriented and a highly competitive economy comprised of people from many different racial and ethnic backgrounds; and

"(C) to continue to desegregate and diversify schools by supporting magnet schools, recognizing that segregation exists between minority and nonminority students as well as among students of different minority groups.

"(5) Desegregation efforts through magnet school programs are a significant part of our Nation's effort to achieve voluntary desegregation in schools and help to ensure equal educational opportunities for all students.

"(b) PURPOSE.—The purpose of this part is to assist in the desegregation of schools served by local educational agencies by providing financial assistance to eligible local educational agencies for—

"(1) the elimination, reduction, or prevention of minority group isolation in elementary schools and secondary schools with substantial proportions of minority students, which shall include assisting in the efforts of the United States to achieve voluntary desegregation in public schools;

"(2) the development and implementation of magnet school programs that will assist local educational agencies in achieving systemic reforms and providing all students the opportunity to meet challenging State academic content standards and student academic achievement standards;

"(3) the development and design of innovative educational methods and practices that promote diversity and increase choices in public elementary schools and public secondary schools and public educational programs;

"(4) courses of instruction within magnet schools that will substantially strengthen the knowledge of academic subjects and the attainment of tangible and marketable vocational, technological, and professional skills of students attending such schools;

"(5) improving the capacity of local educational agencies, including through professional development, to continue operating magnet schools at a high performance level after Federal funding for the magnet schools is terminated; and

"(6) ensuring that all students enrolled in the magnet school programs have equitable access to high quality education that will enable the students to succeed academically and continue with postsecondary education or productive employment.

. . .

"PART D—FUND FOR THE IMPROVEMENT OF EDUCATION

. . .

"TITLE VI—FLEXIBILITY AND ACCOUNTABILITY

. . .

"TITLE VII—INDIAN, NATIVE HAWAIIAN, AND ALASKA NATIVE EDUCATION

"PART A—INDIAN EDUCATION

"SEC. 7101. STATEMENT OF POLICY.

"It is the policy of the United States to fulfill the Federal Government's unique and continuing trust relationship with and responsibility to the Indian people for the education of Indian children. The Federal Government will continue to work with local educational agencies, Indian tribes and organizations, postsecondary institutions, and other entities toward the goal of ensuring that programs that serve Indian children are of the highest quality and provide for not only the basic elementary and secondary educational needs, but also the unique educational and culturally related academic needs of these children.

. . .

"PART B—NATIVE HAWAIIAN EDUCATION

. . .

"PART C—ALASKA NATIVE EDUCATION

. . .

TITLE VIII—IMPACT AID PROGRAM

. . .

"TITLE IX—GENERAL PROVISIONS

SOURCE: Public Law 107-110, *U.S. Statutes at Large*, 115 (2002): 1425.

ANALYSIS

The No Child Left Behind Act of 2001 (NCLBA) was actually a reauthorization of the Elementary and Secondary Education Act of 1965. It was the product of bipartisanship in Congress, as President George W. Bush's administration worked closely with prominent Democrats, most notably senator Ted Kennedy, to draft legislation that would improve the quality of education provided in the nation's schools from Kindergarten to the 12th grade. The law required any schools receiving monies from the federal government to adopt standards-based education. The specific standards to be met were established by the states. To actually receive the funding, the states also had to utilize standardized tests to measure each school's progress toward meeting the standards. Each school and district received a "report card" to show how they measured against their peers statewide. The report cards were subsequently made publicly available. In addition to standards and testing, the NCLBA called for teachers to participate in professional development to improve their pedagogical methods and their knowledge of the subject(s) that they were teaching.

The bipartisanship that resulted in the NCLBA quickly dissipated. Republicans generally viewed the act as a significant step forward since the test results nationwide suggested widespread improvement in student learning outcomes. The one concern that did emerge among some Republican constituencies was that the standards threatened the quality of education provided to the highest-achieving students since the focus of the act was elevating the lowest-achieving students, schools, and districts.

Democrats who had earlier backed the law changed course when major constituent groups like the National Education Association began to oppose many of the NCLBA's components. Among the common criticisms was that the improvements in test scores was due to teachers only teaching the content that would appear on the respective tests. The tests were thus not an accurate assessment of student learning. Another observation that was advanced was that tests were biased against minority groups and people from the lower economic and social classes. Many educators also pointed out that implementing the NCLBA negatively impacted all school districts because it contained a number of under- and unfunded mandates.

By 2009, even supporters of the NCLBA recognized that there were some issues that needed to be addressed. That year, the National Governors Association called upon a panel of experts to create a curriculum that spelled out what students needed to be taught each year in foundational subjects like English and math. The result was the Common Core State Standards. Some states decided to adopt the new standards in whole or in part. Part of the new initiative was a new testing method to gauge progress. Specific answers to narrow questions, which had been the hallmark of most of the testing regimes initially established by the states under the NCLBA, were supplanted by essay tests. It was believed that essays allowed for a more flexible and broader evaluation of student achievement. Although the adoption of the Common Core was not a requirement of the NCLBA, the federal government did encourage its adoption by offering states that utilized it additional funding for implementation. Many of the educators and professional groups that had opposed the NCLBA saw the same issues present in the Common Core. From their perspective, the Common Core prescribed to them what to teach and required tests that were biased against minorities and the poor.

Critics of the NCLBA were buttressed by data that suggested that the divide between higher- and lower-performing schools had grown wider over the course of the NCLBA's lifetime. In addition, it had become obvious that many schools around the country were not going to meet the 2014 deadline of reaching the standards that had been included in the legislation. If a school or district had failed to meet the standard by that time, punitive actions had been promised to bring them into compliance. Congress and President Barack Obama's administration ensured that the measures that were supposed to be triggered in 2014 never came to pass. In fact, by 2014 they were well into drafting the NCBLA's replacement as part of the 2015 reauthorization of the Elementary and Secondary Education Act of 1965. Signed by President Obama on December 10, 2015, the Every Student Succeeds Act not only returned authority to improve the quality of education to the local level, but also included language that barred the federal government from dictating the curriculum to be taught in the nation's schools.

FURTHER READING

Anderson, Lee W. 2007. *Congress and the Classroom: From the Cold War to "No Child Left Behind."* University Park, PA: Pennsylvania State University Press.

Hayes, William. 2008. *No Child Left Behind: Past, Present, and Future*. Lanham, MD: Rowman & Littlefield.

Hess, Frederick M, and Chester E. Finn Jr., eds. 2004. *Leaving No Child Behind? Options for Kids in Failing Schools*. New York: Palgrave Macmillan.

Jennings, Jack. 2015. *Presidents, Congress, and the Public Schools: The Politics of Education Reform*. Cambridge, MA: Harvard Education Press.

McGuinn, Patrick J. 2006. *No Child Left Behind and the Transformation of Federal Education Policy, 1965–2005*. Lawrence: University Press of Kansas.

Rebell, Michael A., and Jessica R. Wolff, eds. 2009. *NCLB at the Crossroads: Reexamining the Federal Effort to Close the Achievement Gap*. New York: Teachers College Press.

Rhodes, Jesse H. 2012. *An Education in Politics: The Origins and Evolution of No Child Left Behind*. Ithaca: Cornell University Press.

Vinovskis, Maris A. 2008. *From A Nation at Risk to No Child Left Behind: National Education Goals and the Creation of Federal Education Policy*. New York: Teachers College Press.

Zarra, Ernest J., III. 2015. *The Wrong Direction for Today's Schools: The Impact of Common Core on American Education*. Lanham, MD: Rowman & Littlefield.

"A New Optional Medicare Prescription Drug Benefit Program"

- ***Document:*** Summary of the Medicare Prescription Drug, Improvement, and Modernization Act of 2003 (Excerpt)
- ***Date:*** December 8, 2003
- ***Where:*** Washington, D.C.
- ***Significance:*** The act provided for the addition of prescription drug coverage to the Medicare program.

DOCUMENT

Medicare Prescription Drug, Improvement, and Modernization Act of 2003—**Title I: Medicare Prescription Drug Benefit** (Sec. 101) Amends title XVIII (Medicare) of the Social Security Act (SSA) to add a new part D (Voluntary Prescription Drug Benefit Program). Establishes a new optional Medicare prescription drug benefit program augmenting with a comprehensive, flexible, and permanent voluntary prescription drug benefit program the limited coverage of certain outpatient prescription drugs, biologicals, and vaccines currently covered under the Medicare program under its original fee-for-service component under both Medicare parts A (Hospital Insurance) and B (Supplementary Medical Insurance) and under its managed care, medical savings account (MSA), and private fee-for-service component under Medicare part C (Medicare+Choice).

Provides under this new prescription drug benefit program for offering eligible Medicare beneficiaries, regardless of income or health status, access to more coverage options, options which provide enhanced benefits, with cost-sharing, and additional beneficiary protections and assistance, such as access to negotiated prices, catastrophic coverage limits, and premium subsidies for certain low-income beneficiaries.

Provides for these options to be offered through both: (1) a new Medicare part C Medicare Advantage (MA) program that integrates basic medical coverage with added prescription drug coverage, including coverage through specialized MA plans for special needs individuals; and (2) a new separate, stand-alone Medicare Prescription Drug plan (PDP) program under Medicare part D that relies on private plans to provide coverage and to bear a portion of the financial risk for drug costs.

Makes this new program effective January 1, 2006.

Provides that until this new permanent prescription drug benefit program is effective, the Secretary of Health and Human Services (HHS) shall establish a program to endorse prescription drug discount card programs in order to provide access to prescription drug discounts through prescription drug card sponsors for discount card eligible individuals throughout the United States and to provide for transitional assistance for transitional assistance eligible individuals enrolled in such endorsed programs. Provides that the program shall not apply to covered discount card drugs dispensed after December 31, 2005, and transitional assistance shall be available after such date to the extent the assistance relates to drugs dispensed on or before such date.

Allows beneficiaries entitled to benefits under Medicare part A or enrolled under Medicare part B (eligible beneficiaries) to elect to enroll under new Medicare part D, and: (1) provided that they are not enrolled in an MA plan, keep their current Medicare fee-for-service coverage and receive qualified prescription drug coverage (as described below) through enrollment in Medicare part D in a new PDP that is offered in the geographic area in which the beneficiary resides; or (2) enroll in the new Medicare part C MA program in an MA plan, give up their current Medicare fee-for-service coverage, and receive qualified prescription drug coverage under the plan along with basic and possibly enhanced medical coverage through health maintenance organization (HMO) or revised MSA coverage options under the new MA program established by this Act under Medicare part C (and as otherwise provided under Medicare+Choice under Medicare part C as discussed more fully below under title II (Medicare Advantage) of this Act).

Provides an exception for MA enrollees: (1) enrolled in MSA plans to receive qualified coverage of prescription drugs through enrollment in a PDP; (2) enrolled in private-fee-for service plans that do not provide qualified prescription drug coverage to receive qualified coverage of prescription drugs through enrollment in PDP plans; and (3) enrolled in an MA prescription drug plan (MA-PD) to receive qualified prescription drug coverage under that plan.

Directs the Secretary to establish a process for the enrollment, disenrollment, termination, and change of enrollment of Medicare part D eligible individuals in prescription drug plans. Establishes an initial enrollment period beginning November 15, 2005.

Directs the Secretary to conduct activities designed to broadly disseminate information to part D eligible individuals (and prospective part D eligible individuals) regarding the coverage under Medicare part D, including information comparing the plans offered by eligible entities under Medicare part D that are available to eligible beneficiaries in an area.

Divides qualified prescription drug coverage into either a standard coverage benefit package or an alternative prescription drug coverage with at least actuarially equivalent benefits, both with access to negotiated drug prices. Outlines the standard coverage package, which includes, for 2006, a $250 deductible, 25 percent cost-sharing for drug costs between $250 and the initial coverage limit of $2,250, then no coverage; except that the beneficiary shall have access to negotiated prices, regardless of the fact that no benefits may be payable under the coverage, until incurring out-of-pocket costs for covered drugs in a year equal $3,600, with the beneficiary thereafter to pay five percent of the cost of a prescription, or a copayment of $2 for a generic drug and $5 for any other drug, whichever is greater. Includes as negotiated prices all discounts, direct or indirect subsidies, rebates, and direct or indirect remunerations. Increases these amounts in future years by the annual percentage increase in average per capita aggregate expenditures for covered drugs for the year ending the previous July.

Includes among the out-of-pocket costs counting toward the annual $3,600 limit any costs paid by the part D eligible individual (or by another person such as a family member) under the Medicaid program or under a State pharmaceutical assistance program for which the individual (or other person) is not reimbursed.

Allows a PDP or an MA plan to provide a different prescription drug benefit design from the standard prescription drug coverage as long as the Administrator of the Medicare Benefits Administration approves of such benefit design.

Directs the Secretary to ensure that each part D eligible individual has available a choice of enrollment in at least two qualifying plans in the area in which the individual resides, at least one of which is a prescription drug plan. Provides that in such case in which such plans are not available the part D eligible individual shall be given the opportunity to enroll in a fallback prescription drug plan.

Establishes beneficiary protection requirements for qualified prescription drug plans, such as requiring each PDP sponsor offering a prescription drug plan to: (1) have a mechanism for providing specific information on a timely basis to enrollees upon request; (2) have in place with respect to covered part D drugs a cost-effective drug utilization management program and a medication therapy management program; and (3) provide that each pharmacy that dispenses a covered part D drug shall inform an enrollee of any differential between the price of the drug to the enrollee and the price of the lowest priced generic covered part D drug under the plan that is therapeutically equivalent and bioequivalent and available at such pharmacy.

Directs the Secretary to establish, and allows the Secretary to revise PDP regions in a manner that is consistent with the requirements below for the establishment and revision of MA regions, and to the extent practicable PDP regions shall be the same as MA regions. Requires a PDP sponsor to submit to the Secretary bid and other described information with respect to each prescription drug plan it offers for review by the Secretary for the purpose of conducting negotiations concerning the terms and conditions of the proposed bid submitted and other terms and conditions of a proposed plan in order for the Secretary to approve or disapprove the plan. Provides that in order to promote competition under new Medicare part D and in carrying out such part, the Secretary may not interfere with the negotiations between drug manufacturers and pharmacies and PDP sponsors and may not require a particular formulary or institute a price structure for the reimbursement of covered part D drugs.

Establishes organizational requirements for PDP sponsors, such as licenses, and requires that they enter into a contract with the Secretary to be eligible to receive payments.

Provides for premium and cost-sharing subsidies for low-income subsidy-eligible individuals.

Provides: (1) for the establishment of risk corridors for each PDP that determines the amount of risk that the PDP shall be exposed to for drug spending, and the resultant adjustment in payment attributable to this risk; and (2) that a PDP sponsor and MA organization that offers a plan that provides supplemental prescription drug benefits shall be at full financial risk for the provision of such supplemental benefits. Prohibits adjustment in payments made by reason of this paragraph from affecting the monthly beneficiary premium or the MA monthly prescription drug beneficiary premium.

Creates within the Federal Supplementary Medical Insurance Trust Fund the Medicare Prescription Drug Account for payments for low-income subsidy payments, subsidy payments, payments to qualified retiree prescription drug plans, and administrative expenses. Authorizes appropriations. Requires transfers to be made to the Medicaid account for increased administrative costs. Requires amounts withheld for late penalties to be deposited into the Fund. Requires States to make payments to the Account for dual eligibles as provided for under Medicaid.

Directs the Secretary to establish requirements for PDPs to ensure the effective coordination between a part D plan and a State Pharmaceutical Assistance Program with respect to payment of premiums and coverage and payment for supplemental prescription drug benefits for part D eligible individuals enrolled under both types of plans. Requires the Secretary to apply such coordination requirements to described Rx plans, which include Medicaid programs and group health plans and the Federal Employees Health Benefit Program (FEHBP), in the same manner as such requirements apply to a State Pharmaceutical Assistance Program.

Requires the prescription drug discount program and the transitional assistance program to be implemented by the Secretary so that interim prescription drug discount cards and transitional assistance are first available by not later than six months after the enactment of this Act in 2004 and 2005 until coverage under the new part D program becomes effective on January 1, 2006. Requires each prescription drug card sponsor that offers an endorsed discount card program to provide each discount card eligible individual entitled to benefits, or enrolled, under Medicare part A (Hospital Insurance) or part B (Supplementary Medical Insurance) with access to negotiated prices and savings on prescription drugs through enrollment in an endorsed discount card program.

Allows card sponsors to charge annual enrollment fees, not to exceed $30. Requires the fee to be uniform for all discount eligible individuals enrolled in the program. Requires a prescription drug card sponsor offering an endorsed discount card program to provide that each pharmacy that dispenses a covered discount card drug shall inform a discount card eligible individual enrolled in the program of any differential between the price of the drug to the enrollee and the price of the lowest priced generic covered discount card drug under the program that is therapeutically equivalent and bioequivalent and available at such pharmacy.

Provides that a discount card eligible individual is an individual whose income is not more than 135 percent of the poverty line and who is entitled to have payment made of any annual enrollment fee and to have payment made, up to $600 in 2004, under such endorsed program of 90 percent of the costs incurred for covered discount card drugs.

Creates within the Federal Supplementary Medical Insurance Trust Fund the Transitional Assistance Account for payments for transitional assistance. Makes necessary appropriations.

SOURCE: U.S. Congress. 2003. Summary: H.R.1, 108th Congress (2003–2004). https://www.congress.gov/bill/108th-congress/house-bill/1.

ANALYSIS

From the early 1990s to 2002, prescription drug prices escalated rapidly. The increases in cost forced many impoverished individuals to do without the medicines that they required. To address the problem, Congress, with significant input from President George W. Bush's administration, crafted the Medicare Prescription Drug, Improvement, and Modernization Act of 2003 (MPDIMA). The MPDIMA created Medicare Part D, which was a voluntary prescription drug benefit for individuals enrolled in Medicare Parts A or B.

Medicare Part D was envisioned as a federally financed but state-managed program. Individual insurance companies would contract with each state to offer several plans in different price ranges to the states' residents enrolled in Medicare Parts A or B. It was anticipated that the competition between the insurers would result in lower costs for the beneficiaries. In order to help control the costs of the benefit, enrollees in stand-alone plans had to agree to an annual deductible of at least $250. After that was met, enrollees were responsible for approximately 20 percent of the cost of each medicine until they had paid another $2,000. Some of the poorest enrollees received some federal financial assistance to offset these costs.

The design of Medicare Part D reflected the political philosophy of "Compassionate Conservatism" that Bush espoused. It was compassionate in terms of caring for the less fortunate and conservative in its dependence on market forces to control the costs of the medicine. Politically, this approach resulted in criticisms from both ends of the political spectrum. Republicans from the right wing of the party were incensed by the creation of what they viewed as another expensive and unnecessary entitlement. Democrats charged that Medicare Part D was too limited. They instead pushed for legislation that would provide a prescription drug benefit to everyone in the United States. Predictably, the prescription drug benefit became an issue of contention during the 2004 presidential contest between Bush and Senator John Kerry.

FURTHER READING

Farley, Joel F., and Stacie B. Dusetzina. 2010. "Medicaid Prescription Drug Utilization and Expenditures Following Part D." *Journal of Health Care for the Poor and Underserved* 21, no. 2: 715–728.

Funigiello, Philip J. 2005. *Chronic Politics: Health Care Security from FDR to George W. Bush.* Lawrence: University Press of Kansas.

Oliver, Thomas R., Philip R. Lee, and Helene L. Lipton. 2004. "A Political History of Medicare and Prescription Drug Coverage." *The Milbank Quarterly* 82, no. 2: 285–354.

"All Americans Must Be Part of the System and Must Have Coverage"

- ***Document:*** Patient Protection and Affordable Care Act: Detailed Summary (Excerpts)
- ***Date:*** March 23, 2010
- ***Where:*** Washington, D.C.
- ***Significance:*** The Patient Protection and Affordable Care Act, derisively known as "Obamacare," enabled millions of citizens to obtain health insurance at greatly reduced costs. For many, it was the first time that they had been able to obtain an insurance plan that allowed them to address long-standing health issues.

DOCUMENT

The Patient Protection and Affordable Care Act Detailed Summary

The Patient Protection and Affordable Care Act will ensure that all Americans have access to quality, affordable health care and will create the transformation within the health care system necessary to contain costs. The Congressional Budget Office (CBO) has determined that the Patient Protection and Affordable Care Act is fully paid for, will provide coverage to more than 94% of Americans while staying under the $900 billion limit that President Obama established, bending the health care cost curve, and reducing the deficit over the next ten years and beyond.

The Patient Protection and Affordable Care Act contains nine titles, each addressing an essential component of reform:

- Quality, affordable health care for all Americans
- The role of public programs
- Improving the quality and efficiency of health care
- Prevention of chronic disease and improving public health
- Health care workforce
- Transparency and program integrity
- Improving access to innovative medical therapies
- Community living assistance services and supports
- Revenue provisions

Title I. Quality, Affordable Health Care for All Americans

The Patient Protection and Affordable Care Act will accomplish a fundamental transformation of health insurance in the United States through shared responsibility. Systemic insurance market reform will eliminate discriminatory practices such as pre-existing condition exclusions. Achieving these reforms without increasing health insurance premiums will mean that all Americans must be part of the system and must have coverage. Tax credits for individuals and families will ensure that insurance is affordable for everyone. These three elements are the essential links to achieve reform.

Immediate Improvements: Achieving health insurance reform will take some time to implement. In the immediate reforms will be implemented in 2010. The Patient Protection and Affordable Care Act will:

- Eliminate lifetime and unreasonable annual limits on benefits
- Prohibit rescissions of health insurance policies
- Provide assistance for those who are uninsured because of a pre-existing condition
- Require coverage of preventive services and immunizations
- Extend dependant coverage up to age 26
- Develop uniform coverage documents so consumers can make apples-to-apples comparisons when shopping for health insurance
- Cap insurance company non-medical, administrative expenditures
- Ensure consumers have access to an effective appeals process and provide consumer a place to turn for assistance navigating the appeals process and accessing their coverage
- Create a temporary re-insurance program to support coverage for early retirees
- Establish an internet portal to assist Americans in identifying coverage options
- Facilitate administrative simplification to lower health system costs

Health Insurance Market Reform: Beginning in 2014, more significant insurance reforms will be implemented. Across individual and small group health insurance markets in all states, new rules will end medical underwriting and pre-existing condition exclusions. Insurers will be prohibited from denying coverage or setting rates based on health status, medical condition, claims experience, genetic information, evidence of domestic violence, or other health-related factors. Premiums will vary only by family structure, geography, actuarial value, tobacco use, participation in a health promotion program, and age (by not more than three to one).

Available Coverage: A qualified health plan, to be offered through the new American Health Benefit Exchange, must provide essential health benefits which include cost sharing limits. No out-of-pocket requirements can exceed those in Health Savings Accounts, and deductibles in the small group market cannot exceed $2,000 for an individual and $4,000 for a family. Coverage will be offered at four levels with actuarial values defining how much the insurer pays: Platinum—90 percent; Gold—80 percent; Silver—70 percent; and Bronze—60 percent. A lower-benefit catastrophic plan will be offered to individuals under age 30 and to others who are exempt from the individual responsibility requirement.

American Health Benefit Exchanges: By 2014, each state will establish an Exchange to help individuals and small employers obtain coverage. Plans participating in the Exchanges will be accredited for quality, will present their benefit options in a standardized manner for easy comparison, and will use one, simple enrollment form. Individuals qualified to receive tax credits for Exchange coverage must be ineligible for affordable, employer-sponsored insurance any form of public insurance coverage. Undocumented immigrants are ineligible for premium tax credits. The Secretary of Health and Human Services (HHS) will establish a national public option—the Community Health Insurance Option—and permit states to opt-out. Federal support will also be available for new non-profit, member run insurance cooperatives. States will have flexibility to establish basic health plans for non-Medicaid, lower-income individuals; states may also seek waivers to explore other reform options; and states may form compacts with other states to permit cross-state sale of health insurance. No federal dollars may be used to pay for abortion services.

Making Coverage Affordable: New, refundable tax credits will be available for Americans with incomes between 100 and 400 percent of the federal poverty line (FPL) (about $88,000 for a family of four). The credit is calculated on a sliding scale beginning at two percent of income for those at 100 percent FPL and phasing out at 9.8 percent of income at 300–400 percent FPL. If an employer offer of coverage exceeds 9.8 percent of a worker's family income, or the employer pays less than 60 percent of the premium, the worker may enroll in the Exchange and receive credits. Out of pocket maximums ($5,950 for individuals and $11,900 for families) are reduced to one third for those with income between 100–200 percent FPL, one half for those with incomes between 200–300 percent FPL, and two thirds for those with income between 300–400 percent FPL. Credits are available for eligible citizens 3 and legally-residing aliens. A new credit will assist small businesses with fewer than 25 workers for up to 50 percent of the total premium cost.

Shared Responsibility: Beginning in 2014, most individuals will be required to maintain minimum essential coverage or pay a penalty of $95 in 2014, $350 in 2015, $750 in 2016 and indexed thereafter; for those under 18, the penalty will be one-half the amount for adults. Exceptions to this requirement are made for religious objectors, those who cannot afford coverage, taxpayers with incomes less than

100 percent FPL, Indian tribe members, those who receive a hardship waiver, individuals not lawfully present, incarcerated individuals, and those not covered for less than three months.

Any individual or family who currently has coverage and would like to retain that coverage can do so under a "grandfather" provision. This coverage is deemed to meet the requirement to have health coverage. Similarly, employers that currently offer coverage are permitted to continue offering such coverage under the "grandfather" policy.

Employers with more than 200 employees must automatically enroll new full-time employees in coverage. Any employer with more than 50 full-time employees that does not offer coverage and has at least one full-time employee receiving the premium assistance tax credit will make a payment of $750 per full-time employee. An employer with more than 50 employees that offers coverage that is deemed unaffordable or does not meet the standard for minimum essential coverage and but has at least one full-time employee receiving the premium assistance tax credit because the coverage is either unaffordable or does not cover 60 percent of total costs, will pay the lesser of $3,000 for each of those employees receiving a credit or $750 for each of their full-time employees total.

Title II. The Role of Public Programs

The Patient Protection and Affordable Care Act expands eligibility for Medicaid to lower income persons and assumes federal responsibility for much of the cost of this expansion. It provides enhanced federal support for the Children's Health Insurance Program, simplifies Medicaid and CHIP enrollment, improves Medicaid services, provides new options for long-term services and supports, improves coordination for dual-eligibles, and improves Medicaid quality for patients and providers.

Medicaid Expansion: States may expand Medicaid eligibility as early as January 1, 2011. Beginning on January 1, 2014, all children, parents and childless adults who are not entitled to Medicare and who have family incomes up to 133 percent FPL will become eligible for Medicaid. Between 2014 and 2016, the federal government will pay 100 percent of the cost of covering newly-eligible individuals. In 2017 and 2018, states that initially covered less of the newly-eligible population ("Other States") will receive more assistance than states that covered at least some non-elderly, non-pregnant adults ("Expansion States"). States will be required to maintain the same income eligibility levels through December 31, 2013 for all adults, and this requirement would be extended through September 30, 2019 for children currently in Medicaid.

Children's Health Insurance Program: States will be required to maintain income eligibility levels for CHIP through September 30, 2019. Between fiscal years 2014 and 2019, states would receive a 23 percentage point increase in the CHIP federal match rate, subject to a 100 percent cap.

Simplifying Enrollment: Individuals will be able to apply for and enroll in Medicaid, CHIP and the Exchange through state-run websites. Medicaid and CHIP programs and the Exchange will coordinate enrollment procedures to provide seamless enrollment for all programs. Hospitals will be permitted to provide Medicaid services during a period of presumptive eligibility to members of all Medicaid eligibility categories.

Community First Choice Option: A new optional Medicaid benefit is created through which states may offer community-based attendant services and supports to Medicaid beneficiaries with disabilities who would otherwise require care in a hospital, nursing facility, or intermediate care facility for the mentally retarded.

Disproportionate Share Hospital Allotments: States' disproportionate share hospital (DSH) allotments are reduced by 50 percent once a state's uninsurance rate decreases by 45 percent (low DSH states would receive a 25 percent reduction). As the rate continues to decline, states' DSH allotments would be reduced by a corresponding amount. At no time could a state's allotment be reduced by more than 65 percent compared to its FY2012 allotment.

Dual Eligible Coverage and Payment Coordination: The Secretary of Health and Human Services (HHS) will establish a Federal Coordinated Health Care Office by March 1, 2010 to integrate care under Medicare and Medicaid, and improve coordination among the federal and state governments for individuals enrolled in both programs (dual eligibles).

Title III. Improving the Quality and Efficiency of Health Care

The Patient Protection and Affordable Care Act will improve the quality and efficiency of U.S. medical care services for everyone, and especially for those enrolled in Medicare and Medicaid. Payment for services will be linked to better quality outcomes. The Patient Protection and Affordable Care Act will make substantial investments to improve the quality and delivery of care and support research to inform consumers about patient outcomes resulting from different approaches to treatment and care delivery. New patient care models will be created and disseminated. Rural patients and providers will see meaningful improvements. Payment accuracy will improve. The Medicare Part D prescription drug benefit will be enhanced and the coverage gap, or donut hole, will be reduced. An Independent Medicare Advisory Board will develop recommendations to ensure long-term fiscal stability.

. . .

Title IV: Prevention of Chronic Disease and Improving Public Health

To better orient the nation's health care system toward health promotion and disease prevention, a set of initiatives will provide the impetus and the infrastructure. A new interagency prevention council will be supported by a new Prevention and Public Health Investment Fund. Barriers to accessing clinical preventive services will be removed. Developing healthy communities will be a priority, and a 21st century public health infrastructure will support this goal.

. . .

Title V—Health Care Workforce

To ensure a vibrant, diverse and competent workforce, the Patient Protection and Affordable Care Act will encourage innovations in health workforce training, recruitment, and retention, and will establish a new workforce commission.

Provisions will help to increase the supply of health care workers. These workers will be supported by a new workforce training and education infrastructure.

. . .

Title VI—Transparency and Program Integrity

To ensure the integrity of federally financed and sponsored health programs, this Title creates new requirements to provide information to the public on the health system and promotes a newly invigorated set of requirements to combat fraud and abuse in public and private programs.

. . .

Title VII—Improving Access to Innovative Medical Therapies

Biologics Price Competition and Innovation: The Patient Protection and Affordable Care Act establishes a process under which FDA will license a biological product that is shown to be biosimilar or interchangeable with a licensed biological product, commonly referred to as a reference product. No approval of an application as either biosimilar or interchangeable is allowed until 12 years from the date on which the reference product is first approved. If FDA approves a biological product on the grounds that it is interchangeable to a reference product, HHS cannot make a determination that a second or subsequent biological product is interchangeable to that same reference product until one year after the first commercial marketing of the first interchangeable product.

More Affordable Medicines for Children and Underserved Communities: Drug discounts through the 340B program are extended to inpatient drugs and also to certain children's hospitals, cancer hospitals, critical access and sole community hospitals, and rural referral centers.

Title VIII—Community Living Assistance Services and Supports

. . .

TITLE IX—REVENUE PROVISIONS

SOURCE: Responsible Reform for the Middle Class n.d. *The Patient Protection and Affordable Care Act: Detailed Summary*. https://www.dpc.senate.gov/healthreformbill/healthbill04.pdf.

ANALYSIS

During his first 100 days in office, President Barack Obama began working with congressional leaders on a package to reform the nation's health system. One element of the plan that proved controversial was the inclusion of an individual mandate that required all citizens to obtain and keep their health insurance. This was inserted to help manage the costs of the program, as young, healthy people would pay more into the system than they would use, which would create a surplus to help pay for the services utilized by the impoverished, elderly, or the sick.

That one requirement ensured that no Republicans would cross party lines to vote for the Patient Protection and Affordable Care Act of 2010 (PPACA). Other parts of the legislation were very popular, such as a requirement that insurance companies could not deny coverage to individuals with preexisting conditions. The various pieces of the legislation were set to go into effect between 2010 and 2020. This upset many critics who observed that the parts of the legislation that were viewed favorably by the populace went into effect immediately. Those that would prove onerous, such as the requirement that everyone had to have health insurance by 2014, went into effect after Obama had stood for reelection. Despite vehement Republican opposition, the Senate passed the PPACA on December 24, 2009, by a vote of 60 to 39. The House of Representatives approved the Senate's version of the bill 219 to 212 on March 21, 2010. President Barack Obama held the signing ceremony two days later.

In every midterm or presidential election to 2016, Republicans used their opposition to the implementation of Obamacare as a means to encourage their political base to vote. This tactic resulted in more than 40 unsuccessful, but symbolic, votes to repeal the PPACA. The real threats to the PPACA's future during the Obama administration came through the court system. From March 26 to 28, 2012, the U.S. Supreme Court heard challenges to the PPACA emerging from the cases *National Federation of Independent Businesses v. Sebelius*, *Florida v. United States Department of Health and Human Services*, and *United States Department of Health and Human Services v. Florida*. Although the cases differed on key points, the hope of conservative activists was that the PPACA would be ruled unconstitutional. On that point, the Supreme Court ruled in a June 28, 2012 opinion authored by Chief Justice John Roberts that the law was in fact constitutional. Despite the Supreme Court's 5–4 decision, legal challenges to the PPACA continued through the end of Obama's presidency.

FURTHER READING

Altman, Stuart H., and David Shactman. 2011. *Power, Politics, and Universal Health Care: The Inside Story of a Century-Long Battle*. New York: Prometheus Books.

Béland, Daniel, Philip Rocco, and Alex Waddan. 2016. *Obamacare Wars: Federalism, State Politics, and the Affordable Care Act*. Lawrence: University Press of Kansas.

Cooper, Richard. 2016. *Poverty and the Myths of Health Care Reform*. Baltimore: Johns Hopkins University Press.

Dawes, Daniel E. 2016. *150 Years of Obamacare*. Baltimore: Johns Hopkins University Press.

Jenkins, Jeffery A., and Sidney M. Milkis, eds. 2014. *The Politics of Major Policy Reform in Postwar America*. New York: Cambridge University Press.

Keller, Morton. 2015. *Obama's Time: A History*. New York: Oxford University Press.

Kinney, Eleanor D. 2015. *The Affordable Care Act and Medicare in Comparative Context*. New York: Cambridge University Press.

"Pay Workers a Living Wage"

- ***Document:*** S.1832—Pay Workers a Living Wage Act
- ***Date:*** July 22, 2015
- ***Where:*** Washington, D.C.
- ***Significance:*** The Living Wage Act was the centerpiece of senator Bernard "Bernie" Sanders's campaign for the Democratic Party's nomination for the presidency in 2016.

DOCUMENT

A BILL

To provide for increases in the Federal minimum wage.

Be it enacted by the Senate and House of Representatives of the United States of America in Congress assembled,

SECTION 1. SHORT TITLE.

This Act may be cited as the "Pay Workers a Living Wage Act."

SEC. 2. MINIMUM WAGE INCREASES.

(a) MINIMUM WAGE.—

(1) IN GENERAL.—Section 6(a)(1) of the Fair Labor Standards Act of 1938 (29 U.S.C. 206(a)(1)) is amended to read as follows:

(1) except as otherwise provided in this section, not less than—

"(A) $9.00 an hour, beginning on January 1, 2016, or the first day of the third month that begins after the date of enactment of the Pay Workers a Living Wage Act, whichever date is later;

"(B) $10.50 an hour, beginning 1 year after the date the wage specified in subparagraph (A) takes effect;

"(C) $12.00 an hour, beginning 2 years after such date;

"(D) $13.50 an hour, beginning 3 years after such date;

"(E) $15.00 an hour, beginning 4 years after such date; and

"(F) beginning on the date that is 5 years after such date, and annually thereafter, the amount determined by the Secretary pursuant to subsection (h)";

(2) DETERMINATION BASED ON INCREASE IN THE MEDIAN HOURLY WAGE OF ALL EMPLOYEES.— Section 6 of the Fair Labor Standards Act of 1938 (29 U.S.C. 206) is amended by adding at the end the following:

"(h)(1) Each year, by not later than the date that is 90 days before a new minimum wage determined under subsection (a)(1)(F) is to take effect, the Secretary shall determine the minimum wage to be in effect pursuant to this subsection for each period described in subsection (a)(1)(F). The wage determined pursuant to this subsection for a year shall be—

"(A) not less than the amount in effect under subsection (a)(1) on the date of such determination;

"(B) increased from such amount by the annual percentage increase in the median hourly wage of all employees, as determined by the Bureau of Labor Statistics; and

"(C) rounded to the nearest multiple of $0.05."

(2) In calculating the annual percentage increase in the median hourly wage of all employees for purposes of paragraph (1)(B), the Secretary through the Bureau of Labor Statistics shall compile data on the hourly wages of all employees to determine such a median hourly wage and compare such median hourly wage for the most recent year for which data are available with the median hourly wage determined for the preceding year."

(b) BASE MINIMUM WAGE FOR TIPPED EMPLOYEES.— Section 3(m)(1) of the Fair Labor Standards Act of 1938 (29 U.S.C. 203(m)(1)) is amended to read as follows:

"(1) the cash wage paid such employee, which for purposes of such determination shall be not less than—

"(A) for the 1-year period beginning on January 1, 2016, or the first day of the third month that begins after the date of enactment of the Pay Workers a Living Wage Act, whichever date is later, $3.15 an hour;

"(B) for each succeeding 1-year period until the hourly wage under this paragraph equals the wage in effect under section 6(a)(1) for such period, an hourly wage equal to the amount determined under this paragraph for the preceding year, increased by the lesser of—

"(i) $1.50; or

"(ii) the amount necessary for the wage in effect under this paragraph to equal the wage in effect under section 6(a)(1) for such period, rounded to the nearest multiple of $0.05; and

"(C) for each succeeding 1-year period after the year in which the hourly wage under this paragraph first equals the wage in effect under section 6(a)(1) for the same period, the amount necessary to ensure that the wage in effect under this paragraph remains equal to the wage in effect under section 6(a)(1), rounded to the nearest multiple of $0.05; and."

(c) TIPS RETAINED BY EMPLOYEES.—Section 3(m) of the Fair Labor Standards Act of 1938 (29 U.S.C. 203(m)) is amended—

(1) in the second sentence of the matter following paragraph (2), by striking "of this subsection, and all tips received by such employee have been retained by the employee" and inserting "of this subsection. Any employee shall have the right to retain any tips received by such employee"; and

(2) by adding at the end the following: "An employer shall inform each employee of the right and exception provided under the preceding sentence."

(d) SCHEDULED REPEAL OF SEPARATE MINIMUM WAGE FOR TIPPED EMPLOYEES.—

(1) TIPPED EMPLOYEES.—Effective on the date described in paragraph (3), section 3(m) of the Fair Labor Standards Act of 1938 (29 U.S.C. 203(m)), as amended by subsections (b) and (c), is amended by striking the sentence beginning with "In determining the wage an employer is required to pay a tipped employee," and all that follows through "of this subsection." and inserting "The wage required to be paid to a tipped employee shall be the wage set forth in section 6(a)(1)."

(2) PUBLICATION OF NOTICE.—Effective on the date described in paragraph (3), section 6(i)(2) of the Fair Labor Standards Act of 1938 (29 U.S.C. 206(i)(2)), as added by subsection (f), is amended—

(A) in subparagraph (A), by inserting "or" after the semicolon;

(B) by striking subparagraph (B); and

(C) by redesignating subparagraph (C) as subparagraph (B).

(3) EFFECTIVE DATE.—The amendments made by paragraphs (1) and (2) shall take effect on the date that is one day after the date on which the hourly wage under

section 3(m)(1)(C) of the Fair Labor Standards Act of 1938 (29 U.S.C. 19 203(m)(1)(C)) takes effect.

(e) YOUTH MINIMUM WAGE.—Section (6)(g)(1) of the Fair Labor Standards Act of 1938 (29 U.S.C. 206(g)(1)) is amended by striking "a wage which is not less than $4.25 an hour and inserting "a wage at a ratc that is not less than the rate prescribed by subsection 25 (a)(1), reduced by $3.00 per hour."

(f) PUBLICATION OF NOTICE.—Section 6 of the Fair Labor Standards Act of 1938 (as amended by subsections (a) and (e)) (29 U.S.C. 206) is further amended by adding at the end the following":

(i)(1) Not later than 60 days prior to the effective date of any adjusted required wage, the Secretary shall publish in the Federal Register and on the website of the Department of Labor a notice announcing the amount of the adjusted required wage.

"(2) In this subsection, the term 'adjusted required wage' means any increase in the minimum wage that is—

"(A) determined under subsection (h);

"(B) required for tipped employees in accordance with subparagraph (B) or (C) of section 3(m)(1) (as applicable); or

"(C) required for employees who have not attained the age of 20 years in accordance with subsection (g)."

(g) EFFECTIVE DATE.—The amendments made by subsections (a), (b), and (f) shall take effect on January 21 1, 2016, or the first day of the third month that begins after the date of enactment of this Act, whichever date is later.

SOURCE: Sanders, Bernard. 2015. *A Bill to Provide for Increases in the Federal Minimum Wage*. http://www.sanders.senate.gov/download/pay-workers-a-living-wage-act?inline=file.

ANALYSIS

During President Barack Obama's presidency, members of the Democratic Party's progressive wing had been calling for the establishment of a living wage. This was a wage that allowed the recipient to be able to afford decent housing and other necessities of life. A living wage was preferred over the traditional minimum wage because, historically, the value of the minimum wage tended to be outpaced by the growth of the cost of living. The progressives pointed to cities, such as New York, New York, and San Francisco, California, where the minimum wage did not allow its recipients to be able to afford to live in the communities where they worked. A living wage would remedy that problem. Within the halls of Congress, proponents of the living wage found its passage impossible due to the Republican Party majority in the U.S. Senate. On the campaign trail, it proved an effective cause to campaign on. Its popularity nearly propelled senator Bernie Sanders to an upset over his opponent for the Democratic Party's presidential nomination, former secretary of state Hillary Clinton. Upon surviving Sanders's challenge, she subsequently adopted a form of the living wage for her unsuccessful campaign against Donald Trump. Although proponents for a living wage saw their fortunes fall as a result of the 2016 election cycle, progressives continue to push for its enactment. Some big cities, most notably New York, New York, and Portland, Oregon, have enacted local living wage laws rather than waiting for federal authorities to act.

FURTHER READING

Putnam, Robert D. 2015. *Our Kids: The American Dream in Crisis*. New York: Simon & Schuster.

Rossi, Michele M., and Karen A. Curtis. 2013. "Aiming at Half of the Target: An Argument to Replace Poverty Thresholds with Self-Sufficiency, or 'Living Wage' Standards." *Journal of Poverty* 17, no. 1: 110–130.

Schumaker, Paul, and Marisa J. Kelly. 2013. "The Public Assistance Policies of Cities and the Justice Concerns of Elected Officials: The Centrality of the Floors Principle in Addressing Urban Poverty." *Policy Studies Journal* 41, no. 1: 70–96.

Sosnaud, Benjamin. 2016. "Living Wage Ordinances and Wages, Poverty, and Unemployment in U.S. Cities." *Social Service Review* 90, no. 1: 3–34.

Swarts, Heidi, and Ion Bogdan Vasi. 2011. "Which U.S. Cities Adopt Living Wage Ordinances? Predictors of Adoption of a New Labor Tactic, 1994–2006." *Urban Affairs Review* 47, no. 6: 743–774.

"To Seek the Prompt Repeal of the Patient Protection and Affordable Care Act"

- ***Document:*** Executive Order Minimizing the Economic Burden of the Patient Protection and Affordable Care Act Pending Repeal
- ***Date:*** January 20, 2017
- ***Where:*** Washington, D.C.
- ***Significance:*** President Donald Trump's executive order was the symbolic first step in his administration's campaign to repeal the Patient Protection and Affordable Care Act of 2010.

DOCUMENT

By the authority vested in me as President by the Constitution and the laws of the United States of America, it is hereby ordered as follows:

Section 1. It is the policy of my Administration to seek the prompt repeal of the Patient Protection and Affordable Care Act (Public Law 111-148), as amended (the "Act"). In the meantime, pending such repeal, it is imperative for the executive branch to ensure that the law is being efficiently implemented, take all actions consistent with law to minimize the unwarranted economic and regulatory burdens of the Act, and prepare to afford the States more flexibility and control to create a more free and open healthcare market.

Sec. 2. To the maximum extent permitted by law, the Secretary of Health and Human Services (Secretary) and the heads of all other executive departments and agencies (agencies) with authorities and responsibilities under the Act shall exercise all authority and discretion available to them to waive, defer, grant exemptions from, or delay the implementation of any provision or requirement of the Act that would impose a fiscal burden on any State or a cost, fee, tax, penalty, or regulatory

DID YOU KNOW?

The Health Care Freedom Act of 2017

The Health Care Freedom Act was unveiled in the Senate on July 27, 2017 just hours before it was to be put to a final vote. Known as the "Skinny Repeal," it promised to eliminate parts of the Patient Protection and Affordable Care Act of 2010 (PPACA), most notably the individual mandate that assessed a financial penalty to people who did not acquire a federally approved health insurance plan. For the Republicans, it was a face-saving move as they had failed to pass much more comprehensive legislation repealing "Obamacare." Although Senators Susan Collins and Lisa Murkowski had announced that they would be joining all of the Democrats in voting no, Republican leaders felt confident that the rest of the caucus would support the repeal. With the votes of the rest of the caucus, all that was required for passage was the tie-breaking vote from Vice President Mike Pence. The one senator who had not signaled his intentions was John McCain, who had just had surgery for a cancerous tumor in his brain. Recognizing the importance of the vote, he had postponed radiation and chemotherapy to be in Washington, D.C. He dramatically cast a no vote, which preserved the PPACA and dealt a major political defeat to both Mitch McConnell, majority leader of the Senate, and President Donald Trump.

burden on individuals, families, healthcare providers, health insurers, patients, recipients of healthcare services, purchasers of health insurance, or makers of medical devices, products, or medications.

Sec. 3. To the maximum extent permitted by law, the Secretary and the heads of all other executive departments and agencies with authorities and responsibilities under the Act, shall exercise all authority and discretion available to them to provide greater flexibility to States and cooperate with them in implementing healthcare programs.

Sec. 4. To the maximum extent permitted by law, the head of each department or agency with responsibilities relating to healthcare or health insurance shall encourage the development of a free and open market in interstate commerce for the offering of healthcare services and health insurance, with the goal of achieving and preserving maximum options for patients and consumers.

Sec. 5. To the extent that carrying out the directives in this order would require revision of regulations issued through notice-and-comment rulemaking, the heads of agencies shall comply with the Administrative Procedure Act and other applicable statutes in considering or promulgating such regulatory revisions.

Sec. 6. (a) Nothing in this order shall be construed to impair or otherwise affect:

(i) the authority granted by law to an executive department or agency, or the head thereof; or

(ii) the functions of the Director of the Office of Management and Budget relating to budgetary, administrative, or legislative proposals.

(b) This order shall be implemented consistent with applicable law and subject to the availability of appropriations.

(c) This order is not intended to, and does not, create any right or benefit, substantive or procedural, enforceable at law or in equity by any party against the United States, its departments, agencies, or entities, its officers, employees, or agents, or any other person.

DONALD J. TRUMP

THE WHITE HOUSE,
January 20, 2017.

SOURCE: Trump, Donald J. 2017. *Executive Order Minimizing the Economic Burden of the Patient Protection and Affordable Care Act Pending Repeal.* Executive Order 13765. 82 Federal Reserve 8351, January 24, 2017.

ANALYSIS

Since the passage of the Patient Protection and Affordable Care Act of 2010 (PPACA), better known as "Obamacare," Republicans had been using its repeal as a campaign issue. In order to curry favor with the party, Donald Trump pledged to make the repeal of the act a priority should he become president. Upon assuming office, Trump made good on his promise through his symbolic Executive Order Minimizing the Economic Burden of the Patient Protection and Affordable Care Act Pending Repeal. While the order did not immediately undo the PPACA, it did signal its demise. A much more direct attack on the act was Trump's selection of Representative Tom Price to serve as Secretary of Health and Human Services, the department responsible for the oversight of the PPACA. While serving in the House of Representatives, Price sponsored the Empowering Patients First Act of 2015, which called for the eradication of the PPACA.

The repeal of the PPACA proved to be much more politically controversial than anticipated. While it was easy to use as a campaign issue, actually taking health insurance from approximately 14 million Americans caused a number of problems. This was especially true since many of those poised to lose their insurance were the very voters who put Trump into office. Whether it was poor messaging by President Barack Obama's administration or great obfuscation by Republicans, many Americans did not realize that the PPACA and Obamacare were the same thing. Many voters who depended on the PPACA for their health care and that of their families thus went to the polls and voted to rid the nation of Obamacare. Upon discovering that their vote was going to deny them health care coverage, they called on their representatives in Congress to protect their health insurance. The resulting morass compounded problems in Congress as those who were trying to rescind the PPACA did not have an alternative plan in place. A number of plans were being circulated by prominent Republicans, such as senator Rand Paul, but consensus did not quickly coalesce around any of the plans. Democrats in Congress argued that the country would be better served by preserving the PPACA in its present form. The political contest between Republicans and Democrats over the replacement of the PPACA promises to shape the midterm elections in 2018.

FURTHER READING

Béland, Daniel, Philip Rocco, and Alex Waddan. 2016. *Obamacare Wars: Federalism, State Politics, and the Affordable Care Act*. Lawrence: University Press of Kansas.

Dawes, Daniel E. 2016. *150 Years of Obamacare*. Baltimore: Johns Hopkins University Press.

Keller, Morton. 2015. *Obama's Time: A History*. New York: Oxford University Press.

Kinney, Eleanor D. 2015. *The Affordable Care Act and Medicare in Comparative Context*. New York: Cambridge University Press.

CHRONOLOGY

1824 In the Yates Report, New York's secretary of state calls for each county to establish poorhouses for the "worthy poor."

1830 The Indian Removal Act is passed. It is used by President Andrew Jackson to force most of the American Indian groups east of the Mississippi River to relocate to Indian Territory.

1848 Pennsylvania passes a minimum-age law in order to discourage the hiring of children in textile industries.

1862 The Pension Act of 1862 provides benefits to Union soldiers who are disabled while fighting in the Civil War. If the soldier dies, the benefits will go to his widow or surviving children up to their 16th birthday.

The Homestead Act allows a head of household over the age of 21 or more to claim a plot of land in the West 160 acres in size for $1.25 per acre plus a filing fee. Those desiring a smaller plot can buy 80 acres for $2.50 an acre plus the filing fee.

1865 The Freedmen's Bureau is established within the War Department to assist former slaves in their transition to life as free men and women.

1882 The Immigration Act of 1882 is intended to generate revenue to pay for inspectors to examine immigrants in order to determine if they are fit to enter the United States.

1888 Congress passes the General Allotment Act, better known as the Dawes Act, to allow American Indians to own a plot of land on their tribes' reservation. Ownership means they can sell their property to non-Indians.

1889 Hull House, a settlement school in Chicago, Illinois, opens. It provides services to immigrants, the working class, and the poor.

1890 Jacob Riis's book *How the Other Half Lives* introduces the populace to the horrid living conditions endured by the poor living in New York City's Lower East Side tenement houses.

1899 The first juvenile court in the nation is created in Cook County, Illinois.

1912 Massachusetts becomes the first state to mandate a minimum wage for women and children.

The U.S. Children's Bureau is created as part of the Department of Labor.

1921 The Sheppard-Towner Maternity and Infancy Act of 1921 is one of the first welfare programs initiated by the federal government.

1933 Among the achievements of President Franklin Delano Roosevelt's first 100 days in office are the Agricultural Adjustment Act, Civilian Conservation Corps, Federal Emergency Relief Act, and the Tennessee Valley Authority Act.

1935 The Social Security Act establishes the Social Security Board, which is charged with the provision of old-age insurance, payments to the unemployed, assisting with the care of the blind and the homeless, and providing aid to crippled and delinquent children.

1938 The Fair Labor Standards Act requires businesses engaged in interstate commerce to pay a minimum wage and to follow prescribed limits on the number of hours an employee can work in a given week.

1944 The Servicemen's Readjustment Act, also known as the G.I. Bill, provides World War II veterans benefits at government expense, which allows them to gain a higher or vocational education and obtain loan guarantees to purchase a home.

1946 The Hospital Survey and Construction Act, also known as the Hill-Burton Act, helps construct medical facilities in rural areas and is used to modernize existing hospitals.

The National School Lunch Act allows for some schools to begin providing a nutritious meal for pupils. The program allows individual schools to make their own determination on who can receive free or reduced lunches. In practice, this means some poor children go hungry, while their more affluent counterparts receive free meals.

1949 The Housing Act enables some individuals to acquire nice homes. It also succeeds in concentrating the urban poor in high-rise slums.

1953 House Concurrent Resolution 108 makes it the policy of the United States to withdraw all federal support to American Indian groups in order to force their members to leave their reservation and assimilate into the general population of the United States.

1964 In his January 8 State of the Union address, President Lyndon B. Johnson declares "unconditional war" on poverty.

Title VII of the Civil Rights Act makes it illegal to discriminate against federal employees on the basis of race, color, religion, sex, or national origin.

1965 The Social Security Amendments create Medicare and Medicaid.

1966 The Child Nutrition Act expands the school lunch program. It also takes the responsibility for determining eligibility for reduced and free lunches away from local officials.

1975 Recognizing that federal actions have done severe damage to American Indians, the Indian Self-Determination and Education Act allows the secretary of the interior to transfer decision-making authority from the Bureau of Indian Affairs to sovereign Indian nations.

The Tax Reduction Act creates the earned income tax credit.

1979 The Food Stamp Act makes food stamps free to all who qualify to receive them.

1986 The Emergency Medical Treatment and Active Labor Act requires all hospitals receiving monies from Medicare to treat all patients in need of emergency care regardless of their ability to pay.

1987 The Stewart B. McKinney Homeless Assistance Act provides federal funds to non-profit organizations and government agencies at the state or local level to assist the homeless.

1996 On August 22, President William "Bill" Clinton signs the Personal Responsibility and Work Opportunity Act of 1996. In doing so, he keeps his 1992 campaign promise to "end welfare as we know it."

2002 The No Child Left Behind Act requires schools receiving federal funding to adopt standards-based education.

2003 President George W. Bush's administration with the support of key Democrats in Congress crafts the Medicare Prescription Drug, Improvement, and Modernization Act. It creates an optional prescription drug benefit for individuals enrolled in Medicare Parts A or B.

2008 From January 2008 to June 2010, the United States is mired in the Great Recession.

2010 On March 23, the Patient Protection and Affordable Care Act is signed into law. Also known as Obamacare, it enables millions of citizens to obtain health insurance at a greatly reduced cost.

BIBLIOGRAPHY

Abu-Lughod, Janet L. 2007. *Race, Space, and Riots in Chicago, New York, and Los Angeles.* New York: Oxford University Press.

Ackerman, Bruce. 2014. *We the People, Volume 3: The Civil Rights Revolution.* Cambridge: Belknap Press of Harvard University Press.

Aldous, Joan. 1997. "The Political Process and the Failure of the Child Labor Amendment." *Journal of Family Issues* 18, no. 1: 71–91.

Altman, Stuart H., and David Shactman. 2011. *Power, Politics, and Universal Health Care: The Inside Story of a Century-Long Battle.* New York: Prometheus Books.

Ambrose, Stephen E. 1989. *Nixon: The Triumph of a Politician 1962–1972.* New York: Simon & Schuster.

Anderson, Hannah L. 2011. "That Settles It: The Debate and Consequences of the Homestead Act of 1862." *The History Teacher* 45, no. 1: 117–137.

Anderson, Lee W. 2007. *Congress and the Classroom: From the Cold War to "No Child Left Behind."* University Park, PA: Pennsylvania State University Press.

Ashmore, Susan Youngblood. 2008. *Carry It On: The War on Poverty and the Civil Rights Movement in Alabama, 1964–1972.* Athens, GA: University of Georgia Press.

Banner, Stuart. 2005. *How the Indians Lost Their Land: Law and Power on the Frontier.* Cambridge, MA: Belknap Press of Harvard University Press.

Barnhart, Bill, and Gene Schlickman. 1999. *Kerner: The Conflict of Intangible Rights.* Champaign: University of Illinois Press.

Baynton, Douglas C. 2016. "Defectives in the Land: Disability and American Immigration Policy, 1882–1924." *Journal of American Ethnic History* 24, no. 3: 31–44.

Beck, David R. M. 2005. *The Struggle for Self-Determination: History of the Menominee Indians since 1854.* Lincoln: University of Nebraska Press, 2005.

Béland, Daniel. 2005. *Social Security: History and Politics from the New Deal to the Privatization Debate.* Lawrence: University Press of Kansas.

Berkowitz, Edward D., and Larry DeWitt. 2013. *The Other Welfare: Supplemental Security Income and U.S. Social Policy.* Ithaca, NY: Cornell University Press.

Bertram, Eva. 2015. *The Workfare State: Public Assistance Politics from the New Deal to the New Democrats.* Philadelphia: University of Pennsylvania Press.

Biles, Roger. 2011. *The Fate of Cities: Urban America and the Federal Government, 1945–2000.* Lawrence: University Press of Kansas.

Bothmer, Bernard von. 2010. *Framing the Sixties: The Use and Abuse of a Decade from Ronald Reagan to George W. Bush*. Amherst: University of Massachusetts Press.

Boulton, Mark. 2014. *Failing Our Veterans: The G.I. Bill and the Vietnam Generation*. New York: New York University Press.

Bowes, John P. 2016. *Land Too Good for Indians: Northern Indian Removal*. Norman: University of Oklahoma Press.

Brown, Thomas J. 1998. *Dorothea Dix: New England Reformer*. Cambridge, MA: Harvard University Press.

Brown, Victoria Bissell. 2003. *The Education of Jane Addams*. Philadelphia: University of Pennsylvania Press.

Burch, John Russell, Jr. 2017. *The Great Society and the War on Poverty: An Economic Legacy in Essays and Documents*. Santa Barbara: Greenwood.

Burch, John Russell, Jr. 2008. *Owsley County, Kentucky, and the Perpetuation of Poverty*. Jefferson, NC: McFarland & Co.

Cave, Alfred A. 2003. "Abuse of Power: Andrew Jackson and the Indian Removal Act of 1830." *The Historian* 65, no. 6: 1330–1353.

Chappell, Marisa. 2010. *The War on Welfare: Family, Poverty, and Politics in Modern America*. Philadelphia: University of Pennsylvania Press.

Chilman, Catherine S. 1992. "Welfare Reform or Revision? The Family Support Act of 1988." *Social Service Review* 66, no. 3: 349–377.

Cimbala, Paul A., and Randall M. Miller, eds. 1999. *The Freedmen's Bureau and Reconstruction*. New York: Fordham University Press.

Clapp, Elizabeth J. 1998. *Mothers of All Children: Women Reformers and the Rise of Juvenile Courts in Progressive Era America*. University Park, PA: Penn State University Press.

Cohen, Alan B., et al., eds. 2015. *Medicare and Medicaid at 50: America's Entitlement Programs in the Age of Affordable Care*. New York: Oxford University Press.

Cole, Olen. 1999. *The African-American Experience in the Civilian Conservation Corps*. Gainesville: University Press of Florida.

Conn, Steven. 2014. *Americans against the City: Anti-Urbanism in the Twentieth Century*. New York: Oxford University Press.

Cooper, Richard. 2016. *Poverty and the Myths of Health Care Reform*. Baltimore: Johns Hopkins University Press.

Cunningham, Sean P. 2014. *American Politics in the Postwar Sunbelt: Conservative Growth in a Battleground Region*. New York: Cambridge University Press.

Cutter, Barbara. 2003. *Domestic Devils, Battlefield Angels: The Radicalism of American Womanhood, 1830–1865*. DeKalb, IL: Northern Illinois University Press.

Dahlquist, Amanda. 2013. "Legislating Motherhood: The History of Mothers' Aid in Montgomery County." *Journal of the Illinois State Historical Society* 106, no. 1: 129–154.

Daniels, Roger. 2015. *Franklin D. Roosevelt: Road to the New Deal, 1882–1939*. Champaign: University of Illinois Press.

David, Sheri I. 1985. *With Dignity: The Search for Medicare and Medicaid*. Westport, CT: Greenwood Press.

Davis, Martha F. 1993. *Brutal Need: Lawyers and the Welfare Rights Movement, 1960–1973*. New Haven, CT: Yale University Press.

Dawes, Daniel E. 2016. *150 Years of Obamacare*. Baltimore: Johns Hopkins University Press.

Day, Jared N. 1999. *Urban Castles: Tenement Housing and Landlord Activism in New York City, 1890–1943*. New York: Columbia University Press.

Deegan, Mary Jo. 1988. *Jane Addams and the Men of the Chicago School, 1892–1918*. New Brunswick, NJ: Transaction Publishers.

Dolkart, Andrew S. 2012. *Biography of a Tenement House in New York City: An Architectural History of 97 Orchard Street*, 2nd ed. Charlottesville: University of Virginia Press.

Domhoff, G. William, and Michael J. Webber. 2011. *Class and Power in the New Deal: Corporate Moderates, Southern Democrats, and the Liberal–Labor Coalition*. Palo Alto, CA: Stanford University Press.

Ellen, Ingrid Gould, and Brendan O'Flaherty, eds. 2010. *How to House the Homeless*. New York: Russell Sage Foundation.

Eller, Ronald D. 2008. *Uneven Ground: Appalachia since 1945*. Lexington: University Press of Kentucky.

Elshtain, Jean Bethke. 2001. *Jane Addams and the Dream of American Democracy: A Life*. New York: Basic Books.

Elshtain, Jean Bethke. 2002. *The Jane Addams Reader*. New York: Basic Books.

Epstein, William M. 2017. *The Masses Are the Ruling Classes: Policy Romanticism, Democratic Populism, and American Social Welfare*. New York: Oxford University Press.

Farley, Joel F., and Stacie B. Dusetzina. 2010. "Medicaid Prescription Drug Utilization and Expenditures Following Part D." *Journal of Health Care for the Poor and Underserved* 21, no. 2: 715–728.

Farmer-Kaiser, Mary. 2010. *Freedwomen and the Freedmen's Bureau: Race, Gender, and Public Policy in the Age of Emancipation*. New York: Fordham University Press.

Faulkner, Carol. 2003. *Women's Radical Reconstruction: The Freedmen's Aid Movement*. Philadelphia: University of Pennsylvania Press.

Finley, Keith M. 2008. *Delaying the Dream: Southern Senators and the Fight against Civil Rights, 1938–1965*. Baton Rouge: Louisiana State University Press.

Fisher, Gordon M. 2008. "Remembering Mollie Orshansky—The Developer of Poverty Thresholds." *Social Security Bulletin* 68, no. 3: 79–83.

Fisher, Louis. 2016. *Congress: Protecting Individual Rights*. Lawrence: University Press of Kansas.

Fixico, Donald L. 1986. *Termination and Relocation: Federal Indian Policy, 1945–1960*. Albuquerque: University of New Mexico Press.

Flamm, Michael W. 2005. *Law and Order: Street Crime, Civil Unrest, and the Crisis of Liberalism in the 1960s*. New York: Columbia University Press.

Fleck, Robert K. 2002. "Democratic Opposition to the Fair Labor Standards Act of 1938." *Journal of Economic History* 62, no. 1: 25–54.

Foglesong, Richard E. 1986. *Planning the Capitalist City: The Colonial Era to the 1920s*. Princeton: Princeton University Press.

Foner, Eric. 1988. *Reconstruction 1863–1877: America's Unfinished Revolution*. New York: Harper & Row.

Frydl, Kathleen J. 2009. *The G.I. Bill*. New York: Cambridge University Press.

Funigiello, Philip J. 2005. *Chronic Politics: Health Care Security from FDR to George W. Bush*. Lawrence: University Press of Kansas.

Gandal, Keith. 1997. *The Virtues of the Vicious: Jacob Riis, Stephen Crane, and the Spectacle of the Slum*. New York: Oxford University Press.

Garrison, Tim Alan. 2002. *The Legal Ideology of Removal: The Southern Judiciary and the Sovereignty of Native American Nations*. Athens: University of Georgia Press.

Genetin-Pilawa, C. Joseph. 2012. *Crooked Paths to Allotment: The Fight over Federal Indian Policy after the Civil War*. Chapel Hill: University of North Carolina Press.

Getis, Victoria. 2000. *The Juvenile Court and the Progressives*. Urbana: University of Illinois Press.

Gillette, Michael L. 2010. *Launching the War on Poverty: An Oral History*, 2nd ed. New York: Oxford University Press.

Gillon, Steven M. 2018. *Separate and Unequal: The Kerner Commission and the Unraveling of American Liberalism*. New York: Basic Books.

Golay, Michael. 2013. *America 1933: The Great Depression, Lorena Hickok, Eleanor Roosevelt, and the Shaping of the New Deal*. New York: Free Press.

Goldberg, Vicki. 1999. *Lewis W. Hine: Children at Work*. New York: Prestel.

Goldstein, Alyosha. 2012. *Poverty in Common: The Politics of Community Action during the American Century*. Durham: Duke University Press.

Gollaher, David. 1995. *Voice for the Mad: The Life of Dorothea Dix*. New York: Free Press.

Goodwin, Joanne. 1997. *Gender and the Politics of Welfare Reform: Mothers' Pension in Chicago, 1911–1929*. Chicago: University of Illinois Press.

Green, James N. 1985. *Mathew Carey, Publisher and Patriot*. Philadelphia: Library Company of Philadelphia.

Greenwald, Emily. 2002. *Reconfiguring the Reservation: The Nez Percés, Jicarilla Apaches, and the Dawes Act*. Albuquerque: University of New Mexico Press.

Gundersen, Craig, and James P. Ziliak. 2014. "Childhood Food Insecurity in the U.S.: Trends, Causes, and Policy Options." *The Future of Children* 24, Research Report, Fall: 1–19.

Halpern-Meekin, Sarah, et al. 2015. *It's Not Like I'm Poor: How Working Families Make Ends Meet in a Post-Welfare World*. Berkeley: University of California Press.

Hamington, Maurice. 2009. *The Social Philosophy of Jane Addams*. Champaign: University of Illinois Press.

Hannon, Joan Underhill. 1984. "Poverty in the Antebellum Northeast: The View from New York State's Poor Relief Rolls." *Journal of Economic History* 44, no. 4: 1007–1032.

Hanson, Kenneth. "Mollie Orshansky's Strategy to Poverty Measurement as a Relationship between Household Food Expenditures and Economy Food Plan." *Review of Agricultural Economics* 30: 572–580.

Hart, Vivien. 1994. *Bound by Our Constitution: Women, Workers, and the Minimum Wage*. Princeton, NJ: Princeton University Press.

Haveman, Christopher D. 2016. *Rivers of Sand: Creek Indian Emigration, Relocation, and Ethnic Cleansing in the American South*. Lincoln: University of Nebraska Press.

Hays, R. Allen. 2012. *The Federal Government & Urban Housing*, 3rd ed. Albany, NY: SUNY Press.

Hayes, William. 2008. *No Child Left Behind: Past, Present, and Future*. Lanham, MD: Rowman & Littlefield.

Heidler, David S., and Jeanne T. Heidler. 1996. *Old Hickory's War: Andrew Jackson and the Quest for Empire*. Mechanicsburg, PA: Stackpole Books, 1996.

Henderson, A. Scott. 2000. *Housing and the Democratic Ideal: The Life and Thought of Charles Abrams*. New York: Columbia University Press.

Hess, Frederick M, and Chester E. Finn Jr., eds. 2004. *Leaving No Child Behind? Options for Kids in Failing Schools*. New York: Palgrave Macmillan.

Hindman, Hugh D. 2002. *Child Labor: An American History*. Armonk, NY: M.E. Sharpe.

Hirota, Hidetaka. 2016. "'The Great Entrepot for Mendicants': Foreign Poverty and Immigration Control in New York State to 1882." In John J. Bukowczyk, ed. *Immigrant Identity and the Politics of Citizenship*. Champaign: University of Illinois Press, 32–59.

Hoffman, Saul D., and Laurence S. Seidman. 2002. *Helping Working Families: The Earned Income Tax Credit*. Kalamazoo, MI: W.E. Upjohn Institute for Employment Research.

Holleran, Philip M. 1996. "Explaining the Decline of Child Labor in Pennsylvania Silk Mills, 1899–1919." *Pennsylvania History: A Journal of Mid-Atlantic Studies* 63, no. 1: 78–95.

Holmes, Amy E. 1990. "'Such Is the Price We Pay': American Widows and the Civil War Pension System." In Maris A. Vinovskis, ed. *Toward a Social History of the American Civil War: Exploratory Essays*. New York: Cambridge University Press, 171–196.

Holt, Marilyn Irvin. 2014. *Cold War Kids: Politics and Childhood in Postwar America, 1945–1960*. Lawrence: University Press of Kansas.

Horne, Gerald. 1995. *Fire This Time: The Watts Uprising and the 1960s*. Charlottesville: University of Virginia Press.

Hoxie, Frederick E. 1984. *A Final Promise: The Campaign to Assimilate the Indians, 1880–1920*. Lincoln: University of Nebraska Press.

Hrach, Thomas J. 2016. *The Riot Report and the News: How the Kerner Commission Changed Media Coverage of Black America*. Amherst: University of Massachusetts Press.

Jenkins, Jeffery A., and Sidney M. Milkis, eds. 2014. *The Politics of Major Policy Reform in Postwar America*. New York: Cambridge University Press.

Johnson, Russell L. 2011. "'Great Injustice': Social Status and the Distribution of Military Pensions after the Civil War." *Journal of the Gilded Age and Progressive Era* 10, no. 2: 137–160.

Johnston, Valerie, and Yuhua Bao. 2011. "Race/Ethnicity-Related and Payer-Related Disparities in the Timeliness of Emergency Care in U.S. Emergency Departments." *Journal of Health Care for the Poor and Underserved* 22, no. 2: 606–620.

Katz, Michael B. 1996. *In the Shadow of the Poorhouse: A Social History of Welfare in America*, rev. ed. New York: Basic Books.

Katz, Michael B. 2015. "What Kind of a Problem Is Poverty? The Archaeology of an Idea." In Ananya Roy and Emma Shaw Crane, eds. *Territories of Poverty: Rethinking North and South*. Athens: University of Georgia Press, 39–78.

Katznelson, Ira. 2012. *Fear Itself: The New Deal and the Origins of Our Time*. New York: Liveright Publishing.

Kennedy, David M. 1999. *Freedom from Fear: The American People in Depression and War, 1929–1945*. New York: Oxford University Press.

Kerr, Norwood Allen. 1990. "Drafted into the War on Poverty: USDA Food and Nutrition Programs, 1961–1969." *Agricultural History* 64, no. 2: 154–166.

Kessler-Harris, Alice. 1990. *A Woman's Wage: Historical Meanings and Social Consequences*. Lexington: University Press of Kentucky.

King, Ronald F. 2000. *Budgeting Entitlements: The Politics of Food Stamps*. Washington, D.C.: Georgetown University Press.

Kinney, Eleanor D. 2015. *The Affordable Care Act and Medicare in Comparative Context*. New York: Cambridge University Press.

Knight, Louise W. 2005. *Citizen: Jane Addams and the Struggle for Democracy*. Chicago: University of Chicago Press.

Knight, Louise W. 2010. *Jane Addams: Spirit in Action*. New York: W.W. Norton.

Koeninger, W. David. 2013. "Statute Whose Name We Dare Not Speak: EMTALA and the Affordable Care Act." *Journal of Gender, Race, and Justice* 16, no. 1: 139–186.

Kohn, Edward P. 2010. *Hot Time in the Old Town: The Great Heat Wave of 1896 and the Making of Theodore Roosevelt*. New York: Basic Books.

Krall, Lisi. 2001. "US Land Policy and the Commodification of Arid Land (1862–1920)." *Journal of Economic Issues* 35, no. 3: 657–674.

Ladd-Taylor, Molly. 1994. *Mother-Work: Women, Child Welfare, and the State, 1890–1930*. Urbana: University of Illinois Press.

Lefkovitz, Alison. 2011. "Men in the House: Race, Welfare, and the Regulation of Men's Sexuality in the United States, 1961–1972." *Journal of the History of Sexuality* 20, no. 3: 594–614.

Levine, Susan. 2008. *School Lunch Politics: The Surprising History of America's Favorite Welfare Program*. Princeton: Princeton University Press.

Lewis, Richard D., Emma M. Laing, and Stephanie M. Foss. 2015. "From the War on Hunger to the Fight against Obesity." In Sharon Y. Nickols and Gwen Kay, eds. *Remaking Home Economics: Resourcefulness and Innovation in Changing Times*. Athens: University of Georgia Press, 109–127.

Lindenmeyer, Kriste. 1997. *"A Right to Childhood": The U.S. Children's Bureau and Child Welfare, 1912–1946*. Urbana: University of Illinois Press.

Littlefield, Daniel F., and James W. Parins, eds. 2011. *Encyclopedia of Indian Removal*. 2 vols. Santa Barbara, CA: Greenwood.

Maher, Neil M. 2007. *Nature's New Deal: The Civilian Conservation Corps and the Roots of the American Environmental Movement*. New York: Oxford University Press.

Mantler, Gordon K. 2013. *Power to the Poor: Black-Brown Coalition and the Fight for Economic Justice, 1960–1974*. Chapel Hill: University of North Carolina Press.

Marten, James. 2014. *America's Corporal: James Tanner in War and Peace*. Athens: University of Georgia Press.

Matlin, Daniel. 2013. *On the Corner: African American Intellectuals and the Urban Crisis*. Cambridge: Harvard University Press.

Matson, Cathy. 2013. "Mathew Carey's Learning Experience: Commerce, Manufacturing, and the Panic of 1819." *Early American Studies* 11, no. 3: 455–485.

McCarthy, Michael P. 1989. "Urban Optimism and Reform Thought in the Progressive Era." *The Historian* 51, no. 2: 239–262.

McClintock, Megan J. 1996. "Civil War Pensions and the Reconstruction of Union Families." *Journal of American History* 83, no. 2: 456–480.

McDonnell, Janet A. 1991. *The Dispossession of the American Indian, 1887–1934*. Bloomington: Indiana University Press.

McFeely, William S. 1994. *Yankee Stepfather: General O. O. Howard and the Freedmen*. New Haven, CT: Yale University Press.

McGuinn, Patrick J. 2006. *No Child Left Behind and the Transformation of Federal Education Policy, 1965–2005*. Lawrence: University Press of Kansas.

Medhurst, Martin J. 2016. "LBJ, Reagan, and the American Dream: Competing Visions of Liberty." *Presidential Studies Quarterly* 46: 98–124.

Metcalf, R. Warren. 2002. *Termination's Legacy: The Discarded Indians of Utah*. Lincoln: University of Nebraska Press.

Mettler, Suzanne. 2005. *Soldiers to Citizens: The G.I. Bill and the Making of the Greatest Generation*. New York: Oxford University Press.

Meyer, Bruce D., and Douglas Holtz-Eakin, eds. 2001. *Making Work Pay: The Earned Income Tax Credit and Its Impact on America's Families*. New York: Russell Sage Foundation.

Meyer, Melissa L. 1994. *The White Earth Tragedy: Ethnicity and Dispossession at a Minnesota Anishinaabe Reservation, 1889–1920*. Lincoln: University of Nebraska Press.

Miles, Tiya. 2010. *The House on Diamond Hill: A Cherokee Plantation Story*. Chapel Hill: University of North Carolina Press.

Milkis, Sidney M., and Jerome M. Mileur, eds. 2005. *The Great Society and the High Tide of Liberalism*. Amherst: University of Massachusetts Press.

Mitchell, Greg. 1992. *The Campaign of the Century: Upton Sinclair's Race for Governor of California and the Birth of Media Politics*. New York: Random House.

Mucciaroni, Gary. 1990. *The Political Failure of Employment Policy, 1945–1982*. Pittsburgh: University of Pittsburgh Press.

Newman, Katherine S. 2010. *Who Cares?: Public Ambivalence and Government Activism from the New Deal to the Second Gilded Age*. Princeton, NJ: Princeton University Press.

Novkov, Julie. 2001. *Constituting Workers, Protecting Women: Gender, Law and Labor in the Progressive Era and New Deal Years*. Ann Arbor: University of Michigan Press.

O'Connor, Alice. 2001. *Poverty Knowledge: Social Science, Social Policy, and the Poor in Twentieth-Century U.S. History*. Princeton: Princeton University Press.

Oliver, Thomas R., Philip R. Lee, and Helene L. Lipton. 2004. "A Political History of Medicare and Prescription Drug Coverage." *The Milbank Quarterly* 82, no. 2: 285–354.

Orleck, Annelise. 2005. *Storming Caesar's Palace: How Black Mothers Fought Their Own War on Poverty*. Boston: Beacon Press.

Orleck, Annelise, and Lisa Gayle Hazirjian, eds. 2011. *The War on Poverty: A New Grassroots History, 1964–1980*. Athens: University of Georgia Press.

Parker, Jacqueline K., and Edward M. Carpenter. 1981. "Julia Lathrop and the Children's Bureau: The Emergence of an Institution." *Social Service Review* 55, no. 1: 60–77.

Parker, Richard. 2005. *John Kenneth Galbraith: His Life, His Politics, His Economics*. New York: Farrar, Straus and Giroux.

Paulsen, George E. 1996. *A Living Wage for the Forgotten Man: The Quest for Fair Labor Standards 1933–1941*. Selingsgrove, PA: Susquehanna University Press.

Perdue, Theda, and Michael D. Green. 2007. *The Cherokee Nation and the Trail of Tears*. New York: Viking, 2007.

Philip, Kenneth R. 1999. *Termination Revisited: American Indians on the Trail to Self-Determination, 1933–1953*. Lincoln: University of Nebraska Press.

Platt, Harold L. 2000. "Jane Addams and the Ward Boss Revisited: Class, Politics, and Public Health in Chicago, 1890–1930." *Environmental History* 5, no. 2: 194–222.

Porterfield, Jason. 2005. *The Homestead Act of 1862: A Primary Source History of the Settlement of the American Heartland in the Late 19th Century*. New York: Rosen Publishing Group.

Portnoy, Alisse. 2005. *Their Right to Speak: Women's Activism in the Indian and Slave Debates*. Cambridge: Harvard University Press, 2005.

Pritchett, Wendell E. 2008. *Robert Clifton Weaver and the American City: The Life and Times of an Urban Reformer*. Chicago: University of Chicago Press.

Prucha, Francis Paul. 1984. *The Great Father: The United States Government and the American Indians*. Lincoln: University of Nebraska Press.

Purdum, Todd S. 2014. *An Idea Whose Time Has Come: Two Presidents, Two Parties, and the Battle for the Civil Rights Act of 1964*. New York: Henry Holt & Company.

Quadagno, Jill. 1994. *The Color of Welfare: How Racism Undermined the War on Poverty*. New York: Oxford University Press.

Rauchway, Eric. 2015. *The Money Makers: How Roosevelt and Keynes Ended the Depression, Defeated Fascism, and Secured a Prosperous Peace*. New York: Basic Books.

Remini, Robert V. 2001. *Andrew Jackson and His Indian Wars*. New York: Viking.

Rhodes, Jesse H. 2012. *An Education in Politics: The Origins and Evolution of No Child Left Behind*. Ithaca: Cornell University Press.

Risen, Clay. 2014. *The Bill of the Century: The Epic Battle for the Civil Rights Act*. New York: Bloomsbury USA.

Rosenbaum, Sara, and Brian Kamoie. 2003. "Finding a Way through the Hospital Door: The Role of EMTALA in Public Health Emergencies." *Journal of Law, Medicine, and Ethics* 31, no. 4: 590–601.

Rosenfeld, Sam. 2010. "Fed by Reform: Congressional Politics, Partisan Change, and the Food Stamp Program, 1961–1981." *Journal of Policy History* 22, no. 4: 474–507.

Ross, William G. 1994. *A Muted Fury: Populists, Progressives, and the Unions Confront the Courts, 1890–1937*. Princeton, NJ: Princeton University Press.

Rossi, Michele M., and Karen A. Curtis. 2013. "Aiming at Half of the Target: An Argument to Replace Poverty Thresholds with Self-Sufficiency, or 'Living Wage' Standards." *Journal of Poverty* 17, no. 1: 110–130.

Rymph, Catherine E. 2017. *Raising Government Children: A History of Foster Care and the American Welfare State*. Chapel Hill: University of North Carolina Press.

Schmidt, James D. 2010. *Industrial Violence and the Legal Origins of Child Labor*. New York: Cambridge University Press.

Schumaker, Paul, and Marisa J. Kelly. 2013. "The Public Assistance Policies of Cities and the Justice Concerns of Elected Officials: The Centrality of the Floors Principle in Addressing Urban Poverty." *Policy Studies Journal* 41, no. 1: 70–96.

Schuman, Michael. 2017. "History of Child Labor in the United States—Part 1: Little Children Working." *Monthly Labor Review* January 2017: 1–19.

Schuman, Michael. 2017. "History of Child Labor in the United States—Part 2: The Reform Movement." *Monthly Labor Review* January 2017: 1–23.

Sealander, Judith. 2003. *The Failed Century of the Child: Governing America's Young in the Twentieth Century*. New York: Cambridge University Press.

Sklar, Kathryn Kish. 1995. *Florence Kelley and the Nation's Work: The Rise of Women's Political Culture, 1830–1900*. New Haven, CT: Yale University Press.

Skocpol, Theda. 1992. *Protecting Soldiers and Mothers: The Politics of Social Provision in the United States, 1870s–1920s*. Cambridge, MA: Harvard University Press.

Smith, Rogers M. 2016. "The Progressive Seedbed: Claims of American Political Community in the Twentieth and Twenty-First Centuries." In Stephen Skowronek, Stephen M. Engel, and Bruce Ackerman, eds. *The Progressives' Century: Political Reform, Constitutional Government, and the Modern American State*. New Haven: Yale University Press, 264–268.

Sosnaud, Benjamin. 2016. "Living Wage Ordinances and Wages, Poverty, and Unemployment in US Cities." *Social Service Review* 90, no. 1: 3–34.

Speakman, Joseph M. 2006. *At Work in Penn's Woods: The Civilian Conservation Corps in Pennsylvania*. University Park, PA: Pennsylvania State University Press.

Speakman, Joseph M. 2002. "The Inspector and His Critics: Child Labor Reform in Pennsylvania." *Pennsylvania History: A Journal of Mid-Atlantic Studies* 69, no. 2: 266–286.

Stanley, Amy Dru. 1992. "Beggars Can't Be Choosers: Compulsion and Contract in Postbellum America." *Journal of American History* 78, no. 4: 1265–1293.

Starr, Kevin. 1996. *Endangered Dreams: The Great Depression in California*. New York: Oxford University Press.

Steensland, Brian. 2008. *The Failed Welfare Revolution: America's Struggle over Guaranteed Income Policy*. Princeton, NJ: Princeton University Press.

Storrs, Landon R. Y. 2000. *Civilizing Capitalism: The National Consumers' League, Women's Activism, and Labor Standards in the New Deal Era*. Chapel Hill: University of North Carolina Press.

Stricker, Frank. 2007. *Why America Lost the War on Poverty—And How to Win It*. Chapel Hill: University of North Carolina Press.

Sugrue, Thomas J. 1996. *The Origins of the Urban Crisis: Race and Inequality in Postwar Detroit*. Princeton: Princeton University Press.

Summers, Mark Wahlgren. 2014. *The Ordeal of the Reunion: A New History of Reconstruction*. Chapel Hill: University of North Carolina Press.

Sutton, John R. 1988. *Stubborn Children: Controlling Delinquency in the United States, 1640–1981*. Berkeley: University of California Press.

Swarts, Heidi, and Ion Bogdan Vasi. 2011. "Which U.S. Cities Adopt Living Wage Ordinances? Predictors of Adoption of a New Labor Tactic, 1994–2006." *Urban Affairs Review* 47, no. 6: 743–774.

Tani, Karen M. 2016. *States of Dependency: Welfare, Rights, and American Governance, 1935–1972*. New York: Cambridge University Press.

Thomas, Karen Kruse. 2006. "The Hill-Burton Act and Civil Rights: Expanding Hospital Care for Black Southerners, 1939–1960." *Journal of Southern History* 72, no. 4: 823–870.

Trattner, Walter I. 1989. *From Poor Law to Welfare State: A History of Social Welfare in America*. New York: Free Press.

Trent, James. 1994. *Inventing the Feeble Mind: A History of Mental Retardation in the United States*. Berkeley: University of California Press.

U.S. Department of Housing and Urban Development, Office of Policy Development and Research. 2015. *HUD at 50: Creating Pathways to Opportunity*. Washington, DC: U.S. Department of Housing and Urban Development, Office of Policy Development and Research.

Ulrich, Roberta. 2010. *American Indian Nations from Termination to Restoration, 1953–2006*. Lincoln: University of Nebraska Press.

Unrau, William E. 2007. *The Rise and Fall of Indian Country, 1825–1855*. Lawrence: University Press of Kansas.

Vacek, Heather H. 2015. *Madness: American Protestant Reaction to Mental Illness across Three Centuries*. Waco: Baylor University Press.

Vale, Lawrence J. 2002. *Reclaiming Public Housing: A Half Century of Struggle in Three Public Neighborhoods*. Cambridge, MA: Harvard University Press.

Van Wienen, Mark W. 2011. *American Socialist Triptych: The Literary-Political Work of Charlotte Perkins Gilman, Upton Sinclair, and W. E. B. Du Bois*. Ann Arbor: University of Michigan Press.

Wagner, David. 2005. *The Poorhouse: America's Forgotten Institution*. Lanham, MD: Rowman & Littlefield.

Waltman, Jerold. 2006. "Supreme Court Activism in Economic Policy in the Waning Days of the New Deal: Interpreting the Fair Labor Standards Act, 1941–1946." *Journal of Supreme Court History* 31, no. 1: 58–80.

Ward, Deborah E. 2005. *The White Welfare State: The Racialization of U.S. Welfare Policy*. Ann Arbor: University of Michigan Press.

Weir, Margaret. 1992. *Politics and Jobs: The Boundaries of Employment Policy in the United States*. Princeton, NJ: Princeton University Press.

Whisnant, David E. 1994. *Modernizing the Mountaineer: People, Power, and Planning in Appalachia*, rev. ed. Knoxville: University of Tennessee Press.

White, Ann Folino. 2015. *Plowed Under: Food Policy Protests and Performance in New Deal America*. Bloomington: Indiana University Press.

Wilkinson, Charles. 2005. *Blood Struggle: The Rise of Modern Nations*. New York: W. W. Norton.

Williams, John Alexander. 2002. *Appalachia: A History*. Chapel Hill: University of North Carolina Press.

Willse, Craig. 2015. *The Value of Homelessness: Managing Surplus Life in the United States*. Minneapolis: University of Minnesota Press.

Wilson, Jan Doolittle. 2007. *The Women's Joint Congressional Committee and the Politics of Maternalism, 1920–30*. Urbana: University of Illinois Press.

Winders, Bill. 2009. *The Politics of Food Supply: U.S. Agricultural Policy in the World Economy*. New Haven: Yale University Press.

Woods, Randall B. 2016. *Prisoners of Hope: Lyndon B. Johnson, the Great Society, and the Limits of Liberalism*. New York: Basic Books.

Woodsworth, Michael. 2016. *Battle for Bed-Stuy: The Long War on Poverty in New York City*. Cambridge: Harvard University Press.

Yochelson, Bonnie. 2014. "The Jacob A. Riis Collection: Photographs for Books and Lantern Lectures." In Ludwig Vogl-Bienek and Richard Crangle, eds. *Screen Culture and the Social Question 1880–1914*. Bloomington: Indiana University Press and John Libbey Press, 83–95.

Zelizer, Julien E. 2015. *The Fierce Urgency of Now: Lyndon Johnson, Congress, and the Battle for the Great Society*. New York: Penguin Press.

Zimmerman, Joan G. 1991. "The Jurisprudence of Equality: The Women's Minimum Wage, the First Equal Rights Amendment, and Adkins v. Children's Hospital, 1905–1923." *Journal of American History* 78, no. 1: 188–225.

Zolberg, Aristide R. 2006. *A Nation by Design: Immigration Policy in the Fashioning of America*. Cambridge, MA: Harvard University Press.

INDEX

ABOUT THE AUTHOR

John R. Burch Jr. earned a PhD in history at the University of Kentucky in 2005. He has authored or coauthored nine books, including *The Great Society and the War on Poverty: An Economic Legacy in Essays and Documents* (Greenwood, 2017). His other publications include *The Encyclopedia of Water Politics and Policy in the United States* (Congressional Quarterly, 2011), coedited with Steven Danver, and *Water Rights and the Environment in the United States: A Documentary and Reference Guide* (Greenwood, 2015), both of which were named Outstanding Academic Titles by CHOICE: *Reviews for Academic Libraries*. He presently serves as library director at the University of Tennessee at Martin.